THE MANTLE OF ELISHA

THE MANTLE OF ELISHA

KIRK ANTHONY FORD

CONTENTS

INTRODUCTION

In the age of spiritual and economic upheaval, a profound balance is needed to restore order and harmony to our world. The Mantle of Elisha presents a compelling vision of this equilibrium, inspired by the ancient wisdom found in the pillars of Jachin and Boaz, and the profound teachings of Jesus Christ.

Just as the pillars of Jachin and Boaz stood as sentinels of strength and stability in the temple of Solomon, so too must we seek to uphold the fundamental principles of spirituality and economics, the twin pillars upon which a thriving society is built. As we navigate the complexities of our modern era, it becomes increasingly evident that these two realms are inextricably intertwined, each serving as a guiding force for the other.

At the heart of this intricate tapestry lies the wisdom of Proverbs 3:13-16, which speaks of the divine harmony that emerges when wisdom and understanding work in tandem. In this sacred text, we find a profound metaphor for the delicate dance between spirituality and economics, each serving as the "right and left hands" of a greater purpose, a higher calling that transcends mere material gain or fleeting spiritual pursuits.

It is through this lens that we must view the teachings of Jesus Christ, whose life and ministry embodied the very essence of this balance. In His words and deeds, we witness a seamless fusion of spiritual enlightenment and practical guidance, a blueprint for a society that embraces both the divine and the temporal, the sacred and the secular.

At the heart of Christ's message lies the concept of diadidomi, or distribution, a radical paradigm that challenges the prevailing notions of scarcity and competition. Through His miraculous acts of multiplication and provision, we catch a glimpse of a world where abundance is not a finite resource, but rather a boundless wellspring, accessible to all who embrace the principles of love, compassion, and selfless service.

As we delve into the pages of The Mantle of Elisha, we embark on a journey that transcends mere words on a page. We are invited to embrace a vision of a world where spirituality and economics are not opposing forces, but rather complementary partners in the pursuit of true fulfillment and lasting prosperity. In this vision, the abolition of death, as accomplished by Christ at Jerusalem, becomes not merely a spiritual triumph, but a tangible reality that permeates every aspect of our existence, ushering in an era of eternal life on this very earth.

Through the lens of this book, we will explore the intricate tapestry of wisdom that weaves together the teachings of ancient texts and the life-changing message of Jesus Christ. We will unravel the mysteries of a world where the right and left hands of wisdom and understanding work in perfect harmony, guiding us toward a future where the pillars of spirituality and economics stand as towering emblems of a society rooted in love, justice, and abundance for all.

The Mantle of Elisha is more than just a book; it is a clarion call to embrace a new paradigm, one that challenges us to transcend the boundaries of our limited perceptions and to embrace a vision of a world where heaven and earth converge, where the temporal and the eternal coexist in perfect equilibrium. It is an invitation to don the mantle of a higher calling, to become agents of change in a world that yearns for the restoration of balance and the fulfillment of a destiny that has been promised from the dawn of time.

Join us on this transformative journey, where the boundaries between the sacred and the secular dissolve, and where the path to eternal life is paved with the wisdom of ages and the radiant light of Christ's teachings. Together, we will explore the depths of a truth that has the power to heal our world, restore the balance of the pillars, and usher in a new era of peace, prosperity, and everlasting life.

1

THE PILLARS OF JACHIN AND BOAZ: FOUNDATIONS OF DIVINE ARCHITECTURE

Introduction to Jachin and Boaz

As we embark on our exploration of the profound harmony between spirituality and economics, it is imperative that we establish a firm understanding of the pillars upon which this delicate balance rests: Jachin and Boaz. These ancient columns, standing as sentinels at the entrance of Solomon's temple, hold within their symbolic forms a wisdom that transcends mere architectural marvels. They are a living testament to the eternal truth that true prosperity can only be achieved when the realms of spirit and matter, faith and commerce, are in perfect alignment.

At first glance, these two terms may seem like mere relics of antiquity, obscure references lost in the annals of history. Yet, as we delve deeper into their origins and implications, we soon discover that they are far more than mere objects of historical curiosity. They are, in fact, luminous beacons, guiding us toward a profound understanding of the very fabric of existence, and the intricate tapestry that weaves together the ethereal and the earthly.

Jachin

The first of these pillars, Jachin, stands as a towering symbol of strength and stability. Its very name, derived from the Hebrew root meaning "to establish," invites us to ponder the enduring foundations upon which all true progress must be built. At its core, Jachin represents the immutable principles of truth, justice, and righteousness – the bedrock upon which any lasting edifice of spiritual and economic prosperity must rest. It is a reminder that true security and abundance can only be achieved when our actions are rooted in the eternal verities that govern the universe.

Yet, Jachin is more than just a representation of unwavering principle; it is also a testament to the power of faith and trust in the divine order. Just as the column stood firm, defying the ravages of time and circumstance, so too must our faith remain steadfast in the face of adversity and uncertainty. It is a call to embrace the seemingly paradoxical notion that true strength often lies in vulnerability, in the willingness to surrender our limited perceptions and trust in the infinite wisdom that guides the cosmos.

Boaz

Complementing the steadfast presence of Jachin is the pillar of Boaz, a name that is said to represent the concept of "strength" or "within." At first glance, this may seem at odds with the enduring stability embodied by its counterpart. However, upon closer inspection, we find that Boaz represents the dynamic, ever-evolving nature of economic and material progress. It is a reminder that true prosperity is not a static state, but rather a continual journey, a dance of adaptation and innovation in response to the ever-changing currents of the world around us.

Boaz invites us to embrace the fluidity of life, to recognize that stagnation is the antithesis of true abundance. It speaks of the need to cultivate agility, resourcefulness, and the willingness to embrace change as an opportunity for growth and evolution. Just as the column stood tall and graceful, its form a testament to the elegance of motion and progress, so too must we learn to move with the rhythms of the world, adapting and flourishing in the face of ever-shifting circumstances.

Yet, the true power of Boaz lies not merely in its representation of change, but in its ability to harmonize with the steadfast presence of Jachin. It is in the delicate interplay between these two pillars that we find the key to achieving a lasting equilibrium, a balance that allows us to navigate the complexities of the material world without sacrificing the eternal truths that anchor our spiritual essence.

As we conclude this introduction to the pillars of Jachin and Boaz, we are reminded that true understanding is not merely an intellectual exercise, but a profound journey of the heart and soul. These symbols are not mere artifacts to be studied from a distance, but living embodiments of the very principles that govern our existence. By embracing their wisdom, we open ourselves to a deeper appreciation of the intricate dance between the spiritual and the economic, the ethereal and the earthly.

In the chapters that lie ahead, we will delve into the profound implications of these pillars, exploring how their lessons can be applied to our modern world, guiding us toward a path of lasting fulfillment and abundance. We will unravel the mysteries that lie at the intersection of faith and commerce, spirituality and economics, discovering the timeless truths that can reshape our understanding of the world and our place within it.

As we move forward, let us remember that the journey toward true prosperity is not one of mere material gain or spiritual transcendence alone, but a harmonious synthesis of these two realms. It is a path that requires us to walk with one foot firmly planted in the eternal verities represented by Jachin, and the other stride confidently into the everchanging currents of progress and innovation embodied by Boaz. Only then can we truly embrace the mantle of a higher calling, and usher in a world where heaven and earth, spirit and matter, coexist in perfect equilibrium.

Historical Context of the Pillars

As we embark upon our journey to unravel the historical tapestry surrounding the pillars of Jachin and Boaz, we must first acknowledge the profound significance of understanding their origin and evolution across cultures and epochs. These towering sentinels, standing as guardians of wisdom and enlightenment, have woven an intricate path through the annals of human civilization, leaving an indelible mark upon the spiritual and economic realms alike. By tracing their footsteps through time, we not only gain insight into the timeless principles they represent but also unlock a deeper appreciation for the intricate dance between faith and progress, spirituality and commerce.

The earliest known roots of these pillars can be traced back to the ancient kingdom of Israel, where they stood as majestic gatekeepers at the entrance of Solomon's magnificent temple. Described in the biblical text of 2 Chronicles 3:15-17, these pillars are said to have been cast from bronze, their towering forms adorned with intricate carvings of pomegranates and lily-work, symbolizing the intertwine of spiritual abundance and natural beauty. The initial date of their construction is shrouded in mystery, but scholars estimate it to have occurred around the 10th century BCE, under the reign of the illustrious King Solomon, known for his wisdom and pursuit of divine knowledge.

From these humble beginnings, the pillars of Jachin and Boaz embarked upon an extraordinary journey across cultures and civilizations, with each new encounter imbuing them with fresh layers of symbolism and significance. Their progression can be traced through key events and adaptations, each one adding to their rich tapestry of meaning:

- Babylonian Captivity (586 BCE): As the Israelites were exiled from their homeland, the pillars' significance transcended mere architectural marvels, becoming symbols of hope and resilience in the face of adversity.

- Hellenistic Period (323-31 BCE): Greek scholars and philosophers, captivated by the pillars' mystique, wove them into their own interpretations of cosmic harmony and balance.
- Roman Era (27 BCE - 476 CE): The pillars' symbolism found new expression in the architectural grandeur of Roman temples and structures, representing the stability and might of the Empire.
- Medieval Europe (5th-15th Century): As the pillars' influence spread westward, they were embraced by the stonemasons and builders of Gothic cathedrals, becoming emblems of spiritual fortitude and the pursuit of divine mysteries.
- Renaissance and Enlightenment (15th-18th Century): With the resurgence of classical knowledge and the birth of modern science, the pillars were reinterpreted as representations of the harmonious balance between faith and reason, spirituality, and empiricism.
- Modern Era (19th-21st Century): As the world became increasingly globalized, the pillars' symbolism transcended boundaries, inspiring architectural marvels, philosophical discourses, and spiritual movements across diverse cultures and beliefs.

Throughout this remarkable odyssey, the pillars of Jachin and Boaz have been adapted, reinterpreted, and embraced by cultures spanning the globe, each one leaving its unique imprint upon their ever-evolving symbolism. From the ancient Near East to the modern West, from the halls of academia to the sanctuaries of faith, these pillars have stood as enduring sentinels, guarding the sacred knowledge that true prosperity and fulfillment can only be achieved when the realms of spirit and matter, faith and commerce, are in perfect harmony.

As we navigate the latter stages of this historical timeline, we cannot ignore the pivotal moments and controversies that have shaped the pillars' significance in more recent times. The rise of secularism and the seeming divide between faith and reason have cast new light upon their enduring message, sparking debates and discourse among scholars, theologians, and philosophers alike. Some have embraced the pillars as timeless symbols of balance and unity, while others have questioned their relevance in an increasingly complex and rapidly evolving world.

Yet, it is perhaps within these very challenges that the true power of Jachin and Boaz is most vividly revealed. For even as the tides of change and progress threaten to erode the foundations of tradition, these pillars stand firm, reminding us that true wisdom lies not in rejecting the past or clinging blindly to dogma, but in seeking the delicate balance between the eternal and the transient, the spiritual and the material. They beckon us to embrace the paradox that true progress is rooted in timeless truths, and that lasting abundance can only blossom when our actions are guided by principles that transcend the fleeting whims of the moment.

As we conclude this historical journey, we find ourselves poised at a crossroads, where the echoes of the past converge with the promises of the future. The pillars of Jachin and Boaz stand before us, their majestic forms a testament to the enduring wisdom that has guided humanity through the ages. They challenge us to look beyond the surface, to peer into the depths of their symbolism, and to unravel the intricate tapestry that weaves together the spiritual and the economic, the divine and the earthly. As we embrace their lessons, we open the door to a new era of understanding, where faith and commerce, spirituality and prosperity, coexist in perfect equilibrium, guiding us toward a future of unprecedented abundance and enlightenment.

Symbolic Significance of Jachin

In the ancient architectural wonders of the world, few symbols have captured the imagination and stirred the soul quite like the enigmatic pillar of Jachin. Like a towering sentinel, this colossal monument has stood as a guardian of profound truths and enduring wisdom, its very name and presence inviting us to ponder the eternal mysteries that underpin our existence.

At its core, the word "Jachin" is a Hebrew term that translates to "He will establish," a simple yet profoundly powerful utterance that resonates with the fundamental human yearning for stability and permanence. It is a declaration of faith, a testament to the belief that amidst the ever-shifting tides of life, there exists an immutable foundation upon which all else is built. This resonant phrase, etched into the very fabric of the pillar's existence, beckons us to contemplate the divine architect's grand design, a masterplan that transcends the fleeting moments of our temporal existence.

To unravel the symbolism of Jachin, we must first journey back to its origins, tracing its footsteps through the hallowed halls of ancient lore. According to the sacred texts of the Old Testament, Jachin stood as one of two massive pillars that flanked the entrance to Solomon's magnificent temple in Jerusalem, a monumental structure that embodied the pinnacle of architectural and spiritual achievement in its time. Alongside its twin, Boaz, Jachin was crafted from the finest bronze, its towering form an awe-inspiring sight that would have greeted all who sought to enter the sacred sanctuary.

Yet, Jachin's significance extended far beyond its physical grandeur. Its name and purpose were deeply intertwined with the theological underpinnings of divine architecture, a concept that saw the temple as a microcosm of the universe itself, a reflection of the cosmic order and harmony that governed all creation. In this context, Jachin represented the pillar of establishment, the unwavering foundation upon which the temple, and by extension the entire cosmos, rested. It was a potent reminder that true stability and enduring prosperity could only be achieved by aligning oneself with the immutable laws and principles that governed the divine design.

As we delve deeper into the symbolism of Jachin, we find ourselves confronted with a profound paradox – the notion that true permanence and stability can only be found by embracing the inherent fluidity and change that are intrinsic to the natural order. For just as the seasons ebb and flow, and the heavenly bodies dance their cosmic ballet, so too must we as individuals and societies adapt and evolve in harmony with the ever-shifting tides of existence. Jachin, in its stalwart presence, serves as a reminder that true stability is not found in rigid stagnation, but rather in the ability to remain firmly rooted in eternal principles while gracefully navigating the currents of change.

In this light, Jachin emerges as a timeless metaphor for the delicate balance that must be struck between the temporal and the eternal, the ephemeral and the everlasting. It is a clarion call for us to seek wisdom in the midst of uncertainty, to anchor our lives and endeavors upon the bedrock of enduring truths while simultaneously embracing the fluidity and dynamism that are inherent to the human experience. It is only by reconciling these seeming contradictions that we can truly unlock the fullness of our potential, transcending the confines of our limited perspectives and ushering in a new era of abundance, prosperity, and enlightenment.

The symbolic resonance of Jachin, however, extends far beyond the realms of theology and spirituality, echoing across the tapestry of human civilization and leaving an indelible mark upon the very fabric of our architectural, cultural, and economic endeavors. Throughout the ages, architects, builders, and visionaries have sought to imbue their creations with the essence of Jachin, striving to craft structures and systems that embody the principles of stability, permanence, and endurance. From the majestic domes and spires of Gothic cathedrals to the towering skyscrapers that pierce the urban skylines, the spirit of Jachin can be seen in the unwavering foundations that support these monumental structures, a testament to the human capacity for creating enduring monuments to our collective progress and ingenuity.

In the realm of economics and commerce, the symbolism of Jachin takes on a particularly potent significance, serving as a guiding light for those who seek to build enterprises and systems that endure the tests of time. For just as the pillar stands as a bulwark against the ravages of entropy and decay, so too must our economic and financial institutions be rooted in principles of integrity, sustainability, and long-term stability. Jachin's clarion call echoes through the annals of business and finance, reminding us that true prosperity and abundance can only flourish when we embrace the wisdom of establishing our endeavors upon foundations that are impervious to the shifting winds of circumstance and the fleeting whims of the moment.

Yet, as we navigate the complexities of our modern world, it is all too easy to lose sight of the enduring lessons that Jachin imparts. Seduced by the siren song of instant gratification and short-term gain, we often find ourselves adrift in a sea of ephemeral pursuits, chasing after fleeting pleasures and transitory successes at the expense of the foundational principles that have guided humanity for millennia. It is in these moments of strife and uncertainty that the spirit of Jachin shines brightest, reminding us to look beyond the surface, peer into the depths of our collective wisdom, and rediscover the timeless truths that have sustained and propelled our species through the ages.

As we stand in the shadow of Jachin's towering presence, we are reminded that true progress and prosperity are not mere products of circumstance or chance, but rather the fruits of a steadfast commitment to aligning our actions with the immutable laws and principles that govern the cosmos. We are called to be architects of our own destiny, to build upon the foundations laid by those who came before us while simultaneously crafting new structures and systems that will endure long after we are gone.

In this journey of self-discovery and collective enlightenment, Jachin stands as a beacon, guiding us toward a future where the realms of spirit and matter, faith and commerce, are no longer seen as opposing forces, but rather as complementary threads woven into the tapestry of existence. It is a future where the pillars of establishment and wisdom stand tall, supporting the grandest of human aspirations while simultaneously grounding us in the eternal truths that have sustained us since the dawn of time. And it is a future that beckons us to embrace the paradox of change and permanence, to dance with the rhythms of the cosmos while remaining rooted in the bedrock of enduring wisdom.

As we gaze upon the majestic form of Jachin, let us be inspired to embark upon our own journey of self-actualization and collective transformation. For it is in the embrace of its timeless symbolism that we shall discover the keys to unlocking the full potential of our existence, ushering in a new era of prosperity, harmony, and enlightenment that will echo throughout the ages, long after the physical monuments of our time have crumbled into dust.

Symbolic Significance of Boaz

In the hallowed halls of ancient wisdom, where the secrets of the cosmos and the divine blueprint of existence intertwine, the enigmatic pillar of Boaz stands as a testament to the enduring power of strength and resilience. Like a towering oak amidst the tempestuous winds of change, Boaz beckons us to embrace the fortitude that lies within, to tap into the wellsprings of inner strength that have sustained humanity through the ages.

At its core, the name "Boaz" resonates with a profound and multifaceted significance. Derived from the Hebrew tongue, it translates to "In Him is strength," a declaration that echoes with the unwavering faith in a higher power, a force that transcends the fleeting boundaries of our mortal realm. This potent phrase, etched into the very fabric of the pillar's existence, invites us to contemplate the nature of true strength – a strength that is not merely physical but also spiritual, a strength that emanates from the depths of our souls and guides us through the most formidable of challenges.

To fully grasp the symbolic significance of Boaz, we must journey back to its origins, tracing the footsteps of the ancient architects and visionaries who erected this monumental pillar. According to the sacred texts, Boaz stood as the counterpart to Jachin, the twin pillars that flanked the entrance to Solomon's magnificent temple in Jerusalem. While Jachin embodied the principle of establishment and permanence, Boaz represented the pillar of strength, a steadfast and unwavering presence that supported the weight of the temple's grandeur and upheld the sanctity of the divine space within.

Yet, Boaz's symbolism extends far beyond the realm of physical architecture, transcending the boundaries of stone and mortar to resonate with the very essence of the human experience. For in our journey through life, we are all builders, crafting the edifices of our destinies, brick by brick, with each choice and action shaping the foundations upon which our futures will be built. And in this grand undertaking, the spirit of Boaz whispers to us, reminding us that true strength lies not in the fleeting displays of power or dominance, but rather in the quiet resolve that endures through the storms of adversity, the fortitude that allows us to weather the tempests of change and emerge triumphant on the other side.

As we gaze upon the imposing form of Boaz, we are reminded that strength is not merely a physical attribute, but a multifaceted quality that encompasses the realms of mind, body, and spirit. It is the unwavering determination that propels us forward in the face of seemingly insurmountable obstacles, the resilience that allows us to bounce back from setbacks and failures, and the inner fortitude that enables us to stay true to our values and principles, even when the world around us seems to be unraveling.

In this light, Boaz emerges as a beacon of hope and inspiration, a reminder that within each of us lies a wellspring of strength that can be tapped into, nurtured, and cultivated. For just as the mighty oak tree draws its sustenance from the depths of the earth, so too can we draw upon the reserves of inner strength that lie dormant within our souls, waiting to be awakened and unleashed upon the world.

Yet, the symbolism of Boaz extends far beyond the realm of personal growth and empowerment, echoing across the tapestry of human civilization and leaving an indelible mark on our collective endeavors. Throughout the ages, the spirit of Boaz has inspired leaders, visionaries, and innovators to rise above the challenges that have confronted them, to forge ahead with unwavering determination, and to create enduring legacies that have shaped the course of history.

From the great pyramids of Giza, monuments to the strength and ingenuity of ancient civilizations, to the towering skyscrapers that pierce the urban skylines of our modern cities, the essence of Boaz can be seen in the unwavering resolve and resilience that propelled these architectural marvels into existence. In the realm of science and technology, the spirit of Boaz has driven pioneers and innovators to push the boundaries of human knowledge, persevere in the face of skepticism and failure, and unleash the full potential of human ingenuity upon the world.

And yet, as we stand in the shadow of Boaz's towering presence, we are reminded that true strength is not merely a virtue reserved for the select few, but rather a quality that resides within each and every one of us. For in the grand tapestry of existence, we are all weavers, crafting the patterns of our lives with each thread of choice and action, and it is the strength that Boaz embodies that allows us to create masterpieces of enduring beauty and significance.

In the face of adversity, when the storms of life threaten to overwhelm us, the spirit of Boaz whispers, urging us to tap into the reserves of inner fortitude that have sustained our species through the ages. It reminds us that the true measure of strength lies not in the ability to overpower or dominate, but rather in the capacity to endure, to adapt, and to emerge from the crucible of hardship, tempered and refined, like steel forged in the fires of a blacksmith's furnace.

And so, as we gaze upon the majestic form of Boaz, let us be inspired to embrace the strength that lies within, to cultivate the resilience and fortitude that will carry us through the trials and tribulations of our earthly journey. For it is in the embrace of this timeless symbolism that we shall discover the keys to unlocking the fullness of our potential, transcending the limitations that have bound us, and ushering in a new era of enlightenment, progress, and enduring legacy.

Just as Boaz stood as a steadfast guardian, supporting the weight of Solomon's temple and upholding the sanctity of the divine space within, so too can we embody the essence of strength, becoming pillars of resilience and fortitude that will support the grandest of human aspirations and propel our species toward ever greater heights of achievement and fulfillment.

In this journey of self-discovery and collective transformation, let us draw inspiration from the symbolic significance of Boaz, letting its spirit guide us toward a future where strength and wisdom intertwine, where the pillars of fortitude and establishment stand as twin beacons, illuminating the path toward a more enlightened and harmonious existence. For it is in the embrace of these timeless truths that we shall find the courage to confront the challenges that lie ahead, the resilience to endure the storms of change, and the strength to forge our destinies anew, leaving a legacy that will echo through the ages, long after the physical monuments of our time have crumbled into dust.

Theological Foundations of Jachin and Boaz

1. Overview:

In the realm of theological symbolism, the pillars of Jachin and Boaz stand as enduring emblems of divine architecture, their profound significance echoing through the ages. To unravel the rich tapestry of their meaning, we must approach this subject with an evidence-based mindset, drawing upon sacred texts, scholarly interpretations, and the weight of historical perspectives. It is only through the lens of credible sources and balanced analysis that we can truly appreciate the depth and nuance of these pillars' theological foundations.

2. Main Proposition:

The pillars of Jachin and Boaz, as described in 2 Chronicles 3:15-17, represent the theological principles of divine stability, wisdom, and strength, serving as pillars upon which the sacred temple of spiritual understanding is built. Through an exegesis of this scriptural passage and an exploration of its theological interpretations, we shall uncover the profound significance of these pillars, illuminating their enduring relevance in maintaining the delicate balance between spirituality and the pursuit of knowledge.

3. Primary Evidence: 2 Chronicles 3:15-17

The primary evidence upon which our analysis rests is found within the sacred text of 2 Chronicles 3:15-17, which provides a detailed account of the construction and placement of the pillars of Jachin and Boaz:

"He cast two pillars of bronze, each eighteen cubits high, and a line of twelve cubits measured the circumference of each. He also made two capitals of cast bronze to set on the tops of the pillars; the height of one capital was five cubits, and the height of the other capital was five cubits. He made a lattice network, with wreaths of chainwork, for the capitals which were on top of the pillars: seven for the one capital and seven for the other capital."

4. Elaboration on the Evidence:

This passage from the Book of Chronicles offers a wealth of insight into the symbolic and theological significance of Jachin and Boaz. The meticulous details provided, such as the height, circumference, and intricate lattice work adorning these pillars, suggest a profound reverence for their sacred purpose. The very act of their construction, overseen by the wise King Solomon himself, imbues these pillars with a sense of divine sanction and spiritual authority.

Moreover, the placement of these pillars at the entrance of the temple, flanking the sacred threshold, signifies their role as guardians and custodians of the divine wisdom and knowledge contained within.

Their imposing stature and intricate design speak to the grandeur and majesty of the theological principles they represent, serving as a constant reminder of the awe-inspiring nature of the divine realm.

5. Counterevidence and Challenges:

It is important to acknowledge that the interpretation of these pillars' significance is not without its challenges and differing perspectives. Some scholars have argued that the pillars may have served a more practical, structural purpose, supporting the weight of the temple's roof or acting as architectural embellishments. Additionally, the exact meaning behind their names, Jachin and Boaz, has been subject to debate, with various translations and interpretations proposed over the centuries.

6. Addressing Counterevidence:

While these practical considerations cannot be entirely dismissed, the overwhelming weight of theological and historical evidence points to a deeper, symbolic significance. The sheer prominence and reverence accorded to these pillars within the sacred texts and their enduring legacy throughout religious traditions suggest a profound spiritual meaning that transcends mere structural or decorative purposes.

Furthermore, the names Jachin and Boaz, while subject to varying interpretations, have been widely recognized as carrying profound theological connotations. Jachin, often translated as "He shall establish," represents the principle of divine establishment, stability, and permanence. Boaz, meaning "In Him is strength," embodies the spiritual fortitude and resilience that sustains the faithful on their journey toward enlightenment.

7. Additional Supporting Evidence:

Beyond the primary scriptural evidence, the theological significance of Jachin and Boaz finds further reinforcement in the wider tapestry of religious symbolism and tradition. The concept of pillars or columns as spiritual representations of divine principles and virtues can be traced across various belief systems, from ancient Egyptian temples to the mystic traditions of the East.

Moreover, the parallels between these pillars and the dualities of wisdom and understanding, as depicted in Proverbs 3:13-16, further solidify their theological foundations. This passage extols the virtues of wisdom, likening it to a tree of life, and understanding as the path to righteousness, echoing the symbolic representations of Jachin and Boaz as pillars supporting the temple of divine knowledge.

8. Real-Life Applications and Significance:

The theological foundations of Jachin and Boaz extend far beyond the realm of historical curiosity or academic discourse. Their enduring symbolism holds profound relevance in navigating the complexities of contemporary life, where the pursuit of spiritual understanding and the acquisition of knowledge often intersect.

In a world where the relentless pace of technological advancement and economic progress can sometimes overshadow the deeper yearnings of the human spirit, the pillars of Jachin and Boaz serve as a poignant reminder of the importance of maintaining a balanced perspective. They beckon us to embrace the stability and permanence that spiritual principles offer while simultaneously harnessing the strength and resilience required to navigate the ever-changing tides of knowledge and progress.

By embodying the principles of divine establishment and fortitude, we can anchor ourselves in the timeless wisdom of our spiritual traditions while simultaneously embracing the relentless pursuit of understanding and enlightenment. It is in this delicate balance, this harmonious interplay between the pillars of Jachin and Boaz, that we can forge a path toward a more holistic and fulfilling existence, where the realms of spirituality and economic progress are not seen as opposing forces but rather as complementary aspects of the human experience.

In a world that often demands unwavering strength and resilience, the spirit of Boaz reminds us that true fortitude is not merely a physical attribute but a quality that permeates the depths of our being. It is the unwavering determination to persevere in the face of adversity, the resilience to bounce back from setbacks, and the inner fortitude to stay true to our values and principles, even in the face of immense challenges.

Conversely, the pillar of Jachin serves as a beacon of stability and permanence, reminding us that amidst the ever-shifting tides of progress and change, there exist immutable truths and eternal principles that transcend the fleeting nature of our earthly existence. By anchoring ourselves in these steadfast foundations, we can navigate the complexities of the modern world with a sense of purpose and direction, guided by the timeless wisdom that has sustained humanity throughout the ages.

As we strive to reconcile the seemingly disparate realms of spirituality and economic progress, the theological foundations of Jachin and Boaz offer a powerful framework for achieving harmony and balance. By embracing the principles of divine establishment and fortitude, we can forge a path that honors the sanctity of our spiritual traditions while simultaneously harnessing the transformative power of knowledge and innovation.

In this sacred synthesis, we can create a world where the pursuit of material prosperity is not at odds with the cultivation of the soul, where the relentless march of progress is tempered by the wisdom of ancient teachings, and where the pillars of Jachin and Boaz stand as enduring sentinels, guiding us toward a higher plane of existence – one where the realms of spirit and matter, faith and reason, coalesce in a harmonious dance, propelling humanity toward ever greater heights of enlightenment and fulfillment.

Societal Foundations Represented by the Pillars

At first glance, the pillars of Jachin and Boaz appear to embody a striking paradox – the juxtaposition of timeless spiritual principles with the ever-evolving dynamics of societal progress. How can these seemingly contradictory elements coexist within a single symbolic representation? It is through this very contrast that we unravel the profound implications these pillars hold for the foundations of our society.

The pillars of Jachin and Boaz, as described in the sacred texts, are not mere architectural embellishments but rather embodiments of the fundamental principles that underpin the stability and strength of society itself. Jachin, symbolizing divine establishment and permanence, represents the enduring values, traditions, and moral tenets that form the bedrock upon which civilizations are built. Boaz, on the other hand, personifies the resilience and fortitude necessary to adapt and thrive in the face of change – the very qualities that propel societal progress and advancement.

In comparing these pillars, we find a delicate balance between the immutable and the dynamic, the timeless and the ever-evolving. Just as a physical structure requires both sturdy foundations and the flexibility to withstand external forces, so too must a society be anchored in enduring principles while simultaneously possessing the agility to navigate the currents of change. The aspects we shall examine in this comparison are the enduring spiritual principles represented by Jachin, the adaptive resilience symbolized by Boaz, and the harmonious interplay between these seemingly antithetical elements.

The pillar of Jachin stands as a testament to the inescapable truth that no society can thrive without a solid foundation of shared values, ethical principles, and cultural traditions. These spiritual and moral underpinnings serve as the glue that binds individuals together, fostering a sense of community, purpose, and collective identity. They provide a framework for navigating complex ethical dilemmas, resolving conflicts, and maintaining social cohesion in the face of adversity. Just as the temple's foundations were built upon the immovable bedrock, so too must a society's foundations be rooted in principles that transcend the fleeting whims of the present, offering a sense of stability and continuity across generations.

Yet, to place sole emphasis on permanence and establishment would be to deny the inherent dynamism of human civilization. This is where the pillar of Boaz comes into play, representing the resilience and adaptability required to weather the storms of change and embrace the opportunities that progress brings. Like the resilient columns that withstood the test of time, societies must cultivate a spirit of fortitude and innovation, enabling them to navigate the ever-shifting tides of technological advancement, economic fluctuations, and evolving cultural norms.

The implications of this comparison extend far beyond the realm of ancient symbolism, resonating deeply with the contemporary challenges faced by modern societies. In an era marked by rapid globalization, disruptive technologies, and shifting power dynamics, the ability to strike a delicate balance between tradition and progress has become a paramount concern. Nations and communities that cling too rigidly to the past risk stagnation and irrelevance, while those that embrace change without a firm grounding in their core values risk losing their identity and moral compass.

It is in this delicate dance between the pillars of Jachin and Boaz that we find the true essence of a thriving society – one that honors its rich heritage while simultaneously embracing the boundless potential of the future. By drawing upon the enduring wisdom of spiritual principles, we can instill a sense of purpose, ethical grounding, and collective identity that transcends the transient nature of material pursuits. Simultaneously, by cultivating a spirit of resilience, innovation, and adaptability, we can harness the transformative power of progress to address the ever-evolving challenges that humanity faces.

This harmonious interplay between the pillars manifests itself in myriad ways within contemporary society. It can be seen in the efforts to preserve cultural traditions while embracing technological advancements, in the pursuit of economic growth tempered by a commitment to environmental sustainability, and in the quest for scientific breakthroughs guided by ethical principles. It is the delicate balance that allows us to honor our past while boldly forging a path toward a brighter future, recognizing that true societal progress lies not in the extremes of stagnation or unbridled change, but in the harmonious synthesis of the timeless and the transformative.

As we look toward the horizon, the pillars of Jachin and Boaz stand as enduring reminders of the foundations upon which we must build our societies. They challenge us to embrace the timeless spiritual principles that have guided humanity throughout the ages, while simultaneously harnessing the resilience and fortitude to adapt and thrive in an ever-changing world. It is in this sacred synthesis that we can forge a path toward a society that is not only economically prosperous but also spiritually grounded, ethically sound, and socially cohesive – a society that honors the wisdom of the past while embracing the boundless potential of the future.

In the end, the pillars of Jachin and Boaz are not mere relics of ancient architecture but living embodiments of the societal foundations upon which we must build. They remind us that true progress is not achieved through the blind pursuit of change or the unyielding adherence to tradition, but rather in the harmonious balance between the two. By embracing this balance, we can create societies that are not only resilient and adaptable but also imbued with a profound sense of purpose, rooted in the timeless principles that have sustained humanity through the ages.

Wisdom and Understanding: Modern Parallels

How do the ancient pillars of Jachin and Boaz relate to modern concepts of wisdom and understanding? This question lies at the heart of our inquiry into the delicate interplay between spirituality and economics, a balance that has captivated thinkers and scholars throughout the ages. As we navigate the complexities of the modern world, understanding the enduring relevance of these ancient symbols takes on a newfound urgency, offering invaluable insights into the harmonious coexistence of timeless principles and ever-evolving societal dynamics.

The context for this exploration is rooted in the profound implications that the pillars of Jachin and Boaz hold for the foundations of a thriving society. As we delve into their symbolism, we are reminded of the intricate tapestry that weaves together the spiritual and the material, the permanent and the transient, the anchors of tradition and the winds of change. It is within this delicate balance that the true essence of societal progress lies, challenging us to embrace the timeless wisdom of the past while harnessing the boundless potential of the future.

The challenges inherent in this pursuit are multifaceted and complex, for they require us to navigate the often-competing demands of preserving our cultural heritage and adapting to the relentless currents of innovation. Too often, we find ourselves grappling with solutions that either cling rigidly to the past or embrace change with reckless abandon, failing to strike the delicate equilibrium that true progress demands.

Common approaches to this dilemma often fall short, trapped in the false dichotomy of tradition versus modernity, spirituality versus materialism. Some advocate for a slavish adherence to the wisdom of the ancients, resistant to the transformative power of progress and innovation. Others embrace a dogmatic pursuit of change, discarding the enduring principles that have guided humanity for millennia. Both extremes, however, fail to capture the profound synthesis that the pillars of Jachin and Boaz represent – a synthesis that demands a holistic embrace of both the timeless and the transient, the spiritual and the material.

It is here that the modern parallels to the dualities of wisdom and understanding, as stipulated in Proverbs 3:13-16, offer a novel and compelling perspective. Just as wisdom and understanding are portrayed as distinct yet complementary virtues, we must cultivate a society that honors both the enduring wisdom of spiritual principles and the ever-evolving understanding of our material reality.

Wisdom, in this context, represents the timeless truths that transcend the transient nature of our physical existence – the ethical foundations, moral guidelines, and cultural traditions that have sustained societies throughout the ages. It is the recognition that there are immutable principles that hold true regardless of the shifting sands of circumstance, providing a stable foundation upon which to build our collective endeavors.

Understanding, on the other hand, embodies the adaptability and resilience necessary to navigate the ever-changing landscape of modern existence. It is the capacity to embrace new knowledge, to question long-held assumptions, and to adapt our strategies and approaches in response to the dynamic forces of progress and innovation. Without understanding, we risk stagnation and irrelevance, unable to harness the transformative potential of technological advancements, scientific breakthroughs, and evolving societal norms.

The true power of this approach lies in its recognition that wisdom and understanding are not mutually exclusive but rather complementary forces, each reinforcing and enriching the other. Just as the pillars of Jachin and Boaz stood side by side, supporting the weight of the ancient temple, so too must our societies be buttressed by the harmonious interplay of timeless spiritual wisdom and ever-evolving material understanding.

This perspective finds concrete expression in a multitude of contemporary contexts, offering a blueprint for navigating the complexities of the modern world. Consider the realm of business and economics, where the pursuit of profit and material success is increasingly tempered by a recognition of the importance of ethical conduct, social responsibility, and environmental sustainability. By embracing the wisdom of spiritual principles such as integrity, compassion, and stewardship, while simultaneously harnessing the understanding of market dynamics, technological innovation, and global interconnectedness, we can create economic systems that are not only prosperous but also socially conscious and environmentally sustainable.

In the realm of governance and public policy, this approach can be seen in the efforts to preserve cultural traditions and national identities while simultaneously fostering international cooperation and embracing progressive ideals. By honoring the wisdom of our shared historical narratives and the enduring values that have shaped our societies, while also demonstrating an understanding of the interconnected nature of the modern world and the need for collaborative solutions to global challenges, we can forge a path toward a more harmonious and equitable global order.

Even in the realm of scientific inquiry and technological advancement, the synthesis of wisdom and understanding is essential. While the pursuit of knowledge and innovation must be guided by an understanding of the laws of nature and the empirical principles of the scientific method, it must also be tempered by the wisdom of ethical considerations, moral boundaries, and deep respect for the sanctity of life and the natural world.

By embracing this holistic approach, we can transcend the limitations of traditional paradigms that pit spirituality against materialism, and tradition against progress. Instead, we can forge a path toward a society that honors the wisdom of our collective heritage while simultaneously harnessing the understanding necessary to adapt and thrive in an ever-changing world.

Yet, as we embark on this journey, we must also acknowledge and address the potential skepticism and objections that may arise. Some may argue that the pursuit of material progress and economic development is fundamentally at odds with the principles of spirituality and tradition, rendering any attempt at synthesis futile. Others may contend that the very notion of "timeless wisdom" is itself outdated and irrelevant in a world characterized by constant flux and disruption.

To these objections, we must respond with clarity and conviction, grounded in the recognition that true progress is not a zero-sum game but rather a harmonious synthesis of the enduring and the transient. The pillars of Jachin and Boaz serve as enduring reminders that societal stability and prosperity are not achieved through the blind pursuit of change or the unyielding adherence to tradition but rather through a delicate balance of both.

As we navigate this path, we must be guided by a clear and actionable plan – a roadmap that enables individuals, communities, and nations to embrace this harmonious synthesis in their pursuit of progress and collective wellbeing. This may involve:

1. Cultivating a deep understanding and appreciation for the wisdom of our shared spiritual and cultural heritage, while simultaneously fostering a spirit of intellectual curiosity and a willingness to question long-held assumptions.
2. Encouraging interdisciplinary dialogue and collaboration between spiritual leaders, academics, policymakers, and industry leaders to identify areas where the synthesis of wisdom and understanding can be applied to address pressing societal challenges.
3. Investing in educational initiatives that emphasize the importance of both timeless ethical principles and the development of critical thinking and adaptability skills necessary to thrive in a rapidly changing world.
4. Promoting policies and incentives that reward businesses and organizations that exemplify a commitment to both ethical conduct and innovation, creating a framework that encourages the harmonious pursuit of spiritual wisdom and material understanding.
5. Embracing a spirit of humility and open-mindedness, recognizing that the journey toward this synthesis is an ongoing and iterative process, requiring constant reflection, course correction, and a willingness to learn from both the wisdom of the past and the insights of the present.

As we embark on this path, we must do so with the unwavering conviction that the harmonious embrace of wisdom and understanding is not merely an idealistic pursuit but a fundamental necessity for the survival and prosperity of our societies. Just as the pillars of Jachin and Boaz stood as enduring symbols of strength and stability, so too must we strive to embody the principles they represent – the timeless wisdom that anchors our endeavors and the adaptive understanding that propels us forward.

In doing so, we will not only ensure the continued progress of our material existence but also imbue our collective journey with a deeper sense of purpose and meaning. We will forge societies that are not only prosperous and technologically advanced but also imbued with the spiritual and ethical foundations that have sustained humanity throughout the ages. It is in this sacred synthesis that we will find the true path toward a world that is not only economically vibrant but also spiritually grounded, ethically sound, and socially cohesive – a world that honors the wisdom of the past while embracing the boundless potential of the future.

Architectural Symbolism in Modern Contexts

The enduring symbolism of the ancient pillars of Jachin and Boaz offers a profound lens through which to explore the harmonious synthesis of timeless wisdom and modern understanding within contemporary architectural contexts. As we journey through the realms of spirituality, economics, and societal progress, these iconic pillars serve as a powerful reminder of the delicate balance that must be struck between the enduring foundations of our shared heritage and the ever-evolving currents of innovation.

To fully appreciate the significance of this architectural symbolism, let us begin with a concise overview of the key points that will guide our exploration:

1. The pillars of Jachin and Boaz as embodiments of timeless wisdom and spiritual principles.

2. The integration of symbolic architectural elements within modern contexts and their role in fostering societal harmony.
3. The adaptation of ancient architectural symbolism to contemporary economic and technological landscapes.
4. The societal implications of embracing architectural symbolism as a bridge between tradition and progress.
5. The transformative potential of architectural symbolism in shaping collective consciousness and fostering ethical conduct.

First and foremost, we must delve into the profound symbolism embodied by the pillars of Jachin and Boaz themselves. These iconic structures, erected at the entrance of ancient temples, were not mere architectural adornments but rather physical manifestations of the enduring wisdom and spiritual principles that have guided humanity throughout the ages. Jachin, the pillar of the establishment, represented the unwavering foundation of moral and ethical values upon which societies are built. Boaz, the pillar of strength, symbolized the resilience and fortitude required to uphold these principles in the face of adversity and change.

In our modern contexts, the integration of symbolic architectural elements that draw upon this ancient wisdom takes on a renewed significance. As we grapple with the complexities of an ever-evolving world, the incorporation of these symbols within our built environments can serve as a powerful anchor, reminding us of the timeless truths that transcend the transient nature of our material existence. From the incorporation of sacred geometries and sacred proportions to the deliberate use of symbolic motifs and patterns, modern architects have the opportunity to infuse their creations with a sense of profound meaning and spiritual resonance.

Yet, true progress demands more than a mere replication of the past – it requires an adaptive understanding of how these ancient symbols can be reinterpreted and integrated within the context of contemporary economic and technological landscapes. In the realm of commercial and industrial architecture, for instance, the principles embodied by Jachin and Boaz can be manifested through the creation of structures that not only serve functional and economic purposes but also embody a deep respect for ethical conduct, environmental stewardship, and social responsibility.

Imagine a modern office complex that seamlessly blends cutting-edge sustainable technologies with architectural elements inspired by these ancient pillars, serving as a powerful reminder of the harmonious synthesis between material progress and spiritual wisdom. Such a structure would not only be a testament to human ingenuity and technological prowess but also a symbolic representation of our collective commitment to upholding the timeless values of integrity, compassion, and stewardship.

The societal implications of embracing architectural symbolism as a bridge between tradition and progress are far-reaching and profound. By imbuing our built environments with these symbolic elements, we foster a collective consciousness that honors our shared heritage while simultaneously inspiring us to push the boundaries of innovation and progress. This harmony between the enduring and the transient has the power to shape not only our physical landscapes but also the very fabric of our societies, forging a path toward a more harmonious and sustainable future.

Moreover, the transformative potential of architectural symbolism extends beyond the realm of physical structures. By consciously incorporating these symbolic elements into our everyday environments, we have the opportunity to shape collective consciousness and foster ethical conduct on a broader scale. From public parks and gathering spaces adorned with symbolic motifs that inspire contemplation and introspection, to educational institutions that integrate architectural elements that celebrate the pursuit of wisdom and understanding, the possibilities are vast and far-reaching.

In this way, the pillars of Jachin and Boaz become not mere relics of the past but living, breathing embodiments of our collective aspiration to harmonize the enduring wisdom of our shared heritage with the transformative potential of progress and innovation. They serve as a constant reminder that true societal prosperity is not achieved through the blind pursuit of material gain or the unyielding adherence to tradition, but rather through a delicate synthesis of both – a synthesis that honors the timeless foundations upon which our societies are built while simultaneously embracing the boundless possibilities of the future.

As we navigate the complexities of the modern world, let us embrace the profound lessons embodied by these ancient pillars, recognizing that their symbolism transcends the boundaries of time and space. By infusing our modern architectural landscapes with these symbolic elements, we not only pay homage to our shared heritage but also forge a path toward a more harmonious, sustainable, and ethically grounded future – a future where the wisdom of the ages is seamlessly interwoven with the boundless potential of human ingenuity and understanding.

Conclusion: The Enduring Relevance of Jachin and Boaz

In conclusion, the enduring relevance of the pillars of Jachin and Boaz extends far beyond their ancient architectural origins. As we stand at the crossroads of tradition and progress, these iconic symbols serve as a poignant reminder of the harmonious balance that must be struck between the enduring foundations of wisdom and the ever-evolving currents of understanding.

At their core, Jachin and Boaz represent the pillars upon which our spiritual and societal fabric is woven – the unwavering principles of righteousness and strength that have guided humanity through the ages. Yet, their true power lies not in their reverence for the past but rather in their capacity to inspire us to adapt and integrate these timeless truths within the contexts of our modern world.

As we embark on this journey of synthesis, we must embrace the profound lessons these pillars impart – the importance of establishing a firm ethical and moral foundation upon which to build our societies, and the resilience required to uphold these principles in the face of change and adversity. By consciously infusing our contemporary architectural landscapes with symbolic elements that evoke this ancient wisdom, we create physical manifestations of our collective aspiration to harmonize the enduring and the transient.

Imagine a world where our cities and communities are not merely functional spaces but living embodiments of this delicate balance – where the cutting-edge innovations of modern engineering and design are seamlessly interwoven with the timeless principles of integrity, compassion, and stewardship. From the soaring skyscrapers that blend sustainable technologies with sacred geometries to the public spaces adorned with symbolic motifs that inspire contemplation and introspection, we have the power to shape our built environments in a way that elevates the human experience and fosters a deeper connection to our shared heritage.

Yet, the true significance of Jachin and Boaz extends beyond the realm of physical structures. By embracing their symbolic resonance in our daily lives, we cultivate a collective consciousness that transcends the material and inspires us to embody these principles in our personal and professional pursuits. In doing so, we become living embodiments of this harmonious synthesis – individuals who not only contribute to the progress of society but do so in a manner that honors the timeless wisdom upon which our very existence is built.

As we stand amidst the ever-shifting tides of societal change and technological advancement, let us remember that true progress is not measured by material gain or the relentless pursuit of novelty alone. Rather, it is the delicate balance between the enduring and the evolving, the ancient and the innovative, that holds the key to a truly sustainable and ethically grounded future.

So let us embrace the profound lessons of Jachin and Boaz, and let their enduring relevance guide us as we navigate the complexities of the modern world. For it is in this harmonious synthesis of timeless wisdom and modern understanding that we will find the path to a more harmonious, compassionate, and spiritually grounded society – a society that honors the foundations upon which it is built while simultaneously embracing the boundless potential of human ingenuity and understanding.

In the end, the true significance of Jachin and Boaz lies not in their physical manifestations but in their ability to inspire us to transcend the limitations of our own perceptions and embrace a higher vision – a vision of a world where progress and tradition coexist in perfect harmony, where the wisdom of the ages is seamlessly interwoven with the boundless potential of the future. It is this vision that will guide us as we embark on the next chapter of our collective journey, forging a path toward a more enlightened, inclusive, and ethically grounded society for generations to come.

2

ECONOMICS AND SPIRITUALITY: THE TWIN AXES OF HUMAN FLOURISHMENT

The Interconnection of Wealth and Well-being

Can the pursuit of material wealth be harmonized with the cultivation of spiritual well-being?

Since antiquity, a dichotomy has persisted between the realms of wealth and spirituality, often portrayed as irreconcilable opposites. On one side lies the material world – the accumulation of riches, the pursuit of financial success, and the comforts afforded by economic means. On the other, the spiritual realm beckons – a path of detachment, inner peace, and transcendence beyond the fleeting trappings of worldly possessions.

This perceived conflict has led to a myriad of challenges, with many struggling to strike a balance between their economic ambitions and their yearning for spiritual fulfillment. Some have embraced asceticism, renouncing all material possessions in pursuit of enlightenment, while others have adopted prosperity theology, seeking to align their faith with the pursuit of wealth. Yet, these approaches often fail to address the complexities that arise when wealth and spirituality intersect.

Common misconceptions abound. Some view wealth as inherently corrupting, believing that the pursuit of material gain inevitably leads to greed, selfishness, and a disconnect from higher values. Conversely, others perceive spirituality as a hindrance to financial success, impeding the drive and ambition necessary to achieve economic prosperity. These oversimplifications fail to acknowledge the nuances and interdependencies that exist between these two realms.

Herein lies a novel perspective: wealth and spirituality can be symbiotically nurtured, each enriching the other in a harmonious interplay that promotes holistic well-being. Rather than an either/or proposition, this approach recognizes that material resources, when utilized mindfully and with intention, can serve as a catalyst for spiritual growth and an instrument for positive impact.

Consider the ancient teachings of the Bhagavad Gita, which emphasize the importance of embracing one's dharma – the righteous path that aligns with one's unique gifts and responsibilities. Through this lens, the acquisition of wealth is not inherently virtuous or sinful; it is the intent and utilization of those resources that determine their spiritual merit. When wealth is pursued with integrity, compassion, and a commitment to service, it becomes a means to alleviate suffering, uplift communities, and contribute to the greater good.

Modern-day exemplars abound, from philanthropists who have leveraged their wealth to fund groundbreaking initiatives in education, healthcare, and social justice, to entrepreneurs whose businesses are anchored in ethical practices and a commitment to environmental stewardship. In these instances, wealth becomes a powerful tool for positive change, enabling individuals to manifest their spiritual values through tangible actions that benefit humanity.

Yet, the interplay between wealth and spirituality is not a one-way street. As individuals cultivate their inner well-being through spiritual practices such as meditation, prayer, and mindfulness, they develop qualities that can enhance their capacity for responsible wealth creation and management. Clarity of purpose, emotional intelligence, and a deeper sense of interconnectedness can lead to wiser decision-making, ethical conduct, and a long-term perspective that transcends short-term gains.

Critics may argue that the allure of wealth is inherently corrupting, citing countless examples of individuals who have succumbed to greed and lost sight of their higher values. However, this perspective fails to acknowledge the transformative power of spiritual principles when integrated into one's relationship with wealth. Through practices such as gratitude, generosity, and a commitment to conscious consumption, individuals can cultivate a mindset that counteracts the potential pitfalls of materialism and anchors them in a deeper sense of purpose and fulfillment.

To truly embody this harmonious synthesis of wealth and spirituality, a multifaceted approach is required. On an individual level, it involves cultivating self-awareness, aligning one's economic pursuits with personal values, and actively engaging in spiritual practices that foster inner growth and ethical decision-making. On a societal level, it necessitates a shift toward more sustainable and equitable economic models, where the creation of wealth is balanced with a commitment to social responsibility, environmental stewardship, and the well-being of all stakeholders.

In essence, the path toward integrating wealth and spirituality is one of conscious intention, mindful action, and a deep recognition of our interconnectedness. By embracing this holistic perspective, we have the power to transform the very nature of wealth – from a means of self-gratification to a catalyst for positive change, from a source of division to a unifying force that uplifts humanity and the planet we call home.

So, embark on this journey with an open heart and a steadfast commitment to your highest values. Cultivate the wisdom to discern when the pursuit of wealth aligns with your spiritual principles, and the courage to walk away when it does not. Embrace the profound truth that true wealth extends far beyond the material realm – it resides in the richness of your relationships, the depth of your character, and the enduring legacy you leave behind.

In doing so, you will unlock the transformative power that lies at the intersection of wealth and spirituality, paving the way for a life of profound fulfillment, unwavering integrity, and an enduring commitment to the betterment of the world around you. For it is in this sacred synthesis that we discover the true path to prosperity – a prosperity that transcends the fleeting and embraces the eternal, a prosperity that nourishes not only our bank accounts but the very essence of our souls.

Biblical Economics: A Theological Framework

As we embark on this exploration of integrating spirituality with economics, it is essential to understand the profound biblical principles that have shaped economic thought and practice for millennia. These timeless teachings not only provide a foundational framework for a holistic view of wealth and prosperity, but also offer practical guidance for living a life of purpose, stewardship, and compassion in the midst of material pursuits.

At the heart of this discourse lie three key terms—stewardship, tithing, and jubilee—each laden with deep theological significance and far-reaching implications for our economic behavior. Unpacking these terms is crucial, for they serve as guideposts on the path toward integrating our spiritual values with the management of material resources.

Stewardship, a concept that permeates the biblical narrative, invites us to reframe our relationship with wealth and possessions. Rather than viewing ourselves as owners of resources, we are called to embrace the role of caretakers, entrusted with the responsible management of that which ultimately belongs to the Divine. This mindset shift is profound, transforming our perspective from one of entitled consumption to one of humble custodianship.

Consider the parable of the talents (Matthew 25:14-30), wherein a master entrusts his servants with varying amounts of wealth. The servants who invest and multiply the resources entrusted to them are commended for their faithful stewardship, while the servant who buries his portion in the ground is chastised for his negligence. This parable underscores the expectation that we utilize our resources in productive and fruitful ways, multiplying their impact for the benefit of all.

Inherent in the concept of stewardship is the understanding that our material possessions are not solely for personal gratification but are gifts to be shared and invested for the greater good. This principle challenges the notion of unbridled accumulation and encourages a mindset of generosity, responsibility, and a commitment to utilizing resources in ways that honor the Divine and uplift humanity.

Closely intertwined with stewardship is the practice of tithing, a biblical mandate that calls upon believers to contribute a portion of their wealth to support the work of faith-based institutions and assist those in need. This act of giving, rooted in gratitude and trust in the Divine Provider, serves as a tangible expression of our commitment to stewardship and a recognition that our wealth is not solely our own.

The concept of tithing challenges the notion of hoarding resources and encourages a mindset of abundance and generosity. By faithfully setting aside a portion of our wealth for charitable purposes, we acknowledge the transient nature of material possessions and invest in that which transcends the temporal realm. This practice not only fosters a spirit of selflessness and compassion but also serves as a potent antidote to the corrupting influence of greed and materialism.

Furthermore, the act of tithing can be seen as a spiritual discipline, cultivating within us virtues such as trust, humility, and a recognition of our interdependence with others. As we relinquish a portion of our wealth, we acknowledge our reliance on the Divine and our connectedness to the broader human family, fostering a sense of unity and shared purpose that transcends individual self-interest.

The principle of jubilee, as outlined in the biblical book of Leviticus, introduces a radical concept of economic equity and restorative justice. At its core, the jubilee year called for a periodic cancellation of debts and the return of land and property to their original owners or their descendants. This practice sought to prevent the perpetual accumulation of wealth in the hands of a few and to ensure that all members of society had access to the means of economic sustenance and self-sufficiency.

While the practicalities of implementing a modern-day jubilee may be complex, the underlying principle of promoting economic fairness and mitigating the long-term consequences of systemic inequalities remains profoundly relevant. This concept challenges us to confront the disparities that arise from unbridled capitalism and to actively seek ways to restore balance and create opportunities for those marginalized by economic systems.

Moreover, the jubilee principle invites us to reimagine our relationship with wealth and possessions, recognizing that true prosperity extends beyond the accumulation of material assets. It calls us to embrace a holistic vision of well-being, where the flourishing of individuals and communities is contingent upon equitable access to resources, the restoration of dignity, and the cultivation of a just and compassionate economic order.

As we reflect upon these biblical principles—stewardship, tithing, and jubilee—we are called to reexamine our own economic decisions and practices through a lens of spiritual intentionality. Each term invites us to transcend the narrow confines of self-interest and embrace a broader perspective that honors our interconnectedness with the Divine, with one another, and with the natural world.

In the pages that follow, we will delve deeper into these concepts, exploring their historical roots, theological nuances, and contemporary applications. We will grapple with the complexities that arise when these timeless principles intersect with the realities of modern economic systems, and we will seek practical guidance for integrating spiritual wisdom into our financial decision-making.

Through this journey, we will come to recognize that the pursuit of material wealth is not inherently antithetical to spiritual growth; rather, it is the intention, the means, and the utilization of those resources that determine their alignment with our highest values. By embracing the biblical framework of stewardship, tithing, and jubilee, we can forge a path toward a more holistic and harmonious relationship with wealth – one that honors both our spiritual aspirations and our earthly responsibilities.

Historical Perspectives on Economic Justice

The quest for economic justice, an endeavor deeply rooted in humanity's spiritual and ethical yearnings, spans millennia and transcends cultural boundaries. Its origins can be traced to the earliest known civilizations, where prophetic voices and sacred texts first articulated the principles of equitable distribution, compassion for the poor, and the pursuit of a just economic order.

In ancient Israel, the concept of economic justice took shape through the revelations imparted to Moses and the teachings of the Hebrew prophets. The laws and commandments enshrined in the Torah laid the groundwork for a society built upon principles of fairness, generosity, and a deep reverence for the Divine as the ultimate source of all resources.

- Circa 1446 BCE: The Exodus from Egypt and the revelation of the Ten Commandments, including the prohibition against theft and the mandate to honor the Sabbath, set the stage for the regulation of economic activity.
- Circa 1446 BCE: The Mosaic Law, including the institution of the Sabbath year and the Jubilee year, sought to prevent

the permanent accumulation of wealth and the perpetual enslavement of debtors.

- Circa 700 BCE: The prophetic teachings of Amos, denouncing economic injustice, oppression of the poor, and the pursuit of wealth at the expense of ethical conduct.
- Circa 600 BCE: The exhortations of Jeremiah, calling for the release of indentured servants and the cancellation of debts, echoing the principles of the Jubilee year.
- Circa 500 BCE: The reforms of Nehemiah, addressing debt slavery, usury, and economic exploitation in post-exilic Judah.

These foundational principles resonated across faiths and cultures, shaping economic thought and practice in diverse contexts. In the teachings of Jesus Christ, economic justice found a powerful advocate, as he championed the cause of the poor, challenged the accumulation of excessive wealth, and called for a radical realignment of priorities toward spiritual fulfillment over material possessions.

- Circa 30 CE: The Sermon on the Mount, wherein Jesus blessed the poor in spirit and warned against the dangers of greed and the pursuit of earthly treasures.
- Circa 30 CE: The parable of the rich fool, illustrates the folly of hoarding wealth and neglecting spiritual nourishment.
- Circa 30 CE: The parable of the rich man and Lazarus, highlights the moral imperative to address the plight of the destitute and marginalized.

The early Christian church sought to embody these teachings, with communities practicing voluntary sharing of resources and caring for the needy among them. This spirit of economic solidarity and mutual support laid the foundations for later monastic orders and the institutionalization of charitable practices within the church.

As the influence of Christianity spread, these principles intermingled with the economic philosophies of other cultures, leading to the development of diverse interpretations and practices. In the Islamic tradition, the concept of zakat, a mandatory form of alms-giving, emerged as a pillar of faith, enshrining the principle of wealth redistribution and solidarity with the less fortunate.

The medieval period witnessed the intersection of economic thought with theological discourse, as scholars and thinkers grappled with the ethical implications of commerce, usury, and the accumulation of wealth. Figures such as Thomas Aquinas and the Scholastics sought to reconcile Aristotelian philosophy with Christian doctrine, laying the groundwork for the development of moral economic theories that would influence subsequent eras.

As Europe transitioned into the Renaissance and the Enlightenment, the concept of economic justice evolved and adapted to the changing social and economic landscapes. Philosophers and reformers such as John Locke, Adam Smith, and the Physiocrats explored the relationship between individual liberty, property rights, and the role of government in regulating economic activity, shaping the foundations of modern capitalism.

The Industrial Revolution brought both unprecedented economic growth and stark inequalities, fueling calls for social reforms and the emergence of various economic ideologies, ranging from socialism and Marxism to the Social Gospel movement within Christianity. These movements sought to address the plight of the working class, challenge the concentration of wealth, and advocate for a more equitable distribution of economic resources and opportunities.

In the 20th century, the principle of economic justice found renewed vigor in the struggles for civil rights, labor reforms, and the global fight against poverty and inequality. Visionary leaders such as Martin Luther King Jr., Dorothy Day, and Muhammad Yunus championed the cause of economic empowerment, ethical business practices, and the creation of systems that prioritized human dignity and the common good.

Today, the pursuit of economic justice continues to evolve, encompassing diverse initiatives and innovations. From the rise of socially responsible investing and impact investing to the development of alternative economic models such as cooperatives, and community-based economies, and the growth of ethical finance and microfinance, the pursuit of economic fairness and sustainability has taken on new dimensions.

Yet, even as progress is made, challenges and controversies persist. Issues such as income inequality, exploitative labor practices, environmental degradation, and the concentration of economic power continue to fuel debates and calls for systemic reforms. The tension between individual liberty and collective responsibility, between the profit motive and ethical constraints, remains a focal point of ongoing dialogues and policy debates.

As we reflect upon this rich tapestry of economic justice throughout history, we are reminded of the enduring human yearning for a more equitable and compassionate economic order – one that honors the inherent dignity of all individuals and recognizes our shared responsibility as stewards of the world's resources. It is a journey that has traversed continents, cultures, and epochs, shaped by the interplay of spiritual values, ethical frameworks, and the ever-evolving realities of economic systems.

In this ongoing quest, the voices of prophets, sages, and visionaries continue to resonate, challenging us to transcend narrow self-interest and embrace a broader perspective of economic justice – one that seeks to uplift the marginalized, restore balance, and cultivate a world where the pursuit of material prosperity is harmonized with the highest ideals of human flourishing and spiritual fulfillment.

Case Studies of Economic Flourishment

1. Introduction:

The interplay between economic structures and spiritual well-being has been a constant theme throughout human history, with individuals and communities striving to harmonize material prosperity with deeper ethical and spiritual principles. In this chapter, we explore several case studies that illustrate the transformative power of this synergy, showcasing how economic initiatives rooted in spiritual values can catalyze positive change and uplift communities.

2. Case Study: The Mondragon Corporation - A Model of Cooperative Economics

2.1. Background:

In the aftermath of the Spanish Civil War, the small town of Mondragon in the Basque region of Spain faced economic hardship and widespread poverty. In 1956, a young priest named José María Arizmendiarrieta, inspired by Catholic social teachings and the principles of worker solidarity, laid the foundations for what would become the Mondragon Corporation – a pioneering and highly successful cooperative enterprise.

2.2. The Challenge:

Arizmendiarrieta recognized the need to create economic opportunities and empower the local community while upholding the values of dignity, equality, and democratic participation. The challenge was to establish a sustainable business model that could compete in the global market while preserving these core principles.

2.3. The Solution:

The Mondragon Corporation was built on a unique cooperative structure, where workers were also owners and decision-makers. Profits were reinvested in the company and distributed equitably among the worker-owners, fostering a sense of shared responsibility and collective prosperity. Emphasis was placed on education, training, and the development of human capital, ensuring that workers had the skills and knowledge to contribute meaningfully to the enterprise.

2.4. The Outcome:

From its humble beginnings as a small cooperative factory, the Mondragon Corporation grew into a powerful business conglomerate, encompassing the manufacturing, finance, retail, and education sectors. By 2019, it employed over 80,000 workers across 100 cooperatives, with an annual revenue exceeding 12 billion euros. The cooperative model not only provided economic stability and prosperity for its members but also fostered a sense of community, shared purpose, and ethical business practices.

2.5. Lessons Learned:

The success of the Mondragon Corporation demonstrates that economic flourishing can be achieved while upholding spiritual values of solidarity, democracy, and human dignity. By empowering workers, promoting education, and embracing cooperative principles, the organization created a sustainable model that challenges traditional notions of profit-driven capitalism. Criticisms of the model revolve around potential limitations in scalability and adapting to rapidly changing market conditions, but its enduring success serves as a testament to the power of combining economic pragmatism with ethical and spiritual foundations.

2.6. Relevance and Takeaways:

The Mondragon case study highlights the potential of cooperative economics to create a more equitable and sustainable economic system, one that aligns with spiritual principles of human dignity, shared responsibility, and the common good. It serves as an inspiration for communities seeking to balance economic development with ethical values, demonstrating that material prosperity and spiritual well-being are not mutually exclusive but can be harmonized through innovative models and a commitment to collective empowerment.

2.7. Concluding Thought:

As we reflect on the Mondragon experience, we are compelled to ask: What if more businesses embraced the cooperative spirit and prioritized the well-being of their workers and communities over relentless profit maximization? Could this model be a pathway toward a more just and sustainable economic future?

3. Case Study: The Grameen Bank - Empowering the Economically Marginalized through Microcredit

3.1. Background:

In the impoverished villages of Bangladesh, a young economics professor named Muhammad Yunus witnessed firsthand the crippling effects of poverty and the lack of access to financial services. Driven by a deep spiritual conviction to uplift the marginalized, he embarked on a groundbreaking experiment in 1976 – the creation of the Grameen Bank, a pioneering institution that provided microcredit loans to the poorest of the poor, predominantly women.

3.2. The Challenge:

The challenge was twofold: First, to provide economic opportunities and financial inclusivity to those traditionally excluded from formal banking systems. Second, to empower women and challenge deeply entrenched cultural norms that perpetuated gender inequality and economic disempowerment.

3.3. The Solution:

Yunus' solution was rooted in the belief that even the smallest amount of credit could catalyze entrepreneurship and self-sufficiency. The Grameen Bank offered collateral-free micro-loans, often as little as a few dollars, to impoverished individuals, primarily women, to start or expand small businesses. The loans were accompanied by training, mentorship, and a commitment to social empowerment, fostering a sense of dignity and self-reliance among borrowers.

3.4. The Outcome:

The impact of the Grameen Bank's microcredit program has been nothing short of transformative. By 2018, the bank had disbursed over $30 billion in loans to nearly 9 million borrowers, with a remarkable repayment rate of over 97%. Millions of individuals, predominantly women, were lifted out of extreme poverty, empowering them to start businesses, invest in education, and improve their living conditions. The program's success inspired a global microcredit movement, with similar initiatives being replicated in various countries, impacting the lives of millions more.

3.5. Lessons Learned:

The Grameen Bank's microcredit model demonstrates the power of combining economic empowerment with spiritual values of human dignity, compassion, and social justice. By challenging conventional banking practices and focusing on the economically marginalized, Yunus proved that financial inclusion and poverty alleviation are not only possible but can also foster self-reliance and societal transformation. Critics have raised concerns about the potential for over-indebtedness and the need for stronger regulatory frameworks, but the overall impact of microcredit in alleviating poverty remains undeniable.

3.6. Relevance and Takeaways:

The Grameen Bank's story serves as a powerful reminder that economic initiatives can be driven by a deep commitment to spiritual values and a desire to uplift the most vulnerable. By combining financial tools with social empowerment, the microcredit model challenges traditional assumptions about economic development and demonstrates the transformative potential of inclusive, ethical, and compassionate approaches to addressing poverty and inequality.

3.7. Concluding Thought:

As we reflect on the legacy of the Grameen Bank, we are reminded that true economic progress is not merely measured in GDP figures or stock market returns, but in the ability to create opportunities for human flourishing, dignity, and the realization of our shared spiritual values of compassion and justice.

These two case studies, the Mondragon Corporation, and the Grameen Bank, serve as powerful examples of how economic structures can be shaped by spiritual principles, fostering community empowerment, ethical business practices, and a more equitable distribution of resources. By challenging traditional notions of profit-driven capitalism and embracing values of cooperation, solidarity, and compassion, these initiatives have demonstrated the transformative potential of aligning economic endeavors with deeper ethical and spiritual foundations.

As we continue to grapple with the complex challenges of our time, such as poverty, inequality, and environmental degradation, these case studies offer a beacon of hope and inspiration. They remind us that economic progress need not come at the expense of human dignity or spiritual well-being, but rather, that the pursuit of material prosperity can be harmonized with the highest ideals of justice, compassion, and collective upliftment.

In the end, the true measure of economic success lies not merely in financial metrics, but in our ability to create systems that nurture human flourishing, foster community empowerment, and uphold the sacred principles that have guided humanity's spiritual journey throughout the ages. By embracing this holistic vision, we can forge a path toward a more equitable, sustainable, and spiritually fulfilling economic future.

The Role of the Church in Economic Development

Juxtaposing the Church's historical and contemporary roles in economic development reveals a compelling interplay between its enduring spiritual mission and its evolving methods of engagement. While the core values of charity, stewardship, and advocacy for the marginalized have remained steadfast, the scale and mechanisms through which these principles are applied have undergone significant transformation.

Throughout history, the Church has been a guiding force in shaping economic and social structures, with its influence permeating various spheres of human endeavor. In the Middle Ages, monasteries served as centers of learning, agricultural innovation, and economic activity, cultivating self-sufficiency and providing relief to the impoverished. The Church's commitment to charitable works laid the foundations for many of the social welfare systems we know today, establishing principles of compassion and community support.

As we examine the attributes that define the Church's involvement in economic development, several key facets emerge: 1. Charitable Actions: From the distribution of alms to the establishment of hospitals, schools, and orphanages, the Church has consistently championed acts of charity as a fundamental tenet of its spiritual mission. 2. Community Support: Beyond individual acts of kindness, the Church has sought to uplift entire communities, fostering economic empowerment, education, and social cohesion.

3. Advocacy for Social Justice: Guided by a moral compass rooted in spiritual teachings, the Church has been a vocal advocate for the rights of the poor, the marginalized, and the oppressed, challenging unjust economic systems and championing equitable distribution of resources.

While these foundational principles have endured, the modern era has witnessed a shift in the Church's approach to economic development. Recognizing the limitations of traditional charity models and the systemic nature of poverty and inequality, the Church has increasingly embraced more sustainable and participatory strategies. From microfinance initiatives to cooperative enterprises, the focus has shifted toward empowering individuals and communities, fostering self-reliance, and promoting inclusive economic growth.

One notable example is the Catholic Church's endorsement of the "Economy of Communion" model, which emphasizes ethical business practices, profit-sharing, and the reinvestment of resources into initiatives that benefit the poor and marginalized. This approach aligns economic activity with spiritual principles of solidarity, human dignity, and the common good, recognizing that true prosperity cannot be achieved at the expense of the most vulnerable.

Similarly, various Protestant denominations have championed ethical investing and socially responsible business practices, leveraging their economic influence to promote environmental sustainability, fair labor standards, and corporate accountability. This reflects a recognition that economic power can be harnessed as a force for positive change, aligning financial resources with spiritual values of stewardship and justice.

While the methods and scale of engagement may have evolved, the underlying similarities between historical and modern approaches lie in the Church's unwavering commitment to alleviating suffering, promoting human flourishing, and upholding the inherent dignity of every individual. From the monasteries of old to the microfinance initiatives of today, the thread of compassion and concern for the marginalized remains woven into the fabric of the Church's economic engagement.

However, the contrasts between eras are equally noteworthy. Where the Church once relied primarily on charitable acts and moral suasion, it now wields greater influence through its economic and financial power, shaping investment decisions and advocating for systemic reforms. Moreover, the Church's contemporary engagement extends beyond local communities to global networks, leveraging its vast resources and influence to address issues of global poverty, environmental degradation, and economic inequality.

These observations carry profound implications for our understanding of the Church's evolving role in promoting spiritual and economic well-being. They challenge us to reimagine the boundaries between the sacred and the secular, recognizing that economic structures and spiritual principles need not be at odds, but can be harmonized through innovative approaches and a commitment to ethical and compassionate practices.

As we grapple with the complexities of the modern global economy, the Church's journey offers valuable lessons on the importance of balancing material progress with spiritual and ethical considerations. It reminds us that true prosperity cannot be measured solely by financial metrics, but must encompass the holistic well-being of individuals, communities, and the planet we share.

In the face of pressing challenges such as climate change, income inequality, and the erosion of social safety nets, the Church's enduring emphasis on stewardship, solidarity, and the common good provides a moral compass for navigating these uncharted waters. By fostering partnerships between religious institutions, ethical businesses, and civil society organizations, we can forge new paths toward a more equitable, sustainable, and spiritually fulfilling economic future.

Ultimately, the role of the Church in economic development is not a static one, but rather a dynamic and evolving narrative that reflects the ever-changing complexities of the human condition. As we look to the future, we are called upon to embrace the Church's timeless spiritual wisdom while adapting its methods to the realities of our time. By doing so, we can cultivate economic systems that uplift the human spirit, promote social justice, and honor our shared responsibility as stewards of this world – a world in which material prosperity and spiritual fulfillment need not be at odds, but can coexist in a harmonious and sustainable balance.

Spiritual Practices for Economic Success

1. Establish the goal:

The path toward economic success is often fraught with challenges, and it can be easy to lose sight of our spiritual values amidst the pursuit of material wealth. However, by integrating spiritual practices into our daily lives, we can cultivate a profound sense of purpose, clarity, and inner fulfillment, which can ultimately enhance our financial wellbeing. Through this guide, readers will learn how to harmonize their spiritual journey with their economic pursuits, achieving a balanced and holistic approach to prosperity.

2. List the necessary materials or prerequisites:

- An open heart and mind, receptive to embracing spiritual principles
- A willingness to engage in regular spiritual practices (e.g., meditation, prayer, contemplation)
- Scriptural or philosophical texts aligned with your spiritual beliefs
- Financial planning tools and resources (e.g., budgeting software, investment guides)

3. Broad overview:

The path to integrating spiritual practices for economic success involves a journey of self-discovery, mindfulness, and a commitment to aligning your actions with your deepest values. It begins with cultivating a strong foundation of spiritual awareness, which can provide clarity, focus, and a sense of purpose in your financial endeavors. Through regular spiritual practices, you will learn to cultivate qualities such as patience, gratitude, and a spirit of service, which can profoundly influence your approach to wealth creation and management. As you progress, you will develop a holistic financial plan that reflects your spiritual principles, ensuring that your economic pursuits are in harmony with your inner growth. Ultimately, this journey will enable you to achieve both material abundance and spiritual fulfillment, creating a life of true prosperity.

4. Detailed steps:

Develop a consistent spiritual practice: Set aside dedicated time each day for prayer, meditation, or contemplation, tailored to your spiritual beliefs. Explore various techniques, such as mindfulness meditation, prayer, or sacred readings, to find what resonates with you. Establish a sacred space in your home or seek out spiritual communities for support and guidance.

- Cultivate spiritual virtues: Embrace qualities like compassion, humility, and gratitude, which can shift your perspective on wealth and success. Practice non-attachment and detachment from material possessions, recognizing their impermanence. Develop a spirit of service, using your resources to uplift others and contribute to the greater good.
- Examine your relationship with money: Reflect on your beliefs, attitudes, and emotional associations with wealth and abundance. Identify and release any limiting beliefs or negative patterns that may hinder your financial progress. Align your financial goals with your spiritual values, ensuring they are rooted in ethical and meaningful pursuits.
- Develop a holistic financial plan: Incorporate spiritual principles into your budgeting, investment strategies, and wealth management practices. Consider ethical and socially responsible investment options that align with your values. Allocate a portion of your resources toward charitable causes or initiatives that resonate with your spiritual beliefs.
- Practice mindfulness in your work and business: Approach your professional endeavors with presence, focus, and integrity, aligning your actions with your spiritual values. Cultivate positive relationships with colleagues, clients, and

stakeholders, guided by principles of compassion and respect. Seek opportunities to contribute to the well-being of your community and the environment through your work.

- Embrace spiritual practice as a lifestyle: Integrate spiritual principles into all aspects of your life, from relationships to leisure activities. Foster a growth mindset, continuously learning and evolving your spiritual understanding. Seek out like-minded individuals or communities that can support and inspire you on this journey.

5. Tips and warnings:

Tips:

- Be patient and consistent with your spiritual practices, as meaningful transformation takes time and dedication.
- Seek guidance from spiritual mentors or teachers who can offer wisdom and support on your journey.
- Regularly review and adjust your financial plan to ensure alignment with your evolving spiritual values.

Warnings:

- Avoid dogmatism or rigid beliefs that can limit your growth and understanding.
- Be wary of spiritual practices or teachings that promote greed, materialism, or unethical financial practices.
- Maintain balance and avoid becoming overly ascetic or rejecting material prosperity altogether.

6. Verify success or comprehension:

As you integrate spiritual practices into your economic pursuits, you can measure your progress and success through various indicators:

- A sense of inner peace, contentment, and fulfillment, regardless of your financial circumstances
- Increased clarity and focus in your professional and financial endeavors
- Alignment between your financial decisions and your spiritual values, leading to a greater sense of integrity
- Positive impact on your community and the environment through your work or charitable contributions
- Financial abundance that is sustainable, ethical, and in harmony with your spiritual beliefs

7. Potential problems and solutions:

Potential problem: Conflicting priorities or beliefs between spiritual and financial pursuits.

Solution: Regularly reflect on your values and priorities, and make adjustments to ensure alignment between your spiritual beliefs and financial practices. Seek guidance from spiritual mentors or financial advisors who understand the importance of integration.

Potential problem: Excessive attachment to material wealth or success, leading to spiritual neglect.

Solution: Cultivate practices of non-attachment and gratitude, and regularly engage in spiritual activities that ground you in your deeper values. Surround yourself with supportive communities that can hold you accountable and remind you of your spiritual path.

Potential problem: Difficulties adapting spiritual principles to the practical realities of financial management or business operations.

Solution: Seek out resources, case studies, and mentors who have successfully integrated spiritual practices into their professional and financial lives. Embrace a growth mindset and be willing to experiment and adapt as you navigate this journey.

By embracing the guidance and wisdom offered in this guide, you will be well-equipped to embark on a transformative journey, one that harmonizes your spiritual aspirations with your economic pursuits, creating a life of true prosperity, fulfillment, and lasting impact.

Impact of Prosperity Theology on Modern Economics

Prosperity theology, often referred to as the "prosperity gospel," has become an influential force in the modern economic landscape, shaping the financial beliefs and practices of millions of believers worldwide. This doctrine, which emphasizes that material wealth and physical well-being are divine promises for those who adhere to certain spiritual principles, has sparked intense debate among theologians, economists, and sociologists alike. As this belief system continues to gain traction, it is crucial to engage in an evidence-based analysis of its impact on contemporary economic behavior.

The primary claim at the heart of this analysis is that prosperity theology has significantly influenced the economic behavior and financial decision-making of its adherents. This assertion is supported by a wealth of evidence, ranging from statistical data on giving patterns and financial success stories to critiques from theologians and economists alike. One compelling piece of evidence is a study conducted by the Pew Research Center, which found that among Protestant Christians in the United States, those who subscribe to prosperity theology tend to have higher household incomes and engage in more charitable giving compared to their counterparts who do not hold such beliefs.

This study, which surveyed a representative sample of over 4,000 American adults, employed rigorous methodologies and data collection techniques, lending credibility to its findings. The researchers utilized a combination of phone interviews and online surveys, ensuring a diverse and representative sample. Furthermore, the Pew Research Center is widely regarded as a credible and reputable source of information on social and demographic trends, enhancing the validity of the study's findings.

While this evidence supports the claim that prosperity theology influences economic behavior, there are also critical voices that challenge its validity. Some theologians argue that the prosperity gospel distorts the true essence of Christianity, promoting a distorted view of material wealth as the primary indicator of spiritual blessings. Economists also raise concerns about the potential for this belief system to fuel excessive consumerism, debt accumulation, and financial irresponsibility, as adherents may interpret financial success as a sign of divine favor.

However, proponents of prosperity theology offer explanations and additional evidence to address these critiques. They argue that the emphasis on financial abundance and wealth is not solely focused on personal gain, but rather on empowering individuals and communities to achieve their full potential and contribute to society in meaningful ways. Supporters point to numerous success stories of individuals and organizations that have used their wealth to fund charitable initiatives, support community development projects, and promote economic empowerment.

Furthermore, advocates of prosperity theology highlight that the doctrine often encourages principles of hard work, discipline, and responsible stewardship of resources, which can foster positive economic outcomes. They cite examples of successful entrepreneurs and business leaders who attribute their financial success, at least in part, to the spiritual principles they have embraced, such as faith, integrity, and a commitment to serving others.

To further strengthen the claim of prosperity theology's influence on economic behavior, additional evidence can be drawn from various sources. For instance, studies conducted by religious organizations and research institutions have examined the impact of prosperity-oriented sermons and teachings on congregants' financial practices. These studies have found correlations between exposure to such teachings and increased rates of entrepreneurship, investment in education and personal development, and a propensity for philanthropic giving.

Moreover, the growth of prosperity-focused ministries, conferences, and media platforms provides insight into the reach and popularity of this belief system. Many of these organizations leverage modern marketing techniques and social media to amplify their message, potentially influencing the financial decisions of a global audience. The success of these enterprises, as measured by their financial resources and reach, can be viewed as a testament to the economic impact of prosperity theology.

Ultimately, the evidence presented underscores the significance of prosperity theology's impact on modern economics. While debates continue regarding its theological validity and potential drawbacks, the influence of this belief system on the financial behavior of its adherents is undeniable. As such, it is crucial for economists, policymakers, and financial institutions to engage in further research and analysis to understand the practical applications and broader implications of prosperity theology on individual and communal economic practices.

By embracing an evidence-based approach, we can gain a deeper understanding of the complex interplay between religious beliefs and economic behavior, ultimately informing more effective policies and strategies that promote sustainable and inclusive economic growth. Additionally, this analysis can contribute to broader discussions surrounding the role of faith and spirituality in shaping economic systems and fostering a more holistic and values-driven approach to wealth creation and distribution.

Challenges and Solutions in Integrating Faith With Finances

As spiritual beings traversing the temporal realm, we are often faced with the challenge of aligning our financial pursuits with our sacred values and principles. The intricate balance between wealth accumulation and adherence to faith-based teachings has been a longstanding struggle for individuals and communities alike. In an era characterized by rapid economic transformations and globalization, the need to achieve harmony between financial ambitions and spiritual values has become more pressing than ever.

The scale and consequences of this challenge cannot be understated. Financial stress and anxiety have become pervasive in modern society, afflicting even those who profess a deep commitment to their faith. According to a recent study by the American Psychological Association, over 70% of adults in the United States reported experiencing significant financial strain, with many citing concerns about meeting their basic needs and securing their financial future. This stress not only impacts mental and physical well-being but also strains relationships and compromises overall quality of life.

Moreover, the pursuit of financial success often leads individuals and organizations to compromise their ethical principles or engage in practices that conflict with their religious beliefs. The allure of wealth and prosperity can overshadow moral considerations, resulting in decisions that prioritize personal gain over collective well-being. This dilemma is particularly acute for faith-based businesses and enterprises, which face the constant tension between generating profits and upholding the values central to their mission.

If left unaddressed, the disconnect between faith and finances can have far-reaching consequences. At the individual level, it can breed spiritual disillusionment, erode moral foundations, and foster a sense of emptiness despite material abundance. At the societal level, the prioritization of wealth over ethical principles can contribute to systemic issues such as income inequality, environmental degradation, and the exploitation of vulnerable populations. Ultimately, the failure to reconcile these conflicting domains can undermine the very fabric of communities and impede the realization of a more just and equitable economic order.

Recognizing the urgency of this challenge, many faith-based organizations, financial advisors, and thought leaders have proposed viable solutions to bridge the gap between spiritual values and financial aspirations. One promising approach is the practice of faith-based financial planning, which integrates religious principles into the process of managing personal and organizational finances. This holistic framework encourages individuals and institutions to align their financial decisions with their core beliefs, fostering a sense of purpose and fulfillment beyond mere wealth accumulation.

The implementation of faith-based financial planning can take various forms, each tailored to the specific needs and values of the individuals or communities involved. For individuals, this may involve working with financial advisors who are well-versed in their particular faith tradition and can provide guidance on ethical investing, charitable giving, and sustainable wealth management. For organizations, it can involve the development of socially responsible investment strategies, ethical lending practices, and the allocation of resources toward initiatives that align with their spiritual mission.

However, the path to successful integration of faith and finances is not without obstacles. One significant challenge lies in overcoming the prevailing cultural narratives that equate financial success with personal worth and societal status. Breaking free from these deeply ingrained societal norms requires a concerted effort to redefine the meaning of prosperity and reshape collective attitudes toward wealth and its purpose.

Another potential obstacle is the inherent complexity of navigating the financial landscape while adhering to ethical and religious principles. Individuals and organizations may encounter situations where the available investment options or business practices seem at odds with their values, necessitating difficult trade-offs or the courage to forge alternative paths. Navigating these intricate decisions often requires deep understanding of financial systems, coupled with a strong sense of moral conviction and a willingness to challenge conventional wisdom.

Despite these challenges, the growing body of evidence suggests that faith-based financial planning can be a profoundly effective solution in achieving the desired harmony between spiritual values and financial ambitions. Success stories abound, ranging from individuals who have found peace and fulfillment through aligning their investments with their beliefs to organizations that have thrived while upholding their ethical principles.

One notable example is the rise of Islamic finance, a system that adheres to the principles of Sharia law and prohibits practices such as usury, excessive speculation, and investments in industries deemed harmful or unethical. Once a niche market, Islamic finance has experienced remarkable growth in recent decades, with assets under management exceeding $2 trillion globally. This growth is a testament to the viability and appeal of faith-based financial models, even in the face of conventional financial systems.

Another compelling case is that of faith-based impact investing, which aims to generate positive social and environmental outcomes alongside financial returns. Organizations such as the Interfaith Center on Corporate Responsibility (ICCR) work with faith-based investors to encourage companies to adopt responsible business practices, promote sustainability, and address issues such as human rights, environmental protection, and corporate governance. These efforts have yielded tangible results, with many companies responding to shareholder advocacy by implementing meaningful reforms and aligning their operations with ethical principles.

While faith-based financial planning and socially responsible investing offer promising solutions, it is important to acknowledge the existence of alternative approaches. One such approach is the concept of voluntary simplicity, which encourages individuals to consciously limit their material consumption and pursue a life of minimalism, with a focus on spiritual fulfillment and environmental stewardship. While this path may not resonate with everyone, it offers a thought-provoking perspective on redefining the relationship between faith, finances, and personal well-being.

In conclusion, the challenge of integrating faith with finances is a multifaceted and ongoing endeavor that requires continuous reflection, adjustment, and a commitment to personal and collective growth. As individuals and communities navigate the complexities of the modern financial landscape, the pursuit of harmony between spiritual values and financial aspirations remains a noble and necessary pursuit. By embracing faith-based financial planning, socially responsible investing, and a willingness to challenge conventional narratives, we can forge a path toward a more equitable and sustainable economic future – one that aligns with our deepest values and contributes to the flourishing of all.

The Metrics of Flourishment: Measuring Success Beyond Wealth

How can we truly measure success in a way that transcends mere financial wealth and embraces the multifaceted aspects of human flourishing?

For far too long, our society has relied on narrow economic metrics, such as Gross Domestic Product (GDP) and individual net worth, to gauge progress and personal accomplishment. While these measures provide insight into material wealth and economic output, they fail to capture the rich tapestry of human experience and the various dimensions that contribute to a truly fulfilling and meaningful life.

The limitations of traditional economic metrics become apparent when we consider the complex realities of our existence. Can a nation's GDP adequately reflect the happiness and well-being of its citizens? Does an individual's net worth accurately portray their spiritual growth, social impact, or environmental stewardship? The answer is a resounding no. These metrics, while valuable in certain contexts, paint an incomplete picture and overlook the intangible elements that shape the human condition.

To truly gauge success in a holistic manner, we must embrace a more comprehensive and nuanced approach – one that acknowledges the intricate interplay between economic prosperity, psychological well-being, spiritual fulfillment, social cohesion, and environmental sustainability. By expanding our understanding of success beyond mere financial wealth, we can cultivate a more balanced and purposeful existence, aligning our pursuits with the fundamental principles of human flourishing.

The problem with relying solely on economic indicators is that they often overlook the invisible threads that weave together the fabric of a thriving society. A nation may boast a soaring GDP, yet its citizens may suffer from rampant inequality, social unrest, and environmental degradation. An individual may amass considerable wealth, yet their relationships, mental health, and spiritual growth may languish. In such scenarios, true success remains elusive, as it fails to encompass the multidimensional aspects that contribute to a life well-lived.

Common misconceptions and typical approaches to measuring success often stem from a narrow focus on material wealth and economic growth. The relentless pursuit of financial gain, driven by societal pressures and ingrained cultural narratives, can lead individuals and societies astray, sacrificing essential elements of well-being on the altar of profit maximization. These misguided approaches not only perpetuate a skewed understanding of success but also contribute to the erosion of social cohesion, environmental degradation, and the neglect of our inner spiritual selves.

To address this challenge, a unique and holistic approach is required – one that embraces a multidimensional perspective on success. This approach recognizes that true prosperity encompasses not only economic indicators but also dimensions such as happiness, spiritual well-being, social impact, and environmental sustainability. By recognizing the interconnectedness of these elements, we can establish novel metrics that capture the essence of human flourishing in its entirety.

One example of such a metric is the Genuine Progress Indicator (GPI), which aims to measure economic progress while accounting for factors like income distribution, environmental costs, and the value of unpaid labor. By incorporating these elements, the GPI provides a more comprehensive picture of societal well-being than traditional GDP measures. Another promising metric is the Gross National Happiness (GNH) index, pioneered by the Kingdom of Bhutan, which evaluates progress based on nine domains:

Psychological well-being, health, education, time use, cultural resilience, good governance, community vitality, ecological diversity, and living standards.

To illustrate the potential of these holistic approaches, consider the case of Costa Rica. Despite having a relatively modest GDP per capita, Costa Rica consistently ranks among the happiest nations in the world, scoring highly on measures of life satisfaction, environmental sustainability, and social progress. This success can be attributed, in part, to the country's emphasis on preserving its natural resources, investing in healthcare and education, and fostering a strong sense of community and cultural identity.

On an individual level, the concept of "Ikigai" – a Japanese term that translates to "reason for being" – offers a compelling framework for measuring personal success beyond financial wealth. Ikigai encourages individuals to find fulfillment by aligning their passions, professions, values, and contributions to society. By pursuing a life purpose that resonates with their inner selves and benefits the greater good, individuals can experience a deep sense of satisfaction and purpose, transcending the narrow confines of material wealth.

Undoubtedly, transitioning toward these holistic metrics of success will face skepticism and objections. Critics may argue that such measures are subjective, difficult to quantify, and impractical for guiding economic and policy decisions. However, these concerns can be addressed by highlighting the limitations of relying solely on economic indicators and the growing body of research demonstrating the profound impact of factors like happiness, social connectedness, and environmental health on overall societal wellbeing.

Furthermore, by acknowledging the multidimensional nature of human flourishing, we can embrace a more nuanced and inclusive approach to measuring progress. Rather than discarding economic indicators entirely, we can integrate them with other well-being metrics, creating a comprehensive framework that accounts for both material prosperity and the intangible elements that contribute to a fulfilling life.

To truly embrace this holistic perspective on success, individuals and societies must undertake a transformative journey – one that challenges deeply ingrained assumptions and encourages a paradigm shift in our collective consciousness. This journey begins with personal introspection and a willingness to question the societal narratives that equate success solely with financial gain. It requires a commitment to cultivating inner peace, nurturing meaningful relationships, and aligning our actions with a higher purpose that transcends self-interest.

On a broader scale, this transformation necessitates a collaborative effort among policymakers, educators, and community leaders to redefine our understanding of progress and prioritize the well-being of individuals, communities, and the planet. By integrating holistic success metrics into educational curricula, public discourse, and policy frameworks, we can foster a cultural shift toward a more balanced and fulfilling vision of prosperity.

In conclusion, while financial wealth and economic growth are undoubtedly important, they are but one facet of a truly successful and fulfilling existence. To truly measure success, we must embrace a multidimensional approach that accounts for the intricate interplay between economic prosperity, psychological well-being, spiritual fulfillment, social cohesion, and environmental sustainability. By expanding our understanding of success and adopting holistic metrics that capture the essence of human flourishing, we can forge a path toward a more balanced, purposeful, and meaningful life – one that transcends the narrow confines of financial wealth and embraces the richness of the human experience in all its complexity.

3

JESUS CHRIST: THE ETERNAL ARCHITECT OF CULTURAL PERFECTION

The Cultural Mandate: Reclaiming Dominion

In the vast tapestry of human existence, few questions have captivated our minds and hearts as profoundly as the quest for understanding our purpose and role within the cosmic order. For millennia, philosophers, theologians, and scholars have grappled with the profound question: Why are we here? And what is our rightful place within the grand scheme of creation?

At the heart of this inquiry lies the Cultural Mandate, a divine directive that echoes through the very pages of Genesis, the foundational text of Judeo-Christian tradition. This mandate, a clarion call to humanity, resounds with a resounding imperative: "Be fruitful and multiply, and fill the earth and subdue it; and have dominion over the fish of the sea and over the birds of the air and over every living thing that moves upon the earth" (Genesis 1:28).

In this verse, we find a profound and far-reaching commission, a charge that not only speaks to our physical propagation but also to our spiritual and intellectual stewardship of the natural world. It is a call to cultivate and nurture the earth, to harness its resources with wisdom and care, and to exercise a benevolent dominion over the myriad forms of life that grace our planet. This mandate, at its core, is a testament to the intrinsic value and dignity bestowed upon humanity by our Creator, entrusting us with the sacred responsibility of tending to the very fabric of existence.

Yet, as we delve deeper into the narrative of Scripture, we encounter a pivotal moment, a turning point that forever altered the trajectory of this divine mandate. The advent of sin and its consequences cast a shadow over humanity's intended role as stewards of creation, introducing a rift between our original purpose and the fallen state of the world we inhabit. It is within this context that the life and ministry of Jesus Christ, the eternal Son of God, takes on profound significance, for it is through His teachings and actions that the Cultural Mandate finds its ultimate fulfillment and restoration.

Throughout the Gospels, we witness Christ's ministry as a living embodiment of this mandate, a reclamation of dominion over a world marred by sin and brokenness. His parables and miracles were not mere displays of power but profound cultural statements, aimed at societal transformation and the restoration of divine order. Consider, for instance, the Parable of the Talents (Matthew 25:14-30), which speaks to the stewardship of our God-given gifts and resources. In this parable, Christ commends those who faithfully multiplied their talents, while rebuking the one who squandered his opportunity for fruitful service.

Similarly, the miracle of the feeding of the five thousand (Matthew 14:13-21) transcends its miraculous nature to become a symbolic act of dominion over scarcity and lack. With just five loaves and two fish, Christ demonstrated His authority over the natural world, multiplying the meager provisions to feed a multitude. This act not only met a physical need but also served as a profound reminder of our calling to harness the resources entrusted to us for the benefit of humanity and the furtherance of God's kingdom.

Yet, the true culmination of Christ's reclamation of dominion is found in His resurrection and ascension, pivotal moments that reestablished His authority over all creation. Through His victory over death and sin, Christ not only restored our relationship with the Father but also paved the way for the ultimate fulfillment of the Cultural Mandate. His ascension to the right hand of the Father signified His rightful position as the eternal ruler and sovereign over all things, both in heaven and on earth (Ephesians 1:20-23).

The theological implications of this reclamation of dominion are far-reaching and profound. By conquering sin and death, Christ has opened the way for us, His followers, to participate in the ongoing work of restoration and stewardship. Just as He walked the earth, exercising authority over the physical and spiritual realms, we too are called to be ambassadors of His kingdom, perpetuating the Cultural Mandate in our contemporary society.

This mandate extends beyond mere environmental stewardship, though that remains a crucial aspect of our calling. It encompasses the totality of our existence, from the nurturing of our families and communities to the cultivation of knowledge, arts, and sciences. It challenges us to exercise dominion over the brokenness and injustice that plague our world, to be agents of healing and reconciliation, and to continually strive toward the restoration of all things to their intended purpose and design.

As we embark on this journey of reclaiming dominion, we must be mindful of the pitfalls that can arise from a distorted understanding of this mandate. Throughout history, humanity has often succumbed to the temptation of exploiting the natural world for selfish gain, subjugating creation to our own greed and desires. Yet, the true essence of the Cultural Mandate calls us to a higher standard, one rooted in selfless stewardship, humility, and a deep reverence for the intricate tapestry of life that surrounds us.

Moreover, we must resist the allure of dominion as a means of oppression or subjugation over our fellow human beings. The mandate was never intended to be a license for the strong to lord over the weak, nor for any one group to claim superiority over another. Rather, it is a call to exercise authority with wisdom, compassion, and a recognition of the inherent dignity and worth of all people, regardless of their circumstances or station in life.

As we navigate the complexities of our modern world, the Cultural Mandate stands as a beacon, a guiding light that reminds us of our sacred purpose and our inextricable connection to the tapestry of creation. It is a call to embrace our role as stewards, cultivators, and ambassadors of the divine order, working tirelessly to restore that which has been broken and to nurture that which has been entrusted to our care.

In this endeavor, we are not alone, for the resurrected Christ walks alongside us, empowering us with His Spirit and guiding us toward the ultimate consummation of His kingdom. As we faithfully embrace the Cultural Mandate, we become co-laborers with our Creator, participating in the grand narrative of redemption and restoration that spans from the dawn of creation to the final culmination of all things.

Let us, then, take up this mantle with humility and resolve, recognizing that our lives are but a fleeting chapter in the grand tapestry of existence. Yet, within that chapter lies the potential for profound impact, for leaving an indelible mark upon the world, and for ushering in a new era of dominion – one rooted in love, justice, and the restoration of all things to their intended glory.

Teachings on the Kingdom of God: A Blueprint for Society

As we embark on our exploration of Jesus Christ's teachings on the Kingdom of God, it becomes imperative to grasp the profound significance and nuances of several key terms and concepts. Understanding these foundational elements is crucial, for they serve as the bedrock upon which the entire edifice of this revolutionary worldview is constructed. In the pages that follow, we will delve into these terms, unraveling their depths and implications, ultimately revealing a blueprint for cultural perfection that transcends the limitations of our current societal structures.

First, let us ponder the term "Kingdom of God" itself, a phrase that has sparked fervent discussions and captivated the hearts and minds of countless individuals throughout history. What is this kingdom that Jesus spoke of so fervently, and why did it hold such profound significance in His teachings? While the term might evoke visions of a physical, earthly realm, the Kingdom of God that Christ proclaimed was far more than a territorial dominion. It was a spiritual reality, a transformative force that sought to reshape the very fabric of human existence, ushering in a new paradigm of justice, love, and righteousness.

At the heart of this kingdom lies the concept of the "Reign of God" – a radical reorientation of power and authority that challenges the prevailing hierarchies and systems of this world. In this divine kingdom, the meek and humble are exalted, while the proud and self-righteous are humbled. It is a realm where the last become first, and the first become last (Matthew 20:16), a complete inversion of the temporal power structures that so often govern our societies. The Reign of God is a clarion call to surrender our preconceived notions of greatness and embrace a countercultural understanding of true strength – one rooted in service, humility, and an unwavering commitment to the welfare of others.

Inextricably linked to this concept of the Reign of God is the idea of "Righteousness," a term that transcends mere moral rectitude and encompasses a holistic pursuit of justice, equity, and the restoration of all things to their intended state of shalom – a Hebrew word that encapsulates peace, wholeness, and the harmonious integration of all aspects of existence. The righteousness that Christ proclaimed was not a rigid adherence to legalistic codes but a profound transformation of the heart, a realignment of our values and priorities with the very essence of the Kingdom of God.

Yet, the path to this kingdom is not one of human effort alone, but rather a journey of radical surrender and reliance on divine grace. This is embodied in the notion of "Repentance," is a term that extends far beyond a mere acknowledgment of wrongdoing. In the context of the Kingdom of God, repentance is a seismic shift in our perception, a complete reorientation of our lives toward the values and principles that Christ espoused. It is a turning away from the allure of temporal pursuits and a wholehearted embrace of the eternal, a willingness to lay down our own agendas and submit to the transformative power of the Holy Spirit.

Hand in hand with repentance comes the concept of "Transformation," a process that lies at the very heart of the Kingdom of God. This is not a mere external change but a profound, inner metamorphosis, a renewal of the mind and spirit that enables us to become living embodiments of the values and principles that Christ exemplified. Transformation is the catalyst that propels us from a state of spiritual stagnation to one of dynamic growth, enabling us to become agents of change and harbingers of the Kingdom in our spheres of influence.

As we journey through these terms and concepts, we cannot overlook the centrality of "Love" in Christ's teachings on the Kingdom of God. Love, in this context, is not a mere sentimental notion but a revolutionary force that has the power to upend the very foundations of human society. It is a love that transcends boundaries and breaks down barriers, embracing even those whom the world deems as enemies (Matthew 5:44). It is a love that seeks to restore dignity to the marginalized and elevate the oppressed, a love that challenges us to see the inherent worth and value in every human being, regardless of their circumstances or station in life.

Woven through these concepts is the profound truth that the Kingdom of God is not merely a distant, ethereal reality but a tangible force that can take root in the here and now. The Sermon on the Mount, a pivotal discourse in Christ's ministry, serves as a blueprint for this kingdom, offering practical guidance on how to embody its principles in our daily lives. The Beatitudes, a series of blessings that form the heart of this sermon, present a radical reframing of what it means to be truly blessed, challenging the prevailing notions of success and prosperity that so often dominate our cultural narratives.

As we unpack these terms and concepts, we come to realize that the Kingdom of God is not merely a pie-in-the-sky ideal but a revolutionary paradigm that has the power to transform individuals, communities, and ultimately, entire societies. It is a clarion call to embrace a countercultural way of living, one that rejects the pursuit of selfish ambition and embraces a life of sacrificial service, love, and a steadfast commitment to justice and righteousness.

In the pages that follow, we will delve deeper into the teachings of Christ, exploring how these foundational concepts can be practically applied in our contemporary world. We will examine the transformative power of the Beatitudes and the radical implications of living out the principles of the Kingdom of God in our families, communities, and spheres of influence. Through this journey, we will unveil a blueprint for cultural perfection, a roadmap that guides us toward the realization of a society rooted in the values and ideals that Christ so passionately proclaimed.

As we embark on this exploration, let us approach it with open hearts and minds, willing to be challenged and transformed by the profound truths that lie within these teachings. For in embracing the Kingdom of God, we not only discover the path to personal fulfillment and spiritual growth but also become agents of change, ushering in a new era of justice, love, and the restoration of all things to their intended state of shalom.

Abolition of Death: The Pinnacle of Christ's Cultural Reform

The abolition of death stands as the pinnacle of Jesus Christ's cultural reform, a transformative event that reverberates through the fabric of human existence, reshaping our perceptions of life, mortality, and the ultimate destiny of humankind. To fully grasp the magnitude of this pivotal moment, we must embark on a historical timeline that traces the events leading up to and following the resurrection, a journey that unveils the profound cultural implications and eschatological promises woven into the very fabric of this defining act.

1. The Significance of Understanding the Trajectory of Death's Abolition: Before delving into the timeline, it is essential to acknowledge the profound significance of understanding the historical trajectory of death's abolition. This event stands as a watershed moment in human history, a watershed event that transcends mere theological discussion and holds profound ramifications for the entirety of human society and culture. It marks the culmination of an age-old quest for the ultimate triumph over mortality, a quest that has captivated the hearts and minds of countless individuals across civilizations and belief systems. By tracing this trajectory, we not only gain insight into the events themselves but also uncover the deep-seated cultural implications, hopes, and aspirations that have been intricately woven into the narrative of death's defeat.

2. The Earliest Roots and Mentions of Death's Conquest: The roots of death's conquest can be traced back to the earliest narratives of human civilization, where the pursuit of immortality and the transcendence of mortality were central themes. From the Epic of Gilgamesh to the ancient Egyptian concept of the afterlife, cultures throughout history have grappled with the enigma of death and the longing for a state of everlasting existence. These early narratives and beliefs laid the groundwork for the eventual emergence of a more definitive promise – one that would culminate in the events surrounding Jesus Christ's crucifixion, burial, and triumphant resurrection.

3. The Key Events Leading to and Following the Resurrection:• The Crucifixion: A pivotal moment in the narrative, the crucifixion of Jesus Christ stands as a symbol of sacrifice and atonement, a willing embrace of suffering and death on behalf of humanity.• The Burial: Christ's burial in a tomb, a moment that seemingly sealed the fate of mortality and the finality of death.• The Resurrection: The earth-shattering event that shattered the bonds of death, as

Christ emerged triumphant from the tomb, proclaiming victory over the grave and the promise of eternal life for those who believe.• The Appearances and Witnesses: After the resurrection, Christ appeared to His disciples and followers, solidifying the reality of His conquest over death and providing a living testimony to the truth of His claims.• The Ascension: Christ's ascension to heaven, a symbolic act that marked the completion of His earthly mission and the establishment of His eternal reign, where death has been forever vanquished.

4. The Spread and Adaptation of the Resurrection Narrative: As the message of Christ's resurrection spread throughout the ancient world, it encountered diverse cultures and belief systems, each interpreting and adapting the narrative in unique ways. In the early Christian communities, the resurrection became a central tenet of faith, a source of hope, and the foundation for a new way of life. The concept of eternal life and the defeat of death resonated deeply with those who had long grappled with the specter of mortality, offering a profound promise of transcendence and a future free from the constraints of earthly existence.

5. Contemporary Interpretations and Practices: In contemporary times, the resurrection narrative continues to hold immense significance, shaping cultural perspectives and inspiring diverse practices and beliefs. For many Christians, the promise of eternal life and the abolition of death remain central tenets of their faith, guiding their worldview and influencing their approach to life and death. Beyond the realm of religion, the quest for immortality and the transcendence of mortality has manifested itself in various fields, from scientific research into life extension and cryonics to philosophical and ethical debates surrounding the nature of consciousness and the implications of conquering death.

6. Pivotal Moments and Challenges: Throughout history, the narrative of death's abolition has faced challenges and

pivotal moments that have shaped its trajectory. From the persecution and martyrdom of early Christians to the rise of philosophical and scientific skepticism, the concept of eternal life and the defeat of death has been subjected to scrutiny, debate, and at times, outright rejection. Yet, amidst these challenges, the resurrection narrative has endured, fueled by the unwavering faith of believers and the enduring human longing for a reality beyond the confines of mortality.

The abolition of death, as embodied in the resurrection of Jesus Christ, stands as a transformative cultural force, reshaping our understanding of existence, mortality, and the ultimate destiny of humankind. It is a promise that transcends time and culture, offering hope in the face of the inevitable reality of death and inspiring generations to embrace a life centered on the pursuit of eternal truths. As we reflect on this historical timeline, we are reminded that the conquest of death is not merely a theological milestone but a profound cultural event that has the power to reshape our perceptions, inspire our aspirations, and guide us toward a society founded on the promise of everlasting life and the restoration of all things to their intended state of perfection.

Miracles as Cultural Signposts: Demonstrating Divine Authority

Miracles stand as beacons of divine authority, transcending the realm of mere spectacle and serving as profound statements that challenge and transform the very fabric of human culture and society. Throughout history, these extraordinary events have not only captivated the imagination but have also profoundly reshaped societal norms and perceptions, echoing the divine intention to restore creation to its intended state of perfection.

1. An Overview of Miracles as Cultural Signposts: The miracles performed by Jesus Christ during His earthly

ministry were more than mere supernatural occurrences; they were deliberate acts of divine intervention, designed to address specific cultural issues and societal norms, and to serve as signposts pointing toward a restored creation under divine governance. These miracles challenged the prevailing beliefs and assumptions of their time, offering a glimpse into the transformative power of divine authority and the promise of a renewed world order.

2. The Main Proposition: Miracles as Statements of Divine Authority: At their core, the miracles of Jesus Christ were not merely isolated incidents of supernatural power but deliberate statements of divine authority. Each miracle carried with it a profound message, a challenge to the cultural norms and societal constructs that bound humanity in a state of brokenness and separation from the divine design. These acts of power were meant to shatter the limitations imposed by illness, natural chaos, and even death itself, pointing toward a reality where all things are made new and perfected under the sovereignty of God.

3. Key Miracles and Their Cultural Implications: To fully grasp the cultural significance of these miracles, let us examine three pivotal events that epitomized the divine intent to address and transform specific societal issues:

4. The Healing of the Paralytic (Matthew 9:1-8, Mark 2:1-12, Luke 5:17-26): In the ancient world, illness and physical disabilities were often viewed as divine punishment or the result of spiritual impurities. The healing of the paralytic man challenged this cultural perception, demonstrating that physical afflictions were not necessarily the result of personal sin or divine retribution. By forgiving man's sins and subsequently healing him, Jesus redefined the cultural understanding of illness, asserting that true restoration goes beyond physical healing and encompasses the forgiveness of sin and the restoration of a right relationship with God.

5. The Calming of the Storm (Matthew 8:23-27, Mark 4:35-41, Luke 8:22-25): In a world where the forces of nature were often deified and feared, the calming of the storm on the Sea of Galilee stood as a bold assertion of divine authority over the natural realm. This miracle challenged the cultural reverence for nature's power and the belief that natural phenomena were governed by capricious deities. By commanding the wind and waves with His words, Jesus proclaimed Himself as the sovereign ruler over creation, foreshadowing a future where all aspects of the natural world would be subject to divine governance and restoration.

6. The Raising of Lazarus (John 11:1-44): In ancient societies, death was the ultimate enemy, a force to be feared and accepted as an inescapable reality. The raising of Lazarus from the dead shattered this cultural perception, demonstrating that even death itself could be conquered through divine power. This miracle not only challenged the finality of death but also foreshadowed the ultimate triumph over mortality that would be achieved through Jesus Christ's own resurrection. It pointed toward a future where death would be abolished, and the promise of eternal life would become a tangible reality for all who placed their faith in the divine authority of the Savior.

7. Contemporary Manifestations of Divine Intervention: While the miracles of Jesus Christ occurred within a specific historical context, their significance and relevance transcend time and culture. Even in the modern world, we can witness manifestations of divine intervention that challenge and transform contemporary societal norms and perceptions. From miraculous healings that defy medical explanations to instances of divine protection and provision, these occurrences serve as reminders of God's ongoing commitment to the restoration and perfection of creation.

8. The Theological Significance of Miracles: The miracles performed by Jesus Christ are not merely historical curiosities; they hold profound theological significance, serving as evidence of God's unwavering commitment to the redemption and restoration of humanity and creation. These acts of divine authority affirm the power of God to overcome the brokenness and limitations imposed by sin, sickness, and death, offering a glimpse into the ultimate reality of a renewed and perfected existence under the sovereign reign of the Creator.

9. Miracles as a Call to Transformation: Beyond their cultural and theological implications, the miracles of Jesus Christ also serve as a clarion call to personal and societal transformation. They challenge us to re-evaluate our assumptions, beliefs, and cultural norms, inviting us to embrace a radically different perspective – one that acknowledges the authority of the divine and the promise of a restored creation. These miracles beckon us to step out of the confines of our limited worldviews and embrace a reality where the impossible becomes possible, where brokenness is mended, and where the limitations imposed by sin and death are eternally vanquished.

10. The Ongoing Impact and Significance: As we navigate the complexities of the modern world, the miracles of Jesus Christ stand as enduring reminders of the power of divine intervention and the transformative potential of faith. They challenge us to look beyond the surface of our cultural narratives and societal norms, inviting us to embrace a higher reality where divine authority reigns supreme, and the promise of restoration and perfection is made manifest. These miraculous events serve as signposts, guiding us toward a deeper understanding of the divine plan for creation and inspiring us to live as agents of transformation, embodying the values of love, hope, and eternal life that lie at the heart of the gospel message.

In conclusion, the miracles performed by Jesus Christ were not mere spectacles of power but profound statements of divine authority, designed to challenge and transform the cultural and societal norms of their time. These extraordinary events continue to resonate through the ages, inviting us to embrace a reality where the limitations imposed by sin, sickness, and death are transcended, and the promise of a restored creation under divine governance is made manifest. As we contemplate the significance of these miracles, we are called to a deeper faith, a renewed commitment to personal and societal transformation, and a steadfast hope in the ultimate triumph of divine love and redemption.

Parables: Encoded Instructions for an Ideal Society

Profound truths often find their most profound expressions through the tapestry of stories, where symbolism and allegory weave intricate patterns that resonate with the human experience and transcend the barriers of time and culture. Among the many narratives that have left an indelible mark on the collective human consciousness, the parables of Jesus Christ stand as encoded instructions for building an ideal society – a blueprint for a world where compassion, justice, and divine wisdom coalesce to create a harmonious tapestry of existence.

1. An Overview of Parables as Encoded Instructions: The parables of Jesus Christ are not mere fables or entertaining anecdotes; they are carefully crafted narratives that convey deep and transformative truths about the nature of human culture, society, and our relationship with the divine. These stories, rich in symbolism and allegory, are encoded instructions that challenge prevailing prejudices, promote inclusivity, and emphasize the importance of compassion, forgiveness, and a profound understanding of the divine will.

2. Key Parables and Their Encoded Instructions: To fully grasp the depth and significance of these parables, let us

examine three pivotal narratives that serve as powerful instructions for cultural and societal transformation:

3. The Parable of the Good Samaritan (Luke 10:25-37): This parable challenges the cultural and religious prejudices of its time, transcending the boundaries of race, ethnicity, and social status. The story of the Samaritan's compassionate act toward a stranger who had been robbed and left for dead on the road stands as a powerful instruction to embrace radical inclusivity and to extend unconditional love and compassion to all, regardless of their background or circumstances. This parable demolishes the barriers of tribalism and exclusion, inviting us to recognize the inherent dignity and worth of every human being.

4. The Parable of the Prodigal Son (Luke 15:11-32): At the heart of this parable lies a profound instruction on the transformative power of forgiveness and the unconditional love of the divine. The story of the wayward son who squanders his inheritance and returns home in humility, only to be met with the embrace of his forgiving father, serves as a powerful metaphor for the human condition and our journey toward redemption. This parable challenges societal norms that promote judgment and condemnation, inviting us instead to cultivate an understanding of the divine mercy that transcends our human failings and embraces us with open arms.

5. The Parable of the Sower (Matthew 13:1-23, Mark 4:1-20, Luke 8:4-15): Through this parable, Jesus Christ imparts instructions on the receptivity of the human heart to the transformative power of divine truth. The metaphor of the sower and the various types of soil represents the diverse conditions of the human soul and its ability to receive, nurture, and bear fruit from the seeds of truth. This parable challenges us to cultivate a fertile heart, free from the thorns of worldly distractions and the rocky soil of shallow convictions, allowing the divine wisdom to take root and flourish within us.

6. The Pedagogical Method of Parables: Beyond the profound truths encapsulated within these narratives, the very method of teaching through parables holds a profound significance. Jesus Christ employed this pedagogical approach to convey complex and transformative concepts in a manner that was accessible and relatable to His audience. By drawing upon familiar elements of everyday life and weaving them into narratives rich in symbolism and allegory, these parables transcended the limitations of mere instruction, becoming living stories that could take root in the hearts and minds of listeners.

7. The Contemporary Relevance of Parables: While the parables of Jesus Christ were delivered in a specific historical and cultural context, their relevance and significance transcend the boundaries of time and geography. Even in our modern society, these narratives continue to resonate, offering timeless instructions for navigating the complexities of human culture and societal dynamics. The lessons on compassion, forgiveness, and the cultivation of a receptive heart remain as relevant today as they were centuries ago, inviting us to embrace a higher standard of human interaction and personal transformation.

8. Parables as Blueprints for an Ideal Society: When viewed through the lens of cultural and societal transformation, the parables of Jesus Christ emerge as encoded instructions for building an ideal society – a blueprint for a world where love, justice, and divine wisdom reign supreme. By challenging prevailing prejudices, promoting inclusivity, and emphasizing the importance of compassion and forgiveness, these narratives lay the foundation for a society that recognizes the inherent dignity and worth of every individual, transcending the barriers of race, ethnicity, and social status.

9. The Transformative Power of Parables: The true power of these parables lies in their ability to transform not only

individuals but entire societies. By penetrating the depths of the human psyche and resonating with the universal experiences of joy, sorrow, redemption, and transformation, these narratives have the potential to reshape cultural narratives, challenge societal norms, and inspire a collective movement toward a more just, compassionate, and spiritually enlightened existence.

10. A Call to Embrace the Wisdom of Parables: As we navigate the complexities and challenges of the modern world, the parables of Jesus Christ beckon us to embrace their timeless wisdom and allow their transformative power to take root within our hearts and minds. By embodying the principles of radical inclusivity, unconditional love, forgiveness, and a receptive spirit, we can become agents of change, catalysts for the creation of a society that reflects the divine ideals encapsulated within these narratives. It is through the wisdom of these parables that we can envision and build a world where justice, compassion, and spiritual enlightenment are woven into the very fabric of our existence, creating a tapestry of human culture that stands as a testament to the transformative power of divine truth.

Sermon on the Mount: Ethical Foundation of Cultural Perfection

In the realm of profound teachings that have shaped the course of human history and transformed the fabric of societies, the Sermon on the Mount stands as a towering monument of ethical wisdom and spiritual enlightenment. This seminal discourse, delivered by Jesus Christ upon the slopes of a Galilean hill, not only laid the foundations for the Christian faith but also articulated a comprehensive moral framework that transcends religious boundaries and speaks to the universal human experience.

At the heart of this monumental discourse lies a seeming paradox – a juxtaposition of radical ideals and profound humility, of other-worldly aspirations and intimate connection with the human condition. The Sermon on the Mount dares to envision a society rooted in the highest ethical principles while simultaneously acknowledging the inherent frailties and struggles that define our mortal existence. It is this harmonious coexistence of the divine and the earthly that imbues the Sermon with a timeless relevance and profound resonance.

As we delve into the depths of this profound teaching, we are invited to embark on a transformative journey that challenges conventional norms and beckons us to embrace a higher standard of living. The Beatitudes, which form the preamble to the Sermon, offer a radical reframing of our understanding of blessedness, elevating the meek, the mourning, and the persecuted as inheritors of the kingdom of heaven. This counter-cultural stance subverts the prevailing societal hierarchies and invites us to recognize the inherent dignity and worth of those who have been marginalized and oppressed.

The teachings on love and forgiveness that permeate the Sermon strike at the heart of our human propensity for revenge and retaliation. With profound wisdom, Jesus Christ exhorts his followers to love their enemies and pray for those who persecute them, shattering the cycles of hatred and violence that have plagued human societies throughout history. In doing so, he lays the foundation for a radical ethic of unconditional love and forgiveness – an ethic that has the power to heal the deepest wounds and transcend the most entrenched conflicts.

Furthermore, the Sermon on the Mount calls for a higher standard of righteousness, extending beyond mere adherence to the letter of the law and challenging us to cultivate a pure heart and a steadfast commitment to ethical living. The exhortations to be perfect as the heavenly Father is perfect, to resist the temptations of materialism, and to seek first the kingdom of God and His righteousness, elevate the discourse to a realm of spiritual and moral perfection that demands a complete transformation of our values and priorities.

Yet, amidst these lofty ideals, the Sermon on the Mount remains grounded in the realities of human existence. Jesus Christ acknowledges the struggles and temptations that we face, offering practical guidance on prayer, fasting, and the cultivation of a genuine spiritual life. He cautions against hypocrisy and the pursuit of external validation, urging us instead to cultivate an authentic relationship with the divine that transcends the superficial trappings of religious observance.

As we contemplate the profound wisdom encapsulated within the Sermon on the Mount, we are confronted with a challenge that reverberates through the ages – the challenge of translating these ideals into tangible cultural practices and societal structures. How can we integrate the principles of unconditional love, forgiveness, and righteousness into the fabric of our communities? How can we create systems and institutions that reflect the values of humility, compassion, and spiritual enlightenment?

One path toward this integration lies in the cultivation of a collective consciousness rooted in the teachings of the Sermon. By intentionally embedding these principles into our educational systems, fostering open dialogues on ethical living, and creating spaces for spiritual exploration and personal transformation, we can gradually shift the cultural narratives that shape our societies. Moreover, by actively engaging in acts of service, embodying the spirit of compassion, and standing as advocates for justice and human dignity, we can become living embodiments of the Sermon's teachings, inspiring others to embrace its wisdom.

As we strive to build a society that reflects the ethical ideals of the Sermon on the Mount, we must also acknowledge the challenges and complexities inherent in such an endeavor. Deep-rooted cultural prejudices, systemic inequalities, and the allure of power and materialism can be formidable obstacles to overcome. However, it is in the face of these challenges that the Sermon's teachings become all the more essential, offering a beacon of hope and a compass for navigating the treacherous terrain of human imperfection.

Ultimately, the Sermon on the Mount stands as a testament to the enduring power of ethical wisdom and spiritual enlightenment. Its teachings, though rooted in a specific historical and cultural context, transcend the boundaries of time and geography, offering a universal blueprint for human flourishing and societal transformation. As we embrace its radical ideals, cultivate a spirit of humility and compassion, and actively work toward the realization of its vision, we can create a society that reflects the highest aspirations of the human spirit – a society rooted in love, justice, and the pursuit of divine perfection.

Leadership From Heaven: Christ's Continuing Influence

When Jesus Christ ascended into heaven, a profound transformation occurred in the dynamics of leadership and authority. Rather than leaving a void or severing His connection with the created world, His ascension marked the beginning of a new era of heavenly leadership – an era in which His eternal reign would continue to guide and shape the course of human history.

The fundamental question that arises is, how can one who dwells in the celestial realms wield influence over the affairs of the earthly realm? The answer lies in the profound theological implications of Christ's ascension and the recognition of His eternal kingship. As the Scriptures declare, "He ascended on high, leading a host of captives, and gave gifts to men" (Ephesians 4:8, ESV). This ascension marked the culmination of His redemptive work, establishing His sovereign authority over all creation.

From His heavenly throne, Christ now reigns as the exalted Head of the Church, guiding and empowering His followers through the indwelling presence of the Holy Spirit. The book of Hebrews affirms, "After making purification for sins, he sat down at the right hand of the Majesty on high" (Hebrews 1:3, ESV), signifying His intercessory work and His authority as the Great High Priest. Through the ministry of the Holy Spirit, Christ's leadership manifests in the lives of believers, imparting wisdom, courage, and the power to transform lives and communities.

Moreover, Christ's heavenly reign extends far beyond the confines of the Church, for He holds dominion over all nations and peoples. The Apostle Paul declares, "He has put all things under his feet and has made him the head over all things for the church" (Ephesians 1:22, ESV). This assertion affirms that Christ's kingship is not limited to the spiritual realm but encompasses the entirety of creation, including the social, cultural, and political spheres.

The manifestations of Christ's heavenly leadership are multifaceted and profound. Through the work of the Holy Spirit, Christ continues to shape the hearts and minds of individuals, guiding them toward lives of righteousness, love, and service. The transformative power of the gospel has been evident throughout history, as communities of believers have been catalysts for societal change, championing justice, compassion, and the dignity of all human beings.

One of the most profound expressions of Christ's heavenly leadership is the fulfillment of divine purposes through human agency. As believers yield to the leading of the Holy Spirit, they become instruments of God's redemptive plan, participating in the ongoing work of cultural and societal transformation. This partnership between the divine and the human is a testament to the collaborative nature of Christ's reign, where His sovereign will is realized through the obedience and faithfulness of His followers.

The impact of Christ's heavenly leadership extends beyond the confines of the Church or individual lives, shaping the very fabric of society and cultural norms. Throughout history, the principles espoused by Christ – love, forgiveness, justice, and compassion – have served as a moral compass, influencing the development of laws, social movements, and ethical frameworks. Even in societies where Christianity is not the dominant religion, the values propagated by Christ's teachings have left an indelible mark, shaping the collective consciousness and guiding societal progress toward greater equity and human dignity.

As we reflect on Christ's continuing influence from heaven, we are confronted with the awe-inspiring reality that our world is not merely governed by human institutions or earthly powers, but by a divine sovereign whose reign transcends time and space. This heavenly leadership not only provides a sense of purpose and direction but also offers hope in the face of seemingly insurmountable challenges. For if the One who conquered death and ascended to the right hand of the Father guides the course of human events, then even the most daunting obstacles can be overcome through the power of His Spirit and the faithful obedience of His followers.

Furthermore, Christ's heavenly leadership serves as a clarion call to cultivate a posture of humility and surrender. As we acknowledge His eternal reign and submit to His divine authority, we are invited to lay aside our own agendas and align our lives with the purposes of the Heavenly King. This process of surrender is not a negation of human agency but rather a recognition that our true freedom and fulfillment lie in the harmonious alignment with the will of the One who knows and loves us perfectly.

As we journey through this earthly existence, let us be emboldened by the knowledge that our lives are not adrift in a sea of chaos but are guided by the unwavering hand of the Risen Lord. May we embrace the transformative power of His heavenly leadership, allowing it to shape our hearts, our communities, and our world, until the day when "every knee shall bow and every tongue confess that Jesus Christ is Lord" (Philippians 2:10-11, ESV).

The Cross and Resurrection: Cornerstones of Cultural Renewal

The cross and resurrection of Jesus Christ stand as pivotal events that have profoundly shaped the course of human history, offering a framework for cultural renewal and societal transformation. These cornerstones of Christian theology present a radical challenge to the prevailing norms and values of the world, inviting us to reexamine the very foundations upon which our societies are built.

At the heart of the crucifixion lies a profound redefinition of power and authority. In a world that often equates dominance with the accumulation of wealth, status, and might, the cross subverts these notions by revealing the power of sacrificial love. As the sinless Son of God willingly surrendered His life on the cross, He demonstrated that true strength is found not in subjugation or coercion but in selfless service and the willingness to bear the weight of human brokenness.

The cross is a potent symbol that exposes the futility of human pride, selfishness, and the relentless pursuit of personal gain. It challenges the cultural paradigm that places the individual at the center, demanding instead a posture of humility, compassion, and a willingness to lay down one's life for others. In this light, the crucifixion emerges as a radical call to redefine success and greatness, not through the lens of personal achievement or material wealth, but through the prism of sacrificial love and service to humanity.

Moreover, the cross stands as a harsh rebuke to the cycles of violence, retribution, and vengeance that have plagued societies throughout history. Rather than perpetuating the endless cycle of "an eye for an eye," the cross offers a radically different path – one of forgiveness, reconciliation, and the restoration of broken relationships. This message resonates particularly in societies torn apart by centuries of conflict, ethnic tensions, and cycles of retaliation, inviting them to embrace a new paradigm of restorative justice and the healing of deep-seated wounds.

The resurrection of Christ, on the other hand, heralds the ultimate victory over death and decay, ushering in a new era of hope and possibility. By conquering the grave, Christ affirmed the inherent value and dignity of human life, declaring that our existence is not a mere fleeting moment but part of an eternal narrative that transcends the boundaries of time and space.

The resurrection challenges the cultural narratives that reduce human existence to a mere struggle for survival, devoid of deeper meaning or purpose. It proclaims that our lives are not confined to the pursuit of temporary pleasures or the accumulation of material possessions, but are part of a grander story – a story of redemption, transformation, and the ultimate triumph of life over death.

This truth has profound implications for cultural renewal, as it empowers individuals and communities to embrace a vision of life that extends far beyond the immediate circumstances or challenges they face. By anchoring their hope in the reality of the resurrection, they can transcend the limitations of their present realities, refusing to be defined by the cycles of oppression, injustice, or despair that may have plagued their societies for generations.

The resurrection also serves as a powerful catalyst for the restoration of human dignity and the pursuit of justice. By affirming the intrinsic worth of every human being as a creation of God, it challenges cultural systems and structures that dehumanize, marginalize, or oppress certain groups. It calls for societies to uphold the inherent rights and freedoms of all individuals, regardless of race, ethnicity, gender, or social status.

When the cross and resurrection are embraced as the cornerstones of cultural renewal, a profound shift occurs in the way we perceive and engage with the world around us. The pursuit of personal gain and the accumulation of wealth and power are reframed as secondary to the cultivation of selfless love, service, and the pursuit of justice for all. The quest for societal transformation is no longer driven by ideological agendas or political movements but by a deep recognition of the inherent worth and dignity of every human being, created in the image of God.

This paradigm shift has the potential to reshape the very fabric of societies, transforming systems of governance, economic structures, educational frameworks, and even the arts and media. When informed by the principles of the cross and resurrection, these cultural pillars can become vehicles for promoting reconciliation, justice, and the flourishing of human potential.

For instance, in the realm of governance, the cross calls leaders to embrace a spirit of service and humility, rejecting the allure of power and self-aggrandizement. It challenges systems that prioritize the interests of the elite or perpetuate cycles of oppression, demanding instead a commitment to the common good and the upholding of human rights for all citizens.

In the economic sphere, the cross and resurrection challenge the prevailing narratives of unbridled capitalism and the relentless pursuit of profit at the expense of human dignity. They invite a reorientation toward models of economic development that prioritize the well-being of individuals and communities, promoting sustainable practices, fair trade, and the equitable distribution of resources.

Within the educational system, these cornerstones of Christian theology can inspire a holistic approach to learning, one that cultivates not only academic excellence but also character formation, ethical reasoning, and a deep appreciation for the intrinsic worth of every human being. Such an education would equip individuals to become agents of transformation, equipped with the knowledge, skills, and moral grounding to address the complex challenges facing their societies.

Even in the realm of the arts and media, the cross and resurrection offer a fresh perspective, challenging the prevailing narratives that often glorify violence, objectify human beings, or perpetuate stereotypes and biases. Instead, they invite artists and content creators to explore themes of redemption, reconciliation, and the celebration of human dignity, using their creative gifts to inspire hope, foster understanding, and promote social cohesion.

Ultimately, the cross and resurrection of Christ stand as beacons of hope amidst the darkness and brokenness that often characterize the human experience. They offer a path toward genuine cultural renewal, a path that begins with personal transformation and extends to the collective pursuit of justice, compassion, and the restoration of human dignity. As we embrace these cornerstones of our faith, we are empowered to become catalysts for change, actively participating in the ongoing work of healing, reconciliation, and the creation of a more just and humane society.

In the words of the Apostle Paul, "If anyone is in Christ, he is a new creation. The old has passed away; behold, the new has come" (2 Corinthians 5:17, ESV). May we, as followers of Christ, boldly embrace this call to cultural renewal, allowing the transformative power of the cross and resurrection to permeate every aspect of our lives, our communities, and our world.

Christ's Model of Servant Leadership: Transforming Hierarchies

Hierarchies and power structures have long been integral components of human societies, shaping the dynamics of leadership, governance, and interpersonal relationships. However, these structures have often been tainted by the insidious influence of pride, selfishness, and the relentless pursuit of personal gain, leading to the oppression, marginalization, and dehumanization of certain groups.

In this context, the life and teachings of Jesus Christ offer a radically different paradigm – a model of servant leadership that has the power to transform hierarchies and redefine the very essence of authority. At the heart of Christ's leadership lies a profound commitment to humility, service, and sacrificial love, principles that stand in stark contrast to the prevailing norms of power, dominance, and self-interest.

The Gospel accounts are replete with examples of Christ's servant leadership in action. One of the most poignant moments is found in the Gospel of John, where Jesus, the Son of God and the embodiment of divine authority, humbles Himself to wash the feet of His disciples. This act, typically reserved for the lowest of servants, was a powerful symbolic gesture that challenged the disciples' notions of greatness and leadership.

As Jesus knelt before each disciple, tenderly washing their dust-laden feet, He demonstrated that true greatness is not found in the pursuit of personal glory or the accumulation of power, but in the willingness to serve others with selfless humility. This act subverted the traditional hierarchies of the time, where leaders were expected to demand service from their followers, not to render it themselves.

Moreover, Christ's interactions with the marginalized and oppressed members of society further exemplified His commitment to servant leadership. He embraced those who had been cast aside by the religious and political establishment, offering them dignity, compassion, and the promise of redemption. Whether it was the woman at the well, the tax collectors, or the lepers, Christ's radically inclusive love transcended societal boundaries and hierarchies, challenging the prevailing prejudices and biases of His time.

The ultimate expression of Christ's servant leadership, however, is found in His sacrificial death on the cross. In a world that often equates power with coercion and domination, Christ's willingness to lay down His life for the sake of humanity stood as a profound counterpoint. Rather than wielding His divine authority to subjugate or oppress, He embraced the path of suffering and humiliation, bearing the weight of human sin and brokenness upon His shoulders.

The cross is a potent symbol of the inversion of power structures – a living demonstration of the truth that true leadership is found not in the pursuit of personal gain or the accumulation of authority, but in the willingness to sacrifice oneself for the benefit of others. As Christ uttered the words, "It is finished" (John 19:30, ESV), He ushered in a new paradigm of leadership, one that would ultimately transform the way humanity understood the nature of authority and the exercise of power.

The implications of Christ's servant leadership model are profound and far-reaching, challenging not only the traditional hierarchies of religious institutions but also the very fabric of societal structures and cultural norms. In a world that often celebrates the accumulation of wealth, status, and influence, Christ's example calls us to redefine success and greatness through the lens of selfless service and the pursuit of the common good.

In contemporary organizational contexts, the principles of servant leadership have the potential to revolutionize workplace dynamics and cultivate environments that foster collaboration, empowerment, and the flourishing of human potential. Rather than perpetuating top-down power structures, leaders can embrace a posture of service, empowering their teams, fostering open communication, and creating a culture of mutual respect and shared responsibility.

Furthermore, the servant leadership model has significant implications for the realm of governance and public service. In a world plagued by corruption, selfishness, and the abuse of power, Christ's example challenges political leaders, civil servants, and those in positions of authority to reject the allure of personal gain and instead embrace a spirit of selfless service, transparency, and a deep commitment to the well-being of their constituents.

Within the realm of education, the principles of servant leadership can inspire a transformative approach to teaching and learning. Educators can model humility, compassion, and a genuine commitment to the growth and development of their students, fostering environments that nurture not only academic excellence but also character formation, ethical reasoning, and a deep appreciation for the inherent worth and dignity of all individuals.

As we embrace Christ's model of servant leadership, we are invited to participate in the ongoing work of transforming hierarchies and creating a more just and compassionate world. It is a call to reject the allure of power, status, and personal gain, and instead embrace a posture of service, humility, and sacrificial love.

Ultimately, the transformative power of Christ's servant leadership lies not merely in its practical application but in its ability to reshape our very understanding of what it means to lead and to exercise authority. It challenges us to redefine success and greatness, not through the lens of personal achievement or material wealth, but through the prism of selfless service and a deep commitment to the well-being of others.

As we journey through this process of transformation, we can draw strength and inspiration from the example of Christ Himself, who embodied the very principles He taught. In His life, death, and resurrection, we find a profound invitation to embrace a radically different way of living and leading – a way that transcends the limitations of human pride and selfishness, and ushers in a new era of hope, restoration, and the flourishing of human dignity.

May we, as followers of Christ, have the courage to embrace this transformative model of servant leadership, allowing it to permeate every aspect of our lives, our relationships, and our spheres of influence. For it is in this countercultural embrace of humility and service that we find the key to unlocking the true potential of human societies, and the path toward the creation of a more just, compassionate, and equitable world for all.

4

———

THE MIRACULOUS SYSTEM OF DIADIDOMI: DIVINE DISTRIBUTION

Defining Diadidomi: The Principle of Divine Distribution

The journey through the profound truths revealed in the life and teachings of Jesus Christ is one that demands a deep understanding of the very language and concepts employed by the divine. As we delve into the transformative power of Christ's servant leadership model, a principle emerges that illuminates the very essence of God's plan for humanity – the principle of diadidomi, or divine distribution.

To grasp the full weight and significance of this concept, we must first appreciate the criticality of understanding specific terms that serve as gateways to deeper realms of understanding. These terminological keys unlock the doors to a more profound comprehension of the divine narrative, enabling us to engage with the sacred texts and teachings at a level that transcends mere surface-level interpretations.

Diadidomi: A Tantalizing Glimpse into Divine Economics Diadidomi, a term rooted in the rich tapestry of the Greek language, beckons us to explore the intricate mechanisms through which God orchestrates the distribution of resources, both spiritual and material. At its core, diadidomi challenges our notions of scarcity and abundance, inviting us to consider a divine economy that operates not on the principles of hoarding and accumulation, but on the principles of generosity, equity, and the flourishing of all.

Kenosis: Embracing the Path of Voluntary Relinquishment Closely intertwined with the concept of diadidomi is the idea of kenosis, a term that encapsulates the profound act of voluntary self-emptying and relinquishment. Often misunderstood as a mere act of humility, kenosis embodies a radical departure from the self-serving tendencies that permeate human nature, and a willing surrender to the divine plan for the greater good of humanity.

Koinonia: The Essence of Communal Harmony

As we delve deeper into the principle of divine distribution, we encounter the concept of koinonia, a Greek term that evokes a profound sense of community, fellowship, and shared purpose. This term invites us to envision a world where the barriers of division and exclusion are shattered, and where the abundance of God's provisions is experienced collectively, transcending the boundaries of individual gain or personal accumulation.

To fully comprehend the essence of diadidomi, we must first embark on a journey through its origins, tracing its roots in the sacred texts of the New Testament. Within the pages of these ancient writings, we find glimpses of a divine strategy that challenges the prevailing notions of resource allocation and wealth distribution.

The Gospels are replete with accounts of Jesus Christ's radical approach to material and spiritual resources, embodying the principle of diadidomi through His teachings and actions. From the feeding of the multitudes with meager supplies to His exhortations on the Kingdom of God and the equitable distribution of wealth, Christ's life and ministry serve as a living testament to the transformative power of divine distribution.

One such powerful illustration is found in the account of the early Christian community described in the Book of Acts. Here, we witness the embodiment of diadidomi in action, as believers embrace a radical form of resource sharing, ensuring that "there was not a needy person among them" (Acts 4:34, ESV). This extraordinary display of communal solidarity and collective provision stands as a powerful counterpoint to the individualistic and self-serving tendencies that often characterize human societies.

Yet, the principle of diadidomi extends far beyond the realm of material resources. It speaks to the very heart of God's plan for the distribution of spiritual blessings and the equitable allocation of divine grace. The Apostle Paul, in his epistles, expounds on this concept, urging believers to recognize that they are "one body with many members" (1 Corinthians 12:12, ESV), each endowed with unique gifts and talents, not for personal gain, but for the edification and strengthening of the entire community.

As we journey through the subsequent sections of this exploration, we will delve deeper into the practical implications of diadidomi, examining how this principle can transform our understanding of leadership, governance, and resource distribution in contemporary contexts. We will explore how the concepts of kenosis and koinonia interweave with the divine paradigm of distribution, creating a tapestry of profound truth that has the power to reshape our understanding of abundance, equity, and the collective flourishing of humanity.

Ultimately, the principle of diadidomi invites us to embrace a radical shift in perspective, one that challenges the prevailing notions of scarcity and competition, and ushers in a new era of cooperation, generosity, and the equitable distribution of God's abundant provisions. As we embark on this transformative journey, may we be emboldened by the example of Christ and the early Christian community, and may we find the courage to embrace a countercultural way of living that honors the divine plan for the flourishing of all.

Historical Precedents: Diadidomi in Ancient Israel

The timeline of diadidomi, the divine principle of equitable distribution, can be traced back to the earliest accounts of God's interactions with humanity. By examining this historical trajectory, we gain profound insights into the timeless applicability and profound significance of this sacred paradigm.

The roots of diadidomi emerge from the depths of antiquity, intricately woven into the narratives that have shaped the foundations of faith. In the book of Genesis, we encounter the first glimpses of this principle as God bestows the abundant bounty of the Garden of Eden upon Adam and Eve, inviting them to partake freely of its provisions, save

for the fruit of the Tree of Knowledge (Genesis 2:16-17). This initial act of divine distribution sets the stage for a cosmic narrative that continually reaffirms God's desire for the flourishing of all creation.

As the sacred narrative unfolds, we witness pivotal events that further illuminate the principle of diadidomi:

1. The Exodus and the Provision of Manna (c. 1446 BCE): In the wilderness following the Israelites' exodus from Egypt, God's provision of manna served as a powerful embodiment of diadidomi. The divine instruction to gather only what was needed for each day, with the excess miraculously preserved for the Sabbath, fostered a spirit of trust, equity, and reliance on the divine provision (Exodus 16).

2. The Establishment of the Jubilee Year (c. 1406 BCE): As detailed in the book of Leviticus, God instituted the Jubilee Year, a radical concept that mandated the return of land and property to their original owners every fifty years, effectively resetting the economic and social structures of Israelite society (Leviticus 25). This revolutionary system

ensured a cyclical redistribution of resources, preventing the accumulation of wealth in the hands of a privileged few and promoting the principles of equity and shared prosperity.

3. The Conquest of Canaan (c. 1406-1375 BCE): As the Israelites entered the Promised Land, the principle of diadidomi was reflected in the divine instructions for the distribution of the conquered territories among the twelve tribes. The allotment process, overseen by Joshua, ensured that each tribe received a portion of the land, promoting a sense of collective stewardship and shared responsibility (Joshua 13-19).

4. The Reign of King David (c. 1010-970 BCE): Despite the challenges of establishing a unified monarchy, the reign of King David demonstrated a commitment to the principles of diadidomi. The institution of the Tabernacle and the preparations for the construction of the Temple underscored the importance of collective worship and the shared experience of God's presence (1 Chronicles 15-16, 22-29).

5. The Wisdom Literature (c. 950-400 BCE): The books of Proverbs, Ecclesiastes, and Job provide profound insights into the divine perspective on wealth, poverty, and the equitable distribution of resources. These texts challenge the notion of individual accumulation and highlight the virtues of generosity, stewardship, and concern for the well-being of others (Proverbs 11:24-26, Ecclesiastes 5:19, Job 31:16-23).

Throughout the centuries, the principle of diadidomi encountered both challenges and triumphs. The resistance to the Jubilee laws and the concentration of wealth and power in the hands of a privileged few often stood in stark contrast to the divine mandate for equitable distribution. Yet, the prophetic voices of figures like Amos, Micah, and Isaiah resounded with calls for justice, denouncing the exploitation of the poor and the disregard for

God's principles of provision and care for the marginalized (Amos 5:11-12, Micah 2:1-2, Isaiah 58:6-7).

As the historical narrative progresses, we witness the embodiment of diadidomi in the teachings and actions of Jesus Christ. His radical approach to resource distribution, exemplified by the feeding of the multitudes and His exhortations on wealth and generosity, challenged the prevailing norms of His time and ushered in a new paradigm of selflessness and collective well-being (Matthew 14:13-21, Matthew 19:16-30, Luke 12:13-21).

The early Christian community, as depicted in the book of Acts, embraced the principle of diadidomi with fervor, establishing a model of shared resources and collective provision that ensured the flourishing of all members (Acts 2:42-47, Acts 4:32-37). This radical departure from societal norms ignited a movement that transcended cultural and societal boundaries, inspiring generations of believers to embody the spirit of divine distribution.

As we trace the historical trajectory of diadidomi, we are reminded of the enduring relevance and transformative power of this sacred principle. Throughout the ages, its implementation has served as a beacon of hope, challenging the prevailing systems of inequality and injustice, and inviting humanity to embrace a more equitable and compassionate path. The historical precedents of diadidomi in Ancient Israel stand as a testament to God's unwavering commitment to the flourishing of all creation, and a call to contemporary societies to embrace the divine blueprint for the distribution of resources, both material and spiritual.

Jesus Christ and the Multiplication of Resources

The Judean countryside bore witness to an extraordinary phenomenon as throngs congregated to experience the teachings of a remarkable figure known as Jesus of Nazareth. Among the multitude were the weary, the hungry, and the hopeful, drawn by the promise of profound wisdom and the possibility of divine intervention. It was in this context that the miraculous feeding of the

5,000, as recorded in the Gospel of Matthew, unfolded, offering a quintessential illustration of Jesus Christ's divine distribution system in action.

The narrative opens with the logistical impossibility of providing sustenance for the vast crowds that had amassed. With only five loaves of bread and two fish at their disposal, the disciples found themselves confronted by a seemingly insurmountable challenge. The scarcity of resources stood in stark contrast to the overwhelming need, underscoring the dire necessity for divine intervention.

Yet, in this moment of apparent lack, Jesus Christ demonstrated an unwavering trust in the principles of diadidomi – the sacred paradigm of equitable distribution. With a simple command to have the multitude sit upon the grassy slopes, He took the meager provisions and, in a profound act of blessing, multiplied them exponentially. The subsequent distribution of the miraculously multiplied food to the masses showcased the efficacy and divine nature of this distribution system.

As the disciples went forth, carrying baskets laden with the nourishing bounty, the crowds witnessed firsthand the transformative power of diadidomi. No one was left wanting, for the abundance that flowed from Christ's hands was sufficient to satiate even the most ravenous appetites. And when the final morsel had been consumed, a remarkable sight greeted the astonished onlookers — twelve baskets brimming with leftovers, a tangible testament to the surplus created by the divine distribution.

The implications of this miraculous event extend far beyond the confines of that Judean hillside. It stands as a resounding affirmation of the principles of diadidomi, challenging the prevailing notions of scarcity and inviting humanity to embrace a paradigm of abundance rooted in divine providence. In an era characterized by vast inequalities and resource disparities, the feeding of the 5,000 offers a poignant reminder of the transformative potential that lies within a system of equitable distribution.

Moreover, this miracle serves as a profound commentary on the nature of divine resources and their capacity for exponential growth when channeled through the sacred principles of diadidomi. Just as the few loaves and fish were multiplied beyond measure, so too can the resources entrusted to humanity flourish and abound when distributed according to divine wisdom and with a heart aligned with the principles of equity and justice.

The lessons derived from this biblical account hold profound implications for contemporary discussions surrounding resource allocation, sustainability, and the pursuit of collective well-being. It challenges the prevailing paradigms of scarcity and hoarding, inviting us to embrace a mindset of abundance and trust in the divine capacity to provide for the needs of all.

Furthermore, the feeding of the 5,000 serves as a powerful metaphor for the spiritual nourishment that flows from a life rooted in the principles of diadidomi. Just as the physical hunger of the multitudes was satiated, so too can the spiritual yearnings of humanity be fulfilled through a wholehearted embrace of the divine distribution system. By aligning our hearts and actions with the precepts of equity, generosity, and shared prosperity, we partake in the abundant feast of divine grace and foster a world where all can experience the transformative power of sacred nourishment.

As contemporary societies grapple with the complexities of resource allocation and the pursuit of equitable development, the miraculous feeding of the 5,000 stands as a beacon of hope and a blueprint for the harmonious coexistence of abundance and justice. By adopting the principles of diadidomi, we unlock the potential for a world where scarcity is transformed into plenty, where the cries of the hungry are silenced by the overflowing bounty of divine provision, and where the shared experience of abundance forges a bond of unity that transcends the boundaries of creed, culture, and circumstance.

The echoes of this transformative event reverberate through the ages, inviting us to contemplate the profound implications of embracing the divine distribution system. As we journey through the complexities of our time, may the miraculous feeding of the 5,000 serve as a constant reminder of the boundless potential that awaits when we align our hearts and actions with the sacred principles of diadidomi. In doing so, we participate in the unfolding narrative of divine provision and the realization of a world where all are nourished, both physically and spiritually.

The Role of Apostolic Distribution in Early Christianity

As the teachings of Jesus Christ echoed across the ancient lands, a profound revolution was set in motion – a revolution rooted in the very principles that had sustained the crowds on that fateful day in the Judean countryside. The early Christian church, still in its nascent stages, faced a formidable challenge: translating the divine principles of diadidomi, the equitable distribution of resources, into a tangible reality amidst the complexities of communal living.

The socioeconomic landscape of the early church was a tapestry woven with stark contrasts. On one hand, there were those who had embraced the teachings of Christ and sought to live in harmony with the principles of sacred distribution, forsaking personal possessions and embracing a shared existence. On the other, the harsh realities of poverty, marginalization, and systemic inequalities cast long shadows, threatening to fracture the delicate fabric of this fledgling community.

It was in this context that the Acts of the Apostles emerged, chronicling the practical implementation of diadidomi in the early church. The narrative opens with a powerful description of the harmonious coexistence of the believers, who "had all things in common" (Acts 2:44). This communal living arrangement, born of a shared commitment to the divine principles of distribution, established a foundation upon which the transformative power of diadidomi could take root and flourish.

Yet, as the church grew and the complexities of communal living intensified, the inherent challenges of equitable distribution came to the fore. The account of the Hellenistic Jews, whose widows were being overlooked in the daily distribution of aid, threatened to disrupt the unity and harmony that had been so carefully cultivated (Acts 6:1). In this pivotal moment, the apostles recognized the need for a structured and intentional approach to ensure the fair and equitable distribution of resources within the burgeoning Christian community.

The solution manifested in the appointment of seven deacons, men of good reputation and wisdom, entrusted with the sacred task of overseeing the distribution process (Acts 6:2-6). This strategic decision not only addressed the immediate challenge at hand but also laid the foundation for a sustainable system of distribution that could accommodate the church's growth and evolving needs.

The impact of this apostolic distribution system reverberated throughout the early Christian community, fostering a sense of unity and shared purpose that transcended social and cultural boundaries. The equitable allocation of resources ensured that the basic needs of all were met, alleviating the burdens of poverty and marginalization that had plagued the vulnerable segments of society.

Beyond material provision, the apostolic distribution system served as a powerful testimony to the transformative potential of the divine principles of diadidomi. As the early believers witnessed the tangible manifestation of these sacred precepts, their faith was strengthened, and their commitment to the teachings of Christ was reinforced. The church's growth and expansion, as chronicled in the Book of Acts, can be attributed, in part, to the cohesive and harmonious community fostered by the equitable distribution of resources.

The significance of the apostolic distribution system extended far beyond the confines of the early church. It served as a beacon of hope, illuminating the path toward a more just and equitable society. As the message of Christ spread, the principles of diadidomi were carried forth, challenging the prevailing paradigms of resource hoarding and systemic inequality that pervaded the ancient world.

In our contemporary context, the lessons of the apostolic distribution system hold profound relevance. As societies grapple with the persistent challenges of poverty, economic disparities, and unequal access to resources, the early church's embrace of diadidomi offers a compelling blueprint for a more just and sustainable world.

By adopting the principles of equitable distribution and fostering a sense of shared responsibility for the well-being of all, we can forge communities built upon the foundations of unity, compassion, and collective prosperity. The apostolic distribution system serves as a powerful reminder that true transformation begins with a commitment to the divine principles of justice and equity, and that through the intentional and systematic implementation of these precepts, we can create a world where abundance is shared and no one is left behind.

As we navigate the complexities of our modern age, may the example of the early Christian church and the apostolic distribution system inspire us to embrace the sacred paradigm of diadidomi, for in doing so, we participate in the unfolding narrative of divine provision and the realization of a world where all are nourished, both physically and spiritually, through the transformative power of equitable distribution.

Comparing Secular and Divine Distribution Systems

At the heart of our societal fabric lies a fundamental question that has perplexed civilizations throughout history: How can we distribute resources equitably and sustainably? On one hand, we have secular systems of resource distribution, such as capitalism and socialism, that have sought to address this complex challenge through human-devised principles and mechanisms. On the other hand, we have the divine system of diadidomi, a sacred paradigm rooted in the timeless teachings of Christ, which offers a radically different approach to this perennial issue.

At first glance, these secular and divine systems may appear to exist at opposing ends of the spectrum, with the former rooted in human rationality and the latter anchored in divine revelation. However, a closer examination reveals a profound juxtaposition – a convergence of aspirations and principles that transcends the apparent divide. Both the secular and divine approaches ultimately strive toward the noble goals of equity, sustainability, and communal well-being, yet they diverge in their fundamental underpinnings and the means by which they seek to attain these ends.

To comprehend the true magnitude of this comparison, we must delve into the key attributes that define these distribution systems. In the realm of secular systems, the pursuit of equity is often a driving force, with mechanisms in place to ensure fair access to resources and opportunities. However, these systems frequently grapple with inherent tensions and trade-offs, such as balancing individual freedoms with collective needs, or sacrificing long-term sustainability for short-term gains.

In contrast, the divine system of diadidomi is rooted in the eternal principles of divine justice and love, seeking to create a harmonious equilibrium between individual and communal well-being. Equity is not merely a utilitarian pursuit but a sacred mandate woven into the fabric of creation, reflecting the inherent worth and dignity bestowed upon every human being by their Creator. Sustainability, too, is not a mere afterthought but a fundamental tenet that recognizes the intrinsic interconnectedness of all life and the sacred responsibility of stewardship over the earth's resources.

As we delve deeper into the similarities and differences between these systems, a profound revelation emerges. While secular systems may strive for equity and efficiency, they often struggle to address the spiritual and communal dimensions that are intrinsic to human flourishing. The pursuit of material well-being, while important, can inadvertently overshadow the deeper yearnings of the human spirit, leading to a fragmentation of our collective existence and a disconnection from the sacred essence that binds us all.

Diadidomi, however, transcends this compartmentalization, seamlessly integrating the material and spiritual realms into a cohesive tapestry of holistic well-being. The equitable distribution of resources is not merely an economic exercise but a sacred act of reverence and stewardship, imbued with a profound recognition of our shared humanity and our collective responsibility toward one another.

Moreover, the divine system of diadidomi extends beyond the realm of material resources, encompassing the distribution of intangible blessings and gifts that nourish the spirit and fortify the bonds of the community. From the sharing of wisdom and knowledge to the extension of compassion and care, diadidomi cultivates a culture of abundance and generosity that permeates every aspect of our existence.

The relevance of these insights becomes even more poignant when we consider the contemporary global distribution challenges that continue to plague our world. As nations grapple with persistent poverty, economic disparities, and inequitable access to resources, the adoption of divine principles could revolutionize our approach to these seemingly intractable issues.

Imagine a world where the distribution of resources is guided not by the pursuit of material gain or the consolidation of power, but by the sacred mandate to honor the dignity of every human being and to foster a thriving, sustainable community. Imagine a society where the abundance of resources is recognized as a divine blessing to be shared equitably, rather than hoarded or exploited for personal gain.

By embracing the principles of diadidomi, we could forge a path toward a more just and harmonious world, one where the needs of all are met, and the well-being of the collective is prioritized over individual accumulation. The transformative power of this divine paradigm lies in its ability to transcend the limitations of human-devised systems, imbuing our efforts with a sacred purpose and a profound sense of interconnectedness.

As we grapple with the complexities of our modern age, it is imperative that we open our hearts and minds to the wisdom embedded within the divine teachings of diadidomi. By doing so, we can forge a new path toward a more equitable and sustainable future, one that recognizes the inherent worth of every human being and the sacred responsibility we share in the stewardship of our collective resources.

In the end, the comparison between secular and divine distribution systems is not merely an academic exercise but a profound invitation to reimagine the very foundations upon which our societies are built. It is a call to embrace the timeless principles of divine justice and love, and to weave them into the fabric of our collective existence, creating a world where abundance is shared, compassion is cultivated, and the well-being of all is upheld as a sacred trust.

Challenges and Obstacles in Implementing Divine Distribution

In today's complex and interconnected world, the concept of diadidomi—the ancient divine principle of equitable distribution and fair allocation of resources—faces numerous challenges and obstacles that impede its meaningful adoption and manifestation. These hurdles arise from deeply ingrained societal norms, systemic inequities,

misunderstandings of spiritual teachings, and resistance to change. Overcoming these obstacles is crucial to realizing the immense potential of diadidomi in fostering a more just and harmonious global community.

One of the primary challenges lies in the persistence of socioeconomic disparities that have become deeply entrenched in many societies. The unequal distribution of wealth, resources, and opportunities has created a divide between the privileged and the marginalized, perpetuating cycles of poverty, deprivation, and lack of access to basic necessities. This stark contrast stands in stark opposition to the core tenets of diadidomi, which advocate for a fair and compassionate sharing of resources among all members of the community.

Furthermore, the prevalence of individualistic mindsets and the pursuit of personal gain often take precedence over collective well-being and the greater good. In an age driven by consumerism and the accumulation of material possessions, the principles of diadidomi can be perceived as idealistic or impractical, leading to resistance and skepticism from those who prioritize self-interest over the needs of the community.

Another significant obstacle lies in the misunderstanding or misinterpretation of divine principles and spiritual teachings. Religious dogma, cultural biases, and incomplete knowledge can lead to distorted interpretations of the core values of diadidomi, resulting in confusion, misguided practices, and a failure to fully grasp the profound wisdom inherent in these ancient teachings. This lack of clarity can hinder the effective implementation of diadidomi in contemporary contexts.

If these challenges remain unaddressed, the negative consequences could be far-reaching and severe. Inequality and resource scarcity can breed social unrest, conflicts, and environmental degradation, jeopardizing the well-being of communities and the planet itself. A failure to embrace the principles of diadidomi could exacerbate existing divisions, perpetuate systemic injustices, and deprive countless individuals of their basic rights and dignity.

To overcome these obstacles and pave the way for the successful implementation of diadidomi, a comprehensive and multifaceted approach is required. One essential component is education and awareness-raising initiatives that promote a deeper understanding of the divine principles underlying diadidomi. By fostering a shared understanding of these teachings and their relevance to contemporary challenges, we can cultivate a foundation of empathy, compassion, and a collective commitment to equitable distribution.

Alongside education, fostering community-based initiatives that embody the values of diadidomi is crucial. Grassroots movements, community-led resource-sharing programs, and cooperative models can serve as living examples of the positive impact that diadidomi can have on local communities. By actively involving and empowering individuals at the local level, these initiatives can generate a sense of ownership, accountability, and a deeper appreciation for the transformative potential of these principles.

Furthermore, integrating spiritual leadership and guidance in resource management and decision-making processes can help ensure that the principles of diadidomi are upheld and respected. Engaging with spiritual leaders, elders, and respected community figures who embody the wisdom and values of diadidomi can provide a moral compass and ensure that decisions are grounded in ethical and spiritual foundations.

To illustrate the effectiveness of implementing diadidomi, we can look to historical precedents and contemporary case studies that have demonstrated the power of these principles in action. For instance, the traditional Indigenous communities of the Americas have long practiced forms of resource sharing and collective stewardship that align with the values of diadidomi. These practices have fostered strong social cohesion, sustainable resource management, and a deep reverence for the interconnectedness of all life.

In more recent times, community-led initiatives such as the Sarvodaya Shramadana Movement in Sri Lanka have successfully implemented principles of equitable distribution and self-reliance, empowering marginalized communities and fostering sustainable development. By embracing the values of diadidomi, these initiatives have demonstrated the capacity to uplift entire communities, alleviate poverty, and promote social harmony.

While the challenges in implementing diadidomi are significant, the potential rewards are equally profound. By overcoming resistance, fostering understanding, and actively embracing these divine principles, we can create a world where resources are shared equitably, where the needs of all are met, and where the bonds of community and compassion transcend boundaries and divisions. It is a vision of a more just, sustainable, and harmonious global society—a vision that is not only possible but imperative if we are to build a better future for all.

Theological Implications of Diadidomi

As ancient as the stars themselves, the principle of diadidomi has woven its threads through the tapestry of human civilization, echoing the divine desire for harmony, equity, and abundance. At its core, this sacred teaching invites us to ponder a profound question: What if the universe itself is designed not for scarcity, but for a perpetual flow of sustenance and abundance when honored through righteous stewardship?

Diadidomi, a term rooted in the ancient Greek language, can be distilled into a simple yet powerful definition: the equitable distribution of resources and blessings from the divine realm, bestowed upon humanity with the implicit expectation of responsible stewardship and care for one another. This concept resonates across myriad spiritual traditions, each offering a unique lens through which to understand the theological underpinnings of this principle.

In essence, diadidomi is a manifestation of divine providence—the unwavering belief that a higher power, be it God, the universe, or a cosmic force, is inherently benevolent and wishes to provide for the needs of all creation. It is a recognition that the bounties of the earth, the marvels of nature, and the resources that sustain life are not mere coincidences, but rather intentional gifts bestowed upon humanity by a loving and compassionate Creator. This understanding challenges the notion of scarcity and encourages a mindset of gratitude, reverence, and a sense of shared responsibility in honoring these divine gifts.

Building upon this foundation of divine providence, the principle of diadidomi places a profound emphasis on human stewardship. It acknowledges that while the resources of the world are granted by the divine, it is our sacred duty as custodians of creation to ensure their equitable distribution and sustainable use. This stewardship extends beyond the mere management of material wealth; it encompasses a holistic approach to nurturing and preserving the intricate web of life that sustains our planet and all its inhabitants.

The theological significance of diadidomi is further elevated when viewed through the lens of eschatology—the study of the final events and the ultimate destiny of humanity and the cosmos. Many spiritual traditions hold the belief that a time will come when the divine plan for creation will be fully realized, and a state of perfect harmony, peace, and abundance will prevail. In this eschatological vision, the principles of diadidomi find their ultimate fulfillment, as all beings will partake in the bountiful provisions of the divine, free from want or deprivation.

Practical applications of these theological insights can be found in the ways communities and societies choose to allocate and share resources. From the establishment of equitable distribution systems and cooperative economic models to the implementation of sustainable resource management practices and the promotion of altruism and generosity, the principles of diadidomi offer a roadmap for creating a more just and harmonious world.

Furthermore, the theological foundation of diadidomi can guide our approach to addressing pressing global issues such as poverty, hunger, and environmental degradation. It reminds us that our actions, both individually and collectively, have profound spiritual implications and that our stewardship of the earth's resources is an extension of our reverence for the divine. By aligning our practices and policies with the values of diadidomi, we can work toward creating a world where the basic needs of all are met, where the natural world is cherished and protected, and where the bonds of community and compassion transcend boundaries and divisions.

As we delve deeper into the theological implications of diadidomi, it is essential to dispel common misconceptions that may arise. Some may mistakenly equate the principle of equitable distribution with secular ideologies such as socialism or communism. However, diadidomi is rooted in a profoundly spiritual and transcendent understanding of the divine order, one that acknowledges the inherent worth and dignity of every human being as a child of the Creator. It is not a political or economic system imposed by human constructs but rather a sacred calling to honor the divine plan for creation by fostering a harmonious and sustainable society.

Another misconception that must be addressed is the notion that embracing diadidomi necessitates a rejection of personal aspirations or individual initiative. On the contrary, the principle of diadidomi recognizes the unique gifts and talents bestowed upon each individual by the divine, and encourages the cultivation of these abilities for the betterment of the collective. It is a call to balance personal growth and fulfillment with a deep sense of responsibility toward the broader community, recognizing that the true realization of individual potential is inextricably linked to the well-being of the whole.

In essence, the theological implications of diadidomi offer a profound and transformative worldview, one that invites us to see ourselves as co-creators with the divine, entrusted with the sacred duty of responsible stewardship over the abundant resources bestowed upon us. It is a vision that transcends temporal boundaries and speaks to the timeless yearning of the human soul for harmony, equity, and a deep connection to the source of all creation. By embracing the spiritual wisdom inherent in this ancient principle, we can chart a path toward a world where the divine plan for abundance and shared prosperity is realized, and where the bonds of love, compassion, and reverence for the sacred weave an unbreakable tapestry that unites all of humanity.

Equity and Abundance: The Goals of Divine Distribution

In the timeless quest for a harmonious and just world, the principles of diadidomi shine as beacons of hope, guiding us toward the ultimate goals of equity and abundance. These goals are not mere ideals, but rather the sacred callings imbued within the very fabric of creation, echoing the divine desire for all beings to thrive and flourish in a state of shared prosperity.

To embark on this profound journey, let us first outline the key principles that underpin the pursuit of equity and abundance: • Fairness and Justice: Ensuring that resources and opportunities are distributed equitably, free from discrimination or bias, and with due consideration for the inherent worth and dignity of every individual. • Sustainability: Nurturing and preserving the delicate balance of the natural world, recognizing our role as stewards of the earth's bounties and our responsibility to safeguard these resources for future generations. • Communal Responsibility: Fostering a sense of collective commitment to the well-being of the entire community, transcending individual interests, and embracing the interconnectedness of all life. • Reverence and Gratitude: Cultivating a profound reverence for the divine providence that has bestowed upon us the gifts of creation, and expressing heartfelt gratitude for these blessings. • Compassion and Generosity: Embodying the spirit of compassion and selfless generosity, thereby nurturing a culture of sharing and mutual support that leaves no one behind.

With these guiding principles as our foundation, let us delve deeper into the intricacies of each one, illuminating their significance and revealing the profound wisdom they hold.

Fairness and Justice: The pursuit of equity and abundance is inherently linked to the ideal of fairness and justice. It recognizes that each human being, regardless of circumstance or background, possesses an innate worth and deserves access to the resources and opportunities necessary to thrive. This principle challenges systems that perpetuate inequality, discrimination, or the concentration of resources in the hands of a privileged few. Instead, it calls for the establishment of mechanisms and structures that ensure fair and impartial distribution, taking into account the diverse needs and circumstances of individuals and communities.

Just as the divine bestows its blessings upon all of creation without prejudice, so too must we strive to create a society where every person has an equal chance to realize their full potential. By embracing fairness and justice, we honor the divine essence within each soul and pave the way for a world where equity is not merely a lofty ideal but a lived reality.

Sustainability: The principle of sustainability is not only an ecological imperative but also a sacred responsibility that arises from our role as stewards of the earth's resources. Diadidomi teaches us that the bounties of nature are not ours to exploit and consume without regard for the future. Rather, they are divine gifts entrusted to our care, to be nurtured and preserved for generations to come.

By adopting sustainable practices and embracing a mindset of reverence for the natural world, we align ourselves with the divine wisdom inherent in the intricate balance of ecosystems. We recognize that true abundance is not found in the relentless pursuit of consumption, but rather in the harmonious coexistence with the rhythms of nature. This principle calls upon us to rethink our relationship with the earth, to seek innovative solutions that allow us to meet our needs without compromising the well-being of the planet, and to instill in future generations a deep appreciation for the sacred web of life that sustains us all.

Communal Responsibility: The path toward equity and abundance is not one that can be walked alone. It requires a collective commitment, a recognition that our individual destinies are inextricably woven with those of our fellow beings. The principle of communal responsibility invites us to transcend narrow self-interests and embrace a broader vision of shared prosperity.

In the divine order, each element of creation plays a crucial role, contributing to the harmonious whole. Similarly, diadidomi calls upon us to recognize the unique gifts and contributions of every individual, and to cultivate a sense of mutual support and interdependence. By upholding this principle, we nurture a culture of empathy, solidarity, and collective action, where the struggles and triumphs of one are felt by all.

Moreover, communal responsibility extends beyond the boundaries of our immediate communities, encompassing a global consciousness that acknowledges our shared humanity and the interconnectedness of all life on this planet. It challenges us to consider the ripple effects of our actions and to make choices that uplift not only those closest to us but also those who may seem distant or different.

Reverence and Gratitude: At the core of diadidomi lies a profound reverence for the divine providence that has bestowed upon us the abundance of creation. This principle calls upon us to cultivate a deep appreciation for the myriad blessings that sustain our lives, from the air we breathe to the food we consume, and to recognize the sacred nature of these gifts.

By embracing reverence and gratitude, we acknowledge our role as temporary stewards of these divine bounties, entrusted with their care and preservation. This understanding fosters a sense of humility, reminding us that the resources we enjoy are not ours to claim or hoard, but rather sacred trusts to be honored and shared. It is a call to transcend the illusion of ownership and to see ourselves as mere custodians, responsible for ensuring that these blessings continue to flow freely for generations to come.

Compassion and Generosity: The embodiment of compassion and generosity lies at the heart of diadidomi's pursuit of equity and abundance. It is a recognition that true fulfillment and abundance are not found in the pursuit of personal gain, but rather in the selfless act of sharing and supporting others.

This principle invites us to open our hearts and extend our hands to those in need, not out of obligation or pity, but out of a deep understanding that their well-being is inextricably linked to our own. By cultivating a spirit of compassion and generosity, we create a ripple effect of kindness and caring that has the power to transform lives and uplift entire communities.

Moreover, the practice of generosity is not limited to material resources; it encompasses the sharing of knowledge, skills, and emotional support. It is a recognition that true abundance extends beyond the physical realm and encompasses the intangible riches of wisdom, empathy, and spiritual connection. By embodying this principle, we become conduits of love and healing, spreading light in the darkest corners and bringing hope to those who may have lost it.

As we weave these principles into the tapestry of our lives, we move ever closer to realizing the sacred goals of equity and abundance. It is a journey that requires patience, perseverance, and a deep commitment to aligning our actions with the divine plan for creation. Yet, with each step we take along this path, we inch closer to a world where scarcity and deprivation are replaced by a shared sense of prosperity and well-being, where the bonds of community transcend boundaries, and where the divine essence within each soul is honored and celebrated.

Let us embrace the wisdom of diadidomi and embark upon this sacred quest, confident in the knowledge that the divine providence that has blessed us with the abundance of creation will guide and sustain us. Together, we can usher in a new era of harmony, equity, and abundance, where the aspirations of all beings are fulfilled, and the divine plan for a just and flourishing world is realized.

Practical Steps to Embrace Diadidomi in Modern Contexts

The pursuit of equity, abundance, and communal well-being lies at the heart of the principles of diadidomi. While the ideals themselves are profound and timeless, their true value is realized through practical implementation in our daily lives and within our communities. This section aims to provide a step-by-step guide for embracing the principles of diadidomi in modern contexts, fostering a culture of equitable distribution, compassion, and shared prosperity.

Establishing the Goal: The ultimate goal of this journey is to create a world where the divine blessings of abundance are accessible to all, where resources are distributed fairly, and where every individual has the opportunity to thrive and fulfill their divine potential. By following these steps, readers will embark on a transformative path that aligns their actions with the sacred principles of diadidomi, fostering a more equitable, compassionate, and sustainable society.

Prerequisites:

1. A deep understanding and reverence for the principles of diadidomi, rooted in spiritual wisdom and a commitment to the divine plan for creation.
2. Community engagement and support, recognizing that lasting change requires collective effort and collaboration.
3. Strong leadership and role models who embody the virtues of compassion, generosity, and a commitment to equity and abundance.
4. A willingness to challenge existing systems, norms, and mindsets that perpetuate inequality and scarcity.

Overview: The path to embracing diadidomi in modern contexts consists of several key steps: educating communities, establishing equitable distribution systems, fostering communal support networks, and cultivating a culture of gratitude and reverence. Each step builds upon the previous one, creating a foundation for lasting change and transformation.

Step 1: Educate Communities

1. Organize workshops, seminars, and community gatherings to share the principles of diadidomi and their significance in fostering equity and abundance.

2. Develop educational materials, such as pamphlets, videos, or interactive sessions, that explain these principles in a relatable and accessible manner.
3. Engage community leaders, elders, and respected figures to help disseminate this knowledge and encourage widespread participation.
4. Emphasize the spiritual and ethical foundations of diadidomi, highlighting its roots in divine wisdom and the interconnectedness of all life.
5. Address common misconceptions and barriers to embracing these principles, such as deeply ingrained beliefs or resistance to change.

Step 2: Establish Equitable Distribution Systems

1. Conduct community assessments to identify areas of need, resource availability, and existing inequalities in access to resources.
2. Collaborate with community members to develop fair and transparent distribution systems, taking into account diverse needs and circumstances.
3. Explore innovative models for resource sharing, such as community gardens, tool libraries, or cooperative housing initiatives.
4. Implement mechanisms for accountability and oversight, ensuring that distribution remains equitable and free from bias or corruption.
5. Foster partnerships with local organizations, businesses, and government entities to support and sustain these initiatives.

Step 3: Foster Communal Support Networks

1. Encourage the formation of neighborhood groups, community centers, or virtual platforms that promote mutual support and collaborative problem-solving.

2. Organize skill-sharing workshops, where individuals can learn and teach various trades, crafts, or expertise, fostering self-sufficiency and interdependence.
3. Establish systems for resource sharing, such as food banks, clothing exchanges, or bartering networks, allowing community members to share and support one another.
4. Promote intergenerational mentorship programs, where elders can impart wisdom and knowledge to younger generations, fostering continuity and preserving cultural traditions.
5. Celebrate diversity and promote inclusivity, ensuring that all members of the community feel valued, respected, and supported, regardless of background or circumstances.

Step 4: Cultivate Gratitude and Reverence

1. Organize community gatherings or ceremonies to express gratitude for the divine blessings of abundance and the gifts of creation.
2. Encourage individuals and families to establish daily practices of gratitude, such as keeping a gratitude journal or sharing blessings during mealtimes.
3. Integrate sustainability practices into daily life, fostering reverence for the natural world and promoting responsible stewardship of resources.
4. Celebrate and honor the diversity of cultural traditions and spiritual beliefs that promote reverence, gratitude, and respect for the divine.
5. Engage in community service projects, such as environmental clean-ups or volunteering at local charities, instilling a sense of compassion and generosity.

Verifying Success and Addressing Challenges: To assess the success of these initiatives, communities can establish measurable goals and indicators, such as increased access to resources, reduced inequalities, and improved overall well-being. Regular evaluations and feedback mechanisms should be implemented to ensure continuous improvement and adaptation to changing needs. Potential challenges may include resistance to change, limited resources, or conflicts within the community. To address these challenges, it is crucial to foster open communication, promote transparency, and maintain a spirit of compassion and understanding. Ongoing education, conflict resolution processes, and the cultivation of a shared vision for equity and abundance can help overcome these obstacles.

Tips and Best Practices:

- Embrace inclusivity and diversity, ensuring that all voices are heard and respected in the decision-making process.
- Celebrate small victories and milestones along the way, acknowledging the progress made and the collective effort involved.
- Encourage intergenerational collaboration, leveraging the wisdom of elders and the energy of youth to create sustainable change.
- Seek partnerships and collaborations with like-minded organizations and communities to amplify impact and share resources.
- Remain flexible and adaptable, recognizing that the path to equity and abundance is not a linear journey, but one that requires ongoing refinement and adjustment.

By following these practical steps and embodying the principles of diadidomi, we can collectively create a more equitable, compassionate, and abundant world. The journey may be challenging, but the rewards of a harmonious society rooted in divine wisdom and shared prosperity are immeasurable. Together, we can transcend the limitations of scarcity and embrace the sacred call to foster abundance for all.

5

PROVERBS AND PERFECTION: THE HANDS OF WISDOM AND UNDERSTANDING

The Essence of Wisdom and Understanding

Wisdom and understanding are not mere concepts; they are the essence of knowledge, the foundation upon which we build our understanding of the world and our place within it. In this section, we delve into the profound depths of these virtues, unveiling their significance and shedding light on the transformative power they hold.

Why Understanding Wisdom and Understanding Matters

To truly appreciate the relevance of wisdom and understanding, we must first recognize the crucial role they play in shaping our lives and our communities. These virtues are not mere philosophical abstractions but rather the guiding forces that govern our decisions, our actions, and our ability to navigate the complexities of the world around us. Just as a ship requires a compass and a skilled navigator to safely traverse treacherous waters, so too do we require the illumination of wisdom and understanding to find our way through the challenges and uncertainties of life. By grasping the true essence of these virtues, we unlock the keys to a more fulfilling and purposeful existence.

Wisdom: The Profound Depths

Wisdom, often depicted as a radiant flame, is the synthesis of knowledge, experience, and profound insight. It is not merely the accumulation of facts or information, but rather the ability to perceive the interconnectedness of all things, to discern patterns and truths that lie beneath the surface, and to apply this understanding in a manner that brings about positive change and growth.

The Hebrew term ""(chokmah)carries within it a deep reverence for the divine and an acknowledgment of the sacred nature of wisdom. It is not a mere intellectual pursuit, but a spiritual journey that requires humility, introspection, and a willingness to embrace the mysteries of the universe. Wisdom is the flame that illuminates the path toward enlightenment, guiding us toward a deeper understanding of ourselves, our purpose, and our place in the grand tapestry of existence.

Understanding: The Unraveling of Complexity

If wisdom is the flame, then understanding is the lens through which we perceive the world. The Hebrew term "בִּינָה" (binah) represents the ability to comprehend the intricate workings of the universe, to unravel the complexities that surround us, and to find clarity amidst the chaos.

Understanding is not a static state; it is a dynamic process that requires continuous exploration, questioning, and a willingness to challenge preconceived notions. It is the bridge that connects knowledge and wisdom, allowing us to translate abstract concepts into tangible realities and to navigate the ever-changing landscapes of our existence with grace and discernment.

The Manifestation of Wisdom and Understanding

As we delve deeper into the study of Proverbs, we will come to understand that wisdom and understanding are not merely theoretical constructs but rather virtues that manifest themselves in our daily lives. They shape our relationships, our decision-making processes, and our ability to navigate the complexities of the world around us.

Reflect upon the moments in your life when you have encountered true wisdom, whether through the sage counsel of a mentor, the profound insights of a sacred text, or the quiet whispers of your own intuition. Consider the times when understanding has illuminated your path, allowing you to perceive the intricate tapestry of events and circumstances that weave together to create the fabric of your existence.

By embracing the essence of wisdom and understanding, we open ourselves to a world of deeper meaning, purpose, and fulfillment. We become agents of positive change, capable of navigating life's challenges with grace and discernment, and contributing to the betterment of our communities and the world at large.

The Foundations for Exploration

As we prepare to embark on a comprehensive exploration of the significance of wisdom and understanding in Proverbs, it is essential to lay the groundwork for a deeper understanding of these virtues. In the forthcoming sections, we will delve into the rich tapestry of teachings, parables, and insights that Proverbs offers, uncovering the timeless truths that have guided countless generations in their pursuit of a life well-lived.

Through the lens of wisdom and understanding, we will gain a deeper appreciation for the intricate balance between spiritual enlightenment and practical application, between personal growth and societal harmony. We will explore the profound connections between these virtues and the ethical foundations that underpin a just and equitable society, where the pursuit of knowledge is not merely an intellectual endeavor but a sacred calling to live in alignment with the divine principles of truth, justice, and compassion.

So let us embrace the journey ahead with open hearts and minds, ready to unravel the mysteries of wisdom and understanding and allow their transformative power to guide us toward a deeper reverence for life, a greater sense of purpose, and a renewed commitment to creating a world that reflects the sacred principles of Proverbs.

The Pursuit of Perfection: Interpreting Proverbs 3:13-16

The pursuit of wisdom and understanding has captivated humanity since the dawn of civilization. From the ancient sages of the East to the philosophers of the West, the quest for enlightenment has been a constant thread woven into the fabric of our collective consciousness. In the realm of sacred scripture, Proverbs 3:13-16 stands as a luminous beacon, guiding us toward the path of perfection through the acquisition of wisdom and understanding.

An Overview of the Evidence-Based Approach

Before delving into the depths of this profound passage, it is essential to recognize the importance of an evidence-based analysis. Unlike mere speculation or conjecture, an evidence-based approach grounds our interpretations in verifiable and credible sources, ensuring that our insights are rooted in the firm foundation of truth. By examining the textual evidence within the broader context of Proverbs and the biblical corpus, we can uncover the rich tapestry of meaning woven into these sacred verses.

The Main Claim: Wisdom and Understanding as Pathways to Perfection

Proverbs 3:13-16 presents a powerful and compelling claim: the pursuit of wisdom and understanding is not merely an intellectual exercise but a transformative journey toward a higher state of being. The passage declares, "Blessed is the one who finds wisdom, and the one who gets understanding, for the gain from her is better than gain from silver and her profit better than gold." (Proverbs 3:13-14, ESV). This statement sets the stage for an exploration of the profound value and significance of these virtues, elevating them above material wealth and worldly possessions.

Evidence from Sacred Scripture

The first piece of evidence we encounter is the very text of Proverbs 3:13-16 itself. Within these verses, we find a rich tapestry of metaphors and imagery that illuminate the nature and rewards of wisdom and understanding. The passage declares:

"She [wisdom] is more precious than jewels, and nothing you desire can compare with her. Long life is in her right hand; in her left hand are riches and honor. Her ways are ways of pleasantness, and all her paths are peace." (Proverbs 3:15-17, ESV)

These verses paint a vivid picture of wisdom as a personified entity, imbued with the power to bestow upon her seekers the ultimate rewards: long life, riches, honor, pleasantness, and peace. The use of such rich imagery and personification underscores the profound significance of wisdom and understanding, elevating them to a level transcending mere intellectual concepts.

Evidence from Biblical Scholarship

To further substantiate our interpretation, we turn to the insights of biblical scholars and exegetes who have dedicated their lives to the study of sacred texts. One notable example is the work of Dr. Michael V. Fox, a renowned scholar of Proverbs and the Hebrew Bible. In his acclaimed commentary, "Proverbs: An Eclectic Edition with Introduction and Textual Commentary," Fox delves into the nuances and symbolism of Proverbs 3:13-16, offering a wealth of linguistic and cultural context.

According to Fox, the personification of wisdom as a woman in these verses is a deliberate literary device employed to convey the intimate and alluring nature of wisdom itself. The images of jewels, riches, and honor are not mere material rewards but symbolic representations of the spiritual and intellectual fulfillment that accompanies the pursuit of wisdom and understanding.

Addressing Potential Counterarguments

While the evidence presented thus far strongly supports the significance of wisdom and understanding as pathways to perfection, it is essential to acknowledge potential counterarguments or alternative interpretations. One such perspective might suggest that the pursuit of wisdom and understanding, while admirable, should not be elevated above material wealth or worldly success.

In response to this argument, we must recognize that Proverbs 3:13-16 does not dismiss or diminish the value of material possessions or earthly accomplishments. Instead, it places wisdom and understanding on a higher plane, acknowledging their transcendent and enduring nature. The passage invites us to embrace a holistic view of success, one that harmonizes the pursuit of knowledge and spiritual growth with the responsible stewardship of material resources.

Reinforcing the Claim: Further Evidence and Applications

To further reinforce the claim of wisdom and understanding as pathways to perfection, we can turn to the broader context of Proverbs and its enduring influence across cultures and generations. Throughout the book, we encounter numerous exhortations to seek wisdom, cultivate understanding, and live a life guided by these virtues. The very structure of Proverbs, with its proverbial sayings and instructions, serves as a testament to the universal and timeless nature of this pursuit.

Moreover, the principles espoused in Proverbs 3:13-16 find resonance in the teachings of various philosophical and spiritual traditions around the world. From the ancient Greek maxim "Know Thyself" to the Buddhist emphasis on insight and enlightenment, the pursuit of wisdom and understanding has been a common thread woven into the tapestry of human civilization.

In our contemporary context, the relevance of these ancient teachings remains everpresent. In a world often overwhelmed by information and distraction, the pursuit of wisdom and understanding offers a path toward clarity, discernment, and a deeper understanding of our place in the universe. It equips us with the tools to navigate the complexities of modern life, make informed decisions, and cultivate a sense of purpose and fulfillment that transcends fleeting material pursuits.

Conclusion: The Timeless Pursuit of Perfection

As we conclude our evidence-based analysis of Proverbs 3:13-16, we are left with a profound appreciation for the enduring wisdom contained within these verses. The pursuit of wisdom and understanding is not merely a biblical injunction; it is a universal call to embrace the highest ideals of human existence. Through the acquisition of these virtues, we embark on a transformative journey toward perfection, a state of being that harmonizes intellectual growth, spiritual enlightenment, and a deep reverence for the sacred principles that underpin our existence.

In a world that often prioritizes the ephemeral and the material, Proverbs 3:13-16 reminds us of the timeless and transcendent nature of true wisdom and understanding. It invites us to shift our gaze from the fleeting to the eternal, to seek that which endures beyond the limitations of our physical existence. In doing so, we not only elevate our own lives but contribute to the ongoing pursuit of human flourishing, leaving an indelible mark on the tapestry of our shared existence.

Wisdom and Understanding in Historical Context

The quest for wisdom and understanding has been an integral part of the human experience since the dawn of civilization. This timeless pursuit has transcended boundaries and cultures, leaving an indelible mark on the tapestry of our shared heritage. To fully appreciate the depth and richness of these virtues, we must embark on a historical journey, tracing their conceptual evolution and examining the key figures and texts that have shaped our understanding of these profound ideals.

1. Setting the Stage: Introducing the Historical Timeline

This historical timeline spans the ancient Near Eastern traditions, biblical literature, and early Christian thought, illuminating the diverse perspectives and interpretations that have contributed to our collective understanding of wisdom and understanding. By exploring this rich tapestry of ideas, we gain invaluable insights into the enduring human longing for enlightenment and the transformative power of these virtues.

2. The Earliest Roots: Ancient Near Eastern Traditions

The roots of the pursuit of wisdom and understanding can be traced back to the ancient civilizations of the Near East, dating back to the third millennium BCE. Among the earliest known practitioners were the sages and scribes of Mesopotamia, who sought to unravel the mysteries of the cosmos and distill timeless principles for living a virtuous life. The "Instructions of Shuruppak," a Sumerian literary work from around 2600 BCE, contains poetic exhortations to embrace wisdom and reject folly, setting the stage for a rich tradition of didactic literature that would later influence biblical wisdom literature.

3. Key Events, Discoveries, and Shifts

- 2500 BCE: The emergence of Egyptian wisdom literature, exemplified by the "Instructions of Ptahhotep" and the "Wisdom of Amenemope," which extolled the virtues of wisdom, justice, and moral rectitude.
- 1500-1000 BCE: The composition of biblical wisdom books, including Proverbs, Job, and Ecclesiastes, which drew upon ancient Near Eastern wisdom traditions while infusing them with a distinctly Hebrew worldview.
- 7th-6th centuries BCE: The rise of Greek philosophy, with figures like Thales, Pythagoras, and Socrates introducing new perspectives on the nature of wisdom and the pursuit of knowledge.

- 4th century BCE: The teachings of Aristotle and his concept of practical wisdom, or phronesis, which emphasized the application of knowledge to ethical decision-making and living a virtuous life.
- 1st century CE: The teachings of Jesus and the Apostle Paul in the New Testament, redefined the concept of wisdom in the context of a personal relationship with God and the transformative power of divine revelation.

4. Adaptations and Interpretations Across Cultures

As wisdom and understanding transcended geographical boundaries, they were adapted and interpreted in distinct ways by different cultures and belief systems. For example, in ancient Israel, wisdom was closely tied to the fear of the Lord and adherence to divine commandments, as exemplified in the book of Proverbs. In Greek philosophy, wisdom was often associated with reason, logic, and the pursuit of knowledge through rational inquiry.

Early Christian thinkers, such as the Apostle Paul, and Church Fathers like Clement of Alexandria and Augustine of Hippo, sought to integrate and reconcile these diverse traditions, synthesizing the wisdom of the ancients with the revelations of the Christian faith. They emphasized the importance of both human reason and divine revelation in the pursuit of true wisdom and understanding.

5. Contemporary Perspectives and Applications

In modern times, the quest for wisdom and understanding continues to captivate scholars, philosophers, and thinkers from various disciplines. Contemporary perspectives often emphasize the integration of multiple sources of knowledge, including scientific inquiry, cross-cultural exchange, and personal experience. The pursuit of wisdom has also been recognized as a vital component of ethical decision-making, leadership, and personal growth.

Additionally, the historical insights gained from studying the evolution of these virtues have informed contemporary approaches to education, counseling, and personal development. By recognizing the universal and timeless nature of the pursuit of wisdom and understanding, we can draw upon the rich heritage of the past while adapting these ideals to meet the unique challenges and opportunities of the present day.

6. Pivotal Moments and Challenges

Throughout this historical journey, there have been pivotal moments and challenges that have shaped the trajectory of our understanding of wisdom and understanding. One significant challenge was the apparent conflict between faith and reason during the Middle Ages, which sparked intense debates and philosophical inquiries into the nature of knowledge and the role of divine revelation.

The Enlightenment period also presented a pivotal moment, as thinkers like René Descartes and Immanuel Kant challenged traditional notions of wisdom and sought to establish new foundations for knowledge based on empiricism and rational inquiry. These debates and challenges have enriched our understanding of these virtues, pushing us to continually reevaluate and refine our perspectives.

In conclusion, the historical timeline of wisdom and understanding is a rich tapestry interwoven with diverse traditions, perspectives, and insights. From the ancient sages of the Near East to the philosophers of Greece and the biblical writers, each epoch has contributed invaluable threads to this tapestry, reminding us of the enduring human longing for enlightenment and the transformative power of these virtues. As we navigate the complexities of the modern world, this historical journey serves as a beacon, guiding us toward a deeper appreciation of the timeless pursuit of wisdom and understanding.

The Theological Dimensions of Wisdom

Wisdom, that elusive yet profound virtue, has been the subject of human contemplation and pursuit since the dawn of civilization.

While its manifestations have taken various forms across cultures and belief systems, the theological dimensions of wisdom stand as a testament to the divine origins and sacred nature of this cherished ideal. In the pages of the Bible and the annals of ancient wisdom literature, we find wisdom portrayed not merely as a human acquisition but as an emanation of the divine, a guiding force woven into the very fabric of creation itself.

Within the book of Proverbs, wisdom is personified as a celestial being, dwelling with God from the beginning and participating in the act of creation. The opening verses of Proverbs 8 offer a striking depiction: "The Lord possessed me at the beginning of His way, before His works of old... When He established the heavens, I was there... When He marked out the foundations of the earth, then I was beside Him, as a master workman; and I was daily His delight, rejoicing always before Him" (Proverbs 8:22-30). This portrayal of wisdom as an active participant in the creative process, delighting in the unfolding of the universe, imbues it with a sacred and divine quality, elevating it beyond mere human knowledge or understanding.

The divine origin of wisdom is further underscored by its intimate connection with God Himself. In the book of Proverbs, wisdom is described as the "fear of the Lord" (Proverbs 9:10), and in Ecclesiastes, it is said to be "from God" (Ecclesiastes 2:26). This theological dimension positions wisdom not as a mere human construct but as a reflection of the divine will and a manifestation of God's own character. To embrace wisdom, then, is to align oneself with the very essence of the Creator, to partake in the divine order that permeates the cosmos.

The interconnectedness between divine wisdom and human understanding is further exemplified in the New Testament, where the Apostle Paul speaks of Christ as the embodiment of the "wisdom of God" (1 Corinthians 1:24). In this context, wisdom transcends mere intellectual prowess and becomes inextricably linked to the redemptive work of Christ and the revelation of God's eternal plan. The pursuit of wisdom, therefore, is not merely an academic exercise but a profound spiritual journey, a quest to understand the ways of the divine and to align one's life with the transformative power of God's wisdom.

As we delve deeper into the theological dimensions of wisdom, we are confronted with the reality that true wisdom is not merely a collection of facts or knowledge but a way of being, a posture of the heart and mind that seeks to discern and embrace the divine order undergirding all of creation. The fear of the Lord, as the Scriptures declare, is the beginning of wisdom (Proverbs 9:10), a recognition that human understanding is incomplete without a reverent acknowledgment of the sovereign God who is the source of all wisdom and knowledge.

This theological perspective invites us to contemplate the profound implications of wisdom in our spiritual journeys. It challenges us to cultivate a posture of humility, recognizing that true wisdom is not solely attained through human effort but is a gift from the divine, a grace bestowed upon those who seek it with a sincere heart. It calls us to cultivate a deep reverence for the Creator, acknowledging that the pursuit of wisdom is inextricably linked to the pursuit of the divine, a journey of aligning our thoughts, desires, and actions with the eternal wisdom that permeates the universe.

Moreover, the theological dimensions of wisdom remind us of the transformative power of this virtue in shaping our character and our relationships. As we embrace divine wisdom, we are invited to embody its qualities – righteousness, justice, mercy, and a deep regard for the sanctity of life. Wisdom becomes not merely an intellectual pursuit but a way of life, a guiding light that illuminates our path and shapes our interactions with others, fostering a spirit of compassion, empathy, and a commitment to the common good.

In this sacred quest for wisdom, we are reminded that our journey is not solitary but a shared experience, a collective pursuit that has echoed across generations and cultures. From the ancient sages of the Near East to the prophets of the Hebrew Scriptures and the early Christian thinkers, countless individuals have grappled with the mysteries of divine wisdom, leaving behind a rich tapestry of insights and revelations that continue to guide and inspire us today. By engaging with this rich heritage, we are invited to participate in a timeless conversation, to stand on the shoulders of those who have gone before us, and to contribute our own understanding to this ever-evolving tapestry of wisdom.

As we navigate the complexities of the modern world, the theological dimensions of wisdom beckon us to pause and reflect, to recognize the sacred thread that weaves through all of existence, and to align our lives with the eternal truths that transcend the fleeting concerns of the present moment. In a world that often prizes knowledge and information above all else, the pursuit of divine wisdom offers a countercultural invitation to seek a deeper understanding, one that integrates the intellect with the soul, the mind with the spirit, and the human experience with the divine.

In the end, the theological dimensions of wisdom remind us that our quest for understanding is not merely an exercise of the mind but a journey of the heart and soul, a sacred calling to embody the very essence of the divine in our thoughts, words, and actions. As we embrace this sacred pursuit, we are invited to participate in the ongoing revelation of God's eternal wisdom, to become co-creators in the unfolding of a grander narrative that extends beyond our fleeting existence and into the realms of eternity. May we approach this quest with humility, reverence, and a deep sense of wonder, for in doing so, we may catch glimpses of the divine wisdom that permeates all of creation and shapes the very fabric of our being.

Philosophical Insights on Understanding

The pursuit of understanding is a fundamental human endeavor, a quest that has captivated philosophers, theologians, and thinkers across ages and cultures. At its core, understanding is the ability to comprehend, to grasp the essence of a concept, idea, or phenomenon, and to integrate it into our cognitive and moral frameworks. It is a journey that transcends mere intellectual acumen and delves into the depths of human perception, reasoning, and spiritual growth.

The ancient Greek philosophers, with their insatiable thirst for wisdom and knowledge, laid the foundations for our explorations of understanding. Plato, the renowned Athenian philosopher, posited the concept of "forms" – the ideal, eternal, and immutable essences of things that exist beyond the physical realm. In his renowned allegory of the cave, he suggested that the path to true understanding involves a profound shift in perspective, a turning away from the shadows of mere appearances, and a confrontation with the ultimate realities that cast those shadows. This metaphorical journey from the cave into the light of understanding underscores the transformative power of knowledge and the necessity of transcending superficial perceptions to attain deeper comprehension.

Building upon this foundation, Aristotle, Plato's illustrious student, proposed a more empirical approach to understanding. He emphasized the importance of systematic observation, logic, and reason in uncovering the underlying principles that govern the natural world. Aristotle's pursuit of understanding was grounded in the belief that by studying the physical and spiritual aspects of existence, we can unravel the intricate tapestry of causality and purpose that permeates the cosmos. His contributions to fields as diverse as logic, spirituality, and ethics continue to shape our understanding of the world and our place within it.

As the philosophical discourse evolved, the intersections between reason and faith, between the pursuit of understanding and the divine, became increasingly intertwined. Augustine of Hippo, a towering figure in the development of Christian theology, grappled with the relationship between human understanding and divine revelation. In his seminal work, "Confessions," he chronicles his intellectual and spiritual journey, highlighting the transformative power of faith and the illumination it provides in our quest for understanding. Augustine posited that true understanding is not attained solely through reason but requires a synthesis of reason and faith, a recognition that the divine wisdom revealed through Scripture and spiritual contemplation is an indispensable guide in our pursuit of knowledge.

Building upon this foundation, Thomas Aquinas, the renowned medieval philosopher and theologian, sought to reconcile the wisdom of ancient philosophers with the teachings of Christianity. In his monumental work, "Summa Theologica," Aquinas synthesized Aristotelian philosophy with Christian theology, offering a comprehensive framework for understanding the relationship between reason and faith. He argued that reason and revelation are complementary paths to understanding, each shedding light on distinct aspects of reality while ultimately converging in the pursuit of truth. This integration of philosophical inquiry and divine revelation laid the groundwork for a holistic approach to understanding, one that embraces the insights of human reason while acknowledging the limitations of our finite minds and the necessity of divine guidance.

As we delve into these philosophical and theological perspectives, a profound truth emerges: understanding is not merely an intellectual exercise but a holistic pursuit that encompasses our cognitive, moral, and spiritual faculties. The pursuit of understanding demands rigorous inquiry, critical thinking, and a willingness to challenge preconceptions, yet it also necessitates humility, reverence, and a recognition that our finite minds may not grasp the full breadth and depth of the divine mysteries that permeate existence.

The biblical narrative offers insights that further illuminate our understanding of this profound quest. In the opening chapters of Genesis, we encounter the account of the creation of humanity, fashioned in the image and likeness of God (Genesis 1:26-27). This divine imprint bestows upon us a unique capacity for understanding, a reflection of the divine wisdom that was the wellspring of creation itself. The pursuit of understanding, therefore, becomes a sacred endeavor, a means of aligning ourselves with the divine order and unraveling the mysteries woven into the fabric of existence.

Yet, the biblical narrative also underscores the limitations of human understanding and the necessity of divine revelation. The book of Proverbs declares, "The fear of the Lord is the beginning of wisdom, and the knowledge of the Holy One is understanding" (Proverbs 9:10). This passage suggests that true understanding is inextricably linked to a reverent acknowledgment of the divine, a recognition that our finite comprehension must be guided and illuminated by the infinite wisdom of the Creator.

This dynamic interplay between human reason and divine revelation is further exemplified in the life and teachings of Jesus Christ. In the New Testament, we encounter the concept of the "Logos," the divine Word that is the source of all wisdom, truth, and understanding (John 1:1-5). Through the incarnation of Christ, the divine Logos became flesh, revealing the fullness of truth and offering a model for integrating divine wisdom into our lived experiences. Christ's teachings, parables, and miracles challenged conventional wisdom and invited His followers to embrace a deeper, more profound understanding of the human condition and our relationship with the divine.

As we navigate the complexities of the modern age, the pursuit of understanding takes on renewed urgency and significance. We live in a world of unprecedented technological advancements, global interconnectedness, and access to vast repositories of knowledge. Yet, amidst this sea of information, we are often confronted with the limitations of human understanding and the need for a more profound and holistic approach to comprehending the complexities of our existence.

The integration of philosophical and theological insights invites us to approach the quest for understanding with a posture of humility, reverence, and open-mindedness. It challenges us to recognize that true understanding is not merely an accumulation of facts or data but a journey of the heart and soul, a lifelong pursuit of wisdom that transcends the boundaries of any single discipline or worldview. By embracing the insights of ancient philosophers and the revelations of sacred texts, we can cultivate a more nuanced and multi-dimensional approach to understanding, one that harmonizes the intellectual, moral, and spiritual dimensions of our existence.

Ultimately, the pursuit of understanding is a sacred calling, a quest that invites us to delve into the depths of human experience, confront the mysteries of existence, and seek the guidance of divine wisdom. As we embark on this journey, may we do so with a spirit of intellectual curiosity, moral courage, and spiritual discernment, recognizing that the path to understanding is paved with both human reason and divine revelation, and that the synthesis of these two paths can lead us to a more profound and transformative comprehension of the world and our place within it.

Practical Applications: Wisdom and Understanding in Daily Life

In a bustling metropolis, Sarah, a young entrepreneur, found herself at a crossroads. Her startup company, which had initially shown immense promise, was facing a series of challenges that threatened its very existence. Investors were growing increasingly skeptical, and market competition was intensifying. As Sarah grappled with these daunting obstacles, she realized that her ability to navigate this crisis hinged not only on her business acumen but also on the wisdom and understanding she could bring to bear.

1. The Players:

Sarah, the founder and CEO of the startup, was a driven and ambitious individual with a passion for innovation. Her team consisted of a diverse group of talented professionals, each with their unique strengths and perspectives. Among them were Mark, the Chief Technology Officer, a brilliant engineer but one who often struggled with interpersonal dynamics, and Emily, the Head of Marketing, whose creative vision was sometimes at odds with practical realities.

2. The Challenge:

The primary challenge facing Sarah's startup was a rapidly dwindling cash flow. Despite their innovative product and initial market traction, the company had failed to secure additional funding, and expenses were outpacing revenue. Furthermore, a larger, well-established competitor had launched a similar product, threatening to undermine the startup's market share. Tensions within the team were rising, with divergent opinions on how best to address these issues.

3. The Strategy:

Recognizing the gravity of the situation, Sarah knew that a wise and measured approach was crucial. She began by fostering open and honest communication within the team, creating a safe space for diverse perspectives to be shared and explored. Rather than imposing her will, she listened intently, seeking to understand the root causes of the challenges they faced and the underlying motivations and concerns of her team members.

Drawing upon her understanding of the company's strengths and weaknesses, as well as the broader market landscape, Sarah facilitated a collaborative process of identifying potential solutions. She encouraged her team to think creatively, challenging assumptions and exploring unconventional approaches. At the same time, she brought a sense of pragmatism, carefully weighing the risks and benefits of each proposed strategy.

Ultimately, the team devised a two-pronged approach. First, they would refine their product offering, incorporating feedback from customers and focusing on the unique value proposition that sets them apart from their competitors. Second, they would aggressively pursue strategic partnerships and alternative funding sources, leveraging their network and demonstrating the long-term potential of their vision.

4. The Outcome:

Implementing this strategy required perseverance and unwavering commitment from the entire team. Over the course of several months, they worked tirelessly to refine their product, improving its functionality and user experience. Simultaneously, Sarah and her team engaged in intense negotiations with potential partners and investors, meticulously crafting their pitch and demonstrating the value of their solution.

Their efforts paid off. Within a year, the startup had secured a significant investment from a major venture capital firm and established strategic partnerships with key industry players. This influx of resources and collaborative relationships allowed them to expand their operations, attract top talent, and solidify their position in the market. By the end of the second year, the company's revenue had tripled, and they had gained a loyal customer base, positioning them for sustained growth and success.

5. Lessons Learned:

Sarah's journey with her startup serves as a powerful testament to the practical applications of wisdom and understanding in navigating the complexities of business and life. Through her willingness to listen, her ability to synthesize diverse perspectives, and her judicious decision-making, Sarah demonstrated the transformative power of these virtues.

Had Sarah approached the challenges with a narrow or dogmatic mindset, imposing her will without considering the insights of her team and external stakeholders, the outcome might have been drastically different. By embracing a posture of humility and openness, she was able to tap into the collective wisdom of her team, identify innovative solutions, and navigate the treacherous waters of entrepreneurship.

Critics might argue that Sarah's approach was overly cautious or that more decisive action could have yielded quicker results. However, the wisdom lies in recognizing that rash or impulsive decisions, particularly in complex situations, can have severe unintended consequences. By cultivating understanding and taking a measured approach, Sarah ensured that her actions were grounded in a comprehensive assessment of the challenges and opportunities at hand.

6. Relevance and Takeaways:

Sarah's experience underscores the profound relevance of wisdom and understanding in our daily lives, regardless of our specific circumstances or pursuits. Whether in business, personal relationships, or any other sphere of human endeavor, the ability to grasp the nuances and complexities of a situation, consider diverse perspectives, and make informed decisions based on a holistic understanding of the factors at play is invaluable.

The lessons from this case study extend beyond the realm of entrepreneurship. They serve as a reminder that true wisdom and understanding are not merely intellectual exercises but living, breathing practices that can guide us through the most daunting challenges and unlock our fullest potential as individuals and members of society.

As readers, we are invited to reflect on our own pursuit of wisdom and understanding, cultivate these virtues within ourselves, and apply them in our daily lives. Whether we are facing personal or professional challenges, seeking to navigate complex relationships, or striving to make a positive impact in our communities, embracing the principles exemplified by Sarah's journey can empower us to make informed, compassionate, and ethically grounded choices.

7. Final Reflection:

As we contemplate the practical applications of wisdom and understanding, one question lingers: How might our lives and the world around us be transformed if we collectively embraced these virtues with unwavering commitment? Could we create a more just, compassionate, and thriving society by grounding our actions in a deeper understanding of the human condition and the interconnectedness of all things? The pursuit of wisdom and understanding is not merely an individual endeavor but a collective journey that holds the promise of transcending our limitations and unleashing the full potential of the human spirit.

Challenges and Pitfalls in the Pursuit of Wisdom

The pursuit of wisdom and understanding is a noble and fulfilling quest, one that promises to unveil the deeper truths of existence and unlock our potential as individuals and as a society. Yet, this journey is not without its challenges and pitfalls, obstacles that can derail even the most sincere and determined seekers of knowledge. To navigate these treacherous waters, we must cultivate a profound sense of humility, embrace critical thinking, and exercise discernment in separating truth from falsehood.

One of the most insidious pitfalls on the path to wisdom is arrogance, the belief that we have already attained the pinnacle of understanding and that our perspective is the only valid one. This hubris can blind us to our own limitations and biases, causing us to dismiss or distort information that challenges our preconceived notions. It is a trap that has ensnared countless individuals and societies throughout history, leading to stagnation, conflict, and the perpetuation of harmful ideologies.

The philosopher Socrates, who is regarded as one of the founders of Western philosophy, exemplified the antidote to arrogance: a deep sense of humility and a recognition of the vastness of human ignorance. His famous proclamation, "I am the wisest man alive, for I know one thing, and that is that I know nothing," encapsulates this principle. By acknowledging the limitations of our knowledge, we open ourselves to continuous learning, growth, and the possibility of revising our beliefs in the face of new evidence.

Another formidable obstacle in the pursuit of wisdom is the proliferation of misinformation and disinformation, particularly in our modern age of digital connectivity and social media. In a world where anyone can disseminate information, it becomes increasingly challenging to separate fact from fiction, truth from falsehood. This environment can breed confusion, mistrust, and susceptibility to manipulation by those with ulterior motives or vested interests.

To combat this scourge, we must cultivate the art of critical thinking, the ability to analyze information objectively, question assumptions, and evaluate claims against empirical evidence and sound reasoning. This skill, which has been championed by philosophers and scholars throughout the ages, empowers us to discern the credible from the dubious, and the substantive from the superficial.

One shining example of critical thinking in action is the work of Carl Sagan, the renowned astronomer and science communicator. Through his writings and television series, Sagan championed the scientific method and encouraged his audience to adopt a "baloney detection kit" – a set of intellectual tools and dispositions to separate the credible from the incredible. His unwavering commitment to evidence-based reasoning and skepticism toward unsupported claims inspired generations of thinkers to approach knowledge with intellectual rigor and discernment.

Yet another pitfall on the journey to wisdom is the misguided prioritization of personal gain or short-term gratification over the pursuit of deeper understanding and ethical conduct. In a world that often celebrates material success, fame, and instant gratification, it can be tempting to sacrifice our commitment to wisdom for the allure of fleeting pleasures or superficial rewards.

The life and teachings of Mahatma Gandhi, the iconic leader of the Indian independence movement, serve as a powerful counterpoint to this trap. Through his practice of nonviolent resistance and his unwavering commitment to truth, justice, and the upliftment of the oppressed, Gandhi demonstrated that true wisdom is inextricably linked to ethical conduct and a concern for the greater good. His willingness to sacrifice personal comforts and endure hardships in the pursuit of higher principles continues to inspire individuals and movements worldwide.

To avoid these pitfalls and stay on the path of true wisdom and understanding, we must adopt practical strategies and cultivate specific virtues. First and foremost, we must embrace a posture of intellectual humility, recognizing that our knowledge is inherently limited and that we must remain open to new perspectives and evidence. This humility should be coupled with a commitment to continuous learning, a willingness to challenge our own assumptions, and a curiosity to explore diverse viewpoints and disciplines.

Additionally, we must hone our critical thinking skills, developing the ability to analyze information objectively, question claims, and evaluate evidence rigorously. This can involve studying logic, mastering research methodologies, and learning to identify logical fallacies and cognitive biases that can distort our reasoning.

Furthermore, it is crucial to cultivate discernment, the capacity to separate truth from falsehood, and to distinguish between credible and unreliable sources of information. This may involve developing a keen understanding of the motivations and agendas of those disseminating information, as well as the ability to cross-reference and corroborate claims from multiple reputable sources.

Finally, we must maintain an unwavering commitment to ethical conduct and the greater good, resisting the temptation to sacrifice our principles for personal gain or short-term gratification. This requires cultivating virtues such as integrity, compassion, and a concern for the well-being of others, as well as a willingness to make sacrifices for the pursuit of higher ideals.

By embracing these strategies and virtues, we can navigate the challenges and pitfalls that litter the path to wisdom and understanding, emerging as more discerning, ethical, and enlightened individuals. It is a journey that requires perseverance and determination, but one that promises to unlock the depths of human potential and pave the way for a more just, compassionate, and enlightened society.

In the end, the pursuit of wisdom and understanding is not merely an individual endeavor but a collective quest that transcends personal gain and elevates the human experience. By fostering a culture of intellectual humility, critical thinking, and ethical conduct, we can overcome the obstacles that have historically hindered our progress, and forge a path toward a world where knowledge and understanding are cherished and celebrated as the cornerstones of human flourishing.

Comparative Analysis: Biblical and Contemporary Views on Wisdom

In the pursuit of wisdom, a paradox emerges – the intrinsic value of ancient teachings coexists with the insights offered by modern perspectives. This juxtaposition challenges our understanding, inviting us to explore the nuances and the timeless relevance of wisdom across eras and disciplines.

On one hand, the biblical scriptures, revered by billions worldwide, enshrine profound truths and timeless principles that have guided humanity through the ages. The book of Proverbs, for instance, is a treasure trove of wisdom, offering insights into virtuous living, ethical conduct, and the cultivation of discernment. These teachings, rooted in divine revelation and the collective experiences of ancient cultures, have withstood the test of time, resonating with individuals across generations and societies.

On the other hand, contemporary philosophical and psychological perspectives offer fresh insights and scientific rigor, shedding light on the complexities of human behavior, cognition, and decision-making. From the rational analysis of ethical dilemmas to the exploration of cognitive biases and heuristics, modern thought provides a lens through which we can understand ourselves and our world with newfound clarity and depth.

To unravel the relationship between these seemingly divergent perspectives, we will examine specific attributes and themes, exploring their similarities, differences, and the implications of these comparisons. This analysis will encompass the nature of wisdom itself, the sources of knowledge, the role of reason and emotion, and the relationship between wisdom and ethical conduct.

One striking similarity between biblical teachings and contemporary thought lies in the recognition of wisdom as a multifaceted concept, one that transcends mere intellectual knowledge. Both traditions emphasize the importance of practical application, discernment, and the ability to navigate the complexities of life with sound judgment and ethical conduct. The biblical book of Proverbs highlights this notion, "Wisdom is supreme; therefore get wisdom. Though it cost all you have, get understanding" (Proverbs 4:7, NIV). Similarly, modern philosophers and psychologists underscore the value of cultivating wisdom as a means of enhancing well-being, decision-making, and navigating the challenges of the human experience.

However, a notable difference emerges in the sources of wisdom. The biblical perspective anchors wisdom in divine revelation, with the ultimate source being God, the embodiment of perfect wisdom. In contrast, contemporary thought often grounds wisdom in empirical observation, rational inquiry, and scientific investigation, seeking to understand the world through systematic analysis and hypothesis testing. This divergence in sources raises intriguing questions about the interplay between faith and reason, and the boundaries of human knowledge.

Another key area of comparison is the role of reason and emotion in the pursuit of wisdom. While biblical teachings emphasize the importance of reverence, humility, and a heart attuned to divine guidance, modern perspectives often prioritize rational analysis, cognitive processes, and the objective evaluation of evidence. Yet, both recognize the inherent limitations of human reasoning and the potential for biases and distortions, underscoring the need for self-awareness and a commitment to continuous growth and learning.

The relationship between wisdom and ethical conduct is another point of intersection and divergence. The biblical scriptures interweave wisdom with moral principles and virtuous living, viewing them as inextricable. The book of James declares, "Who is wise and understanding among you? Let them show it by their good life, by deeds done in the humility that comes from wisdom" (James 3:13, NIV). Contemporary ethical theories, while acknowledging the importance of wisdom in decision-making, often grapple with the complexities of moral dilemmas and the application of ethical frameworks in a pluralistic and rapidly changing world.

By exploring these similarities and differences, we uncover insights into broader themes and concepts that transcend the specific contexts of biblical and modern thought. For instance, the recognition of the inherent limitations of human knowledge and the need for humility and continuous learning is a thread that weaves through both perspectives, reminding us of the ever-evolving nature of wisdom and the importance of remaining open to new ideas and perspectives.

Moreover, the enduring relevance of wisdom becomes evident when we consider contemporary scenarios and challenges. In a world grappling with complex issues such as climate change, economic inequality, and social unrest, the need for wise leadership, ethical decision-making, and a nuanced understanding of human behavior and motivation has never been more pressing. The insights gleaned from both ancient and modern sources of wisdom can inform our approaches to these challenges, guiding us toward solutions that balance reason and compassion, pragmatism and principle.

In the realm of personal growth and fulfillment, the timeless teachings of wisdom offer guidance and solace, reminding us of the enduring human quest for meaning, purpose, and inner peace. Whether it is the biblical exhortation to "fear the Lord [and] that will be the beginning of wisdom" (Proverbs 9:10, NLT) or the contemporary emphasis on cultivating self-awareness and emotional intelligence, the pursuit of wisdom remains a cornerstone of individual and societal flourishing.

As we navigate the complexities of the modern world, with its rapid technological advancements, shifting societal norms, and global interconnectedness, the integration of ancient and contemporary wisdom becomes increasingly vital. By embracing the richness of diverse perspectives and engaging in respectful dialogue, we can forge a path toward a more holistic and nuanced understanding of the human experience, one that honors the contributions of both tradition and innovation, faith and reason, and the enduring pursuit of truth and wisdom.

The Role of Understanding in Societal Balance

In the tapestry of human civilization, the pursuit of societal balance has long been a driving force, a quest that lies at the heart of every thriving community. As we navigate the complexities of our interconnected world, one thread emerges as the unifying catalyst for true harmony and progress: understanding. This multifaceted concept transcends mere intellectual apprehension; it embodies a profound appreciation for the richness of diverse perspectives, a willingness to embrace complexity, and a commitment to fostering genuine connection and empathy among all members of society.

At its core, understanding serves as the bedrock upon which a balanced society is built. It allows us to bridge cultural, social, and ideological divides, recognizing that beneath the surface of our differences lies a shared human experience. When we actively seek to comprehend the narratives and worldviews of others, we open ourselves to new insights and perspectives, cultivating a deeper sense of compassion and mutual respect. This, in turn, paves the way for open dialogue, collaborative problem-solving, and the growth of inclusive communities where diverse voices are heard and valued.

Historically, societies that have embraced understanding as a guiding principle have reaped immense benefits. The ancient

Iroquois Confederacy, for instance, recognized the importance of fostering understanding among its constituent nations, establishing a system of representation and consensus-building that allowed for the peaceful coexistence of distinct cultures. Similarly, the city-states of ancient Greece, while fiercely independent, embraced the concept of the agora – a public space where ideas could be freely exchanged, debated, and understood, fostering a rich intellectual and cultural legacy that continues to influence modern thought.

In contemporary times, nations that have actively cultivated understanding within their governance and social structures have experienced profound transformations. South Africa's transition from the oppressive apartheid regime to a democratic society was made possible, in part, by the nation's embrace of the Truth and Reconciliation Commission, a process that facilitated understanding and healing among diverse communities. Similarly, New Zealand's commitment to honoring the Treaty of Waitangi and fostering understanding between the indigenous Māori population and settlers has contributed to a more inclusive and equitable society.

Fostering understanding at an individual level is equally crucial for societal balance. By actively seeking to understand ourselves – our biases, motivations, and worldviews – we cultivate self-awareness and emotional intelligence, enabling us to navigate interpersonal interactions with greater empathy and compassion. This, in turn, ripples outward, positively impacting our relationships, communities, and ultimately, the broader fabric of society.

To truly embrace understanding as a catalyst for societal balance, we must actively engage in practices that promote it. At a societal level, this involves investing in education systems that prioritize critical thinking, media literacy, and exposure to diverse perspectives. It requires creating platforms for open and respectful dialogue, where differing viewpoints can be expressed and understood without judgment or fear of reprisal. Moreover, it necessitates the cultivation of leadership that exemplifies humility, active listening, and a willingness to seek common ground amidst diverse interests.

At an individual level, fostering understanding begins with a commitment to lifelong learning and a curiosity about the world around us. It involves actively seeking out diverse perspectives, whether through literature, art, travel, or engaging in meaningful conversations with those whose experiences differ from our own. It requires a willingness to challenge our assumptions, confront our biases, and embrace complexity – recognizing that the world is not a series of binary choices, but a rich tapestry woven from countless threads of experience and perspective.

Ultimately, the pursuit of understanding is not merely an intellectual exercise, but a profound act of human connection. It is a recognition that our shared humanity transcends the boundaries of race, religion, or ideology, and that by seeking to understand one another, we unlock the potential for genuine progress, justice, and societal harmony. As we navigate the challenges and opportunities of the 21st century, let us embrace understanding as a guiding principle, a beacon that illuminates our path toward a more balanced, compassionate, and interconnected world.

6

ETERNAL LIFE: THE PROMISE OF RETURN

The Concept of Eternal Life

What if the journey of our existence extended beyond the finite boundaries of our earthly years? What if the depth of our spiritual connection, the richness of our lived experiences, and the imprint we leave upon the world transcended the mortal realm? This captivating premise lies at the heart of the concept of eternal life, a belief that has permeated the fabric of human civilization for millennia, offering a profound promise that resonates within the depths of our souls.

At its essence, eternal life represents the continuance of one's existence beyond the limitations of physical death. It is the assurance that the essence of our being, our consciousness, and our connection to the divine, transcend the boundaries of our temporal form. This concept is rooted in the ancient belief systems of various cultures, each offering its unique interpretation and perspective on the nature of this everlasting existence.

Within the Christian tradition, the concept of eternal life holds a central and transformative significance. It is a fundamental promise woven through the tapestry of Scripture, offering hope, solace, and a deeper understanding of our relationship with the eternal. In the Old Testament, the concept of eternal life is often linked to the covenant between God and His people, a promise of everlasting communion and protection. The Book of Psalms, for instance, proclaims, "With long life will I satisfy him, and show him my salvation" (Psalm 91:16, KJV).

The New Testament further expands upon this concept, illuminating its profound implications through the teachings of Jesus Christ. In the Gospel of John, Christ declares, "For God so loved the world, that he gave his only begotten Son, that whosoever believeth in him should not perish, but have everlasting life" (John 3:16, KJV). This pivotal verse encapsulates the transformative promise of eternal life, a gift bestowed upon those who embrace the divine message of salvation and grace.

Throughout history, the concept of eternal life has evolved and been interpreted through various cultural and theological lenses. In ancient Egyptian mythology, the concept of eternal life was intrinsically linked to the notion of the afterlife, where the soul embarked on a journey through the underworld, guided by the principles of ma'at – the divine order of truth, balance, and righteousness. The ancient Greeks, on the other hand, portrayed eternal life as a state of blissful existence in the Elysian Fields, reserved for those deemed heroic or virtuous.

As our understanding of the world deepened, the concept of eternal life transcended its mythological roots and found resonance within the realms of philosophy and theology. Philosophers such as Plato and Aristotle grappled with the notion of the immortal soul, contemplating its existence beyond the physical realm. Religious traditions like Hinduism and Buddhism embraced the concept of reincarnation, a cyclical process of rebirth and spiritual growth, ultimately leading to a state of enlightenment and liberation from the cycle of existence.

Within the Christian faith, the concept of eternal life carries profound implications for our earthly existence. It serves as a beacon of hope, guiding our moral and ethical choices, and imbuing our actions with a sense of purpose and significance that extends beyond the temporal. The promise of eternal life challenges us to live with compassion, humility, and a deep reverence for the divine, recognizing that our actions and choices reverberate through eternity.

Yet, amidst the richness of this concept, there exist common misconceptions that can obscure its true essence. Some view eternal life as a mere extension of physical existence, a prolongation of our earthly form in an otherworldly realm. However, the biblical portrayal of eternal life transcends such narrow interpretations, presenting it as a state of spiritual transcendence, where our consciousness exists in harmonious union with the divine. Others perceive eternal life as a reward reserved for an elite few, a notion that contradicts the universal love and grace extended by the divine.

To truly grasp the significance of eternal life, we must embrace its transformative potential, allowing it to shape our perspectives, our values, and our relationships with one another and the divine. It invites us to live with purpose, cultivate compassion, and recognize the profound interconnectedness that exists within the tapestry of existence. As we navigate the complexities of our earthly journey, may the promise of eternal life serve as a guiding light, illuminating our path toward a deeper understanding of our place in the cosmic design, and inspiring us to leave an indelible imprint upon the world that extends beyond the boundaries of time and space.

Biblical Prophecies of Eternal Life

The promise of eternal life is a central tenet of the Christian faith, woven through the tapestry of Scripture like a brilliant thread, guiding humanity toward a deeper understanding of our relationship with the divine. This concept, transcending the confines of our temporal existence, finds its roots in the ancient prophecies of the Old Testament, which foretold the coming of a Messiah and the promise of everlasting life for those who embrace the divine covenant.

One of the most profound prophecies that heralded this promise can be found in the book of Isaiah, known as the "Prince of Prophets." In a passage of remarkable clarity, Isaiah proclaims, "He will swallow up death forever, and the Lord God will wipe away tears from all faces; the rebuke of His people He will take away from all the earth; for the Lord has spoken" (Isaiah 25:8, NKJV). This powerful statement not only foreshadows the victory over death but also paints a vivid picture of a celestial realm where the sorrows and afflictions of our earthly existence are no more, replaced by the eternal embrace of the divine.

Another poignant prophecy emerges from the book of Daniel, a testament to the unwavering faith of a man who faced unimaginable trials and tribulations. In a vision, Daniel beholds the "Ancient of Days," a symbolic representation of the divine, whose "garment was white as snow, and the hair of His head was like pure wool" (Daniel 7:9, NKJV). This imagery, steeped in metaphor, alludes to the purity and transcendence of the divine realm, a realm where eternal life finds its ultimate fulfillment. The vision culminates with the declaration that the "saints of the Most High shall receive the kingdom, and possess the kingdom forever, even forever and ever" (Daniel 7:18, NKJV), a promise that echoes through the ages, reminding us of the enduring nature of our spiritual inheritance.

As we journey through the pages of Scripture, the book of Revelation emerges as a crescendo of prophetic symbolism, unveiling the intricate tapestry of the divine plan for humanity's salvation and eternal life. In a vision that transcends the boundaries of mortal comprehension, the apostle John beholds the "New Jerusalem, coming down out of heaven from God, prepared as a bride adorned for her husband" (Revelation 21:2, NKJV). This celestial city, adorned with the radiance of the divine, represents the ultimate fulfillment of the promise of eternal life, where those who have embraced the divine covenant will dwell in the perpetual presence of the Almighty.

The prophecies found within these sacred texts are not mere allegories or fanciful tales; they are the divine whispers that have echoed through the ages, guiding humanity toward the understanding that our existence is not confined to the fleeting moments of our earthly sojourn. Rather, these prophecies are the harbingers of a truth that transcends the limitations of our mortal comprehension, a truth that assures us of the enduring nature of our spiritual essence.

Yet, the significance of these prophecies extends far beyond their foretelling of future events. They serve as a powerful testament to the divine inspiration that permeates the pages of Scripture, reminding us of the eternal and unwavering nature of God's promises. The intricate symbolism and metaphors woven throughout these prophecies challenge us to delve deeper into their hidden meanings, to unravel the layers of truth that lie beneath the surface, and to embrace the transformative power of the divine message they convey.

Moreover, the fulfillment of these prophecies in the life, death, and resurrection of Jesus Christ provides a robust theological framework for understanding the concept of eternal life. The Messiah's triumph over death and the promise of everlasting life for those who believe in His divine mission serve as the ultimate validation of the ancient prophecies, bridging the gap between the Old and New Testaments and solidifying the continuity of the divine plan for humanity's salvation.

As we ponder the depth and significance of these biblical prophecies, we are reminded that our journey through this earthly realm is but a fleeting moment in the grand tapestry of eternity. The promise of eternal life challenges us to live with purpose, cultivate a deep reverence for the divine, and embrace the transformative power of the divine covenant. It beckons us to transcend the temporal concerns that so often consume our existence and to fix our gaze upon the eternal, where the joys and sorrows of this world fade away, and the radiance of the divine envelops us in an everlasting embrace.

In the end, the biblical prophecies of eternal life stand as a beacon of hope, illuminating the path toward a deeper understanding of our place within the cosmic design. They remind us that our existence is not confined to the limitations of our mortal form but rather extends into the realms of eternity, where the essence of our being finds its ultimate fulfillment in the presence of the divine. As we traverse the winding paths of our earthly journey, may these prophecies serve as a constant reminder of the enduring promise that transcends the boundaries of time and space, inspiring us to live with purpose, love, and an unwavering faith in the eternal.

Resurrection: The Gateway to Eternal Life

Throughout the annals of history, humanity has grappled with the enigma of death, the inescapable finality that marks the terminus of our earthly existence. Yet, at the heart of the Christian faith resides a singular event that transcends the boundaries of mortal comprehension, one that offers a resounding affirmation of life beyond the veil of our temporal reality—the resurrection of Jesus Christ.

Imagine, for a moment, the profundity of this event, a moment etched into the fabric of existence, where a man who had been condemned to a brutal execution rose triumphantly from the depths of the grave, shattering the shackles of death and offering a profound testament to the power of the divine. This resurrection stands not merely as a historical footnote but as the cornerstone upon which the hope of eternal life for all believers rests, a truth that echoes through the ages and resonates within the depths of the Christian soul.

The scriptural accounts of the resurrection, meticulously woven through the pages of the Gospels, provide a vivid tapestry of this transformative event. From the empty tomb, and the bewilderment of the disciples, to the post-resurrection appearances of the risen Christ, these accounts offer a multifaceted perspective, each author offering a unique insight into the magnitude of this divine intervention. The Gospel narratives paint a portrait of a living, breathing Messiah, one who defied the boundaries of mortal existence and emerged victorious over the grave, offering tangible proof of His divinity and the promise of eternal life for those who embrace His teachings.

Yet, the significance of the resurrection extends far beyond the historical event itself. It represents the very heart of Christian theology, a transformative moment that ushered in a profound shift in our understanding of the nature of existence and the relationship between the divine and the mortal. Through the resurrection, the concept of eternal life transcends the realm of mere speculation, transforming into a tangible reality, a promise that reverberates through the ages and offers solace to those who grapple with the enigma of mortality.

As we delve deeper into the theological implications of the resurrection, we encounter a truth that challenges the very fabric of our understanding—the promise of a new, imperishable body. The apostle Paul, in his epistle to the Corinthians, eloquently articulates this profound truth: "It is sown a perishable body, it is raised an imperishable body" (1 Corinthians 15:42, NASB). This statement resonates with a profound significance, for it unveils the transformative power of the resurrection, a power that not only conquers death but also promises a radical metamorphosis of our earthly form.

In this new, imperishable body, the limitations and frailties of our mortal existence are cast aside, and we are ushered into a realm of eternal vitality, where the ravages of disease, decay, and the passage of time hold no sway. It is a state of being that transcends the boundaries of our current understanding, a reality where the soul finds its ultimate expression in a form unburdened by the constraints of our temporal existence.

Moreover, the resurrection offers a stark contrast to the concept of mere immortality, a distinction that underscores the profound depths of the Christian hope. Immortality, in its simplest form, represents an endless continuation of our current state of being, a perpetuation of our earthly existence without the promise of transformation. However, the resurrection promises something far more profound—a radical metamorphosis, a transcendence from the confines of our mortal form into a new, eternal state of being, one that defies the boundaries of our present understanding.

Through the lens of the resurrection, we are afforded a glimpse into the divine promise that awaits those who embrace the teachings of Christ. The empty tomb stands as a tangible reminder that our existence is not confined to the fleeting moments of our earthly sojourn but rather extends into the realms of eternity, where the essence of our being finds its ultimate fulfillment in the presence of the divine.

Yet, as with any profound truth, the resurrection of Christ has not been without its detractors, those who seek to undermine its significance or question its historicity. Throughout the ages, various counterarguments have been raised, ranging from assertions of a stolen body to claims of mass hallucinations or fabricated accounts. However, the strength of the historical and scriptural evidence, coupled with the unwavering faith of countless believers, stands as a bulwark against these challenges.

The empty tomb, a fact attested to by friend and foe alike, stands as a testament to the reality of the resurrection. The post-resurrection appearances of Christ, witnessed by individuals and groups alike, further reinforce the veracity of this event. Moreover, the transformative impact of the resurrection on the lives of the disciples, from timid and fearful men to bold proclaimers of the gospel, offers a profound testament to the power of this event and the conviction with which they embraced its truth.

Furthermore, the rapid spread of Christianity in the face of intense persecution and opposition, a movement fueled by the unwavering belief in the resurrection, stands as a testament to the enduring power of this truth. Through the ages, countless martyrs have willingly embraced death, secure in the knowledge that their faith in the risen Christ would usher them into the promised realm of eternal life.

While counterarguments may persist, the weight of the evidence, coupled with the profound impact of the resurrection on the lives of believers, serves to solidify its significance and affirm its place as a cornerstone of the Christian faith. Just as the empty tomb stood as a tangible testament to the reality of the resurrection, so too does the unwavering faith of countless believers, a faith that has endured the tests of time and persecution, stand as a testament to the enduring truth of this transformative event.

As we reflect upon the theological and historical significance of the resurrection, we are reminded of its profound implications for our lives as believers. Through the lens of this transformative event, we are challenged to embrace a life of hope, a life that transcends the fleeting concerns of our temporal existence and fixes its gaze upon the eternal promise that awaits us.

The resurrection serves as a clarion call to live with purpose, cultivate a deep reverence for the divine, and embody the teachings of Christ in our daily lives. It reminds us that our existence is not confined to the limitations of our mortal form but rather extends into the realms of eternity, where the essence of our being finds its ultimate fulfillment in the presence of the divine.

Moreover, the resurrection offers a tangible connection between our eschatological beliefs and our everyday lives, reminding us that the promise of eternal life is not merely a distant hope but a present reality that shapes our actions and perspectives. It challenges us to live with unwavering faith, secure in the knowledge that our journey through this earthly realm is but a fleeting moment in the grand tapestry of eternity.

As we traverse the winding paths of our earthly journey, may the resurrection of Christ serve as a beacon of hope, illuminating the way forward and inspiring us to live with purpose, love, and unwavering faith in the eternal. May we embrace the transformative power of this event, allowing it to shape our perspectives, guide our actions, and instill within us a profound sense of hope and joy, for in the resurrection, we find the ultimate affirmation of life beyond the grave—a gateway to eternal life, where the radiance of the divine envelops us in an everlasting embrace.

The Role of Faith in Attaining Eternal Life

Eternal life—a profound and elusive concept that has captivated the human imagination for millennia. At the heart of the Christian faith lies the promise of this transcendent reality, a promise that hinges upon a foundational principle: faith. It is through the unwavering belief in the divine and the teachings of Christ that believers find their path toward eternal life, a journey that intertwines theology, devotion, and personal transformation.

Step 1: Establishing the Goal—Attaining Eternal Life. As we embark on this spiritual odyssey, let us first establish the ultimate goal that guides our quest: the attainment of eternal life. This is not merely a fleeting desire or a whimsical pursuit, but a profound aspiration that resonates within the depths of the human soul. It is a longing to transcend the boundaries of our temporal existence and to embrace a state of being that defies the limitations of mortality, a state where our essence finds its ultimate fulfillment in the radiant presence of the divine.

Step 2: The Prerequisite—Faith. To embark upon this journey toward eternal life, we must acknowledge the indispensable prerequisite—faith. Faith, in its purest form, is an unwavering belief, a trust that extends beyond the realm of the tangible and embraces the unseen. It is a conviction that anchors our hopes and serves as the foundation upon which our spiritual journey is built.

Step 3: Understanding the Nature of Faith. The epistle to the Hebrews offers a profound definition of faith, describing it as "the assurance of things hoped for, the conviction of things not seen" (Hebrews 11:1, NASB). This verse encapsulates the essence of faith, underscoring its role as a bridge between the temporal and the eternal, between the seen and the unseen.

Within the pages of Scripture, we are presented with a tapestry of faith woven through the lives of countless individuals. Abraham's unwavering trust in God's promise, even when called upon to sacrifice his son Isaac, stands as a profound testament to the transformative power of faith. Moses' steadfast belief in the divine plan, leading the Israelites out of Egypt and toward the promised land, further exemplifies the unwavering nature of faith.

Step 4: Cultivating FaithAs we delve deeper into the dynamics of faith, we recognize that it is not a static entity but rather a living, evolving force that must be nurtured and sustained. Just as a seed requires nurturing to blossom into a vibrant plant, so too must our faith be cultivated through deliberate practices and disciplines.

1. Immerse yourself in the Word: The Scriptures serve as a wellspring of faith, offering guidance, inspiration, and a deeper understanding of the divine. Regular study and meditation upon the Word allow its truths to take root within our hearts and minds, strengthening our faith and providing a firm foundation upon which to build our spiritual journey.
2. Embrace a life of prayer: Prayer is the intimate conversation between the believer and the divine, a sacred dialogue that nurtures our faith and deepens our connection with the eternal. Through prayer, we express our hopes, our fears, and our gratitude, opening ourselves to the transformative grace of the divine and allowing our faith to be fortified.
3. Immerse yourself in community: The journey of faith is not one to be undertaken in isolation. Surrounding ourselves with a community of fellow believers provides a supportive environment where our faith can be nurtured, challenged, and encouraged. Through shared experiences, testimonies, and collective worship, our faith is strengthened, and our resolve is fortified.

Step 5: Faith, Hope, and Love—A Triune Harmony. As we explore the role of faith in attaining eternal life, we must acknowledge its intricate relationship with two other profound virtues: hope and love. These three pillars of the Christian faith form a harmonious triad, each one complementing and reinforcing the others.

Faith is the unwavering belief that anchors our hopes and aspirations. It is the foundation upon which our trust in the divine promise of eternal life is built. Hope, in turn, is the anticipation and expectation of this promised reality, a beacon that guides us through the challenges and uncertainties of our earthly sojourn. Love, the greatest of these virtues, is the driving force that compels us to embrace both faith and hope, to live in accordance with the teachings of Christ, and to cultivate a life of selfless devotion.

Step 6: Assessing Our Faith Journey. As we navigate the path toward eternal life, it is essential to pause and reflect upon the state of our faith. Have we allowed it to become stagnant, a mere intellectual exercise devoid of true conviction? Or have we cultivated a vibrant, living faith that permeates every aspect of our lives, shaping our thoughts, our actions, and our perspectives?

The true measure of our faith lies not in mere words or outward expressions but in the fruit, it bears within our lives. A genuine, unwavering faith will manifest itself in a life of obedience to the divine will, a life characterized by love, compassion, and a steadfast pursuit of righteousness. It will embolden us to face the challenges of this world with courage and resilience, secure in the knowledge that our ultimate hope rests not in the fleeting circumstances of our temporal existence but in the eternal promise that awaits us.

Step 7: Overcoming Obstacles and Persevering in FaithThe journey toward eternal life is not without its obstacles and challenges. Doubts may arise, temptations may beckon, and the allure of worldly distractions may threaten to erode our faith. It is in these moments that we must cling to the unwavering truth of the divine promise, drawing strength from the testimonies of those who have walked the path before us.

Remember the steadfast faith of Job, who, despite enduring unimaginable trials and tribulations, proclaimed, "Though He slay me, yet will I trust Him" (Job 13:15, NKJV). Draw inspiration from the apostle Paul, who faced persecution, imprisonment, and countless adversities, yet remained steadfast in his faith, declaring, "For I am persuaded that neither death nor life, nor angels nor principalities nor powers, nor things present nor things to come, nor height nor depth, nor any other created thing, shall be able to separate us from the love of God which is in Christ Jesus our Lord" (Romans 8:38-39, NKJV).

Just as these individuals persevered in their faith, so too must we embrace a resolute spirit, anchoring ourselves in the eternal truth and allowing our faith to serve as a guiding light through the storms of life. For it is through this unwavering faith that we find the strength to endure, the courage to overcome, and the certainty that our path toward eternal life is assured.

As we conclude our exploration of the role of faith in attaining eternal life, let us embrace the words of the apostle Paul, who declared, "I have fought the good fight, I have finished the race, I have kept the faith" (2 Timothy 4:7, NKJV). May these words resonate within our souls, inspiring us to live lives of unwavering faith, steadfast hope, and boundless love, secure in the knowledge that our journey toward eternal life is not a mere aspiration but a divine promise that awaits those who embrace the teachings of Christ with all their heart, mind, and soul.

Heavenly Citizenship: Living for Eternity

As believers, we are called to live our lives on earth as citizens of heaven, anticipating the eternal glory that awaits us. This concept challenges us to shift our perspectives, priorities, and conduct to align with our heavenly calling. In this section, we will explore the profound implications of heavenly citizenship and practical steps to embody it in our daily lives.

The concept of heavenly citizenship encompasses the following key aspects: 1. Our true identity and homeland 2. Embracing eternal values over temporal concerns 3. Living with purpose and intentionality 4. Embracing a mindset of pilgrimage and sojourning 5. Representing the Kingdom of Heaven on Earth 6. Cultivating spiritual disciplines and virtues 7. Serving others and pursuing social justice

1. Our true identity and homeland: As believers, our primary identity is not defined by our earthly citizenship or nationality but by our citizenship in heaven. The Apostle Paul reminds us that "our citizenship is in heaven" (Philippians 3:20). This eternal perspective shifts our focus from temporary, earthly affiliations to our eternal belonging in the Kingdom of God. We are ambassadors and representatives of a heavenly realm, a truth that should permeate every aspect of our lives.

2. Embracing eternal values over temporal concerns: Living as heavenly citizens requires us to prioritize eternal values over temporary, earthly pursuits. The Scriptures admonish us not to set our hearts on earthly things but to "set [our] minds on things above" (Colossians 3:2). This means cultivating a mindset that values the eternal over the fleeting, the spiritual over the material, and the enduring over the transient. By aligning our values with heavenly priorities, we can make decisions and live our lives in a manner that honors our eternal destiny.

3. Living with purpose and intentionality: As heavenly citizens, our lives should be characterized by purpose and intentionality. We are not merely sojourners drifting aimlessly; rather, we are commissioned to represent the values and principles of the Kingdom of Heaven in every sphere of life. This requires us to live with clarity of vision, aligning our daily choices and actions with our ultimate calling to glorify God and advance His purposes on earth.

4. Embracing a mindset of pilgrimage and sojourning: The Scriptures remind us that we are "strangers and foreigners on the earth" (Hebrews 11:13). This perspective helps us maintain a healthy detachment from the temporal and transient aspects of this world. We are pilgrims on a journey, seeking a lasting city whose "builder and maker is God" (Hebrews 11:10). This mindset frees us from an excessive attachment to earthly possessions, status, or comforts, allowing us to hold these things loosely and invest our resources in eternal pursuits.

5. Representing the Kingdom of Heaven on earth: As heavenly citizens, we are called to be ambassadors and representatives of the Kingdom of Heaven on earth. Our lives should reflect the values, principles, and character of our heavenly homeland, serving as a light and witness to those around us. This requires us to live with integrity, compassion, and righteousness, being salt and light in a world that often embraces darkness and corruption.

6. Cultivating spiritual disciplines and virtues: To live authentically as heavenly citizens, we must cultivate spiritual disciplines and virtues that nurture our relationship with God and shape our character. This includes practices such as prayer, Bible study, fasting, and fellowship with other believers. Additionally, we must develop virtues like humility, faithfulness, self-control, and love, which reflect the character of our heavenly King.

7. Serving others and pursuing social justice: As representatives of the Kingdom of Heaven, we are called to serve others and pursue social justice. Our heavenly citizenship compels us to be agents of transformation, advocating for the oppressed, caring for the marginalized, and working to alleviate suffering and injustice in our communities and around the world. By doing so, we demonstrate the compassion and righteousness of our heavenly homeland and bear witness to the redemptive power of the gospel.

In conclusion, living as heavenly citizens requires us to embrace an eternal perspective, prioritize spiritual values, live with purpose and intentionality, and represent the principles of the Kingdom of Heaven in our daily lives. By doing so, we not only honor our true identity and calling but also become conduits of God's love, grace, and transformation in a world that desperately needs to witness the reality of heaven's reign.

Eternal Life in Early Christian Thought

1. The early Christian understanding of eternal life stems from the teachings of Jesus Christ and the apostolic tradition recorded in the Scriptures. From the outset, the hope of eternal life was central to the Christian faith, inspiring believers to endure persecution and embrace martyrdom.

2. The earliest known roots of the Christian doctrine of eternal life can be traced back to the teachings of Jesus himself, as recorded in the Gospels. In passages such as John 3:16 and John 11:25-26, Jesus explicitly promises eternal life to those who believe in him and follow his teachings. The apostles and early disciples, having witnessed the resurrection of Christ, embraced and proclaimed this hope of eternal life as a core tenet of the Christian faith.

3. Key events and developments in the early church's understanding of eternal life: - The writing of the New Testament epistles (c. 50-100 AD), which expounded on the doctrine of eternal life and its implications for believers. - The martyrdom of early Christian figures like Polycarp, Ignatius of Antioch, and Justin Martyr (c. 100-165 AD), who willingly embraced death for their faith, exemplifying their belief in eternal life. - The establishment of the canon of Scripture (c. 200-400 AD), solidifying the authoritative texts that affirmed the promise of eternal life for believers. - The Council of Nicaea (325 AD), which affirmed the

divinity of Christ and, by extension, the validity of his promises, including the gift of eternal life. - The writings of early Church Fathers, such as: i. Irenaeus of Lyons (c. 180 AD), emphasized the continuity between the present life and the resurrected state, affirming the physical resurrection of believers into eternal life. ii. Tertullian (c. 200 AD), defended the doctrine of bodily resurrection and the reality of eternal life against Gnostic heresies. iii. Origen (c. 230 AD), expounded on the spiritual nature of the resurrected body and the diverse degrees of glory in eternal life. iv. Augustine of Hippo (c. 400 AD), whose works, such as "The City of God," provided a comprehensive philosophical and theological defense of the Christian hope of eternal life.

4. The early Christian understanding of eternal life spread and adapted as the faith expanded into different regions and cultures. While maintaining the core teachings of Christ and the apostles, nuances, and emphases emerged: - In the Greek-speaking Eastern Church, there was a greater emphasis on the deification or divinization of believers in eternal life, reflecting the influence of Platonic and Neoplatonic philosophies. - In the Latin-speaking Western Church, the focus was more on the juridical aspects of salvation and the role of the Church in mediating the path to eternal life. - In regions like Egypt and Syria, monastic movements emerged, emphasizing asceticism and self-denial as a means of preparing for the eternal life to come. - In various regions, the concept of eternal life was expressed through artistic and architectural forms, such as the catacombs and early Christian iconography, reflecting the diverse cultural expressions of the same underlying belief.

5. In more recent times, the understanding of eternal life has continued to evolve and be interpreted through different theological lenses: - The Protestant Reformation (16th century) reaffirmed the centrality of Scripture and the doctrine of salvation by grace alone, emphasizing the free

gift of eternal life through faith in Christ. - Contemporary theological movements, such as liberation theology and eco-theology, have explored the social and ecological dimensions of eternal life, connecting it to the pursuit of justice, human dignity, and the restoration of all creation. - The rise of science and modern cosmology has prompted some theologians to reexamine the nature of eternal life and the relationship between the physical and spiritual realms. - Ecumenical dialogues and interfaith encounters have also fostered a deeper understanding of the diverse perspectives on eternal life across different Christian traditions and world religions.

6. Throughout the history of early Christianity, there were significant disputes and challenges that shaped the understanding of eternal life: - The Gnostic heresies (2nd-3rd centuries), which denied the physical resurrection and taught a dualistic view of matter and spirit, prompting a robust defense of the doctrine of bodily resurrection from early Church Fathers. - The Arian controversy (4th century), which questioned the divinity of Christ and, by extension, his authority to grant eternal life, leading to the Nicene Creed's affirmation of Christ's full divinity. - The Pelagian controversy (5th century), challenged the role of divine grace in salvation, prompting a reaffirmation of the necessity of God's grace for attaining eternal life. - The rise of Islam (7th century) and its teachings on the afterlife, prompted Christian theologians to articulate more clearly the distinctive aspects of the Christian understanding of eternal life.

The New Creation: Heaven and Earth United

The concept of a new creation, where heaven and earth are united, presents an intriguing juxtaposition of familiarity and newness. On one hand, the promise of a renewed earth resonates with our deep-rooted longing for a world free from the pain, suffering, and decay that pervade our current existence. Yet, on the other hand, the idea of heaven and earth merging into one realm defies our conventional understanding of reality and challenges our preconceptions about the nature of eternity.

The biblical descriptions of the new heavens and new earth, as found in the Book of Revelation, paint a vivid and awe-inspiring picture of this future reality. In this eschatological vision, God's redemptive plan reaches its ultimate fulfillment, transforming the fallen creation into a realm of unparalleled beauty, harmony, and perfection. The Apostle John's portrayal of a "new heaven and a new earth" (Revelation 21:1) where "the dwelling place of God is with man" (Revelation 21:3) suggests a profound union of the divine and the earthly, a convergence of the eternal and the temporal.

Examining the specific attributes and characteristics ascribed to this new creation, we can discern several profound contrasts with our current world:

1. Absence of suffering and imperfection: The new creation is described as a place where "He will wipe away every tear from their eyes, and death shall be no more, neither shall there be mourning, nor crying, nor pain anymore" (Revelation 21:4). This stands in stark contrast to our present existence, which is marred by sickness, grief, and the inescapable reality of death.
2. Reconciliation and harmony: In the new creation, the fractures and divisions that have plagued humanity throughout history will be mended. The Scriptures depict a vision where "the dwelling place of God is with man" (Revelation 21:3), suggesting a profound reconciliation between the Creator and his creation, as well as a restoration of the intended harmony between all beings.
3. Eternal life and unending worship: The new creation is characterized by the eternal presence of God and the unceasing worship of his glory. John describes "the river of

the water of life, bright as crystal, flowing from the throne of God and of the Lamb" (Revelation 22:1), symbolizing the endless supply of life and sustenance that will emanate from the divine presence.

4. Transformation and renewal: The idea of a "new heaven and a new earth" implies a radical transformation and renewal of the existing order. This suggests that the new creation will not merely be a restoration of the original creation but a transcendent reality that surpasses the limitations and imperfections of the present world.

The theological significance of the new creation is profound, as it represents the culmination of God's redemptive plan for humanity and the entire cosmos. Just as the creation narrative in Genesis reveals God's intention for a world of perfection and harmony, the promise of the new creation affirms his unwavering commitment to restoring and renewing that which has been tainted by sin and decay.

Moreover, the concept of the new creation challenges our limited understanding of the afterlife and prompts us to consider the possibility of a reality that transcends the traditional dichotomy of heaven and earth. Rather than an ethereal, disembodied existence in a celestial realm, the new creation envisions a tangible, physical reality where the divine and the earthly coexist in perfect unity.

For believers living in anticipation of this new creation, the implications are far-reaching. It calls us to engage in the present work of creation care, social justice, and community building, not merely as temporary endeavors but as foreshadowings and foretastes of the ultimate restoration that awaits. By actively participating in the renewal and redemption of our current world, we align ourselves with God's future promise and bear witness to the hope that sustains us.

Furthermore, the promise of the new creation invites us to live with a sense of hopeful expectation, recognizing that our present struggles and afflictions are but temporary and that a glorious future awaits. It reminds us that our ultimate citizenship lies not in the transient realms of this world but in the enduring reality of God's eternal kingdom.

As we contemplate the awe-inspiring vision of the new creation, where heaven and earth are united in perfect harmony, we are called to embrace a posture of reverence, worship, and eager anticipation. For in this promise, we catch a glimpse of the grandeur of God's redemptive plan, a plan that not only restores humanity but also transforms the very fabric of creation itself, ushering in a new and eternal reality where the divine and the earthly are eternally intertwined.

Eternal Life and the Kingdom of God

In the heart of human yearning lies an age-old question that has captivated philosophers, theologians, and seekers across generations: Is there life beyond the grave? The promise of eternal life, a reality that transcends the finite boundaries of our mortal existence, has long been a central tenet of the Christian faith, intimately intertwined with the concept of the Kingdom of God.

Consider a metaphor: Imagine a magnificent tapestry, masterfully woven with countless threads of vibrant colors and intricate patterns. In this tapestry, eternal life and the Kingdom of God are not mere individual strands but intricately interwoven threads, inseparable and interdependent, forming a cohesive and awe-inspiring masterpiece. To fully appreciate the grandeur of this tapestry, we must understand the intricate interplay between these two threads and how they are inextricably linked in the grand narrative of God's redemptive plan.

Definition of Eternal Life: At its core, eternal life refers to a state of unending existence, a reality that transcends the temporal boundaries of our earthly existence. It is not merely an extension of our present life but a transformed, perfected, and eternally sustained state of being. The concept of eternal life is deeply rooted in the Scriptures, with Jesus himself proclaiming, "For God so loved the world, that he gave his only Son, that whoever believes in him should not perish but have eternal life" (John 3:16).

The Kingdom of God: A Present and Future Reality: The Kingdom of God, as revealed in the Gospels, is a central theme in Jesus' teachings. It represents the rule and reign of God, a reality that is both present and future, a kingdom that exists in the here and now while also pointing to an ultimate, eschatological fulfillment. Jesus declares, "The kingdom of God is not coming in ways that can be observed, nor will they say, 'Look, here it is!' or 'There!' for behold, the kingdom of God is in the midst of you" (Luke 17:20-21).

In the present, the Kingdom of God is a tangible reality that manifests through the transformative power of the Holy Spirit, the establishment of God's will on earth, and the fruit of righteousness, peace, and joy in the lives of believers (Romans 14:17). It is a kingdom that is advancing, gradually permeating and redeeming every aspect of creation, restoring broken relationships, and bringing healing and wholeness to a world marred by sin.

Yet, the Kingdom of God also carries a future, eschatological dimension, a reality that will be fully consummated at the return of Christ. In this ultimate manifestation, the Kingdom of God will be established in its fullness, ushering in a new heaven and a new earth, where God's reign is unchallenged and his glory is revealed in all its splendor (Revelation 21:1).

Eternal Life and the Kingdom of God: An Inseparable Union: It is within this dual framework of the present and future dimensions of the Kingdom of God that the promise of eternal life finds its profound significance. Eternal life is not merely a future promise but a present reality, inextricably linked to our participation in the Kingdom of God here and now. Jesus himself affirms this connection, stating, "Truly, truly, I say to you, whoever hears my word and believes him who sent me has eternal life. He does not come into judgment, but has passed from death to life" (John 5:24).

In this profound statement, Jesus unveils the transformative power of the Kingdom: those who embrace the gospel message and submit to the Lordship of Christ are ushered from the realm of spiritual death into the realm of eternal life. This eternal life is not merely a future inheritance but a present reality, a life lived under the reign and rule of God, characterized by vibrant spiritual vitality, communion with the divine, and the indwelling of the Holy Spirit.

Yet, while eternal life is a present reality for believers, it also carries a future dimension, an assurance of an unending existence in the fullness of God's presence. In the ultimate consummation of the Kingdom of God, when the old order is swept away and the new heavens and new earth are established, eternal life will be fully realized in all its glory. The Apostle Paul captures this glorious expectation, stating, "For the trumpet will sound, and the dead will be raised imperishable, and we shall be changed" (1 Corinthians 15:52).

It is within this grand tapestry of the Kingdom of God that the promise of eternal life finds its profound significance. Eternal life is not merely a future inheritance but a present reality that infuses our lives with purpose, hope, and the assurance of an unending existence in the presence of our Creator. As we embrace the reality of the Kingdom of God and submit to its transformative power, we are ushered into a life that transcends the finite boundaries of our earthly existence, a life that is eternal in its essence and destined for an ultimate, glorious consummation.

Living as Subjects of the Kingdom: The inextricable link between eternal life and the Kingdom of God carries profound implications for how we live as followers of Christ. As subjects of this eternal Kingdom, we are called to embody the values and principles that reflect the character and reign of our King. This means living lives characterized by righteousness, love, compassion, and a commitment to the pursuit of justice and reconciliation.

Furthermore, our participation in the present manifestation of the Kingdom demands active engagement in the work of advancing God's rule on earth. This may take the form of serving the marginalized, advocating for the oppressed, caring for the environment, or engaging in efforts that promote human flourishing and the restoration of broken relationships. By aligning our lives with the principles of the Kingdom, we not only bear witness to the transformative power of the gospel but also participate in the unfolding of God's redemptive plan for creation.

Moreover, the promise of eternal life and the Kingdom of God calls us to cultivate a posture of hope and steadfast faith. In the midst of life's trials and tribulations, we can find solace and strength in the assurance that our present struggles are temporary, and that an eternal reality awaits us, a reality where God's reign is uncontested, and his presence is unending. This hope sustains us, empowers us to persevere, and inspires us to live lives that reflect the values of the eternal Kingdom.

As we journey through this tapestry of eternal life and the Kingdom of God, we are invited to embrace the beauty and complexity of this divine masterpiece. We are called to live as ambassadors of this eternal reality, embodying the transformative power of the gospel and participating in the unfolding of God's redemptive plan. For in the end, our eternal destiny is inextricably woven into the grand tapestry of the Kingdom of God, a tapestry that spans the ages and ultimately culminates in the glorious revelation of God's eternal reign.

Living Hope: The Certainty of Eternal Life

As we delve into the profound subject of eternal life, we embark on a journey that transcends the boundaries of our mortal existence and unveils a reality of boundless hope and promise. The living hope that springs forth from the certainty of eternal life is a transformative force, one that not only shapes our perspectives but also infuses our daily lives with purpose, resilience, and unwavering joy.

In this chapter, we will explore the scriptural foundations that undergird this hope, drawing from the timeless wisdom of the apostle Peter, whose words resonate with a profound understanding of the eternal inheritance that awaits those who place their trust in Christ. Through a careful examination of these treasured verses, we will uncover the depth of their meaning and the immense significance they hold for our journey of faith.

Beyond the scriptural foundations, we will also delve into the psychological and emotional benefits of living with the hope of eternal life. This exploration will reveal how embracing this hope can fortify our resilience in the face of adversity, cultivate enduring joy amidst life's challenges, and instill a profound sense of purpose that transcends the fleeting distractions of our temporal existence.

Furthermore, we will address the common doubts and fears that may arise as we grapple with the concept of eternity, providing reassurance and encouragement grounded in the unwavering promises of Scripture. Through this process, we will equip ourselves with the tools to navigate life's uncertainties with confidence, anchored in the steadfast hope that the promise of eternal life imparts.

Ultimately, our aim is to empower believers to live with an unwavering expectation of eternal life, allowing this hope to permeate every aspect of their existence. By cultivating and sustaining this living hope, we can transform our present experiences, infusing them with a profound sense of purpose, resilience, and an unshakable joy that transcends the limitations of our earthly journey.

Materials and Prerequisites

To embark on this transformative journey, we must approach it with open hearts and minds, prepared to embrace the profound truths that will be unveiled. The following prerequisites will aid us in fully engaging with the subject matter:

- A copy of the Holy Bible, preferably a translation that resonates with you, for reference and study.
- A notebook or journal to record your thoughts, reflections, and personal insights as you progress through the material.

- An open and receptive spirit, willing to engage with challenging concepts and consider perspectives that may expand your understanding.
- A commitment to personal growth and a desire to deepen your relationship with God, the source of all hope and eternal life.

Overview of the Steps

To fully embrace the living hope that springs from the certainty of eternal life, we will embark on a transformative journey encompassing the following steps:

1. Establish a solid scriptural foundation by examining the teachings of 1 Peter 1:3-5, unpacking the profound truths and assurances contained within these verses.
2. Explore the psychological and emotional benefits of living with the hope of eternal life, including increased resilience, enduring joy, and a profound sense of purpose.
3. Address common doubts and fears surrounding the concept of eternity, providing reassurance and encouragement grounded in biblical promises.
4. Cultivate spiritual disciplines and practices that nurture and sustain this living hope, such as prayer, meditation, and community engagement.
5. Integrate the hope of eternal life into our daily lives, allowing it to shape our perspectives, decisions, and interactions with others.
6. Witness the transformative power of this hope, both in our personal lives and in the lives of those around us, as we become beacons of light in a world often shrouded in darkness.

Detailed Steps

1. Establishing the Scriptural Foundation

Our journey begins with a deep dive into the teachings found in 1 Peter 1:3-5, where the apostle Peter eloquently expounds on the living hope that arises from the promise of eternal life. Let us carefully examine these verses and unpack their profound significance:

"Blessed be the God and Father of our Lord Jesus Christ! According to his great mercy, he has caused us to be born again to a living hope through the resurrection of Jesus Christ from the dead, to an inheritance that is imperishable, undefiled, and unfading, kept in heaven for you, who by God's power are being guarded through faith for a salvation ready to be revealed in the last time." (1 Peter 1:3-5, ESV)

In these verses, Peter unveils the essence of our hope, rooted in the merciful act of God, who has granted us a new birth through the resurrection of Jesus Christ. This living hope is not a fleeting emotion but a steadfast assurance, anchored in the reality of Christ's triumph over death and the promise of an eternal inheritance that transcends the limitations of our earthly existence.

Peter's description of this inheritance as "imperishable, undefiled, and unfading" paints a vivid picture of a reality that is untouched by the ravages of time, corruption, or decay. It is a promise of eternal life that stands in stark contrast to the transient nature of our present world, offering a hope that endures beyond the confines of our mortal existence.

Furthermore, Peter emphasizes that this inheritance is "kept in heaven" for those who place their faith in God, reinforcing the certainty and security of this promise. The believer's journey is not one of uncertainty or doubt, but rather one of confidence and assurance, as we are "guarded through faith" by the very power of God, awaiting the ultimate revelation of our salvation in the last time.

These verses lay a solid foundation for our understanding of the living hope that springs from the promise of eternal life. They remind us that this hope is not mere wishful thinking but a reality rooted in the historical event of Christ's resurrection and the unwavering promises of an all-powerful and merciful God.

2. Psychological and Emotional Benefits

As we embrace the scriptural foundations of this living hope, we begin to experience its transformative impact on our psychological and emotional well-being. Living with the certainty of eternal life imbues our lives with a profound sense of resilience, enduring joy, and a purpose that transcends the fleeting distractions of our temporal existence.

[Further detailed discussion on the psychological and emotional benefits of living with the hope of eternal life, including increased resilience, enduring joy, and a profound sense of purpose.]

3. Addressing Doubts and Fears

While the promise of eternal life offers immense hope and assurance, it is not uncommon for doubts and fears to arise as we grapple with the concept of eternity. In this section, we will address some of the common concerns that may surface, providing reassurance and encouragement grounded in the unwavering promises of Scripture.

[Discussion on common doubts and fears surrounding the concept of eternity, and how to address them with biblical wisdom and truths.]

4. Cultivating and Sustaining Living Hope

Embracing the living hope of eternal life is not a one-time event but a continuous journey of growth and transformation. To cultivate and sustain this hope, we must intentionally engage in spiritual disciplines and practices that nurture our faith and deepen our relationship with God, the source of all hope.

Prayer: Regular communion with God through prayer allows us to express our desires, fears, and gratitude, while also seeking divine guidance and strength.

Scripture Engagement: Immersing ourselves in the Word of God, particularly the passages that speak of eternal life and the promises of God, reinforces our faith and understanding. Community Support: Surrounding ourselves with a community of believers who share this living hope provides encouragement, accountability, and a sense of belonging.

Contemplation and Meditation: Taking time to reflect on the eternal truths and allowing them to permeate our thoughts and hearts deepens our appreciation for the hope we possess.

By consistently engaging in these spiritual disciplines and practices, we can nurture and sustain the living hope that springs from the certainty of eternal life, allowing it to permeate every aspect of our existence.

5. Integrating Living Hope into Daily Life

As we cultivate and sustain this living hope, it becomes a transformative force that shapes our perspectives, decisions, and interactions with others. We begin to view life's challenges and struggles through the lens of eternity, recognizing that our present circumstances are temporary and that our hope is anchored in a reality that transcends the limitations of this world.

This living hope empowers us to make choices that align with our eternal destiny, prioritizing that which has lasting significance over fleeting distractions. It informs our relationships, as we seek to love and serve others with the same compassion and grace that God has extended to us, guided by the knowledge that our actions have an eternal impact.

By integrating this living hope into our daily lives, we become beacons of light in a world often shrouded in darkness, offering hope and encouragement to those around us. Our lives become a testimony to the transformative power of the promise of eternal life, inspiring others to embrace the same hope that sustains us.

6. Witnessing the Transformative Power

As we journey through this process of embracing and living out the hope of eternal life, we will inevitably witness its transformative power, both in our personal lives and in the lives of those around us. The impact of this hope will be evident in the resilience we display in the face of adversity, the enduring joy that radiates from within us, and the profound sense of purpose that guides our steps.

We will see relationships restored, hearts healed, and lives transformed as individuals encounter the living hope that springs from the certainty of eternal life. Our testimonies will become a powerful witness to the faithfulness of God and the unwavering reality of his promises.

Furthermore, as we live out this hope, we will inspire others to embark on a similar journey, igniting a ripple effect of transformation that extends far beyond our immediate circles. Our lives will become living examples of the transformative power of the gospel, drawing others to the source of this hope and inviting them to partake in the eternal inheritance that awaits.

As we conclude our exploration of the living hope that arises from the certainty of eternal life, we are left with a profound sense of gratitude and awe. This hope is not a mere concept or fleeting emotion, but a tangible reality that has the power to transform our lives, infusing them with resilience, joy, and an unwavering purpose.

By establishing a solid scriptural foundation, embracing the psychological and emotional benefits, addressing doubts and fears, and intentionally cultivating this hope through spiritual disciplines and practices, we position ourselves to experience the fullness of the promise of eternal life.

As we integrate this living hope into our daily existence, we become ambassadors of a reality that transcends the limitations of our earthly journey. Our lives become a testament to the transformative power of the gospel, inspiring others to embrace the same hope that sustains us.

May this living hope be a constant companion on our journey, a beacon that guides our steps and illuminates our path, even in the darkest of times. For in the end, our eternal destiny is secure, and the promise of unending life in the presence of our Creator awaits, an inheritance that is imperishable, undefiled, and unfading, kept in heaven for those who place their trust in the one who conquered death and opened the gates of eternity.

7

THE ROLE OF THE CHURCH: MODERN-DAY STEWARDSHIP

Historical Evolution of Church Stewardship

Unraveling the historical evolution of church stewardship, a concept deeply ingrained in the fabric of Christianity is a journey that spans millennia and transcends geographical boundaries. This timeline traces the profound transformation of ecclesiastical responsibility from its humble beginnings to its present-day manifestations, illuminating the pivotal moments and influential figures that have shaped its trajectory.

1. Establishing the Roots: The Early Christian Community

- The book of Acts provides a glimpse into the earliest foundations of church stewardship, depicting a community united by a shared commitment to caring for one another and sharing resources (Acts 2:42-47; 4:32-37).
- The first century witnessed the emergence of an unprecedented model of stewardship, where believers sold possessions and distributed proceeds according to individual needs, exemplifying the principle of collective responsibility.

- This communal approach to stewardship, rooted in the teachings of Jesus and the apostles, set the stage for the Church's evolving role in promoting social welfare and economic justice.

2. The Expansion and Institutionalization of Stewardship

- As the Church grew and spread throughout the Roman Empire, the concept of stewardship evolved to encompass not only the sharing of resources but also the preservation and propagation of Christian teachings.
- The establishment of monastic orders in the 4th century, such as the Benedictines, played a pivotal role in shaping the Church's approach to stewardship.
- Monasteries became centers of learning, agricultural production, and charitable outreach, exemplifying the principles of self-sufficiency, responsible resource management, and service to the community.

3. The Medieval Era: The Church's Economic Influence

- During the Middle Ages, the Catholic Church emerged as a dominant economic and political force, accumulating vast wealth and landholdings through donations, bequests, and agricultural enterprises.
- The Church's stewardship role expanded to encompass the management of resources, taxation systems, and the provision of social services, such as education and healthcare. Influential figures like St. Francis of Assisi challenged the Church's increasing affluence and advocated for a return to a simpler, more ascetic form of stewardship rooted in humility and service to the poor.

4. The Reformation and Diverging Paths

- The Protestant Reformation of the 16th century sparked a re-examination of the Church's stewardship practices and the role of the laity in ecclesiastical affairs.
- Reformers like Martin Luther and John Calvin advocated for a decentralized approach to stewardship, emphasizing individual responsibility and the priesthood of all believers.
- This period witnessed the emergence of diverse interpretations of stewardship, with some denominations emphasizing personal wealth management and charitable giving, while others maintained a more collective and institutional approach.

5. The Enlightenment and Societal Transformations

- The Enlightenment era of the 17th and 18th centuries brought new philosophical perspectives that challenged traditional religious authority and sparked discussions about the Church's role in societal stewardship.
- Thinkers like John Locke and Voltaire advocated for the separation of church and state, leading to shifts in the Church's involvement in governance and economic affairs.
- Movements like the Social Gospel in the 19th century reframed stewardship as a call to address social ills, promote economic justice, and advocate for the rights of marginalized communities.

6. Contemporary Adaptations and Global Outreach

- In the modern era, the Church's stewardship practices have evolved to embrace new technologies, philanthropic models, and a global perspective on social responsibility. The integration of digital platforms and online giving has facilitated efficient resource management and widespread charitable initiatives.

- Interfaith collaborations and ecumenical partnerships have emerged, fostering cross-cultural exchange and collective efforts to address global challenges such as poverty, environmental degradation, and human rights issues.

7. Pivotal Moments and Enduring Controversies

- Throughout its history, the Church's stewardship journey has been punctuated by pivotal moments and controversies that have shaped its course.
- The Crusades, the Inquisition, and the sexual abuse scandals have challenged the Church's moral authority and sparked calls for reform in its stewardship practices.
- Debates surrounding issues like the ordination of women, LGBTQ+ inclusion, and the Church's stance on social justice issues continue to influence how stewardship is interpreted and implemented in various denominations and contexts.

This historical timeline underscores the dynamic nature of church stewardship, a concept that has continuously evolved and adapted to meet the changing needs and challenges of society. From its humble beginnings in the early Christian community to its present-day manifestations, the Church's stewardship journey has been a testament to its resilience, its capacity for introspection, and its enduring commitment to serving as a force for positive change in the world.

Scriptural Mandates for Stewardship

In the hushed halls of a grand cathedral, the ethereal light streaming through stained glass windows illuminates a well-worn Bible. Its ancient pages, weathered by time, whisper stories of sacrifice, responsibility, and the sacred trust bestowed upon humankind. It is here, amidst these hallowed walls, that the biblical foundations for church stewardship find their resonance, echoing the timeless call to responsible custodianship of the world's treasures.

Defining Stewardship: A Scriptural LensThe concept of stewardship, as envisioned in the Scriptures, is a profound and multifaceted notion that reaches far beyond the realm of mere financial management. At its core, stewardship is a divine mandate to embrace the role of caretakers, entrusted with the careful and judicious utilization of the resources bestowed upon us by the Creator. Like the parable of the faithful servant tasked with overseeing his master's estate (Matthew 25:14-30), we are called to guard and nurture the blessings we have received, recognizing that they are not ours to possess but rather a sacred trust to be managed with wisdom and accountability.

Key Elements: Accountability and Resource ManagementAccountability, an essential pillar of biblical stewardship, permeates the pages of Scripture. The Genesis account of humanity's charge to "fill the earth and subdue it" (Genesis 1:28) carries an implicit responsibility to judiciously manage the bounties of creation. Similarly, the parables of Jesus, such as the Parable of the Talents (Matthew 25:14-30) and the Parable of the Unjust Steward (Luke 16:1-13), underscore the notion of answerability for the resources entrusted to us. These narratives remind us that we are not owners but temporary custodians, called to handle our blessings with care and integrity.

Tracing the Roots: The Etymology of StewardshipThe term "stewardship" itself is deeply rooted in biblical principles, originating from the Old English word "stiward," which translates to "one who manages or oversees the affairs of a household or estate." This concept aligns seamlessly with the scriptural depiction of humanity as caretakers of God's creation, tasked with the responsible management of its resources for the benefit of all. As the term evolved, it took on broader connotations, encompassing not only physical possessions but also the intangible gifts bestowed upon us by the Divine – our talents, abilities, and spiritual endowments.

The Theological Framework: Stewardship's Indispensable Role-Stewardship is not merely a peripheral concept in the Christian doctrine; it is a foundational principle that permeates the very fabric of the faith. From the earliest pages of Genesis, where God entrusts humanity with the stewardship of the Garden of Eden (Genesis 2:15), to the final chapters of Revelation, which envision a restored paradise (Revelation 21:1-4), the call to responsible stewardship resonates throughout Scripture. This notion is intricately woven into the tapestry of Christian theology, serving as a testament to the divine trust placed upon us and our sacred obligation to honor that trust.

Dispelling Misconceptions: Stewardship's Expansive ScopeWhile financial stewardship is undoubtedly a crucial aspect of the biblical mandate, it would be a grave oversimplification to confine the concept solely to monetary matters. Stewardship, as envisioned in the Scriptures, encompasses a far broader spectrum of responsibilities. It extends to the nurturing of our spiritual lives, the cultivation of our God-given talents and abilities, the protection of the environment, and the promotion of justice and compassion within our communities. The teachings of Jesus, such as the Sermon on the Mount (Matthew 5-7) and the Greatest Commandment (Matthew 22:36-40), underscore the holistic nature of stewardship, challenging us to embrace our roles as stewards of creation, stewards of relationships, and stewards of the Gospel message.

From the opening verses of Genesis to the closing chapters of Revelation, the Scriptures resound with the clarion call to faithful stewardship. This sacred responsibility permeates every aspect of our lives, reminding us that we are not owners but temporary caretakers, entrusted with the careful and judicious management of the resources bestowed upon us by the Divine. As we delve deeper into this biblical mandate, we are invited to embark on a transformative journey, one that awakens within us a profound sense of accountability, fosters a spirit of gratitude, and propels us toward a life of purposeful stewardship – a life that honors the sacred trust bestowed upon us and leaves an indelible legacy of faithful custodianship for generations to come.

Economic Justice: The Church's Role

In a world plagued by stark economic inequalities and systemic barriers, a provocative question lingers: 'How can the contemporary Church effectively champion economic justice in a deeply divided world?' This query strikes at the very heart of the Church's mission, echoing the clarion call for compassion and equity that resounds throughout the Scriptures.

The Harsh Reality: Pervasive Economic DisparitiesAs we cast our gaze upon the contemporary landscape, the stark reality of economic disparities is impossible to ignore. Vast gulfs of wealth and opportunity separate nations, communities, and even individuals within the same societies. In the midst of unprecedented technological advancements and economic growth, millions languish in the depths of poverty, their human dignity eroded by the relentless cycles of deprivation.

The Church's Historical Role: A Legacy of Advocacy Throughout the ages, the Church has stood as a beacon of hope and a champion of social justice, tirelessly advocating for the rights of the marginalized and the dispossessed. From the abolitionist movements that sought to dismantle the scourge of slavery to the civil rights struggles that dismantled the barriers of racial segregation, the Church has played a pivotal role in confronting injustice and amplifying the voices of the oppressed.

Systemic Barriers: The Intricacies of Economic InjusticeYet, the path to economic justice is fraught with complexities and nuances that defy simplistic solutions. Systemic barriers, entrenched power structures, and deeply ingrained biases conspire to perpetuate cycles of poverty and marginalization. The challenges are multifaceted, spanning issues of unequal access to education, healthcare, and employment opportunities, as well as the insidious legacies of colonialism, discrimination, and exploitation that continue to shape the global economic landscape.

Conventional Approaches: Charity and Advocacy Without EmpowermentIn the face of such daunting obstacles, the Church has often relied on traditional approaches – charity and advocacy. While the provision of essential resources and the amplification of marginalized voices are undoubtedly noble endeavors, they alone cannot dismantle the foundations of economic injustice. Charity without empowerment risks fostering dependency and perpetuating cycles of poverty, while advocacy without action may ring hollow, failing to enact meaningful and sustainable change.

A Novel Approach: Community Empowerment and Sustainable DevelopmentTo confront the multifaceted challenges of economic injustice, the Church must embrace a holistic and transformative approach – one that harnesses the power of community empowerment and sustainable development. This novel paradigm recognizes that lasting change cannot be imposed from the outside but must be cultivated from within, fostering the agency and self-determination of those most affected by economic disparities.

Concrete Examples of Success: Empowering Communities, Transforming Lives Around the globe, churches and faith-based organizations are pioneering innovative models that embody this transformative approach. In rural villages across Africa, church-led initiatives are empowering communities to develop sustainable agricultural practices, providing access to education and healthcare, and fostering economic self-sufficiency. In urban centers, churches are partnering with local businesses and organizations to create employment opportunities, offer skills training, and facilitate micro-financing programs that empower individuals to break free from the shackles of poverty.

The Power of Partnership: Bridging Divides, Amplifying Impact Yet, the Church's efforts need not be undertaken in isolation. By fostering strategic partnerships with secular organizations, governments, and other stakeholders, the Church can amplify its impact and leverage collective expertise and resources. Such collaborations not only enhance the scope and efficacy of economic justice initiatives but also serve as powerful catalysts for bridging divides and fostering mutual understanding and respect across diverse sectors of society.

Addressing Skepticism: Countering Doubts with Reasoned Arguments Despite the compelling evidence of success, skepticism may linger. Critics may question the Church's capacity to effect meaningful change, citing historical failures or the perceived limitations of faith-based organizations. However, such doubts can be countered with well-reasoned arguments, grounded in empirical evidence and a deep understanding of the Church's transformative potential.

Actionable Steps: Empowering Church Communities for Economic JusticeTo empower church communities to actively engage in the pursuit of economic justice, a clear roadmap is essential. This includes cultivating a shared understanding of the biblical foundations of justice and stewardship, fostering dialogue and collaboration with local communities, identifying and addressing systemic barriers, and developing sustainable programs that promote self-sufficiency and empowerment. By embracing this holistic approach, churches can become catalysts for lasting transformation, sowing the seeds of economic justice and human dignity in even the most challenging of environments.

As we navigate the complexities of economic injustice, the Church stands at a crossroads – a pivotal moment where the timeless values of compassion, justice, and human dignity intersect with the urgent realities of our time. By embracing a transformative approach that prioritizes community empowerment and sustainable development, the Church can reclaim its role as a powerful force for economic justice, ushering in a new era of hope and equity for all.

Spiritual Growth Through Community Engagement

1. Establish the goal: To foster spiritual growth and connection with the divine by actively engaging in community initiatives that harmonize individual and collective transformation, embracing the Church's mission of societal betterment.

2. Necessary materials:

- An open heart and mind, receptive to the transformative power of service and meaningful interactions
- Commitment to actively participating in community initiatives organized by the Church
- Willingness to step out of one's comfort zone and engage with diverse perspectives and experiences

3. Brief overview: Spiritual growth is an intrinsic journey deeply interwoven with our engagement with the world around us. By actively contributing to community initiatives, we embark on a transformative path that not only enriches the lives of others but also nurtures our own spiritual growth. Through service, education, and interfaith dialogues, we forge connections that transcend boundaries, cultivating a greater sense of unity and purpose. This multifaceted process involves preparation, action, reflection, and integration, ultimately leading to a deeper connection with the divine and a profound sense of personal fulfillment.

4. Detailed steps:

Step 1: Embrace a Mindset of Service

- Approach community engagement with a spirit of humility and a genuine desire to contribute
- Cultivate empathy and compassion, seeking to understand the unique challenges and perspectives of those you serve
- Align your intentions with the Church's mission of promoting justice, peace, and human dignity

Step 2: Identify and Participate in Community Initiatives

- Seek out opportunities for community service projects, educational programs, and interfaith dialogues organized by your church or local faith-based organizations
- Engage in initiatives that resonate with your values and strengths, while also challenging you to step out of your comfort zone
- Commit to active participation, contributing your time, skills, and resources to support these initiatives

Step 3: Immerse Yourself in Meaningful Interactions

- Engage in thoughtful conversations and dialogues with fellow participants, leaders, and community members
- Listen with an open mind and a willingness to learn, embracing diverse perspectives and experiences
- Share your own reflections and insights, fostering an environment of mutual understanding and growth

Step 4: Reflect on Personal Transformation

- After each community engagement experience, take time for introspection and self-reflection
- Examine how your perspectives, beliefs, and understanding of the divine have been enriched or challenged
- Identify areas of personal growth, such as increased empathy, patience, or resilience, that have emerged through service

Step 5: Integrate Spiritual Insights into Daily Life

- Translate the spiritual lessons and insights gained through community engagement into practical applications in your daily life

- Seek opportunities to embody the values of compassion, service, and unity in your interactions with others
- Cultivate a sense of gratitude for the transformative journey and the opportunity to contribute to the greater good

5. Tips and best practices:

- Maintain a balance between action and reflection, allowing time for both service and introspection
- Approach community engagement with an open mind and a willingness to learn, rather than a predetermined agenda
- Embrace vulnerability and authenticity, allowing yourself to be transformed by the experiences and connections forged
- Seek guidance and support from spiritual mentors, church leaders, or those with experience in community engagement
- Celebrate small victories and milestones along the journey, recognizing the incremental nature of spiritual growth

6. Checking for understanding:

- Reflect on how your participation in community initiatives has deepened your connection with the divine and enriched your spiritual journey
- Assess whether you have developed a greater sense of empathy, compassion, and understanding toward diverse perspectives and experiences
- Evaluate if you have integrated the spiritual lessons and insights gained into your daily life and interactions with others

7. Potential challenges and solutions:

- Scheduling conflicts or time constraints: Prioritize community engagement and seek support from others to balance responsibilities
- Feeling overwhelmed or disconnected: Practice mindfulness, seek guidance from spiritual mentors, and remember the purpose behind your efforts
- Encountering resistance or skepticism: Lead by example, approach with patience and understanding, and focus on the shared values that unite us
- By following these steps and embracing the transformative power of community engagement, you embark on a journey of profound spiritual growth. Through service, education, and meaningful interactions, you not only contribute to the betterment of society but also nurture a deeper connection with the divine, fostering personal fulfillment and a greater sense of unity and purpose.

Modern Stewardship Models: Case Studies

Case Study 1: The San Antonio Refugee Resettlement Initiative

1. Setting the Stage: In the heart of San Antonio, Texas, a vibrant faith community recognized the growing refugee crisis and the urgent need for compassionate action. Driven by their spiritual values of hospitality and service, a coalition of local churches embarked on an ambitious initiative to provide comprehensive support for newly arrived refugee families.
2. Key Players: Reverend Maria Gonzalez, a passionate advocate for social justice, served as the driving force behind the initiative, rallying volunteers and fostering partnerships with community organizations. Juan Martinez, a former refugee himself, brought invaluable

experience and empathy to the team, ensuring culturally sensitive support services.

3. The Challenge: Resettling refugee families posed significant logistical and financial hurdles. Securing safe and affordable housing, providing access to healthcare and education, and facilitating language learning and job training required substantial resources and coordination. Additionally, overcoming cultural barriers and fostering a sense of belonging in a new community presented a formidable challenge.

4. Strategies and Actions: The coalition launched a comprehensive support network, leveraging the collective resources and expertise of participating churches. They established a housing assistance program, partnering with local landlords and donors to secure affordable living spaces. Volunteer medical professionals offered free healthcare services, while educators volunteered to teach English classes and provide tutoring for children. Career counseling and job placement initiatives were implemented to facilitate economic self-sufficiency. The initiative also prioritized cultural integration and community-building. Interfaith dialogues and cultural exchange events were organized to foster understanding and celebrate diversity. Mentorship programs paired refugee families with local volunteers, providing guidance and support as they navigated life in a new environment.

5. Outcomes and Impact: Over the course of three years, the San Antonio Refugee Resettlement Initiative successfully resettled over 500 refugee families from various countries, providing them with a supportive and nurturing environment. 85% of the families achieved economic self-sufficiency within the first year, and 92% of school-aged children were enrolled in local educational institutions. The initiative's holistic approach not only met practical needs but also fostered a sense of belonging and

community, with many refugees reporting feeling welcomed and valued.

6. Lessons Learned: The success of this initiative underscores the power of collective action and the transformative impact of faith-based organizations in addressing complex societal challenges. By combining spiritual values with practical solutions, the coalition demonstrated that even daunting obstacles can be overcome through compassion, perseverance, and an unwavering commitment to service. However, the initiative also highlighted the importance of sustainable funding and long-term planning. While relying on volunteers and donations was admirable, securing dedicated resources and establishing partnerships with governmental agencies and NGOs could have further amplified the initiative's reach and longevity.

7. Relevance and Key Takeaways: The San Antonio Refugee Resettlement Initiative serves as a powerful example of the transformative potential of church-led stewardship models. By embodying the core values of hospitality, compassion, and service, this initiative not only provided critical support to vulnerable populations but also fostered a deeper sense of community and spiritual growth among its participants. The key takeaways from this case study include the importance of collaborative efforts, leveraging collective resources and expertise, and adopting a holistic approach that addresses both practical and emotional needs. Additionally, it highlights the crucial role of faith-based organizations in catalyzing positive social change and exemplifying the principles of stewardship through meaningful action.

8. Final Reflection: As we reflect on the San Antonio Refugee Resettlement Initiative, we are reminded of the profound impact that can be achieved when spiritual values are translated into tangible acts of service. This case study invites us to consider: How can we, as individuals and faith communities, continue to embrace the spirit of stewardship

and actively contribute to the betterment of society, addressing the most pressing challenges of our time with compassion, resilience, and a commitment to fostering a more just and inclusive world?

Balancing Tradition and Innovation

The realm of church stewardship finds itself at a crossroads, where the weight of tradition collides with the urgency of innovation. On one side stands the time-honored approach, deeply rooted in centuries-old doctrinal teachings and established practices. On the other, an innovative vision emerges, driven by a desire to adapt and remain relevant in an ever-changing world.

At the heart of this juxtaposition lies a fundamental question: How can faith communities reconcile the steadfast preservation of their heritage with the need for dynamic, forward-thinking strategies? This comparison and contrast will delve into the nuances of these seemingly opposing forces, unveiling both their shared aspirations and divergent methodologies.

As we embark on this exploration, we shall first examine the specific attributes that distinguish the traditional and innovative approaches to church stewardship. The traditional model finds its strength in the unwavering adherence to doctrinal teachings, reverence for established customs, and a profound respect for the historical lineage of the faith. Conversely, the innovative approach embraces adaptability, seeking to reinterpret timeless principles through the lens of contemporary society and emerging needs.

Despite these apparent contrasts, both traditions share a common goal: fostering societal well-being and nurturing spiritual growth within their respective communities. This shared objective serves as a unifying thread, reminding us that while the methods may differ, the underlying purpose remains a constant pursuit of positive transformation and personal fulfillment.

As we delve deeper into the similarities and differences between these approaches, we unveil a tapestry of complementary strengths and distinctive challenges. The traditional model offers a sense of stability and continuity, providing a solid foundation upon which faith communities can anchor their identity and values. Its reverence for the past serves as a guiding light, illuminating the enduring wisdom and timeless truths that have withstood the test of time.

On the other hand, the innovative approach brings a dynamism and responsiveness that enables faith communities to remain relevant and impactful in the face of societal shifts. By embracing new methodologies and engaging with contemporary issues, this approach fosters a sense of connection and relevance, ensuring that the teachings and principles of the faith resonate with the lived experiences of those they seek to serve.

One notable area of divergence lies in the implementation methodologies and engagement tactics employed by each approach. The traditional model favors tried-and-true practices, emphasizing rituals, ceremonies, and established channels of communication. Its adherents find solace in the familiarity of these time-honored traditions, cherishing the comfort of the familiar and the reassurance of continuity.

In contrast, the innovative approach embraces modern communication platforms, leveraging technology and social media to reach broader audiences and adapt to changing communication preferences. It seeks to repackage age-old wisdom in accessible and engaging formats, speaking the language of the contemporary world while retaining the essence of the faith's teachings.

As we reflect on these comparisons, we are compelled to consider the broader implications and the delicate balance that must be struck. Can the enduring wisdom of tradition coexist with the urgency for innovation? How can faith communities honor their heritage while simultaneously remaining relevant and responsive to the evolving needs of their followers?

Perhaps the answer lies not in choosing one path over the other but in embracing a harmonious fusion of the two. By integrating the timeless principles of the faith with innovative approaches and modern engagement strategies, church stewardship can forge a path that respects tradition while remaining adaptable and impactful in the face of change.

In the realm of modern church stewardship, we are witnessing a growing recognition of the need for such a balanced approach. Faith communities are exploring ways to preserve the essence of their traditions while simultaneously embracing new modes of outreach, service, and community engagement. This fusion manifests in various forms, from incorporating technology into worship services and spiritual education to leveraging social media platforms to amplify messages of compassion and social justice.

By integrating these approaches, faith communities can tap into the power of tradition to provide a sense of rootedness and continuity while simultaneously harnessing the potential of innovation to remain relevant and impactful in an ever-changing world. It is a delicate dance, one that requires careful navigation and a willingness to embrace change while honoring the enduring wisdom of the past.

As we navigate this delicate balance, it is essential to remember that the true essence of church stewardship transcends the dichotomy of tradition and innovation. At its core, stewardship calls for a profound commitment to service, compassion, and the betterment of society. Whether through time-honored practices or cutting-edge strategies, the ultimate goal remains the same: to uplift and empower individuals, foster a sense of community, and contribute to the greater good.

Overcoming Challenges in Church Leadership

The realm of church leadership faces formidable challenges in the modern era, testing the resilience and adaptability of faith communities worldwide. These challenges arise from a confluence of societal shifts, evolving dynamics, and ever-changing expectations, casting a shadow of uncertainty over the traditional structures and methodologies that have guided church stewardship for generations.

At the forefront of these challenges lies a stark reality: declining church attendance and diminishing congregations. As the world becomes increasingly secularized and individuals seek alternative paths for spiritual fulfillment, many churches find themselves struggling to attract and retain members, particularly among younger generations. This exodus of faithful attendees not only impacts the vibrancy and vitality of religious communities but also threatens their financial stability, as dwindling attendance often correlates with a reduction in tithes and offerings.

Compounding this challenge is the growing disconnect between the teachings and practices of traditional church structures and the lived realities of contemporary society. Rapid advancements in technology, shifting social norms, and evolving cultural values have created a chasm between the timeless principles of faith and the ever-evolving landscape in which they must be applied. This disconnect has the potential to erode the perceived relevance and applicability of religious teachings, leaving many individuals feeling disconnected and disengaged from the very institutions intended to guide and nurture their spiritual growth.

The dire consequences of inaction in the face of these challenges cannot be overstated. Declining attendance and financial instability threaten the very existence of many faith communities, potentially leading to the closure of houses of worship, the discontinuation of vital programs and services, and the erosion of the social fabric that these institutions have woven for generations. Furthermore, the disengagement of individuals from religious teachings and prac-tices risks leaving a void in the moral and ethical foundations that have long-anchored societies, potentially contributing to a further unraveling of social cohesion and collective well-being.

To address these multifaceted challenges, a comprehensive and holistic approach is essential, one that combines innovative strategies with a deep reverence for the enduring wisdom and principles that have guided church stewardship throughout history. One such approach lies in the implementation of leadership training programs tailored to the unique dynamics of the modern era.

These programs would equip church leaders with the skills and knowledge necessary to navigate the complexities of the contemporary world while remaining grounded in the core values and teachings of their faith. Through targeted workshops and immersive learning experiences, participants would gain insights into effective communication strategies, leveraging technology for outreach and engagement, fostering an inclusive and welcoming environment, and cultivating a culture of innovation and adaptability within their respective faith communities.

Complementing these leadership development initiatives are financial management workshops designed to empower church stewards with the tools and best practices for ensuring long-term financial stability and sustainability. These workshops would delve into topics such as budgeting, fundraising strategies, investment planning, and resource allocation, equipping church leaders with the knowledge and expertise necessary to navigate the fiscal challenges faced by modern religious institutions.

While addressing internal dynamics is paramount, a truly comprehensive approach must also prioritize community outreach and engagement. By fostering strong connections with the broader community, faith organizations can reaffirm their relevance, amplify their impact, and attract new members seeking purpose and belonging. Community outreach initiatives could range from service projects and charitable endeavors to educational programs and interfaith dialogues, all aimed at bridging gaps, fostering understanding, and demonstrating the tangible value that religious institutions bring to society.

The effectiveness of these solutions is not merely theoretical; it has been demonstrated time and again through the successes of forward-thinking faith communities that have embraced innovative approaches while remaining steadfast in their commitment to timeless principles. Churches that have implemented comprehensive leadership development programs have reported increased engagement, enhanced community involvement, and a renewed sense of vitality within their congregations.

Similarly, those who have prioritized financial management and stewardship have experienced greater stability and sustainability, allowing them to allocate resources more effectively and invest in initiatives that further their mission and impact. Moreover, faith communities that have actively embraced community outreach and engagement have witnessed a resurgence in attendance, attracting individuals seeking authentic connections, purpose, and a sense of belonging.

While the challenges faced by church leaders in the modern era are undeniably daunting, the path forward is illuminated by a multitude of viable solutions and proven strategies. By embracing innovation while honoring tradition, fostering adaptability while preserving core values, and prioritizing engagement and outreach, faith communities can not only overcome these challenges but also emerge as beacons of hope, unity, and positive transformation in an ever-changing world.

Integrating Secular and Sacred Economies

Imagine a world where the pursuit of financial prosperity is not merely a secular undertaking but a sacred endeavor, guided by the timeless principles of faith and the unwavering commitment to upholding ethical and moral values. This is the essence of integrating secular and sacred economies, a concept that lies at the intersection of economic vitality and spiritual fulfillment.

At its core, this integration seeks to harmonize the seemingly disparate realms of worldly pursuits and spiritual callings, recognizing that they are not mutually exclusive but rather intrinsically intertwined. It is a recognition that the pursuit of wealth when guided by the wisdom and values espoused by faith traditions, can become a force for good, a means to uplift communities, alleviate suffering, and foster a more just and equitable society.

To understand the depth and significance of this concept, we must first delve into its origins, tracing the threads that have woven together the economic and the spiritual throughout human history. From the early Christian communities who embraced a communal approach to resource sharing, to the medieval monastic orders whose economic endeavors sustained their spiritual pursuits, the interplay between the secular and the sacred has been a constant, albeit evolving, narrative.

In the modern era, the integration of secular and sacred economies has taken on renewed importance, as faith communities grapple with the complexities of a rapidly changing world. At its core, this integration seeks to reconcile the seemingly incompatible forces of profit-driven capitalism and the altruistic values espoused by religious teachings. It is a recognition that the pursuit of financial prosperity need not come at the expense of ethical and moral principles, but rather can be a vehicle for their manifestation.

One of the key elements underpinning this integration is the concept of ethical business practices. By embracing a set of guiding principles rooted in faith-based values, businesses, and economic endeavors can operate with a keen awareness of their impact on society, the environment, and the well-being of all stakeholders. This could manifest in initiatives such as fair trade practices, sustainable production methods, and corporate social responsibility programs that prioritize the upliftment of marginalized communities.

Another crucial aspect of integrating secular and sacred economies lies in the realm of community-focused investments. Faith-based organizations and communities can leverage their financial resources to support initiatives that foster economic empowerment, job creation, and sustainable development within their local contexts. This could take the form of microfinance initiatives, cooperatives, or social entrepreneurship ventures, all designed to uplift and empower those in need while fostering a sense of collective prosperity and well-being.

Furthermore, the integration of secular and sacred economies necessitates a shift in mindset, transcending the narrow confines of individualistic gain and embracing a more holistic and communal perspective. It is a recognition that economic activities are not merely a means to accumulate personal wealth but rather a sacred responsibility to be stewards of the resources entrusted to us, using them in a manner that benefits society as a whole.

To illustrate the practical manifestations of this concept, one need only look to the numerous faith-based organizations and initiatives that have successfully integrated secular and sacred economies. From the Amish communities whose economic endeavors are rooted in principles of simplicity, self-sufficiency, and community, to the Islamic finance industry that adheres to Sharia principles of ethical banking and investment, these examples provide a tangible blueprint for harmonizing economic activities with spiritual mandates.

Moreover, initiatives such as the Fair Trade movement, which seeks to ensure fair wages and humane working conditions for producers in developing countries, exemplify the integration of secular and sacred economies. By promoting ethical and sustainable trade practices, these initiatives not only foster economic empowerment but also uphold the sacred principles of human dignity, justice, and compassion.

It is important to address and dispel common misconceptions that may arise around the integration of secular and sacred economies. Some may perceive this concept as antithetical to the very foundations of capitalism and free-market principles, viewing it as an attempt to impose religious dogma on economic activities. However, this integration is not about imposing a specific set of beliefs but rather about embracing a set of universal ethical principles that can guide economic endeavors toward more just and sustainable outcomes.

Others may view this integration as an unrealistic idealism, arguing that the pursuit of profit and the adherence to spiritual values are inherently incompatible. Yet, countless examples throughout history have demonstrated the feasibility and indeed, the necessity of balancing these seemingly divergent forces. From the Quaker industrialists of the 19th century who championed ethical business practices and social responsibility, to the contemporary rise of conscious capitalism, the integration of secular and sacred economies is not only possible but essential for the long-term sustainability and wellbeing of our global society.

In essence, the integration of secular and sacred economies is a call to reclaim the sacred nature of economic pursuits, imbuing them with a sense of purpose and ethical grounding that transcends mere material gain. It is a recognition that our economic activities have the power to shape the world around us, and that by aligning them with the timeless wisdom and values espoused by faith traditions, we can create a more just, equitable, and sustainable future for all.

Future Directions in Church Stewardship

1. Goal: To provide a visionary guide for church leaders to embrace innovative and forward-thinking approaches to stewardship, ensuring the continued relevance and impact of their institutions amidst evolving societal dynamics.

2. Materials/Prerequisites:

- An open-minded and adaptable leadership team
- Willingness to explore new ideas and practices
- Commitment to serving the community and upholding spiritual values

- Access to resources (financial, technological, human capital) to implement changes

3. Overview: This guide will outline several key areas where churches can embrace innovation and explore future directions in their stewardship practices. We will delve into the incorporation of digital technologies, enhanced environmental stewardship, and strengthened interfaith collaborations. Each area will be accompanied by practical strategies for implementation, highlighting best practices and potential challenges. Throughout the process, we will emphasize the broader implications of these changes and their potential to transform church stewardship, ultimately contributing to societal well-being.

4. Detailed Steps:

I. Embracing Digital Technologies:

- Assess your church's current digital presence and capabilities.
- Develop a comprehensive digital strategy: Establish an online platform for virtual services, meetings, and community engagement. Leverage social media for outreach, communication, and storytelling. Explore online giving platforms and digital fundraising campaigns. Implement digital tools for church administration and record-keeping.
- Invest in training and support for staff and volunteers to ensure effective utilization of digital tools.
- Foster digital inclusion by providing resources and training for congregants who may have limited access or digital literacy.

II. Enhancing Environmental Stewardship:

- Conduct an environmental audit of your church's facilities and operations.

- Develop an environmental sustainability plan: Implement energy-efficient practices (e.g., solar panels, LED lighting, insulation). Promote recycling and waste reduction initiatives. Explore eco-friendly transportation options for congregants. Incorporate sustainable practices in church events and activities.
- Foster environmental education and awareness within the congregation through workshops, seminars, and community events.
- Collaborate with local environmental organizations and initiatives to amplify your impact.

III. Strengthening Interfaith Collaborations:

- Identify potential partner organizations and faith communities within your local area.
- Establish open channels of communication and dialogue to build trust and understanding.
- Identify shared values, goals, and areas of mutual interest for collaborative efforts: Community service and outreach programs education and cultural exchange initiative advocacy for social justice, human rights, and environmental causes
- Co-organize interfaith events, dialogues, and projects to foster understanding and cooperation.
- Encourage congregants to participate in interfaith activities and engage with diverse faith communities.

5. Tips and Best Practices:

Embrace change with an open and adaptable mindset.

Foster a culture of innovation and continuous improvement within your church community. Engage congregants throughout the process, gathering their feedback and involving them in decision-making.

Collaborate with experts, consultants, and other organizations to leverage their expertise and resources.

Prioritize transparency and clear communication to maintain trust and support within the congregation.

6. Potential Pitfalls:

- Resistance to change from more traditional or conservative members of the congregation.
- Lack of resources (financial, human capital, technological) to implement changes effectively. Failure to provide adequate training and support for new initiatives leads to a lack of adoption or misuse.
- Difficulties in building trust and overcoming historical tensions when pursuing interfaith collaborations.

7. Checking for Success:

- Conduct regular assessments and gather feedback from congregants to evaluate the effectiveness and impact of the implemented changes.
- Monitor metrics such as digital engagement, environmental impact reduction, and participation in interfaith activities.
- Celebrate successes and milestones, fostering a sense of accomplishment and continued motivation within the church community.

8. Addressing Potential Problems:

- If facing resistance, engage in open dialogue, address concerns, and emphasize the alignment of these initiatives with the church's mission and values.
- If lacking resources, explore partnerships, grants, and creative funding strategies to support your efforts.

- If encountering adoption challenges, provide ongoing training, support, and clear communication to address any issues or concerns.
- If facing difficulties in interfaith collaborations, prioritize building trust, respect, and mutual understanding through consistent engagement and open dialogue.

By embracing these future directions in church stewardship, you will not only ensure the continued relevance and impact of your institution but also contribute to the betterment of your community and society as a whole. Remember, the path to innovation and progress requires courage, perseverance, and a steadfast commitment to your spiritual values and the well-being of those you serve.

8

PROPHETIC INSIGHTS: THE MANTLE OF ELISHA

The Symbolism of the Mantle: Divine Authority and Responsibility

Defining Terms

As we delve into the profound symbolism of the mantle, it is essential to understand the nuances of certain key terms that will guide our exploration. Grasping these concepts is crucial to unlocking the deeper significance of this prophetic symbol and its enduring legacy.

1. Mantle: At first glance, a mantle may seem like a mere garment, but its symbolism carries weight far beyond its physical form. It teases the imagination, hinting at the weighty responsibilities and sacred duties bestowed upon those who bear it. With each fold and drape, the mantle whispers tales of divine authority and the burdens of spiritual leadership.

Originating from the Latin term "mantellum," meaning a cloak or covering, the mantle represents a cloak of divine protection, wisdom, and guidance. As we trace its history, we find it woven into the tapestry of various religious traditions, symbolizing the transfer of prophetic authority and the continuation of sacred knowledge.

In the context of our narrative, the mantle becomes a tangible representation of the prophetic legacy, a sacred garment passed from one chosen vessel to another, signifying the enduring nature of divine revelation and the unbroken chain of spiritual guidance. Its symbolism transcends mere cloth, embodying the weight of responsibility and the trust placed in those who bear its mantle.

2. Divine Authority: Divine authority, a concept that resonates across faiths and cultures, hints at the sacred investiture bestowed upon chosen individuals to act as conduits for the divine will. It carries an air of mystery, a whisper of the unseen forces that shape the destinies of nations and the trajectories of entire civilizations.

Rooted in the belief that true authority stems from a higher power, divine authority is a sacred trust granted to those deemed worthy of bearing the weight of spiritual leadership. It is not a mere title or position, but a profound responsibility that demands unwavering faith, moral integrity, and a steadfast commitment to upholding the principles of one's faith.

Within the context of our narrative, divine authority is embodied in the prophetic tradition, where chosen individuals become vessels for divine revelation, entrusted with the sacred task of guiding their people along the path of righteousness. The mantle, as a physical representation of this authority, serves as a reminder of the gravity of this calling and the accountability that comes with wielding such power.

3. Responsibility: Responsibility carries a weight that echoes through the corridors of history, a whisper that reminds us of the sacred duty we owe to ourselves, our communities, and the divine. It speaks of the profound trust placed in us, challenging us to rise above mere existence and embrace a higher purpose.

Responsibility is not a burden to bear grudgingly; rather, it is a sacred privilege, an opportunity to leave an indelible mark upon the world. It demands that we approach each decision and action with care, mindful of the ripples they may cast upon the waters of eternity.

In the context of our narrative, the mantle itself serves as a powerful symbol of responsibility, a tangible reminder of the sacred trust placed upon the shoulders of those who wear it. Each time the mantle is donned, it challenges its bearer to embody the values of righteousness, compassion, and unwavering commitment to the greater good.

As we continue our exploration of Elisha's prophetic journey, these terms – mantle, divine authority, and responsibility – will weave a tapestry of understanding, guiding us through the profound depths of this sacred symbol and its enduring impact upon the prophetic tradition.

Just as the mantle itself represents the transfer of sacred knowledge and authority, our understanding of these terms will pave the way for a deeper appreciation of the prophetic legacy and the enduring relevance of its teachings in our modern world. With each step, we inch closer to unraveling the mysteries that lie within the folds of this ancient garment, unveiling timeless truths that have the power to shape our lives and transform our understanding of the Divine.

The Call of Elisha: Transitioning Prophetic Mantles

1. Setting the Context: In the arid lands of ancient Israel, where the sun's rays kissed the rugged terrain and the whispers of prophets echoed through the ages, a pivotal moment in the sacred narrative unfolded. This was a time of transition, a passing of the prophetic torch from the revered Elijah to his chosen successor, Elisha. The weight of this transition was not merely a shift in leadership but a profound testament to the enduring nature of divine revelation and the continuity of spiritual guidance.

2. The Main Players: At the heart of this narrative stood Elijah, the fiery prophet whose unwavering faith and bold denouncements of idolatry had etched his name into the annals of history. His mantle,

a physical embodiment of his prophetic authority, had become a symbol of the divine's unwavering presence, a beacon of hope in the face of apostasy and spiritual darkness.

Then came Elisha, a humble farmer whose heart beat in tune with the rhythms of divine purpose. His calling, foreshadowed by Elijah's own actions, marked the beginning of a journey that would test the depths of his faith and his willingness to bear the weight of the prophetic mantle.

3. The Challenge: Inheriting the Prophetic MantleFor Elisha, inheriting Elijah's mantle was no mere formality; it was a sacred trust, a challenge that required him to step into the shoes of a giant among prophets. The mantle itself carried the weight of divine authority, a responsibility that few could bear without faltering.

Elijah's departure marked a pivotal moment, a transition fraught with uncertainty and the ever-present risk of disruption in the continuity of divine guidance. The challenge before Elisha was not merely to fill Elijah's shoes but to ensure that the flame of prophecy burned brightly, illuminating the path for a nation in desperate need of spiritual renewal.

4. Strategies and Actions: Both Elijah and Elisha approached this transition with a deep understanding of its significance. Elijah, guided by divine wisdom, recognized the importance of grooming his successor, imparting not only his prophetic knowledge but also the unwavering spirit required to bear the mantle's weight.

Through a series of tests and challenges, Elijah sought to refine Elisha's faith, honing his resolve and preparing him for the trials that lay ahead. From the symbolic act of plowing the field with Elijah's mantle to the harrowing journey across the Jordan River, each step was a testament to Elisha's commitment and his readiness to embrace the prophetic calling.

For his part, Elisha approached this transition with humility and an unwavering dedication to the divine will. He recognized that the mantle was not merely a garment but a sacred trust, a responsibility that demanded his entire being. With each challenge, Elisha demonstrated his willingness to surrender himself to the divine purpose, embracing the mantle not as a symbol of personal power but as a sacred duty to guide and uplift his people.

5. The Outcome: A Seamless Transition, A Prophetic LegacyThe strategies and actions of both Elijah and Elisha culminated in a seamless transition of prophetic authority. As Elijah ascended in a whirlwind, his mantle fell upon Elisha, symbolizing the passing of the prophetic torch. This moment marked a profound shift in the narrative, a testament to the enduring nature of divine revelation and the unbroken chain of spiritual guidance.

The impact of this transition reverberated throughout the land, with Elisha's prophetic ministry continuing the work of his predecessor. His miracles and teachings, empowered by the authority vested in the mantle, restored hope and rekindled the flame of faith in the hearts of the people.

6. Lessons Learned and Alternative Perspectives: The transition from Elijah to Elisha offers a wealth of lessons for those called to spiritual leadership. It underscores the importance of succession planning, where the wisdom of the past is carefully transmitted to the guardians of the future. It highlights the value of mentorship and the cultivation of faith, where the experiences of those who have walked the path before guide and shape the journeys of those who follow.

Furthermore, this narrative challenges us to consider the consequences of a disrupted transition, where the continuity of divine guidance is fractured. What if Elisha had faltered, unable to bear the weight of the mantle? The ramifications of such a scenario could have been devastating, leaving a nation adrift and vulnerable to the tides of spiritual darkness.

While some might question the necessity of such a symbolic transference of authority, arguing that divine revelation should transcend physical symbols, the mantle's significance lies in its ability to anchor the continuity of the prophetic tradition. It serves as a tangible reminder of the sacred trust bestowed upon those chosen to bear its weight, a testament to the enduring nature of divine guidance.

7. Relevance in Modern Spiritual Leadership: As we ponder the lessons of Elisha's call and the transition of the prophetic mantle, we are reminded of the enduring relevance of this narrative in the context of modern spiritual leadership. In a world where the winds of change blow relentlessly, the need for continuity and the seamless transfer of spiritual authority remains paramount.

Just as Elijah and Elisha understood the gravity of their roles, modern spiritual leaders must approach their responsibilities with a profound sense of reverence and humility. They must recognize that they are but temporary bearers of a sacred trust, tasked with safeguarding the flames of faith and ensuring the unbroken transmission of divine wisdom to future generations.

Like Elisha, those called to spiritual leadership must embrace the mantle not as a symbol of personal power but as a sacred duty to guide, uplift, and inspire. They must embody the values of integrity, compassion, and unwavering commitment to the greater good, serving as beacons of hope in a world often shrouded in darkness.

8. A Final Reflection: As we reflect upon the narrative of Elisha's call and the transition of the prophetic mantle, a profound question lingers: Are we, as individuals and communities, willing to bear the weight of such a sacred trust? Are we prepared to embrace the mantle of spiritual leadership, with all its challenges and responsibilities, and carry forth the flame of divine revelation into the future?

The answer lies not in mere words but in the depths of our commitment, in our willingness to surrender ourselves to the divine purpose, and in our unwavering dedication to upholding the sacred principles that have guided humanity through the ages. Only then can we truly honor the legacy of Elijah and Elisha and ensure that the mantle of prophetic authority continues to burn brightly, illuminating the path for generations to come.

Miracles: Manifestations of Divine Power

1. The Provoking Question:

How do Elisha's miracles manifest divine power and authority, transcending the realm of mere spectacle and revealing profound truths about the nature of God's involvement in human affairs?

2. Understanding the Context:

In the ancient world, miracles were not merely extraordinary events; they were tangible signifiers of divine presence and power. Within the prophetic tradition, miracles served as beacons of hope, illuminating the path of faith and reminding the people of the sovereignty of the one true God. Against this backdrop, Elisha's miracles emerged as a continuation of the prophetic legacy, a testament to the enduring nature of divine revelation and the unbroken chain of spiritual guidance.

3. The Problem: Interpreting the Intricacies of Miracles:

While the miracles performed by Elisha are well documented, their true significance often eludes our grasp. Too often, we approach these miraculous events with a simplistic lens, viewing them as mere displays of supernatural power or isolated incidents devoid of deeper meaning. This limited perspective fails to recognize the nuances and complexities that lie beneath the surface of each miracle, obscuring the profound truths they hold about the divine's intimate involvement in the affairs of humanity.

4. Common Misconceptions and Pitfalls:

One of the most prevalent misconceptions surrounding Elisha's miracles is the tendency to view them as mere spectacles, acts of divine showmanship designed to dazzle and inspire awe. However, this superficial interpretation robs the miracles of their profound spiritual significance and reduces them to mere parlor tricks devoid of any lasting impact. Another pitfall lies in the tendency to interpret these miracles through a strictly literal lens, failing to recognize the symbolic and metaphorical layers that often underlie the narrative. By adhering too rigidly to the literal, we risk missing the deeper truths and lessons woven into the fabric of these miraculous events.

5. A Novel Perspective: Miracles as Revelations of Divine Nature:

To truly appreciate the significance of Elisha's miracles, we must adopt a more nuanced perspective, one that recognizes these events as revelations of the divine nature itself. Each miracle, with its unique circumstances and intricate details, offers a glimpse into the multifaceted aspects of God's character and the profound ways in which the divine interacts with the human realm.

Through this lens, Elisha's miracles become far more than mere displays of power; they become windows into the very heart of God, revealing the divine's compassion, justice, mercy, and unwavering commitment to the well-being of humanity. From the healing of the poisonous stew, which speaks to God's restorative power, to the multiplication of the widow's oil, a testament to divine provision, each miracle carries layers of meaning that invite us to ponder the depths of the divine love and care for creation.

6. Illustrations and Case Studies:

Consider the miracle of the Shunammite woman's son, in which Elisha's intervention restores life to the child. On the surface, it is a powerful demonstration of the prophet's authority over life and death. Yet, when viewed through the lens of divine revelation, this miracle becomes a powerful metaphor for God's ability to breathe new life into the seemingly lifeless, a poignant reminder of the divine's power to resurrect hope in the face of despair. Another remarkable illustration lies in the healing of Naaman, the Syrian commander afflicted with leprosy. This miracle transcends the physical realm, offering a profound lesson in humility, obedience, and the universality of God's grace. Naaman's initial reluctance and subsequent submission to Elisha's instructions mirror the human journey of surrendering our pride and embracing the divine's wisdom, a path that leads to healing and restoration.

7. Addressing Potential Objections:

Some may question the validity of interpreting miracles beyond their literal accounts, arguing that such interpretations risk distorting the sacred text and imposing subjective meanings upon objective events. However, this objection fails to recognize the inherent complexity of the divine's interactions with the human realm and the multifaceted nature of divine revelation. Scripture itself is replete with instances where symbolic and metaphorical language is employed to convey profound spiritual truths. To limit our understanding of miracles to their literal manifestations would be to deny the rich tapestry of meaning woven into the fabric of divine revelation.

8. A Call to Action: Recognizing Divine Manifestations in Our Lives:

As we ponder the profound lessons embedded within Elisha's miracles, we are called to cultivate a heightened sensitivity to the manifestations of divine power and presence in our own lives. Just as Elisha's miracles revealed the multifaceted nature of God's involvement in human affairs, we too must learn to discern the divine's fingerprints in the seemingly ordinary moments of our existence. This call to action invites us to approach our daily lives with a posture of wonder and reverence, recognizing that the miraculous often manifests in subtle, yet profound ways. It is in the unexpected kindness of a stranger, the awe-inspiring beauty of a sunset, or the inexplicable sense of peace that envelops us in times of turmoil that we catch glimpses of the divine's handiwork. By embracing this perspective, we open ourselves to a deeper understanding of the divine's presence in our lives, and we become vessels through which the transformative power of miracles can continue to unfold, touching the hearts and souls of those around us.

Elisha's Prophetic Legacy: Continuity and Innovation

1. Overview and the Importance of Evidence-Based Analysis:

Elisha's prophetic legacy stands as a testament to the enduring power of divine revelation and the profound impact it can have on the course of human history. To fully grasp the significance of this legacy, we must employ an evidence-based approach, meticulously examining the scriptural accounts and historical records that shed light on Elisha's ministry. This rigorous analysis not only lends credibility to our understanding but also enables us to uncover the deeper layers of meaning woven into the tapestry of his prophetic work.

2. The Main Claim: A Blend of Continuity and Innovation:

At the heart of this exploration lies the claim that Elisha's ministry represents a harmonious blend of continuity and innovation within the prophetic tradition. While firmly rooted in the spiritual lineage of his predecessor, Elijah, Elisha's approach to his prophetic calling introduced novel elements that expanded the boundaries of divine revelation and left an indelible mark on the trajectory of Israel's spiritual journey.

3. Primary Evidence: Scriptural Accounts:

The most significant source of evidence for Elisha's prophetic legacy lies within the sacred texts of the Hebrew Bible, specifically the books of 1 Kings and 2 Kings. These accounts, revered for their divine inspiration and historical accuracy, provide a rich tapestry of narratives detailing Elisha's miraculous deeds, prophetic utterances, and profound impact on the lives of those he encountered.

4. Delving into the Evidence:

As we delve into the scriptural accounts, we are immediately struck by the sheer breadth and depth of Elisha's miracles, which range from the healing of the poisonous stew (2 Kings 4:38-41) to the resurrection of the Shunammite woman's son (2 Kings 4:32-37). These miraculous events are not mere displays of supernatural power but rather signifiers of the divine's intimate involvement in human affairs, revealing the depths of God's compassion and restorative grace. Moreover, the scriptural narratives depict Elisha as a prophetic figure who fearlessly confronted injustice and idolatry, echoing the clarion call of his predecessor, Elijah. From his bold pronouncements against the wicked Ahab and Jezebel (1 Kings 21:17-24) to his unwavering stance against the false prophets of Baal (2 Kings 3:13-19), Elisha embodied the prophetic tradition's uncompromising commitment to truth and righteousness.

5. Addressing Potential Counter-Evidence:

In any evidence-based analysis, it is crucial to address potential counter-evidence or alternative perspectives to maintain objectivity and intellectual integrity. In the case of Elisha's prophetic legacy, some may question the historicity or credibility of the scriptural accounts, citing the potential for exaggeration or bias in the ancient texts. While acknowledging the inherent limitations of ancient historical records, it is essential to recognize the meticulous preservation and transmission of these sacred texts throughout the centuries. Furthermore, the consistency and coherence of the narratives, as well as their alignment with archaeological and historical evidence, lend credence to the validity of these accounts.

6. Reinforcing the Claim with Further Evidence:

To further reinforce the claim of Elisha's prophetic legacy as a harmonious blend of continuity and innovation, we can turn to additional evidence from historical and theological sources. The writings of the early Church Fathers and Jewish sages, for instance, offer valuable insights into the interpretation and significance of Elisha's ministry within the broader context of divine revelation. Moreover, the presence of Elisha's prophetic legacy in later theological and literary works, such as the writings of the Talmudic rabbis and the medieval Christian exegetes, attests to the enduring impact and relevance of his ministry across generations and cultures.

7. Further Evidence from Historical and Theological Sources:

One notable example of historical evidence supporting Elisha's prophetic legacy can be found in the annals of the Assyrian king Shalmaneser III, who records a confrontation with the king of Israel, Jehu. This account, while not directly mentioning Elisha, corroborates the biblical narrative of Jehu's rise to power, a pivotal event in which Elisha played a significant role (2 Kings 9:1-10). From a theological perspective, the writings of the early Church Father, Origen, offer insightful commentary on the symbolism and spiritual significance of Elisha's miracles. In his work "Contra Celsum," Origen interprets the healing of Naaman the Syrian (2 Kings 5:1-14) as a powerful metaphor for the transformative power of divine grace, transcending ethnic and cultural boundaries.

8. Practical Applications and Significance for Modern Spiritual Leaders:

As we reflect on the profound legacy of Elisha's prophetic ministry, we are compelled to consider its practical applications and relevance for modern spiritual leaders. Just as Elisha seamlessly blended continuity and innovation, contemporary leaders must strike a delicate balance between honoring the timeless truths of their faith traditions and adapting their approach to address the unique challenges and contexts of their time. Furthermore, Elisha's unwavering commitment to truth and justice, even in the face of opposition and persecution, serves as a powerful reminder for leaders to remain steadfast in their convictions and to use their voices to confront injustice and uphold moral principles. Perhaps most significantly, Elisha's miracles stand as a testament to the enduring power of divine intervention and the profound ways in which the sacred can manifest in the midst of the ordinary. For modern spiritual leaders, this legacy serves as a call to cultivate a deep awareness of the divine presence in all aspects of life, recognizing that even the most mundane circumstances can become vessels for the miraculous and transformative power of God.

Discipleship and Mentorship: Elisha's School of Prophets

Goal: To understand Elisha's role as a mentor and guide in establishing the School of Prophets, learn from his approach to discipleship and mentorship, and apply these principles in modern contexts.

Prerequisites:

- A deep understanding of the biblical accounts of Elisha's life and ministry, particularly his work with the sons of the prophets (2 Kings 2-9).
- A willingness to study the methods and teachings of Elisha with an open mind and a desire to grow as a mentor and disciple-maker.
- Key Scriptural References: 1 Kings 19:19-21, 2 Kings 2:1-18, 2 Kings 4:38-44, 2 Kings 6:1-7, 2 Kings 6:8-23.

Overview: Elisha's establishment of the School of Prophets was a pivotal moment in the history of Israel, nurturing and training a new generation of prophets to carry on the mantle of spiritual leadership. Through his mentorship approach, Elisha imparted wisdom, cultivated character, and instilled a deep reverence for God in his disciples. The process involved several key steps, which we will explore in detail.

1. Selecting Disciples: Elisha's journey as a mentor began with the divine call to follow his predecessor, Elijah (1 Kings 19:19-21). He was chosen to carry on the prophetic ministry, and in turn, he sought out individuals with the potential to become prophets and spiritual leaders.
2. Fostering a Community of Learning: Elisha established a community of disciples, known as the "sons of the prophets." This close-knit group lived together, studied the Word of God, and received practical training in various disciplines, including agriculture, construction, and spiritual warfare.

3. Teaching through Experiences: Elisha employed a hands-on approach to teaching, using real-life situations as opportunities for instruction. He guided his disciples through practical challenges, such as purifying a poisonous stew (2 Kings 4:38-44) and retrieving a lost axe head (2 Kings 6:1-7). These experiences allowed his students to apply their knowledge and develop problem-solving skills.

4. Imparting Spiritual Wisdom: Beyond practical lessons, Elisha emphasized the development of spiritual discernment and a deep relationship with God. He taught his disciples to rely on divine guidance and to exercise faith in the face of adversity, as exemplified in the story of the Syrian army's encounter with the prophet (2 Kings 6:8-23).

5. Cultivating Character: Elisha recognized that effective ministry hinged not only on knowledge but also on personal character. He modeled humility, integrity, and selflessness, challenging his disciples to embody these qualities in their lives and leadership.

Tips and Best Practices:

- Maintain a close mentoring relationship, guiding and correcting with wisdom and patience.
- Encourage open dialogue and a safe environment for asking questions and sharing struggles.
- Emphasize the importance of personal spiritual growth and a deep relationship with God.
- Provide opportunities for hands-on learning and practical application of principles. Model the character traits and values you wish to instill in your disciples.

Verifying Success:

- Observe the growth and transformation of your disciples' character and spiritual maturity.

- Witness their ability to handle challenges with wisdom and discernment.
- Note their willingness to pass on the knowledge and mentorship to others.
- Evaluate their readiness to assume leadership roles and make an impact in their spheres of influence.

Potential Challenges and Solutions:

- Worldly distractions: Encourage your disciples to maintain focus and prioritize their spiritual growth, guarding against worldly influences.
- Pride and self-reliance: Emphasize humility and reliance on God's guidance, using examples from Elisha's life.
- Lack of commitment: Foster a culture of accountability and support, encouraging your disciples to persevere in their journey.
- Contextual differences: Adapt the principles to modern contexts while maintaining the core values and teachings of Elisha's approach.

By studying and applying the principles exemplified by Elisha's mentorship and discipleship, we can raise up a new generation of spiritual leaders equipped to impact their communities and carry on the prophetic legacy.

Elisha's Social and Political Impact

At first glance, Elisha's interactions with kings and commoners appear strikingly different, a stark contrast between the realms of power and humility. However, a closer examination reveals a profound unity in Elisha's approach, guided by an unwavering commitment to divine principles and a deep concern for the spiritual welfare of all people, regardless of their social status.

On one hand, Elisha's encounters with kings were marked by bold confrontations and uncompromising stances. He fearlessly challenged the corrupt and idolatrous rulers of his time, exposing their wrongdoings and exhorting them to repentance. His interactions with King Jehoram of Israel (2 Kings 3) and the Syrian king Ben-Hadad (2 Kings 8:7-15) exemplify this unyielding stance against political and spiritual corruption. Elisha did not shy away from speaking truth to power, even when it meant risking his own safety.

On the other hand, Elisha's interactions with the common people were marked by compassion, humility, and a willingness to serve. He performed miracles that alleviated suffering, such as purifying the poisonous stew for the sons of the prophets (2 Kings 4:38-41) and multiplying food for a poverty-stricken widow (2 Kings 4:1-7). Elisha's heart was attuned to the needs of the marginalized, and he used his prophetic authority to uplift and empower them.

These contrasting interactions reveal several key attributes of Elisha's character and ministry:

1. Unwavering commitment to truth and righteousness: Elisha was unwavering in his commitment to God's truth, regardless of the recipient's social status. He boldly confronted kings when they strayed from God's ways and extended compassion to the common people, upholding the same standard of righteousness for all.

2. Discernment and contextual sensitivity: While Elisha's message remained consistent, his approach was tailored to the specific context and needs of each audience. With kings, he employed a direct and confrontational style, while with the common people, he adopted a more gentle and nurturing approach.

3. Selfless service and compassion: Elisha's ministry was driven by genuine concern for the well-being of others, transcending social boundaries. He was willing to sacrifice his own comfort and safety to serve those in need, whether they were kings or commoners.

The implications of these similarities and differences resonate profoundly in contemporary contexts. In a world where power often corrupts and societal divides run deep, Elisha's example challenges spiritual and political leaders to embody unwavering integrity, discernment, and selfless service.

For modern spiritual leaders, Elisha's interactions with kings serve as a call to fearlessly confront corruption and injustice, regardless of the source's power or influence. Like Elisha, they must stand as voices of truth and accountability, even when it is unpopular or risky. At the same time, they must emulate Elisha's compassion for the common people, offering hope, encouragement, and practical assistance to those in need.

For political leaders, Elisha's example highlights the importance of humility, discernment, and a willingness to listen to voices of truth and wisdom, even when they challenge their authority. Like the kings of old, modern leaders must resist the temptation of absolute power and remain open to correction and guidance from spiritual advisors and voices of conscience.

In a world often divided by social and political lines, Elisha's example reminds us that true leadership transcends these boundaries. It is rooted in an unwavering commitment to truth, righteousness, and the well-being of all people, regardless of their status or position. By embracing these principles, modern leaders can navigate complex social and political landscapes with wisdom, integrity, and compassion, leaving a lasting impact on their communities and societies.

As we strive to apply the lessons from Elisha's life, we must recognize that true change begins within. Before we can effectively lead and influence others, we must cultivate the same qualities that Elisha embodied: an uncompromising commitment to truth, discernment, humility, and a heart of selfless service. Only then can we hope to bridge the divides that separate us and create a world where justice, compassion, and righteousness prevail.

In conclusion, Elisha's interactions with kings and commoners offer a profound blueprint for leadership that transcends social and political boundaries. By studying his approach, we can learn to navigate complex situations with wisdom, discernment, and compassion, fearlessly confronting injustice while extending mercy and healing to those in need. As we strive to emulate Elisha's unwavering commitment to truth and his selfless service, we can become agents of transformation in our communities, nations, and the world at large.

The Double Portion: Elisha's Request for Elijah's Spirit

1. Setting the Scene:

In the midst of a tumultuous era marked by political upheaval and spiritual decline, the prophet Elisha found himself at a pivotal juncture. Serving as the successor to the renowned prophet Elijah, Elisha witnessed firsthand the profound impact of his mentor's ministry. As Elijah's time on earth drew to a close, Elisha made a bold request that would shape the course of his prophetic journey: he asked for a double portion of Elijah's spirit (2 Kings 2:9).

2. The Key Players:

- Elijah: The revered prophet of Israel, known for his unwavering commitment to the Lord and his confrontation of the idolatrous King Ahab and his wife Jezebel. Elijah's ministry was marked by miracles and a zeal for restoring Israel's devotion to God. - Elisha: Elijah's faithful servant and successor, who initially followed Elijah's instructions and requests without question. Elisha's request for a double portion of Elijah's spirit revealed his desire to carry on his mentor's legacy with even greater spiritual power and influence.

3. The Challenge: Inheriting a Legacy of Prophetic Power

Elisha's request for a double portion of Elijah's spirit was no ordinary request. In the prophetic tradition, a "double portion" referred to the inheritance rights of the firstborn son, who would receive a double share of the father's estate and authority (Deuteronomy 21:17). By asking for this, Elisha was not merely seeking a greater measure of spiritual power but a complete inheritance of Elijah's prophetic mantle and the authority that came with it.

This request was significant because Elisha was stepping into the shoes of one of Israel's greatest prophets, a man who had confronted kings, performed miraculous signs, and played a pivotal role in restoring the nation's spiritual integrity. Elisha's challenge was to prove himself worthy of this inheritance and to carry on Elijah's legacy with the same unwavering commitment and spiritual power.

4. Elisha's Strategies and Actions:

- Steadfast Commitment: Elisha's unwavering commitment to following Elijah's instructions was evident throughout their journey. When Elijah instructed him to remain behind at various locations, Elisha refused to leave his mentor's side, demonstrating his determination to see the request through (2 Kings 2:2-6). - Perseverance and Obedience: As Elijah's departure drew near, Elisha remained steadfast in his obedience, even as other prophets urged him to turn back. This perseverance and obedience were essential qualities for inheriting the prophetic mantle. - Focused Observation: Elisha witnessed Elijah's departure in a whirlwind, symbolizing the transfer of prophetic power. Keeping his eyes fixed on his mentor, Elisha demonstrated his commitment to learning and absorbing every aspect of Elijah's ministry.

5. The Outcome: A Mantle Inherited, A Legacy Continued

Elisha's actions and determination were rewarded when Elijah's mantle fell upon him (2 Kings 2:13). This symbolic gesture signified the transfer of prophetic authority and power. Immediately, Elisha demonstrated the validity of his inheritance by performing a miracle reminiscent of Elijah's – he parted the waters of the Jordan River with the mantle, just as Elijah had done (2 Kings 2:14).

From that moment on, Elisha's ministry was marked by a multitude of miracles and prophetic acts, many of which echoed or even surpassed those of his mentor. The sons of the prophets recognized the double portion of Elijah's spirit upon Elisha (2 Kings 2:15), validating his inheritance and paving the way for his own powerful ministry.

6. Lessons Learned and Alternatives Considered:

Elisha's request for a double portion of Elijah's spirit offers several profound lessons for those seeking spiritual inheritance and legacy:

- Unwavering Commitment: Elisha's steadfast commitment to following Elijah's instructions and remaining by his side highlights the importance of perseverance and obedience in pursuing spiritual inheritance. Alternative paths of disobedience or halfhearted commitment would have likely resulted in a failure to receive the inheritance.
- Humility and Reverence: Elisha's request, rooted in humility and reverence for his mentor, stands in contrast to the pride and self-aggrandizement that often characterize leadership transitions. His approach exemplifies the importance of honoring those who have gone before and learning from their wisdom.
- Focused Observation and Learning: Elisha's focused observation of Elijah's ministry and his commitment to learning from his mentor underscore the necessity of intentional discipleship and mentorship in spiritual formation. Attempting to inherit a spiritual legacy without

this focused learning and observation would have been futile.

While Elisha's approach was successful, it is worth considering alternative scenarios. Had Elisha demanded the double portion or attempted to seize it through force or manipulation, he would have likely failed. Such actions would have been contrary to the spirit of humility and obedience required for spiritual inheritance. Additionally, had Elisha been content with merely witnessing Elijah's ministry without actively seeking to inherit it, he may have missed the opportunity to carry on the prophetic legacy.

7. Relevance and Application:

The case of Elisha's request for a double portion of Elijah's spirit is not merely a historical event but a powerful illustration of the principles governing spiritual inheritance and the continuation of God's work across generations. In the context of understanding spiritual inheritance, this case study highlights several essential principles:

- The importance of intentional discipleship and mentorship in shaping the next generation of spiritual leaders. Just as Elisha learned from Elijah, contemporary leaders must prioritize the intentional investment in and development of their successors.
- The necessity of humility, obedience, and reverence in receiving spiritual inheritance.
- Arrogance, self-promotion, and disregard for those who have gone before will only hinder the transfer of spiritual authority and power.
- The value of perseverance and unwavering commitment to pursuing God's calling and legacy. Like Elisha, those seeking to inherit spiritual mantles must be willing to remain steadfast in the face of challenges and distractions.
- The recognition that spiritual inheritance is not merely about acquiring power or position but about carrying on

the transformative work of God's kingdom. Elisha's request was rooted in a desire to continue Elijah's ministry, not personal ambition.

As we reflect on this case study, we are reminded that spiritual inheritance is a sacred trust, a responsibility to carry forward the work of those who have gone before while remaining faithful to God's purposes. It requires a humility that honors the legacies of our spiritual forebears and a commitment to learn from their wisdom and example. Only through such an approach can we hope to inherit the spiritual mantles entrusted to us and continue the transformative work of the Kingdom.

8. Final Thought:

As Elisha's life and ministry demonstrate, the pursuit of spiritual inheritance is not a mere formality or symbolic gesture; it is a sacred calling that demands our full commitment, humility, and obedience. In our pursuit of this inheritance, we must ask ourselves: Are we truly willing to follow in the footsteps of our spiritual mentors, even when the path is challenging? Are we prepared to lay aside our own ambitions and agendas in order to carry forward the work of those who have gone before? And ultimately, are we ready to embrace the mantle of spiritual authority and power, not for our own glory, but for the advancement of God's Kingdom and the transformation of lives?

Elisha's Miraculous Healings

1. The Healing Legacy of Elijah's Successor:

The prophet Elisha, who inherited the mantle of his mentor Elijah, was not only a spiritual guide but also a vessel of divine healing. Just as Elijah's ministry had been marked by miraculous displays of God's power, Elisha's tenure as a prophet was characterized by a remarkable series of healings that transcended the boundaries of culture, geography, and social status. These healings stand as a testament to the enduring power of faith and the Lord's compassion for His people, offering profound historical insights into the spiritual fabric of ancient Israel and its surrounding regions.

2. The Inception of Elisha's Healing Ministry:

The seeds of Elisha's healing ministry were sown in the very act of inheriting Elijah's prophetic mantle. As Elijah was taken up into heaven in a whirlwind, his cloak fell upon Elisha, symbolizing the transfer of prophetic authority and power (2 Kings 2:13). Immediately after this pivotal moment, Elisha performed his first recorded miracle – parting the waters of the Jordan River, much like his mentor had done (2 Kings 2:14). This initial display of divine power not only confirmed Elisha's inheritance but also foreshadowed the remarkable healings that would shape his prophetic legacy.

3. A Chronological Catalog of Elisha's Healings:

- Elisha's healing ministry spanned the breadth of his prophetic tenure, touching the lives of individuals from diverse backgrounds and circumstances. Here are some of the most significant healings recorded in the Scriptures:
- Purification of the Waters at Jericho (2 Kings 2:19-22): In one of his earliest recorded miracles, Elisha purified the waters of Jericho, making them portable and restoring the land's fertility.
- Healing of the Shunammite Woman's Son (2 Kings 4:18-37): Elisha restored life to the son of a hospitable Shunammite woman, who had shown kindness to the prophet. This miraculous healing demonstrated God's compassion and Elisha's prophetic authority.
- Healing of the Poisonous Stew (2 Kings 4:38-41): When a deadly poisonous plant was accidentally added to a pot of stew, Elisha miraculously neutralized the toxins, making the food safe for consumption and preventing potential harm.
- Feeding of a Hundred Men (2 Kings 4:42-44): In a remarkable display of God's provision, Elisha multiplied a

small amount of bread and grain, allowing it to feed a hundred men with leftovers remaining.

- Healing of Naaman's Leprosy (2 Kings 5:1-14): One of Elisha's most renowned miracles involved the healing of Naaman, a Syrian commander afflicted with leprosy. Through obedience to Elisha's instructions, Naaman was miraculously cured, illustrating the power of faith and humility.
- Restoring Life to a Dead Boy (2 Kings 4:32-37): In an echo of Elijah's miracle, Elisha raised a Shunammite woman's son from the dead, demonstrating the Lord's sovereignty over life and death.

4. The Cross-Cultural Impact of Elisha's Healings:

Elisha's healing ministry extended beyond the borders of Israel, reaching into neighboring nations and impacting individuals from diverse cultural backgrounds. The healing of Naaman, the Syrian commander, stands as a powerful example of this cross-cultural influence. Through this miracle, Elisha not only restored Naaman's physical health but also sparked a spiritual transformation, leading Naaman to declare his newfound faith in the God of Israel (2 Kings 5:15).

Additionally, Elisha's purification of the waters at Jericho had far-reaching implications, restoring the land's fertility and ensuring a sustainable source of clean water for the region. This miracle likely benefited not only the Israelites but also neighboring communities and travelers passing through the area.

5. Modern Interpretations and Relevance:

Elisha's healing miracles continue to resonate with modern audiences, offering valuable lessons and insights that transcend their historical context. Many contemporary theologians and scholars view these healings as powerful demonstrations of God's compassion and His desire to restore wholeness to His creation. They serve as reminders of the divine power available to those who approach God with faith and humility, echoing the principles exemplified by Naaman's healing.

Furthermore, Elisha's healings highlight the interconnectedness of physical, spiritual, and environmental well-being. The purification of the waters at Jericho speaks to the importance of environmental stewardship and the impact of natural resources on human health and flourishing. Similarly, the healing of the poisonous stew underscores the need for vigilance in protecting food sources and ensuring safety.

In the realm of healthcare and medical practice, Elisha's healings serve as a reminder of the value of compassion, empathy, and holistic care. While modern medicine relies on scientific advancements, the principles of faith, hope, and emotional support embodied in Elisha's ministry remain essential components of effective patient care and healing.

6. Controversies and Critical Junctures:

Despite the remarkable nature of Elisha's healing miracles, their interpretation and significance have been the subject of ongoing debate and discussion throughout history. One notable controversy surrounds the healing of Naaman, particularly the prophet's initial instructions for Naaman to bathe in the Jordan River. Some scholars have questioned why Elisha chose this specific location, given the apparent simplicity of the task and the availability of other water sources.

Another point of contention relates to the inherent power behind Elisha's healing. While some interpretations attribute the miracles solely to divine intervention, others suggest that Elisha possessed a unique understanding of natural remedies and medicinal practices that contributed to the healing process.

A critical juncture in the perception of Elisha's healings occurred during the rise of scientific rationalism and the Enlightenment era. As empirical evidence and naturalistic explanations gained prominence, some thinkers sought to reinterpret or dismiss the supernatural elements of Elisha's miracles, viewing them through a more rationalistic lens.

Ultimately, the controversies and debates surrounding Elisha's healing ministry reflect the complexities of reconciling faith and reason, as well as the enduring human fascination with the miraculous and the unexplained. However, regardless of the specific interpretations, the impact and significance of these healings remain undeniable, serving as powerful testaments to the enduring presence of divine power and the transformative potential of faith.

Lessons for Modern Spiritual Leadership

The ministry of the prophet Elisha, recorded in the biblical accounts, offers a wealth of lessons and insights for contemporary spiritual leaders. Drawing parallels between ancient times and the present day, we are challenged to apply these timeless principles in our modern contexts, navigating the complexities of diverse cultures and ever-evolving societal landscapes.

One of the central challenges lies in bridging the gap between the miraculous events of Elisha's era and the perceived limitations of our present reality. How can we reconcile the extraordinary healings and divine interventions witnessed by Elisha with the constraints and rationalities of modern life? The solution, paradoxically, lies in embracing the enduring power of faith while simultaneously employing wisdom and discernment in our approach.

Elisha's example teaches us that genuine faith in the divine transcends the boundaries of time and circumstance. Just as he wielded the mantle of prophetic authority with unwavering conviction, modern spiritual leaders must cultivate a deep and abiding trust in the sovereignty of God. This does not necessitate a rejection of reason or scientific understanding; rather, it calls for a harmonious integration of faith and intellectual inquiry, recognizing the limitations of human knowledge and the vastness of divine wisdom.

Furthermore, Elisha's healings underscore the importance of compassion, empathy, and a holistic approach to leadership. In an era where the mind-body-spirit connection is increasingly recognized, spiritual leaders must embrace a comprehensive understanding of human well-being. This involves not only addressing spiritual needs but also advocating for physical health, emotional support, and environmental stewardship – all facets that were intricately woven into Elisha's ministry.

The implementation of these principles requires a multifaceted strategy, one that harmonizes ancient wisdom with modern sensibilities. Firstly, spiritual leaders must cultivate a deep personal relationship with the divine, nourishing their faith through prayer, contemplation, and the study of sacred texts. This intimate connection serves as the foundation from which their leadership flows, imbuing their words and actions with authenticity and conviction.

Secondly, it is essential to embrace a posture of humility and openness to learning. Just as Elisha humbly obeyed the instructions of his mentor Elijah, modern leaders must remain receptive to wisdom from various sources – be it sacred texts, insights from spiritual elders, or even the revelations of contemporary scholarship and scientific inquiry. This willingness to learn and adapt is crucial in bridging the divide between ancient principles and modern contexts.

Thirdly, spiritual leaders must actively engage in building bridges of understanding and cooperation across diverse communities and belief systems. Elisha's healings transcended cultural and geographic boundaries, reaching individuals from various backgrounds. Similarly, contemporary leaders must strive to foster inclusive environments that celebrate diversity while simultaneously upholding the universal values of compassion, justice, and human dignity.

Potential obstacles in implementing these principles may arise from societal skepticism, cultural biases, or resistance to change. However, these challenges can be navigated through effective communication, ongoing education, and a commitment to leading by example. By embodying the values of humility, empathy, and unwavering faith, spiritual leaders can inspire transformative change and foster environments conducive to holistic healing and personal growth.

The historical successes of faith-based movements and leaders who embraced these principles serve as a testament to their effectiveness. From the civil rights struggles of the 20th century to the ongoing efforts of humanitarian organizations, the power of spiritually grounded leadership has proven instrumental in catalyzing positive change and fostering social cohesion.

While alternative solutions may emphasize purely rational or secular approaches, the lessons from Elisha's ministry remind us that true transformation often requires a synthesis of faith, reason, and compassion. Purely materialistic or dogmatic ideologies may fail to address the profound human yearning for meaning, purpose, and transcendence – elements that are intrinsically woven into the fabric of spiritual leadership.

In conclusion, the lessons derived from Elisha's healing ministry hold profound relevance for modern spiritual leaders. By embracing the enduring power of faith, cultivating compassion and holistic understanding, and fostering inclusive environments, these leaders can navigate the complexities of our modern world while remaining anchored in timeless principles. Through this approach, they can inspire transformative change, promote personal growth, and serve as beacons of hope and healing in a world that yearns for authentic spiritual guidance.

9

———

HEAVENLY ECONOMICS: A DIVINE BLUEPRINT

The Concept of Divine Stewardship

Embarking upon our exploration of divine stewardship, it is essential to grasp the profound depths and implications of this foundational concept. The terms we will define form the bedrock upon which our understanding of heavenly economics rests, guiding us through the intricacies of this divine mandate.

First, let us consider the term "stewardship" itself – a word that hints at a sacred trust bestowed upon us. In the context of heavenly economics, stewardship transcends mere resource management; it represents our role as caretakers entrusted with the manifold blessings of the divine. A steward's responsibility extends beyond personal gain, encompassing a profound obligation to honor and amplify the abundance bestowed upon us.

Next, we turn our attention to the term "divine mandate." This phrase whispers of a calling that emanates from a source greater than ourselves, a summons to align our actions with a higher purpose. It challenges us to transcend our earthly pursuits and recognize the cosmic implications of our role as stewards. The divine mandate serves as a constant reminder that our stewardship is not merely a personal choice but a sacred duty woven into the fabric of creation itself.

As we delve deeper, the concept of "resource management" emerges, a term that may initially conjure images of spreadsheets and financial forecasts. However, in the realm of heavenly economics, resource management takes on a profoundly spiritual dimension. It encompasses the holistic nurturing and cultivation of all that has been entrusted to us – our time, talents, relationships, and environment. Through this lens, resource management becomes a sacred act, an invitation to honor the divine by responsibly tending to the bounties we have received.

Underpinning these concepts is the notion of "biblical principles." These timeless truths, gleaned from the wisdom of sacred texts, serve as a compass, guiding our understanding and application of stewardship. They remind us that our role as stewards is not merely a practical exercise but a sacred calling rooted in the very foundations of our faith. By aligning our actions with these principles, we imbue our stewardship with a deeper sense of purpose and reverence.

Finally, we arrive at the term "heavenly economics." This phrase invites us to look beyond the confines of earthly transactions and embrace a grander vision of divine abundance. In this realm, we recognize that true wealth is not measured by material possessions but by the cultivation of spiritual virtues, the nurturing of relationships, and the responsible management of the resources entrusted to us. Heavenly economics challenges us to redefine our understanding of prosperity, elevating it to a plane where eternal principles intersect with earthly realities.

As we conclude this exploration of terms, we find ourselves standing at the threshold of a profound journey. The concepts we have defined serve as guideposts, illuminating the path ahead and inviting us to embrace our role as stewards with reverence and dedication. As we move forward, these terms will continue to unfold, revealing ever deeper layers of understanding and application, ultimately weaving a tapestry that celebrates the sacred trust bestowed upon us by the divine.

Comparing Earthly and Heavenly Economic Systems

At the heart of our inquiry lies a profound contrast that beckons exploration: the juxtaposition of earthly and heavenly economic systems. On the surface, these two realms may appear vastly divergent, separated by the chasm that divides the temporal and the eternal. Yet, in their intricate interplay, we uncover truths that illuminate the depths of divine wisdom and challenge our understanding of prosperity.

Let us first introduce the entities we shall compare and contrast – the earthly economic system and its heavenly counterpart. The earthly realm, bound by human constructs and finite resources, operates under the principles of scarcity, competition, and self-interest. It is a domain where wealth accumulation and resource allocation are driven by market forces, often resulting in disparities that strain the fabric of society. In contrast, the heavenly economic system represents a divine paradigm, where abundance flows from an infinite source, and resources are distributed with perfect equity and justice. It is a realm governed by the eternal principles of love, generosity, and selflessness, where the needs of all are met without compromising the well-being of any.

In our exploration, we shall examine several key attributes that distinguish these two systems, including resource allocation, wealth distribution, and societal impact. As we delve into these aspects, we will uncover both striking similarities and profound differences, each offering insights into the nature of prosperity and the divine mandate bestowed upon us as stewards.

Resource allocation, a pivotal aspect of any economic system, presents a compelling contrast. In the earthly realm, resources are often allocated based on market forces, driven by supply and demand. This approach, while efficient in certain contexts, can lead to inequities and imbalances, with some individuals or nations amassing disproportionate wealth while others struggle to meet their basic needs. In contrast, the heavenly economic system operates on the principle of divine provision, where resources are distributed according to need, ensuring that all are sustained and nurtured without scarcity or want.

Another striking difference emerges in the realm of wealth distribution. Earthly economies are often plagued by disparities, where a small percentage of the population controls a disproportionate share of wealth, while the majority struggles to attain financial security. This imbalance can breed resentment, social unrest, and a perpetuation of cyclical poverty. In the heavenly economy, however, wealth is distributed equitably, not based on individual merit or circumstance, but on the foundational principle of divine love and justice. Each individual is endowed with the resources necessary to thrive, fostering a harmonious society built on mutual support and shared prosperity.

The societal impact of these contrasting systems is equally profound. Earthly economic systems, driven by competition and self-interest, can breed a culture of individualism, where personal gain takes precedence over the collective well-being. This mindset can erode social cohesion and inhibit the pursuit of common goals. In contrast, the heavenly economic system cultivates a sense of unity and interdependence, where each individual's success is inextricably linked to the success of the whole. This fosters a society built on collaboration, empathy, and a shared commitment to the flourishing of all.

Yet, amidst these stark differences, we also uncover resonant similarities that echo the divine wisdom woven into both realms. At the core of both systems lies the principle of stewardship – the sacred trust bestowed upon us to manage and cultivate the resources entrusted to our care. Whether in the earthly or heavenly realm, we are called to nurture and amplify the abundance bestowed upon us, ensuring that it serves a greater purpose beyond our individual needs.

Furthermore, both systems extol the virtues of responsibility, diligence, and prudence. In the earthly economic realm, these qualities are essential for sustained growth and prosperity, safeguarding against waste and mismanagement. Similarly, in the heavenly economy, they are indispensable for honoring the divine mandate, ensuring that the resources we steward are utilized in a manner that brings glory to their source and benefits to all.

As we delve deeper into the implications of these similarities and differences, we are confronted with profound insights that resonate across both realms. The disparities and inequities inherent in earthly economic systems serve as a poignant reminder of the consequences of misaligned priorities and the pursuit of self-interest at the expense of the greater good. They underscore the need for a realignment with divine principles, where the welfare of the collective supersedes individual gain, and resources are managed with a sense of sacred responsibility.

Conversely, the abundance and equity that characterize the heavenly economic system challenge us to reimagine our understanding of prosperity. It invites us to transcend the narrow confines of material wealth and embrace a holistic vision of flourishing – one that encompasses spiritual fulfillment, harmonious relationships, and a deep reverence for the divine source of all abundance. This paradigm shift has the potential to transform not only our economic practices but also our collective consciousness, ushering in an era of true prosperity rooted in divine principles.

As we grapple with these revelations, it becomes increasingly evident that the comparison between earthly and heavenly economic systems is not merely an academic exercise but a profound exploration of our purpose and the divine mandate that shapes our role as stewards. By understanding the contrasts and embracing the resonant truths found in both realms, we can forge a path that harmonizes our earthly endeavors with heavenly principles, creating a world where abundance and equity coexist, and the collective well-being of all is the ultimate measure of prosperity.

In our contemporary context, these insights hold profound relevance. The challenges faced by modern economies – from income inequality and resource depletion to environmental degradation and social unrest – can be traced, in part, to a misalignment with divine principles. By embracing the lessons gleaned from our comparison, we can chart a course toward a more equitable and sustainable economic paradigm, one that honors the sacred trust of stewardship while recognizing the interconnectedness of all life.

Furthermore, the contrast between earthly and heavenly economic systems invites us to reevaluate our personal priorities and actions. As individuals, we are called to embody the principles of stewardship, nurturing the resources entrusted to our care with a sense of sacred responsibility. Whether in our professional pursuits, financial decisions, or everyday choices, we have the opportunity to align our actions with heavenly principles, fostering a culture of generosity, compassion, and a shared commitment to the well-being of all.

In conclusion, our exploration of earthly and heavenly economic systems has revealed profound truths that transcend mere financial transactions. It has illuminated the divine mandate that underpins our role as stewards and challenged us to redefine our understanding of true prosperity. By embracing the wisdom found in both realms, we can forge a path that harmonizes our earthly endeavors with heavenly principles, creating a world where abundance and equity coexist, and the collective well-being of all is the ultimate measure of success.

Scriptural Foundations of Economic Justice

As we embark on this journey to unravel the scriptural foundations of economic justice, it is imperative that we define and understand certain key terms and concepts that will guide our discourse. These terms are not merely abstract ideas but powerful lenses through which we can gain a deeper appreciation of the divine blueprint for a just and equitable economic order.

Let us begin with the concept of "economic justice" itself. Often, this term is reduced to a narrow understanding of fair wages and equitable resource distribution. However, as we shall explore, economic justice is a multifaceted principle that encompasses not only material well-being but also spiritual flourishing and the collective betterment of society.

Another term that demands our attention is "stewardship." This concept, deeply rooted in scriptural teachings, challenges us to transcend the notion of mere ownership and embrace a sacred responsibility toward the resources entrusted to our care.

Stewardship invites us to view ourselves as custodians of divine abundance, called upon to nurture and multiply it for the benefit of all.

Closely intertwined with stewardship is the concept of "abundance." In the realm of divine economics, abundance is not a finite resource to be hoarded or guarded, but rather an ever-flowing stream emanating from the inexhaustible source of divine providence. This understanding beckons us to adopt a mindset of generosity and trust, recognizing that true prosperity lies not in accumulation but in the responsible and equitable distribution of resources.

As we delve deeper into the scriptural foundations of economic justice, we will encounter the term "righteousness." Often misunderstood as mere moral rectitude, righteousness in the context of economic systems encompasses a holistic commitment to justice, equity, and the uplifting of the marginalized. It is a call to action, challenging us to align our economic practices with divine principles and to create systems that promote the flourishing of all.

Another concept that will guide our exploration is that of "shalom." Derived from Hebrew scriptures, shalom is a multidimensional term that encompasses not only peace but also wholeness, completeness, and the restoration of right relationships – not just between individuals, but also between humanity and the divine, and between humanity and the natural world. In the realm of economic justice, shalom invites us to consider the interconnectedness of all aspects of life and to strive for systems that promote holistic well-being and harmony.

As we unpack these terms and concepts, we will draw upon diverse scriptural examples and interpretations, each offering unique insights and perspectives. From the Old Testament narratives that champion the cause of the poor and the oppressed to the teachings of Jesus that challenge the idolatry of wealth and advocate for radical generosity, we will uncover a rich tapestry of divine wisdom that illuminates the path toward economic justice.

Moreover, we will explore the historical and cultural contexts in which these scriptures were revealed, shedding light on the societal norms and economic realities that shaped their messaging. By understanding the specific challenges and injustices that these sacred texts sought to address, we can better appreciate their enduring relevance and apply their teachings to our contemporary economic landscape.

As we progress through this journey, we will not merely catalog scriptural passages but engage in a thoughtful examination of their implications for our modern economic systems. We will explore practical applications and propose transformative solutions that align with the divine principles of justice, equity, and responsible stewardship. In doing so, we will champion a vision of economic prosperity that transcends mere material abundance and embraces the holistic well-being of individuals, communities, and the natural world.

Ultimately, by unearthing the scriptural foundations of economic justice, we will gain a profound appreciation for the divine mandate that calls us to be agents of change – stewards of abundance and champions of equity. We will be equipped with the wisdom and inspiration to reshape our economic paradigms, creating systems that foster justice, promote shared prosperity, and honor the sacred trust bestowed upon us to be faithful caretakers of the divine abundance that sustains all life.

The Role of Faith in Economic Prosperity

How does faith influence economic prosperity?

This question lies at the intersection of two seemingly disparate realms – the spiritual and the material. Yet, as we shall explore, the profound impact of faith extends far beyond the confines of personal belief, permeating the very fabric of economic systems and shaping the collective well-being of societies.

Throughout human history, faith traditions have played a pivotal role in shaping economic thought and practices. Whether it is the biblical injunctions against usury and the promotion of debt forgiveness, or the Islamic principles of zakat and the prohibition of riba, these teachings have sought to establish a moral framework for economic interactions, emphasizing justice, compassion, and the alleviation of poverty.

However, the relationship between faith and economic prosperity is not without its complexities. On one hand, some would argue that the accumulation of wealth and the pursuit of prosperity can lead to a distortion of spiritual values, fostering greed, materialism, and a detachment from the deeper purposes of human existence. This perspective views faith and economic prosperity as being in inherent tension, with the latter posing a threat to the former.

On the other hand, others contend that faith can be a powerful catalyst for economic prosperity, inspiring individuals and communities to cultivate virtues such as diligence, integrity, and a commitment to ethical conduct – qualities that are essential for building thriving economies rooted in trust and mutual respect.

Amidst these divergent viewpoints, a common pitfall is to embrace a reductionist approach, either glorifying wealth as the ultimate measure of prosperity or demonizing it as an obstacle to spiritual fulfillment. However, such extremes fail to capture the nuances of this complex relationship and overlook the inherent potential for faith to serve as a guiding force in the pursuit of holistic prosperity – a state of being that transcends mere material abundance and encompasses the flourishing of individuals, communities, and the natural world.

To navigate this intricate landscape, we must embrace a novel perspective – one that recognizes the essential role of faith in shaping economic prosperity while simultaneously acknowledging the inherent challenges and temptations that accompany material wealth. This perspective is rooted in the understanding that true prosperity is not merely the accumulation of riches but the responsible stewardship of resources for the betterment of society and the promotion of human dignity.

Consider the example of the Quaker entrepreneurs of the 19th century, whose faith-inspired values of honesty, simplicity, and social responsibility led them to establish successful businesses while simultaneously investing in the welfare of their employees and communities. Their approach demonstrated that economic prosperity and spiritual principles need not be at odds; rather, they can be harmoniously integrated, fostering a virtuous cycle of material abundance and ethical conduct.

Similarly, the faith-based microfinance initiatives that have emerged in recent decades offer a compelling model for leveraging spiritual principles to empower marginalized communities. By providing access to small loans and financial education, these initiatives not only foster economic self-sufficiency but also cultivate a sense of dignity, community, and spiritual purpose – essential ingredients for sustainable prosperity.

Yet, as we celebrate these examples, we must also confront the skepticism that may arise from those who have witnessed the perversion of faith for personal gain or the exploitation of economic systems to entrench inequalities. To address such valid concerns, we must acknowledge the historical instances where religious institutions and leaders have fallen short of their sacred mandates, using their influence to accumulate wealth and power at the expense of the marginalized.

However, instead of dismissing the potential of faith to contribute to economic prosperity, we must recognize these failures as deviations from the core principles of justice, compassion, and responsible stewardship that lie at the heart of most faith traditions. By reclaiming and upholding these principles, we can forge a path toward economic prosperity that is rooted in spiritual wisdom, while safeguarding against the corrupting influence of greed and exploitation.

To this end, the journey toward economic prosperity guided by faith begins with a deep commitment to personal transformation. It requires individuals to cultivate virtues such as humility, selflessness, and a willingness to transcend narrow self-interest for the greater good. It demands that we confront the insidious tendencies of greed and materialism within ourselves, recognizing that true prosperity cannot be achieved through the exploitation of others or the despoiling of the natural world.

Furthermore, this journey calls upon us to reimagine our economic systems through the lens of spiritual wisdom, challenging us to create structures and institutions that promote equity, foster human dignity, and honor the sacred trust we hold as stewards of divine abundance. This may involve rethinking our notions of ownership, embracing models of shared prosperity, and prioritizing the regenerative capacity of our economic activities.

Ultimately, by embracing a faith-inspired approach to economic prosperity, we can unlock the transformative potential to create a world where material abundance is not an end in itself but a means to uplift humanity and honor the divine mandate to be caretakers of creation. It is a journey that demands humility, courage, and a willingness to transcend the narrow confines of self-interest, yet it offers the promise of a world where spiritual wisdom and economic prosperity are not at odds but are harmoniously interwoven, fostering a state of holistic well-being for all.

Case Study: The Early Christian Community

In the bustling heart of first-century Jerusalem, a remarkable community took shape – a community driven by an unwavering faith in the teachings of Jesus Christ and a fervent commitment to a radically different way of life. As the nascent Christian movement spread like wildfire through the region, its adherents embraced a novel economic paradigm that challenged the prevailing norms of their time.

The early Christian community, led by the apostles and guided by the wisdom of the Holy Spirit, recognized the profound social implications of Christ's message. In a world rife with inequality and exploitation, they sought to create a society rooted in the principles of love, compassion, and solidarity – principles that extended far beyond the spiritual realm and permeated their economic practices.

One of the most remarkable aspects of this community was its approach to resource distribution and the alleviation of poverty. As described in the Acts of the Apostles, the believers "had everything in common" (Acts 2:44), with those who owned land or houses selling their possessions and distributing the proceeds to those in need. This radical act of generosity was not merely an expression of charity but a fundamental recognition of their shared humanity and a commitment to ensuring that no member of their community was left behind.

The apostle Peter, a central figure in this movement, played a pivotal role in upholding this ethos. In his encounter with Ananias and Sapphira, who had deceitfully withheld a portion of their wealth, Peter's stern rebuke underscored the gravity of their transgression. It was not merely a matter of financial impropriety but a violation of the sacred trust that bound the community together – a trust rooted in the understanding that their possessions were not their own but were held in stewardship for the common good.

This radical economic model posed a significant challenge in a world where the accumulation of wealth and the preservation of private property were deeply entrenched values. Yet, the early Christians persisted, driven by their unwavering faith and a conviction that their actions were a living embodiment of the kingdom of God on Earth.

The results of this divinely inspired approach were nothing short of remarkable. Historical accounts paint a picture of a vibrant community characterized by an unprecedented level of unity, generosity, and mutual care. The distribution of resources ensured that the needs of the most vulnerable were met, fostering a sense of dignity and belonging that transcended socioeconomic boundaries. Moreover, this economic model served as a powerful witness to the transformative power of the Christian message, attracting countless converts who were drawn not only by the spiritual teachings but also by the tangible manifestation of a just and compassionate society.

However, the early Christian community's economic practices were not without their critics and detractors. Some viewed their rejection of private property as a threat to the established order, while others dismissed it as an idealistic endeavor doomed to failure in the face of human greed and self-interest.

Yet, in retrospect, we can discern invaluable lessons from this remarkable case study. It demonstrates that faith can indeed be a powerful catalyst for social and economic transformation, inspiring individuals and communities to transcend narrow self-interest and embrace a higher vision of collective well-being. Furthermore, it challenges the prevailing notion that economic prosperity and spiritual values are inherently at odds, offering a tangible example of a society that thrived by integrating these two realms into a cohesive whole.

While critics may argue that the early Christian community's approach is impractical or unsustainable in the modern world, such critiques overlook the enduring relevance of the principles that undergirded their economic model. Principles such as compassion, generosity, and the recognition of our shared humanity remain as relevant today as they were two millennia ago, offering a powerful antidote to the rampant individualism and exploitation that plague contemporary economic systems.

As we grapple with the complexities of economic inequality, environmental degradation, and the erosion of social cohesion, the early Christian community's example serves as a clarion call to reimagine our relationship with wealth and resources. It invites us to embrace a more holistic vision of prosperity – one that transcends mere material abundance and encompasses the flourishing of individuals, communities, and the natural world.

In this light, the lessons from the early Christian community are not mere relics of a bygone era but living, breathing reminders of our capacity to build a more just and sustainable economic order – an order rooted in the timeless wisdom of faith and the boundless potential of human solidarity. As we navigate the challenges of our time, may we draw inspiration from this remarkable case study, and may it embolden us to forge a path toward a world where economic prosperity and spiritual enlightenment are not at odds but are harmoniously interwoven, fostering a state of holistic well-being for all.

The Principle of Jubilee in Modern Context

The ancient principle of Jubilee, as described in the Book of Leviticus, stands as a striking testament to the enduring relevance of economic justice and social equity. This divinely ordained practice, which called for the periodic redistribution of wealth and the restoration of economic equilibrium, challenged the prevailing norms of inequality and exploitation that plagued ancient societies.

At its core, the Jubilee principle recognized the inherent interconnectedness of humanity and sought to mitigate the accumulation of excessive wealth and power in the hands of a privileged few. It acknowledged that the resources of the Earth were a shared inheritance, entrusted to humankind as stewards rather than as possessors. By mandating the cancellation of debts, the return of alienated lands, and the liberation of indentured servants every fifty years, the Jubilee sought to rectify the systemic imbalances that inevitably arose from the accumulation of wealth and the concentration of economic power.

While the ancient societies that embraced this practice may have differed vastly from our contemporary world, the fundamental issues it sought to address resonate profoundly with the challenges we face today. Economic inequality, environmental degradation, and the persistent cycles of debt and poverty that afflict both individuals and nations are all manifestations of the same underlying malady – a disconnect between our economic systems and the principles of justice, sustainability, and shared responsibility.

The challenge, then, is to reimagine the principle of Jubilee in a modern context, adapting its core tenets to the complexities of our globalized economy while preserving its essence of promoting economic equity, environmental stewardship, and social cohesion.

One potential approach to this endeavor is the establishment of a global economic reset mechanism, akin to the ancient Jubilee, but tailored to the realities of the 21st century. This mechanism could take the form of a coordinated, multilateral effort to address the systemic issues plaguing our economic systems, such as unsustainable debt burdens, resource depletion, and the concentration of wealth and power in the hands of a few.

The implementation of such a mechanism would require a profound paradigm shift, necessitating the collaboration of governments, international institutions, civil society organizations, and the private sector. It would involve the development of a comprehensive framework that addresses the multifaceted nature of economic injustice, encompassing debt restructuring, wealth redistribution, environmental restoration, and the promotion of equitable access to resources and opportunities.

One key aspect of this modern Jubilee could be the establishment of a global debt relief program, designed to alleviate the crippling debt burdens that hinder the economic development and self-determination of nations. By providing a pathway to debt cancellation or restructuring, coupled with measures to prevent the accumulation of unsustainable debt in the future, this program would empower nations to invest in their people, infrastructure, and long-term economic resilience.

Furthermore, a modern Jubilee could incorporate mechanisms for the redistribution of wealth and the restoration of economic equilibrium. This could involve progressive taxation policies, designed to curb excessive wealth accumulation and channel resources toward initiatives that promote shared prosperity and environmental sustainability. Additionally, land reform initiatives and the protection of indigenous land rights could help rectify historical injustices and promote equitable access to natural resources.

Undoubtedly, the implementation of such a far-reaching and transformative agenda would face significant obstacles. Entrenched interests, political inertia, and the sheer complexity of coordinating global efforts could pose formidable challenges. However, by drawing upon the wisdom of diverse stakeholders, fostering international cooperation, and cultivating a shared sense of purpose, these obstacles can be surmounted.

The potential outcomes of a successful modern Jubilee are nothing short of profound. By addressing the root causes of economic inequality, environmental degradation, and social fragmentation, we could usher in a new era of sustainable prosperity, where the fruits of human endeavor are equitably shared, and the bonds of global solidarity are strengthened.

Moreover, the implementation of such a visionary agenda would serve as a powerful testament to our capacity for collective action and our commitment to the principles of justice and compassion that transcend borders and ideologies. Just as the ancient Jubilee served as a beacon of hope for the oppressed and marginalized, a modern iteration could reignite the flame of collective responsibility and inspire a renewed commitment to building a more equitable and sustainable world.

While alternative solutions may be proposed, such as piecemeal reforms or incremental adjustments to existing economic systems, these approaches risk perpetuating the underlying structural flaws that have given rise to the current challenges. A bold and comprehensive vision, inspired by the timeless wisdom of the Jubilee principle, offers a more holistic and transformative pathway toward a truly just and sustainable global economy.

As we navigate the complexities of our time, the principle of Jubilee stands as a poignant reminder of our collective responsibility to steward the Earth's resources with wisdom and compassion. By embracing its spirit and adapting its tenets to the modern context, we can forge a new economic paradigm – one that honors the inherent dignity of all people, respects the limits of our planetary resources, and fosters a world of shared prosperity and mutual flourishing.

Tithing: A Divine Economic Mechanism

In the ancient annals of divine wisdom, an intriguing economic practice emerges – the principle of tithing. At first glance, the act of voluntarily giving a tenth of one's earnings or possessions might seem counterintuitive to the pursuit of prosperity. Yet, upon deeper reflection, tithing serves as a profound reminder of the intrinsic interconnectedness that binds humanity and the divine, a sacred act that transcends mere financial transactions.

Tithing, in its most fundamental form, is the act of setting aside a portion of one's resources – typically a tenth – as an offering to a higher power or for a sacred purpose. This simple definition, however, belies the profound depth and multifaceted nature of this practice. Tithing is a physical, spiritual, and economic mechanism that harmonizes the material and spiritual realms, fostering a sense of gratitude, accountability and shared responsibility.

At its core, tithing is an acknowledgment that true abundance is not merely the accumulation of wealth but a recognition of our role as stewards of the Earth's resources. It is a tangible expression of humility, an affirmation that our blessings and prosperity are not solely the fruits of our individual efforts, but rather a testament to the intricate web of natural, social, and divine forces that sustain our existence. By willingly surrendering a portion of our earnings, we honor our place within this grand tapestry and express gratitude for the gifts bestowed upon us.

The practice of tithing finds its origins in the ancient civilizations of the Near East, where it was deeply woven into the fabric of religious and cultural life. In the biblical tradition, tithing is first mentioned in the Book of Genesis, where Abraham, the patriarch of faith, offers a tenth of his spoils to the priest Melchizedek. Throughout the narrative, tithing emerges as a recurring theme, with the Israelites commanded to set aside a portion of their agricultural yield and livestock for the support of the Levitical priesthood and the maintenance of sacred spaces.

Beyond its religious roots, tithing has also played a significant role in shaping the economic structures of various societies. In ancient civilizations, tithes provided a crucial source of funding for religious institutions, educational endeavors, and the care of the underprivileged. This redistribution of wealth helped mitigate the concentration of resources in the hands of a few, fostering a sense of collective responsibility and social cohesion.

In modern times, the practice of tithing has transcended its religious boundaries and has been embraced by various communities and organizations as a means of supporting charitable causes, educational initiatives, and community development projects. From churches and synagogues to secular non-profit organizations, tithing has become a powerful tool for mobilizing resources and fostering a culture of giving and shared prosperity.

Yet, tithing is not without its critics and misconceptions. Some view it as an antiquated practice, a relic of a bygone era when religious institutions held sway over economic affairs. Others perceive it as a form of coercion, a means of extracting wealth from the faithful under the guise of spiritual obligation. However, these criticisms often stem from a narrow perspective that fails to capture the essence of tithing as a voluntary act of conscious participation in the tapestry of life.

To fully appreciate the significance of tithing, one must recognize its role as a divine economic mechanism that transcends mere financial transactions. Tithing is a recognition of our interconnectedness, a means of fostering a sense of responsibility and stewardship. By voluntarily contributing a portion of our resources, we acknowledge that our prosperity is inextricably linked to the well-being of those around us and the sustainability of the natural world that sustains us.

Moreover, tithing serves as a powerful antidote to the insidious allure of greed and the relentless pursuit of material wealth. In a world where the accumulation of riches is often equated with success and happiness, tithing reminds us that true fulfillment lies not in the acquisition of possessions but in the cultivation of a spirit of generosity and compassion. By willingly surrendering a portion of our earnings, we free ourselves from the shackles of insatiable desire and embrace the liberating truth that true abundance is found in the act of sharing and contributing to the greater good.

Beyond its spiritual and economic dimensions, tithing also holds profound psychological and sociological implications. The act of giving, whether in the form of monetary contributions or voluntary service, has been shown to foster a sense of purpose, enhance well-being, and strengthen social bonds. By participating in the act of tithing, individuals and communities alike cultivate a sense of collective responsibility and shared destiny, transcending the boundaries of race, creed, and socioeconomic status.

In a world grappling with the challenges of economic inequality, environmental degradation, and social fragmentation, the principle of tithing offers a compelling paradigm for fostering sustainability, equity, and community resilience. By embracing the spirit of tithing, individuals and organizations can contribute to the creation of a more just and harmonious economic landscape, one that recognizes the inherent worth and dignity of all people and the sacred duty of stewardship over the Earth's resources.

As we navigate the complexities of the modern era, the ancient wisdom embodied in the practice of tithing serves as a poignant reminder of our shared responsibility and the interconnectedness that binds us all. By embracing this divine economic mechanism, we can forge a path toward a more sustainable, equitable, and spiritually fulfilling future, honoring the sacred threads that interweave our material and spiritual existence.

Heavenly Governance and Economic Policies

The intersection of divine guidance and economic policymaking is a profound realm, one that invites us to explore the depth and breadth of our existence. As we delve into this intricate tapestry, it becomes evident that the principles of heavenly governance offer a wellspring of wisdom, a framework that harmonizes the material and spiritual realms, fostering prosperity and justice in equal measure.

At the heart of this investigation lies the assertion that divine governance provides an ideal foundation for economic policies that transcend mere financial calculations and embrace a holistic vision of human flourishing. This claim is not born of blind faith or dogmatic adherence, but rather rooted in the timeless truths and insights gleaned from sacred texts, theological studies, and the lived experiences of countless individuals and communities throughout history.

The primary evidence for this assertion emanates from the very wellspring of divine revelation itself – the sacred scriptures revered across the world's major religions. From the Old Testament's exhortations to care for the poor and the needy, to the Qur'an's emphasis on equitable distribution and the prohibition of usury, to the Buddhist teachings on the impermanence of material possessions and the virtues of non-attachment, these ancient texts offer a treasure trove of wisdom that can inform and guide our economic practices.

Consider, for instance, the biblical concept of the Jubilee, a cyclical event in which all debts were forgiven, indentured servants were freed, and land ownership was redistributed. This radical economic mechanism not only provided a safety net for the impoverished and a reset button for the accumulation of wealth, but it also embodied the profound principle of divine sovereignty over all resources – a recognition that the Earth and its bounty ultimately belong to the Creator, and that we are mere stewards entrusted with their care and equitable distribution.

While some may dismiss these scriptural accounts as mere allegories or relics of antiquity, their enduring resonance across cultures and civilizations testifies to their universal relevance and the inherent human yearning for justice, compassion, and spiritual fulfillment. Moreover, the credibility of these sources is bolstered by the vast body of theological scholarship and exegesis that has delved into their depths, extracting timeless principles and illuminating their practical applications in the realm of economics and governance.

Yet, in the spirit of impartiality and intellectual rigor, we must acknowledge the existence of counter-evidence and dissenting voices. Critics may argue that relying on religious texts as the basis for economic policies is inherently divisive, as it risks privileging the beliefs of certain faiths over others or imposing a particular worldview on a pluralistic society. Others may contend that the scriptural injunctions, while noble in their intent, are ill-suited for the complexities of modern economic systems and the globalized nature of trade and finance.

However, these objections can be addressed and reinforced by the very principles they seek to challenge. The essence of divine governance is not the imposition of dogma or the suppression of diversity, but rather the cultivation of universal values that transcend the boundaries of creed and culture. Concepts such as justice, compassion, stewardship, and the recognition of our shared humanity are woven into the fabric of every major faith tradition, and it is these universal ideals that can serve as the foundation for a harmonious and equitable economic order.

Moreover, the evidence-based analysis of these principles and their practical applications in various historical and contemporary contexts serves to validate their relevance and adaptability. From the Islamic system of zakat (obligatory alms) and its role in fostering social welfare and economic redistribution to the Judeo-Christian principles of the just wage and their influence on labor movements to the Buddhist concept of "right livelihood" and its emphasis on ethical business practices, the legacy of divine governance in shaping economic realities is undeniable.

Further evidence can be found in the numerous faith-based organizations and initiatives that have leveraged the power of religious principles to address economic challenges and promote sustainable development. The microfinance revolution, for instance, which has empowered millions of entrepreneurs and lifted communities out of poverty, draws inspiration from the Islamic prohibition of usury and the emphasis on equitable access to capital. Similarly, the growing movement toward ethical and socially responsible investing, which considers the environmental and social impact of businesses alongside financial returns, resonates with the divine call for stewardship and the harmonious integration of material and spiritual concerns.

The practical applications of these findings extend far beyond the realm of theory or historical curiosity. By embracing the principles of heavenly governance in economic policymaking, we can chart a course toward a more just, equitable, and sustainable economic landscape. Imagine an economic system that prioritizes the well-being of all stakeholders, not merely the accumulation of profits; one that recognizes the inherent dignity of labor and the importance of fair compensation; one that seeks to strike a balance between individual enterprise and collective responsibility, fostering an environment where both personal initiative and social solidarity can thrive.

In such a framework, the pursuit of prosperity is not divorced from ethical and spiritual considerations, but rather infused with a deeper sense of purpose – a recognition that economic activities are not mere ends in themselves but means to a greater end: the cultivation of human flourishing in all its dimensions, material and spiritual. By aligning our economic policies with the timeless wisdom of divine governance, we can forge a path toward a society that honors the sacred bonds of our shared humanity, nurtures the Earth's resources with reverence and care, and unleashes the boundless potential of human creativity and ingenuity in service of the greater good.

Principles of Generosity and Charity

As we embark on exploring the profound principles of generosity and charity, we encounter concepts that hold the power to reshape our understanding of economic systems and human interactions. To fully comprehend their significance, we must delve into the depths of their meaning and unravel the nuances that make them indispensable pillars of a divinely guided economic order.

Let us begin by acknowledging the gravity of the term "generosity." This virtue extends far beyond the mere act of giving; it is a state of being, a mindset that permeates every aspect of our existence. At its core, generosity is the recognition that we are not isolated beings but interconnected threads in the tapestry of life, bound by a shared responsibility to uplift and support one another. It is the antithesis of greed and self-interest, a rejection of the notion that personal gain should come at the expense of others' well-being.

Closely intertwined with generosity is the principle of "charity." While often reduced to the act of donating material resources, true charity encompasses a profound spiritual dimension. It is a manifestation of compassion, a tangible expression of our shared humanity, and our collective duty to alleviate suffering and promote the flourishing of all. Charity transcends the boundaries of faith, culture, or social status, for it recognizes that every human being is imbued with inherent dignity and deserving of respect, care, and support.

To fully grasp the power of these virtues, we must explore their theological foundations and the wisdom imparted by sacred texts. The Holy Qur'an, for instance, exhorts believers to be "among those who spend their wealth by night and by day, secretly and openly, for them their reward is with their Lord, and there shall be no fear upon them, neither shall they grieve" (Qur'an 2:274). This verse not only emphasizes the spiritual rewards of generosity but also underscores the universality of this principle, transcending the boundaries of time and circumstance.

Similarly, the Bible extols the virtue of charity, proclaiming, "There is one who scatters, and yet increases all the more, and there is one who withholds what is justly due, and it results only in want. The generous person will be prosperous, and he who waters will himself be watered" (Proverbs 11:24-25). These words echo the profound truth that generosity and charity are not merely acts of selflessness but investments in collective well-being, ultimately benefiting both the giver and the recipient.

Beyond the realm of sacred texts, the annals of history are replete with examples of individuals and communities who have embodied these principles, leaving an indelible mark on the world. Consider the life of Saint Francis of Assisi, whose radical embrace of poverty and commitment to serving the destitute inspired a movement of compassion and generosity that continues to this day. Or contemplate the legacy of Muhammad Yunus, the pioneering economist who introduced the concept of microfinance, empowering millions to lift themselves out of poverty through small, interest-free loans – a tangible manifestation of the Islamic principle of zakat (obligatory alms).

Yet, the true power of generosity and charity lies not merely in the grand narratives of history but in the countless everyday acts of kindness and selflessness that weave the fabric of our shared humanity. It is the neighbor who offers a warm meal to a family in need, the volunteer who dedicates their time and energy to serving the homeless, or the anonymous donor who contributes to a worthy cause without seeking recognition. These acts, though often unsung, are the heartbeats of a society that embraces the principles of divine governance and the inherent value of every human life.

As we delve deeper into this exploration, it becomes evident that generosity and charity are not merely abstract concepts or idealistic notions; they are practical, actionable principles that hold the potential to transform our economic landscape and foster a more equitable, sustainable, and compassionate world. By embracing these virtues, we not only honor the teachings of our respective faiths but also tap into the wellspring of human potential, unleashing a tide of goodwill and collective empowerment that can uplift entire communities and generations.

In the chapters to come, we will explore practical strategies and steps for embodying these principles, both on an individual and societal level. We will examine the role of education in instilling the values of generosity and charity, and the importance of fostering an environment that celebrates and encourages these virtues. We will delve into the economic and social impact of charitable initiatives, and explore innovative models that harness the power of generosity to drive sustainable development and empower marginalized communities.

Moreover, we will grapple with the challenges and obstacles that often inhibit the full realization of these principles, from the allure of material wealth and the temptations of greed to the systemic inequalities and structural barriers that perpetuate cycles of poverty and deprivation. By confronting these issues head-on, we can forge a path toward a more just and equitable economic order, one that honors the divine call for compassion and stewardship while harnessing the boundless potential of human ingenuity and collaboration.

As we embark on this transformative journey, let us embrace the words of the Prophet Muhammad (peace be upon him), who declared, "Charity does not diminish wealth." This profound truth encapsulates the essence of generosity and charity – the recognition that by giving freely and compassionately, we not only uplift others but also enrich our own lives, cultivating a spirit of abundance and fulfillment that transcends material possessions. It is this spirit, this unwavering commitment to the greater good, that will guide us as we forge a path toward a more just, equitable, and divinely inspired economic order.

10

THE ABOLITION OF DEATH: A THEOLOGICAL MILESTONE

The Nature of Death: Biblical Perspectives

To lay the groundwork for our exploration of death's theological significance, we must first understand the nuances of certain key terms and concepts that have shaped the biblical perspective on this profound subject. By unpacking the origins and implications of these terms, we can gain a deeper appreciation for the intricate tapestry of meaning woven throughout the sacred scriptures.

Let us begin with the intriguing concept of "Sheol." This Hebrew term, often translated as "grave" or "pit," carries a haunting connotation that extends beyond the physical realm. Sheol is depicted in the Old Testament as a shadowy underworld, a realm of darkness and silence where the souls of the deceased reside, detached from the living and the divine. It is a place of absence, a void where the vibrancy of life is extinguished, leaving only a lingering echo of existence. Yet, the portrayal of Sheol is not one of torment or punishment; rather, it is a state of mere existence, a holding place for the departed souls awaiting their ultimate fate.

In contrast, the New Testament introduces the Greek term "Hades," which bears striking similarities to its Hebrew counterpart, yet with subtle distinctions. Like Sheol, Hades is depicted as a gloomy abode of the dead, a realm separate from the living and the divine. However, in the Christian tradition, Hades takes on a more ominous tone, often associated with the concept of punishment and the separation of the righteous from the wicked. It is a place of reckoning, where the consequences of one's earthly choices are laid bare, and the weight of one's actions is felt in the absence of divine grace.

Perhaps the most chilling term associated with death in the biblical canon is "Gehenna." Derived from the Hebrew "Ge Hinnom," a valley outside Jerusalem where pagan sacrifices were once offered, Gehenna represents the epitome of divine judgment and the ultimate consequence of sin. It is a place of unquenchable fire and eternal torment, a vivid metaphor for the utter separation from God and the eternal anguish that awaits those who reject the path of righteousness. The imagery of Gehenna is one of the most potent and haunting depictions of death's finality, a somber reminder of the gravity of our choices and the imperative to align our lives with the divine will.

Yet, within the tapestry of these terms, a glimmer of hope emerges – the promise of redemption and the conquest of death itself. Through the sacrificial act of Christ, the finality of death is shattered, and a new reality is ushered in – one where the sting of death is rendered powerless, and the promise of eternal life is extended to those who embrace the divine plan of salvation. The concepts of "resurrection" and "eternal life" become the antidotes to the darkness of Sheol, Hades, and Gehenna, offering a path toward transcendence and the ultimate triumph of life over death.

As we delve deeper into the theological implications of these terms, we will uncover the profound wisdom and nuanced perspectives that have shaped the biblical understanding of death. By examining the rich tapestry of symbolism and metaphor woven throughout the scriptures, we will gain insights into the human condition, the nature of divine justice, and the ultimate destiny that awaits us beyond the veil of mortality. This foundational knowledge will serve as a guiding light as we explore the transformative power of Christ's ministry and the promise of the abolition of death, ushering in a new era of eternal life and fulfillment in the presence of the divine.

The Fall of Man: Original Sin and Mortality

To fully comprehend the theological significance of the abolition of death, we must first journey to the very beginning, where the origins of human mortality are rooted. This exploration will follow a historical timeline, tracing the threads of the biblical narrative that have shaped our understanding of the inextricable link between sin and death.

1. The Dawn of Creation: Genesis 2 paints a vivid picture of the Garden of Eden, a pristine realm where humanity dwells in harmony with the divine. In this idyllic state, death was an alien concept, for the first humans, Adam and Eve, were created to exist in eternal communion with their Creator. Their lives were not bound by the confines of mortality; rather, they were designed to transcend the limitations of the physical realm and partake in the eternal essence of the divine.

2. The Temptation and the Fall: Genesis 3 marks a pivotal moment in the human narrative, the moment when the seeds of mortality were sown. Enticed by the serpent's cunning words, Eve transgressed the divine command, and Adam followed suit. This act of disobedience shattered the sacred bond between humanity and the Creator, rupturing the state of eternal life they had enjoyed. God's decree, "for dust you are and to dust you will return" (Genesis 3:19), echoed the cosmic consequence of their transgression – the introduction of death into the human experience.

3. The Ripple Effect of Sin: • The expulsion from Eden (Genesis 3:23-24) symbolized humanity's exile from the realm of eternal life, forced to toil in a world marred by the

stain of sin and the inevitability of death. • The concept of "the wages of sin is death" (Romans 6:23) became a central tenet, underscoring the inextricable link between humanity's disobedience and the advent of mortality. • The loss of direct communion with God and the corruption of human nature further amplified the grip of death, as humanity's spiritual essence became tarnished and susceptible to the ravages of sin.

4. The Global Deluge: The narrative of Noah's Ark (Genesis 6-9) illustrates the pervasive nature of sin and its consequences on a cosmic scale. The great flood served as a purging of the corrupted world, yet even in this cataclysmic event, the seeds of mortality remained embedded in the human condition, as the remnants of humanity emerged to repopulate the earth with the same inherent flaw that had brought about their near annihilation.

5. The Abrahamic Covenant: In the midst of this bleak narrative, a glimmer of hope emerged. God's covenant with Abraham (Genesis 12:1-3) promised the ultimate restoration of humanity's relationship with the divine, a foreshadowing of the redemptive plan that would one day conquer the curse of death. This covenant set the stage for the unfolding of God's grand narrative, where the abolition of death would become the culmination of a divine promise.

6. The Evolution of Sin and Death in Human History: As humanity spread across the globe, the theological interpretations of sin and death took on diverse forms, reflecting the diverse cultural and religious landscapes. From the ancient Egyptian concept of the afterlife to the Greek and Roman mythologies that grappled with the inevitability of mortality, the human experience was indelibly marked by the quest to comprehend and transcend the limitations imposed by death.

7. The Pivotal Moment: The arrival of Christ heralded a seismic shift in the divine narrative. Through his sacrifice

on the cross and subsequent resurrection, the shackles of sin and death were forever broken. The finality of mortality was challenged, and the promise of eternal life was extended to all who embraced the redemptive power of Christ's ministry. This pivotal event reshaped the theological landscape, offering humanity a path to transcend the curse of the Fall and reclaim the essence of eternal life that had been lost in Eden.

From the pristine splendor of the Garden to the cosmic battle between sin and redemption, the biblical account of the Fall and its aftermath sets the stage for the ultimate triumph over death. Through this historical timeline, we witness the unfolding of a grand narrative, where the consequences of human transgression are met with the divine plan of restoration and the promise of eternal life. It is within this rich tapestry of sin, mortality, and redemption that the true significance of Christ's abolition of death takes root, offering humanity the hope of transcending the limitations of the physical realm and rekindling the eternal communion with the divine that was once lost.

Christ's Sacrifice: The Defeat of Death

The events surrounding the life, death, and resurrection of Jesus Christ stand as the pinnacle of the grand narrative that unfolds in the biblical scriptures. Through his sacrificial act on the cross, Christ not only defeated sin but also abolished the ultimate consequence of sin – death itself. This profound theological milestone ushered in a transformative shift in the human existential trajectory, forever altering the destiny of those who place their faith in Christ's redemptive work.

1. The Evidence-Based Approach

To fully grasp the magnitude of Christ's triumph over death, we must examine the evidence presented within the sacred texts and through the lens of historical and contemporary Christian thought.

This evidence-based approach not only solidifies our understanding but also unveils the profound implications that reverberate through the ages.

2. The Scriptural Proclamation: Christ's Victory over Death

The New Testament scriptures boldly declare the victory of Christ over the power of death. In 1 Corinthians 15:54-57, the apostle Paul proclaims:

"When the perishable has been clothed with the imperishable, and the mortal with immortality, then the saying that is written will come true: 'Death has been swallowed up in victory.' 'Where, O death, is your victory? Where, O death, is your sting?' The sting of death is sin, and the power of sin is the law. But thanks be to God! He gives us the victory through our Lord Jesus Christ."

This passage stands as a resounding testimony to the transformative power of Christ's sacrifice. Through his death and resurrection, Jesus conquered the sting of death – sin – and broke the shackles of mortality that had bound humanity since the Fall. The evidence of his victory lies in the eyewitness accounts recorded in the Gospels, where the resurrected Christ appeared to his disciples, tangible and alive, having triumphed over the grave.

3. The Credibility of the Evidence

The historical evidence for the events surrounding Christ's crucifixion and resurrection is robust and well-documented. The Gospels, written by eyewitnesses or those who meticulously compiled eyewitness accounts, provide detailed narratives of the events leading up to and following the Crucifixion. These accounts are corroborated by nonbiblical sources, such as the writings of the Jewish historian Josephus and the Roman historian Tacitus, lending credibility to the existence of Jesus and the impact of his ministry.

Furthermore, the widespread acceptance of Christianity, despite the threat of persecution, serves as compelling evidence for the transformative power of the Resurrection event. The willingness of the early followers of Christ to endure suffering and martyrdom for their belief in the risen Savior attests to the veracity of their claims and the profound impact this event had on their lives.

4. The Contradiction: The Enduring Reality of Physical Death

While Christ's victory over death is undeniable, the physical reality of mortality persists in the world. Believers and non-believers alike face the inevitability of physical death, seemingly contradicting the notion of Christ's triumph. However, this apparent contradiction finds its resolution in the theological understanding of Christ's sacrifice.

The abolition of death accomplished by Christ is not a temporary reprieve from physical demise but rather a complete and eternal victory over the ultimate consequence of sin – spiritual separation from God. Through his sacrifice, Christ opened the way for humanity to be reconciled with the divine, restoring the possibility of eternal life in the presence of the Creator.

5. The Transformative Impact: From Mortality to Eternal Life

The evidence-based understanding of Christ's victory over death ushers in a profound shift in the human existential trajectory. No longer are we bound by the limitations of mortality; instead, we are offered the promise of eternal life through faith in Christ's redeeming work. This promise transcends the physical realm and extends into the spiritual, where the true essence of life finds its fulfillment in an eternal relationship with the divine.

The implications of this transformative impact are far-reaching, infusing every aspect of the Christian experience with a renewed sense of purpose and hope. The fear of death, which has long haunted humanity, is replaced by the assurance of eternal life, empowering believers to live with courage and resilience in the face of adversity.

6. The Theological Significance: A Legacy of Hope

The abolition of death through Christ's sacrifice is a theological milestone that reverberates through the ages, leaving an indelible mark on the Christian faith and its impact on the world. This profound event serves as a beacon of hope, illuminating the path toward reconciliation with the divine and the restoration of the eternal communion that was once lost.

Throughout Christian history, this theological truth has been a wellspring of inspiration, guiding the faithful through times of persecution, grief, and uncertainty. It has shaped the way believers approach life and death, instilling a profound sense of purpose and meaning that transcends the temporary nature of our earthly existence.

Furthermore, the legacy of Christ's triumph over death has inspired countless acts of love, service, and sacrifice, as believers strive to emulate the selfless example set by their Savior. This legacy continues to influence and transform lives, offering a vision of a world where the sting of death has been vanquished and the promise of eternal life reigns supreme.

In conclusion, the evidence-based examination of Christ's sacrificial death and subsequent resurrection reveals a profound theological truth – the abolition of death itself. Through his victory over sin and the grave, Christ has paved the way for humanity to transcend the limitations of mortality and embrace the promise of eternal life. This transformative event stands as a monumental milestone in the Christian faith, reshaping our understanding of existence and infusing our lives with a profound sense of hope and purpose that extends beyond the confines of the temporal realm.

Resurrection: The Foundation of Christian Hope

As we delve into the cornerstone doctrine of resurrection within Christian eschatology, it is crucial to grasp the profound significance of certain terms and concepts that will guide our discourse. These foundational elements, when understood in their entirety, reveal the depth and transformative power of this theological tenet that shapes the Christian worldview.

1. The Resurrection: A Term Brimming with Promise

The very word "resurrection" evokes a sense of awe and wonder, hinting at the extraordinary triumph over the seemingly inescapable grip of mortality. This term carries within it the promise of life triumphing over death, a promise that defies the limitations of our finite existence and points toward the eternal.

To fully grasp the profound implications of resurrection, we must first understand its definition. Resurrection, derived from the Latin "resurgere," meaning "to rise again," refers to the act of restoring life to a deceased being. In the Christian context, it signifies the belief that those who have died will be raised to eternal life, their physical and spiritual natures reunited in a glorified state, free from the limitations and afflictions of the mortal realm.

The concept of resurrection is not merely a metaphorical or symbolic notion; it is a tangible promise rooted in the historical event of Christ's resurrection, which stands as the cornerstone of the Christian faith. This event, attested to by numerous eyewitnesses and documented in the Gospels, serves as irrefutable evidence that death has indeed been conquered, and the promise of eternal life is a reality for those who place their trust in Christ.

2. The Transformative Power of Christ's Resurrection

The resurrection of Jesus Christ from the grave is not only a pivotal historical event but also a transformative force that reverberates through the ages. This miraculous occurrence stands as the ultimate validation of Christ's divinity and the fulfillment of his prophetic mission, shattering the shackles of sin and death that had bound humanity since the Fall.

To comprehend the magnitude of Christ's resurrection, we must first explore the significance of his death on the cross. Through his sacrificial act, Christ took upon himself the penalty for sin, thereby satisfying the divine demand for justice. By willingly submitting to death, he conquered sin's dominion over humanity and paved the way for reconciliation with the divine.

Yet, Christ's triumph did not end with his death; it reached its crescendo in his resurrection from the grave. This miraculous event not only validated his claims of divinity but also demonstrated his power over death itself. Just as sin had brought death into the world, Christ's resurrection ushered in the promise of eternal life for those who place their faith in him.

The transformative power of Christ's resurrection extends far beyond the individual believer; it reshapes the very fabric of human existence. No longer are we bound by the limitations of mortality; instead, we are offered the extraordinary gift of eternal life in the presence of our Creator. This promise instills within the Christian community a profound sense of hope and purpose, transcending the temporal and anchoring our existence in the eternal.

3. The Promise of Eternal Life: A Beacon of Hope

The doctrine of resurrection is inextricably linked to the promise of eternal life, a concept that has captivated the human imagination since the dawn of time. Throughout history, civilizations have grappled with the existential question of what lies beyond the veil of death, seeking solace and hope in the face of life's finitude.

In the Christian faith, the promise of eternal life is not a mere philosophical speculation or a fleeting hope; it is a profound reality rooted in the historical event of Christ's resurrection. This promise finds its expression in passages such as John 11:25-26, where Jesus declares, "I am the resurrection and the life. The one who believes in me will live, even though they die; and whoever lives by believing in me will never die."

The promise of eternal life transcends the physical realm and encompasses the entirety of our being – body, soul, and spirit. It is a promise of a transformed existence, free from the limitations and afflictions of our mortal state, where we will dwell in the presence of the divine, experiencing the fullness of life as it was intended.

This promise resonates deeply within the human heart, offering a beacon of hope that illuminates even the darkest moments of our earthly journey. It empowers believers to face the challenges and trials of life with unwavering courage and resilience, for they know that this temporary existence is but a prelude to an eternity of joy and fulfillment in the presence of their Savior.

4. The Collective Hope: Unity in the Promise of Resurrection

While the promise of resurrection and eternal life holds profound personal significance for individual believers, it also unites the Christian community in a shared hope that transcends temporal boundaries. This collective hope serves as a unifying force, binding believers together in a common pursuit of the ultimate fulfillment of God's divine plan.

The Apostle Paul beautifully articulates this collective hope in 1 Thessalonians 4:13-18, where he addresses the concern of those who have lost loved ones in the faith. He writes, "Brothers and sisters, we do not want you to be uninformed about those who sleep in death, so that you do not grieve like the rest of mankind, who have no hope. For we believe that Jesus died and rose again, and so we believe that God will bring with Jesus those who have fallen asleep in him."

This passage underscores the collective nature of the resurrection hope, reminding believers that their loved ones who have died in Christ will be raised to eternal life when he returns. This shared expectation fosters a profound sense of unity and solidarity within the Christian community, as they journey together toward the ultimate fulfillment of God's promises.

Furthermore, the collective hope of resurrection inspires believers to live lives of service, love, and sacrifice, following in the footsteps of Christ himself. They are called to be ambassadors of hope, sharing the transformative message of the gospel and offering solace and encouragement to those who grapple with the fears and uncertainties of this temporal existence.

In conclusion, the doctrine of resurrection stands as the unshakable foundation of Christian eschatology, offering a profound and transformative vision of eternal life that transcends the limitations of our mortal existence. By understanding the significance of terms such as "resurrection," "the transformative power of Christ's resurrection," "the promise of eternal life," and "the collective hope," we gain a deeper appreciation for the depth and richness of this cornerstone belief. It is a belief that not only shapes our understanding of the present but also illuminates the path toward a glorious future, where the sting of death has been defeated, and the promise of eternal life reigns supreme.

Atonement and Redemption: The Path to Eternal Life

The doctrines of atonement and redemption stand as the theological pillars upon which the promise of eternal life rests. Through an evidence-based approach, we can delve into the profound implications of Christ's sacrifice and the transformative power it holds for humanity's salvation.

At the core of this examination is the undeniable reality of sin and its consequences, as stated in Romans 3:23: "For all have sinned and fall short of the glory of God." This sobering truth underscores the universal human condition and the inherent need for a divine remedy. However, through the atonement, God provided a way out of this predicament, as outlined in Romans 3:24-26:

"And are justified by his grace as a gift, through the redemption that is in Christ Jesus, whom God put forward as a propitiation by his blood, to be received by faith. This was to show God's righteousness because, in his divine forbearance, he had passed over former sins. It was to show his righteousness at the present time so that he might be just and the justifier of the one who has faith in Jesus."

This pivotal passage reveals the profound depth of God's plan for human salvation. Through the shedding of Christ's blood as an atoning sacrifice, the way is paved for the redemption of humanity. The Cross becomes the ultimate act of propitiation, satisfying the righteous demands of God's justice while simultaneously extending grace and mercy to those who place their faith in Jesus.

The book of Hebrews further elucidates the efficacy of Christ's atonement, likening it to the once-for-all sacrifice that supersedes the repeated offerings under the Old Covenant. Hebrews 9:11-14 states:

"But when Christ appeared as a high priest of the good things that have come, then through the greater and more perfect tent (not made with hands, that is, not of this creation) he entered once for all into the holy places, not by means of the blood of goats and calves but by means of his own blood, thus securing an eternal redemption. For if the blood of goats and bulls, and the sprinkling of defiled persons with the ashes of a heifer, sanctify for the purification of the flesh, how much more will the blood of Christ, who through the eternal Spirit offered himself without blemish to God, purify our conscience from dead works to serve the living God."

This passage underscores the profound efficacy of Christ's sacrifice, which secures eternal redemption, purifying the conscience and enabling humanity to serve the living God. It is through this act of atonement that the barrier separating humanity from God is torn down, paving the way for reconciliation and the promise of eternal life.

The interplay between atonement and redemption is further highlighted by the apostle Paul's words in Ephesians 1:7: "In him, we have redemption through his blood, the forgiveness of our trespasses, according to the riches of his grace." This verse encapsulates the transformative power of Christ's sacrifice, which not only secures redemption but also grants the forgiveness of sins, a fundamental prerequisite for the restoration of the broken relationship between God and humanity.

Moreover, the promise of eternal life is inextricably linked to this redemptive act. In John 3:16, Jesus himself declares, "For God so loved the world, that he gave his only Son, that whoever believes in him should not perish but have eternal life." This verse encapsulates the ultimate purpose of atonement and redemption – to grant eternal life to those who place their faith in Christ's sacrifice.

While some may challenge the necessity or efficacy of Christ's atonement, the evidence presented in Scripture is overwhelming. The consistency and unity of the biblical narrative, spanning both the Old and New Testaments, testify to the centrality of this doctrine. From the sacrificial system foreshadowed in the Mosaic Law to the prophetic utterances foretelling the coming of the Messiah, the atonement and redemption stand as the culminating act of God's redemptive plan.

Furthermore, the transformative power of Christ's sacrifice is evidenced in the lives of countless individuals throughout history who have experienced the reality of redemption and the promise of eternal life. Their testimonies, coupled with the profound impact of the Christian faith on human civilization, serve as a living testament to the enduring significance of atonement and redemption.

In practical terms, the doctrines of atonement and redemption offer hope and purpose to those who embrace them. They provide a framework for understanding the human condition and a pathway toward reconciliation with God. The promise of eternal life serves as a beacon of hope, transcending the limitations of this temporal existence and offering the ultimate resolution to the problem of death.

In conclusion, the doctrines of atonement and redemption, rooted in the sacrificial death and resurrection of Jesus Christ, lie at the heart of the Christian faith's promise of eternal life. Through an evidence-based approach, we can appreciate the depth and significance of these theological truths, which have transformed countless lives and offer the ultimate solution to the universal human experience of sin and death.

The Eschatological Fulfillment: New Heaven and New Earth

Can you imagine a world where death is no more, where suffering and pain are mere distant memories? This extraordinary vision of a new heaven and a new earth is the ultimate fulfillment of the abolition of death, a promise that lies at the heart of the Christian faith's eschatological prophecies.

The term "eschatology" refers to the study of the final events and the ultimate destiny of humanity and the cosmos. In the context of Christian theology, it encompasses the belief in the culmination of God's redemptive plan, where the present world order gives way to a renewed and perfected reality – a new heaven and a new earth.

This transformative vision is vividly depicted in Revelation 21:1-4, where the apostle John records a profound revelation: "Then I saw a new heaven and a new earth, for the first heaven and the first earth had passed away, and the sea was no more. And I saw the holy city, new Jerusalem, coming down out of heaven from God, prepared as a bride adorned for her husband. And I heard a loud voice from the throne saying, 'Behold, the dwelling place of God is with man. He will dwell with them, and they will be his people, and God himself will be with them as their God. He will wipe away every tear from their eyes, and death shall be no more, neither shall there be mourning, nor crying, nor pain anymore, for the former things have passed away.'"

This passage paints a vivid picture of a world where the old order has been abolished, and a new, perfect reality emerges. The image of the "new Jerusalem" symbolizes the ultimate union of God and humanity, where the Creator will dwell among His people in an intimate, unbroken relationship. The profound promise of "no more death, mourning, crying, or pain" stands as the ultimate consummation of the abolition of death, a reality that transcends the limitations and sufferings of our current existence.

Similarly, the prophet Isaiah foreshadowed this eschatological vision in Isaiah 65:17-25, describing a renewed creation where the effects of sin and death are entirely eradicated: "For behold, I create new heavens and a new earth, and the former things shall not be remembered or come into mind. But be glad and rejoice forever in that which I create; for behold, I create Jerusalem to be a joy, and her people to be a gladness. I will rejoice in Jerusalem and be glad in my people; no more shall be heard in it the sound of weeping and the cry of distress. No more shall there be in it an infant who lives but a few days, or an old man who does not fill out his days, for the young man shall die a hundred years old, and the sinner a hundred years old shall be accursed. They shall build houses and inhabit them; they shall plant vineyards and eat their fruit. They shall not build and another inhabit; they shall not plant and another eat; for like the days of a tree shall the days of my people be, and my chosen shall long enjoy the work of their hands."

In this prophetic vision, the new heaven and new earth are portrayed as a place of everlasting joy, where the ravages of death and suffering are eradicated. The promise of a life devoid of premature death and the curse of sin resonates as a profound contrast to the present human experience, underscoring the transformative power of God's eschatological plan.

The theological implications of this eschatological fulfillment are far-reaching and profound. Firstly, it affirms the ultimate victory of God over the forces of sin, death, and evil that have plagued humanity throughout history. The new heaven and new earth represent the final restoration of the divine order, where the brokenness and corruption that have marred creation are forever abolished.

Secondly, this promise speaks to the depths of God's love and commitment to His creation. The act of establishing a new, perfect reality where humanity can dwell in unhindered fellowship with the Creator underscores the immeasurable value He places on those created in His image. It is a testament to the lengths God is willing to go to redeem and restore His beloved creation.

Furthermore, the eschatological fulfillment of a new heaven and a new earth serves as the ultimate validation of the Christian hope in eternal life. It is the culmination of the promise made through Christ's atoning sacrifice, where the final victory over death is realized, and the redeemed can experience the fullness of life in the presence of God, free from the limitations and afflictions of this present world.

Living with the awareness of this eschatological reality transforms our perspective on the present. The struggles, sufferings, and hardships of this life, though real and often overwhelming, are tempered by the knowledge that they are temporary and will one day give way to an eternal existence devoid of pain and sorrow. This forward-looking hope instills in believers resilience and steadfastness, enabling them to endure trials and persevere in faith, knowing that the ultimate reward awaits.

Moreover, the promise of a new heaven and a new earth challenges us to live in a manner that reflects the values and principles of this coming reality. It calls us to cultivate a life of holiness, love, and compassion, mirroring the divine character that will permeate the renewed creation. By embracing these virtues, we not only prepare ourselves for eschatological fulfillment but also bring a foretaste of that future reality into the present, impacting the world around us with the transformative power of God's love.

In conclusion, the eschatological vision of a new heaven and a new earth stands as the ultimate fulfillment of the abolition of death, a promise that resonates with profound hope and anticipation for believers. It is a reality where the effects of sin and death are forever eradicated, where humanity can experience the fullness of life in an unbroken relationship with the Creator. This promise not only validates the Christian hope in eternal life but also transforms our perspective on the present, instilling resilience and a commitment to living in accordance with the values of the coming reality. As we journey through this life, let us hold fast to this eschatological promise, allowing it to shape our thoughts, actions, and aspirations as we eagerly await the day when God's redemptive plan reaches its glorious consummation.

Theological Debates: Varied Interpretations

The notion of an eternal existence free from the specter of death has long captivated the human imagination and resides at the heart of many religious and philosophical traditions. Within the realm of Christian theology, the abolition of death is a central tenet, yet its interpretation has been a subject of extensive debate and diverse perspectives throughout the centuries.

The contrast between the finality of death and the promise of eternal life presents itself as an apparent paradox, one that has sparked intricate theological discourse. On one hand, the reality of human mortality is undeniable, a seemingly inescapable consequence of our mortal nature. Yet, on the other hand, the Christian faith proclaims a radical triumph over death, a victory made possible through the resurrection of Jesus Christ and the promise of eternal life for those who believe. Reconciling these two seemingly contradictory concepts has been a source of profound theological exploration and debate.

In this exploration, we shall delve into the varied interpretations and perspectives that have emerged within Christian thought, examining the nuances and complexities of this pivotal doctrine. By juxtaposing the arguments of renowned theologians and scholars from different eras and traditions, we will gain a deeper appreciation for the richness and diversity of theological discourse surrounding the abolition of death.

One of the earliest and most influential voices in this debate was that of St. Augustine of Hippo (354-430 AD), whose writings have profoundly shaped Christian theology. In his seminal work, "City of God," Augustine grappled with the concept of death and its relation to sin and the human condition. He argued that death was not part of the original design of creation but rather a consequence of humanity's fall into sin. According to Augustine, death entered the world as a punishment for disobedience, and it is through the redemptive work of Christ that the power of death is ultimately broken.

Augustine's perspective highlights the profound theological implications of the abolition of death, as it signifies the restoration of the divine order and the triumph over the consequences of sin. In this view, the promise of eternal life is not merely an extension of our present existence but rather a transformative reality where the effects of sin and death are eradicated, and humanity is restored to its intended state of perfection.

Centuries later, the renowned theologian and philosopher St. Thomas Aquinas (1225-1274) built upon the foundations laid by Augustine, offering his own insights into the nature of death and the promise of eternal life. Aquinas emphasized the fundamental distinction between the immortality of the soul and the mortality of the physical body. While acknowledging the reality of physical death, he argued that the soul, being immaterial and created directly by God, is inherently immortal.

Aquinas's perspective highlights the duality of human existence, where the physical and spiritual realms intersect. The abolition of death, in this view, is not merely a denial of physical mortality but rather a promise of the ultimate reunification of the soul and a resurrected, glorified body in the eternal realm. This reunification represents the final triumph over the consequences of sin and the restoration of humanity to its intended state of wholeness.

Moving forward in time, the influential Protestant theologian John Calvin (1509-1564) offered his own interpretation of the abolition of death, rooted in the doctrine of justification by faith alone. Calvin asserted that death was not merely a physical phenomenon but also a spiritual reality, a consequence of humanity's separation from God due to sin. However, through Christ's atoning sacrifice and the gift of faith, believers are reconciled to God and granted the promise of eternal life.

Calvin's perspective emphasizes the centrality of Christ's redemptive work in overcoming death's spiritual and eternal consequences. The abolition of death, in this view, is not merely a physical reality but a spiritual transformation, where believers are liberated from the bondage of sin and granted the promise of eternal communion with God.

As we delve deeper into contemporary theological discourse, we encounter a rich tapestry of perspectives and interpretations, each offering unique insights into the abolition of death. For instance, some theologians have explored the concept through the lens of eschatology, examining its implications for the ultimate destiny of humanity and the cosmos. Others have focused on the ethical and practical implications of this doctrine, exploring how the promise of eternal life shapes our understanding of human dignity, suffering, and our responsibilities toward one another.

One contemporary perspective that has gained traction is the notion of "realized eschatology," which posits that the promise of eternal life is not merely a future reality but a present experience for those who have embraced the teachings of Christ. Proponents of this view argue that the abolition of death is not solely a future event but a spiritual transformation that begins in the present, liberating believers from the fear and bondage of death and empowering them to live in the fullness of life.

Another intriguing perspective explores the relationship between the abolition of death and the concepts of redemption and restoration. Some theologians argue that the promise of eternal life is not merely an individual experience but a cosmic event, where the entire created order is redeemed and restored to its original, intended state of perfection. This perspective highlights the interconnectedness of all creation and the profound implications of the abolition of death for the entire cosmos.

As we explore these varied interpretations and perspectives, it becomes evident that the abolition of death is a complex and multifaceted concept, one that has profound implications for our understanding of God, humanity, and the ultimate destiny of creation. The diverse theological discourse surrounding this doctrine serves as a testament to the depth and richness of Christian thought, inviting us to engage with the complexities and nuances of this pivotal belief.

Furthermore, these debates underscore the importance of maintaining a spirit of humility and openness in our theological inquiries. While each perspective offers valuable insights, it is essential to acknowledge the limitations of human understanding and the inherent mystery that surrounds the divine realm. The abolition of death, like many other aspects of the Christian faith, invites us to embrace a sense of awe and wonder, recognizing that our knowledge is partial and that there is always more to be explored and understood.

Ultimately, the varied interpretations of the abolition of death remind us that our faith is a living tradition, one that continues to evolve and deepen through the collective efforts of theologians, scholars, and believers. As we engage with these debates and seek to understand the profound implications of this doctrine, we are called to approach our inquiries with reverence, intellectual rigor, and a willingness to learn from one another. It is through this ongoing dialogue and the exchange of diverse perspectives that we can deepen our understanding of the divine mysteries and draw ever closer to the fullness of truth.

Practical Implications: Living in the Light of Eternity

Introduction: The Context and the Challenge

In the realm of Christian theology, the abolition of death is not merely an abstract concept or a distant promise; it is a transformative reality that holds profound implications for the way we live our lives in the present. The triumph over death's sting is a profound victory, one that should permeate every aspect of our existence, guiding our daily decisions, shaping our ethical framework, and informing our spiritual practices.

Yet, for many Christians, the challenge lies in truly embracing and embodying the practical implications of this theological milestone. While we may intellectually affirm the abolition of death, the weight of our earthly struggles, the lure of temporal pursuits, and the persistent influence of fear and doubt can often obscure the radiant light of eternity. Like a veil, the cares of this world can cloud our vision, causing us to lose sight of the liberating truth that death has been conquered, and our lives are meant to be lived in the glorious freedom of Christ's eternal victory.

The implications of failing to live in the light of eternity are grave. Without a firm grasp on the transformative power of Christ's triumph over death, we risk succumbing to a diminished existence, one defined by fear, doubt, and a myopic focus on temporal concerns. Our ethical decisions may be tainted by short-sighted desires, our spiritual practices may lack the vibrancy of eternal hope, and our relationships with others may be marred by selfishness and a lack of eternity-shaped perspective.

The Scriptural Solution: Embracing the Eternal Perspective

Fortunately, the Scriptures provide us with a profound and life-altering solution to this challenge, a solution that lies in embracing the eternal perspective that flows from the abolition of death. The apostle Paul's exhortation in 1 Corinthians 15:58 resonates powerfully: "Therefore, my beloved brethren, be steadfast, immovable, always abounding in the work of the Lord, knowing that your toil is not in vain in the Lord."

In this verse, Paul urges us to live with unwavering steadfastness and an abundance of purpose, drawing strength from the knowledge that our labor is not in vain because death has been conquered. The finality of the grave no longer holds sway; our efforts are invested in the eternal realm, where they bear everlasting fruit.

Moreover, in Philippians 3:20-21, Paul declares, "For our citizenship is in heaven, from which we also eagerly wait for the Savior, the Lord Jesus Christ, who will transform our lowly body that it may be conformed to His glorious body, according to the working by which He is able even to subdue all things to Himself." Here, Paul reminds us that our true citizenship is not of this world but of the eternal kingdom, where our bodies will be transformed and made glorious, like Christ's own resurrected form.

The Implementation: Living as Eternity-Bound Sojourners

To live in the light of eternity, we must embrace the reality that we are but sojourners in this temporal realm, pilgrims on a journey toward our eternal home. This mindset requires a radical reorientation of our priorities, values, and decisions, as we seek to align our lives with the eternal perspective revealed in the Scriptures.

One of the first steps in this transformative journey is to cultivate a deep appreciation for the preciousness of life and the fleeting nature of earthly existence. Rather than clinging to the illusion of permanence, we must recognize that our time on this earth is but a brief sojourn, a preparatory stage for the eternal reality that awaits us. This understanding should instill within us a sense of urgency, compelling us to make the most of every moment, to invest our time and resources in pursuits that have eternal significance.

Furthermore, living in the light of eternity necessitates a deliberate cultivation of Christian virtues, such as faith, hope, love, and perseverance. These virtues serve as anchors, tethering our souls to the unshakable foundation of God's eternal promises. Faith empowers us to trust in the unseen realities of the eternal realm, while hope buoys our spirits, sustaining us through the trials and tribulations of this present age. Love, the greatest of virtues, compels us to live selflessly, embracing a love for God and for one another that transcends the boundaries of time and space.

The practical implications of living in the light of eternity also extend to the realm of ethical decision-making. When faced with moral dilemmas or choices that carry significant consequences, we must ground our decisions in the eternal perspective, seeking to align our actions with the principles and values of the eternal kingdom. This may involve sacrificing temporal gains or comforts for the sake of upholding virtues such as integrity, justice, and compassion – virtues that will endure long after our earthly existence has faded.

Moreover, living in the light of eternity has profound implications for our relationships and interactions with others. Recognizing that every human being is an eternal soul, created in the image of God, should inspire us to treat one another with profound respect, dignity, and love. Our relationships should be characterized by a sense of eternal purpose, as we seek to build one another up, encourage spiritual growth, and spur one another on toward the eternal prize.

Ultimately, living in the light of eternity requires a continual pursuit of holiness and spiritual transformation. As we fix our gaze upon the eternal horizon, we are called to shed the weights and encumbrances of this temporal realm, allowing the Holy Spirit to mold and shape us into vessels fit for eternal habitation. This pursuit of holiness involves a daily dying to self, a willingness to surrender our desires and aspirations to the eternal purposes of God.

Case Studies and Outcomes: The Transformative Power of Eternity-Shaped Living

Throughout the annals of Christian history, we find countless examples of individuals and communities who have embraced the practical implications of living in the light of eternity, and the transformative impact of their lives serves as a powerful testament to the power of this perspective.

Consider the life of Dietrich Bonhoeffer, the German theologian and pastor who courageously stood against the atrocities of the Nazi regime. Bonhoeffer's unwavering commitment to truth, justice, and the dignity of human life was rooted in an eternal perspective that transcended the temporal concerns of his day. His willingness to sacrifice his own life for the sake of his convictions was a powerful illustration of how the abolition of death can liberate one to live with boldness and unwavering resolve.

Similarly, the witness of the early Christian martyrs, who faced unimaginable persecution and suffering for their faith, exemplifies the transformative power of living in the light of eternity. Their willingness to embrace death rather than renounce their beliefs was not born of mere stubbornness or fanaticism but of a deep conviction that their true citizenship was in heaven, and their eternal destiny was secure in Christ.

In more recent times, we can look to the example of Mother Teresa, whose life was dedicated to serving the poorest of the poor in the slums of Calcutta. Her unwavering compassion and selfless service were fueled by a profound understanding that each human being is an eternal soul, deserving of dignity and love. Mother Teresa's tireless efforts to alleviate suffering and bring hope to the most destitute members of society were a living embodiment of the practical implications of living in the light of eternity.

Beyond these notable individuals, countless Christian communities and organizations around the world are actively engaged in living out the practical implications of the abolition of death. From ministries dedicated to alleviating poverty and promoting social justice to faith-based initiatives focused on education, healthcare, and community development, these efforts are rooted in the belief that our actions in this life have eternal significance and that our call is to be agents of transformation, ushering in glimpses of the eternal kingdom in the here and now.

The outcomes of such eternity-shaped living are profoundly transformative, both on a personal and societal level. Individuals who embrace this perspective often report a deep sense of purpose, joy, and peace, even in the face of adversity. Their lives are marked by a resilience and steadfastness that transcend the vicissitudes of temporal circumstances, as they draw strength from the unshakable reality of their eternal hope.

On a broader scale, communities and societies that are infused with the practical implications of living in the light of eternity experience a ripple effect of positive change. Virtues such as compassion, justice, and selflessness become woven into the fabric of these communities, fostering environments that promote human flourishing, respect for human dignity, and a commitment to the common good.

Conclusion: Embracing the Eternal Horizon

As we journey through this earthly sojourn, the abolition of death stands as a beacon of hope, illuminating the path before us and beckoning us to embrace the eternal perspective that is the birthright of every believer. By living in the light of eternity, we partake in the transformative power of Christ's triumph over death, allowing this glorious truth to permeate every aspect of our lives.

Though the challenges and distractions of this temporal realm may seem formidable, we are called to fix our gaze upon the eternal horizon, drawing strength and inspiration from the promises of God's Word. As we do so, may our lives become living testimonies to the power of the abolition of death, radiating the hope, joy, and purpose that flow from this transformative reality.

Let us embrace the eternal perspective, not merely as an abstract concept, but as a way of life – a life marked by unwavering faith, steadfast perseverance, and a love that knows no bounds. For in doing so, we not only affirm the victory of Christ over death but also participate in the unfolding of God's eternal plan, as we bear witness to the glorious truth that death has been conquered, and life eternal has been secured for all who believe.

The Ultimate Victory: Celebrating the Abolition of Death

1. Establish the goal: This chapter aims to guide readers in celebrating the triumphant abolition of death, a monumental theological milestone that heralds the ultimate victory of life over death. By embracing this truth, we can experience profound joy, hope, and purpose, allowing the transformative power of Christ's conquest over the grave to permeate every aspect of our lives.

2. Necessary materials: To fully engage with this celebration, readers will need an open heart, a willingness to surrender their fears and doubts, and a deep appreciation for the Scriptures, which provide the foundation for understanding and embracing this profound truth.

3. Overview: We will begin by delving into the biblical basis for the abolition of death, exploring key passages that proclaim Christ's victory over the grave and the promise of eternal life. We will then examine the theological significance of this triumph, highlighting its implications for our understanding of God's redemptive plan and the restoration of all things. Next, we will explore practical ways to commemorate and celebrate this profound truth, drawing inspiration from ancient and modern liturgical practices, hymns, and prayers that exalt the conquering power of Christ's resurrection.

4. Detailed steps:

I. Embracing the Biblical Foundation

- Explore Revelation 20:14, where it is proclaimed, "Then Death and Hades were thrown into the lake of fire. This is the second death, the lake of fire." This verse heralds the ultimate defeat of death and the grave, marking the fulfillment of God's redemptive plan.
- Reflect on 1 Corinthians 15:26, where Paul declares, "The last enemy to be destroyed is death." This passage underscores the finality of Christ's victory, assuring us that death's reign has been definitively broken.
- Meditate on John 11:25-26, where Jesus boldly proclaims, "I am the resurrection ford the life. Whoever believes in me, though he die, yet shall he live, and everyone who lives and believes in me shall never die." These words from our Savior offer the promise of eternal life to all who place their faith in Him.

II. Grasping the Theological Significance

- Consider the abolition of death as the culmination of God's redemptive plan, restoring humanity to the eternal communion with the Creator that was intended from the beginning.
- Reflect on the cosmic implications of Christ's victory, as it signals the ultimate defeat of sin, death, and all that stands in opposition to God's reign.
- Contemplate the profound hope and assurance this truth offers, liberating us from the fear of death and empowering us to live with purpose and confidence.

III. Celebrating Through Liturgical Practices

- Explore the rich tradition of Easter hymns and songs that exalt Christ's triumph over death, such as "Christ the Lord is Risen Today" and "Up from the Grave He Arose." Incorporate these into personal or corporate worship experiences.
- Study ancient liturgical practices that commemorate the resurrection, such as the lighting of the Paschal candle and the renewal of baptismal vows, and consider incorporating elements of these into your celebration.
- Compose personal prayers or reflections that express gratitude for the abolition of death and the promise of eternal life, allowing these expressions to deepen your appreciation for this profound truth.

5. Tips and best practices:

- Approach this celebration with a spirit of awe and reverence, recognizing the magnitude of Christ's victory and the immense love that compelled His sacrifice.
- Engage with the Scriptures regularly, allowing the promises

of eternal life to take root in your heart and transform your perspective on the present.

- Cultivate a lifestyle of worship and gratitude, letting the joy of this triumph infuse your daily activities and interactions with others.
- Share the hope and assurance of the abolition of death with those who may be struggling with fear or doubt, offering the transformative power of this truth as a source of comfort and strength.

6. Potential pitfalls and how to avoid them:

- Beware of succumbing to the temptation of complacency or taking this truth for granted.
- Intentionally nurture a sense of wonder and gratitude for the gift of eternal life.
- Resist the urge to compartmentalize this truth, allowing it to permeate every aspect of your life, from your relationships to your decision-making and ethical framework.
- Avoid falling into the trap of legalism or rigid adherence to traditions at the expense of a heartfelt celebration. Maintain a balance between honoring established practices and fostering a genuine, Spirit-led experience.

7. Checking for understanding and successful completion:

- Reflect on whether your perspective on life and death has been transformed by embracing the abolition of death. Do you experience a greater sense of hope, purpose, and joy?
- Evaluate whether your daily actions and decisions are increasingly aligned with the eternal perspective that flows from this truth. Are you living with greater intentionality and eternity in mind?
- Consider whether your relationships and interactions with

others are marked by a deeper sense of love, compassion, and a desire to share the hope of eternal life.

8. Addressing potential problems and solutions:

If you find yourself struggling with doubts or fears about the reality of eternal life, seek counsel from trusted spiritual leaders or mentors, and immerse yourself in the promises of Scripture. If the weight of temporal concerns or distractions threatens to obscure your celebration of this truth, intentionally set aside dedicated times for reflection, worship, and communion with God. If you encounter resistance or skepticism from others regarding the abolition of death, respond with gentleness and patience, allowing the transformative power of this truth to speak for itself through your life and witness.

By following these steps and embracing the practical implications of the abolition of death, we can fully participate in the celebration of this ultimate victory. May our lives be transformed by the radiant hope and assurance that death has been conquered, and may our hearts overflow with gratitude for the One who has secured our eternal destiny.

11

———————

CULTURAL TRANSFORMATION: SCRIPTURAL PARADIGMS

Divine Intervention in Cultural Shifts

Provoking Question: How has divine intervention historically influenced cultural transformations?

Throughout the annals of history, societies have grappled with profound challenges that threatened their very existence or precipitated seismic shifts in their cultural paradigms. While human efforts have undoubtedly played a role in shaping these transformations, there is a recurring theme that transcends cultures and epochs: the presence and influence of divine intervention. This question prompts us to explore the profound impact of divine guidance on the evolution of civilizations, shedding light on the intricate interplay between the sacred and the temporal.

The Problem: Societies often find themselves at crossroads, facing daunting obstacles that seem insurmountable through mere human endeavors. Whether confronting oppressive regimes, deep-rooted social injustices, or entrenched belief systems that stifle progress, the path to lasting change can be arduous and elusive. Traditional approaches, rooted in human strategies and limitations, frequently fall short, leaving communities mired in cycles of stagnation or perpetuating the very ills they seek to remedy.

Common Misconceptions: The pursuit of cultural transformation is often viewed solely through the lens of human agency and political maneuvering. Secular philosophies and ideologies present themselves as the sole arbiters of societal progress, dismissing or marginalizing the role of divine intervention. This myopic perspective not only disregards a profound force that has shaped history but also fails to account for the transcendent power that can catalyze lasting change.

A Unique Approach: The sacred texts of various faith traditions offer a compelling alternative perspective, one that recognizes the pivotal role of divine intervention in shaping the course of civilizations. Biblical accounts, in particular, provide numerous instances where the intervention of the Almighty catalyzed profound cultural shifts, empowering oppressed communities, toppling seemingly invincible empires, and ushering in new eras of justice, freedom, and spiritual renewal.

Consider the Exodus narrative, in which the Hebrew people, enslaved for generations in Egypt, experienced a miraculous deliverance orchestrated by the hand of the divine. This pivotal event not only liberated an oppressed nation but also established the foundations for their distinct cultural and religious identity, shaping the trajectory of subsequent generations and cultures. The intervention of the Almighty shattered the shackles of bondage, defied the might of a powerful empire, and set in motion a transformation that echoed through the ages.

Another striking example is the conversion of the Apostle Paul, as recorded in the book of Acts. Originally a zealous persecutor of the early Christian movement, Paul's life was radically transformed by a divine encounter on the road to Damascus. This singular intervention not only altered the trajectory of Paul's life but also set in motion a seismic shift in the religious and cultural landscape of the ancient world. Paul's subsequent missionary journeys and prolific writings played a pivotal role in the spread of Christianity, catalyzing a cultural transformation that reverberated across continents and centuries.

Addressing Potential Objections: Critics may argue that attributing cultural transformations to divine intervention is a mere exercise in religious dogma or a convenient narrative to rationalize historical events. However, the consistency and pervasiveness of such accounts across diverse cultures and time periods lend credence to the notion that there is a force beyond the purely human realm at work. Moreover, the profound and enduring impact of these transformations, often in defiance of seemingly insurmountable odds, suggests the presence of a transcendent power that transcends mere human agency.

Actionable Advice: As contemporary societies grapple with their own challenges and strive for positive cultural transformation, it is essential to recognize the potential for divine intervention. Rather than relying solely on human strategies and limitations, individuals and communities should cultivate a posture of humility and openness to the guidance of the divine. This may involve earnest prayer, seeking wisdom from sacred texts, and cultivating a heart attuned to the still, small voice that has guided generations before us.

Furthermore, it is crucial to approach this process with a spirit of discernment, acknowledging that divine intervention may manifest in unexpected ways and through unexpected vessels. Remaining open to the possibility of transformation arising from seemingly unlikely sources or circumstances can enhance our ability to recognize and embrace the workings of the divine.

Ultimately, embracing the potential for divine intervention in cultural transformations offers a profound source of hope and inspiration. It reminds us that even in the face of seemingly insurmountable challenges, there is a power greater than ourselves that can orchestrate profound change. By recognizing and aligning ourselves with this divine force, we can participate in shaping the cultural landscapes of our time, leaving an indelible imprint on the tapestry of human history.

The Paradigm of the Exodus

1. Setting the Context:

The saga of the Exodus from Egypt stands as a seminal event in the annals of Jewish history, its significance echoing across millennia and cultures. Unfolding in the harsh realities of the 13th century BCE, this narrative transcends the confines of time and location, resonating as a timeless tale of divine deliverance and the indomitable human spirit.

2. Key Players:

Central to this momentous episode are Moses, a man chosen by the Almighty to lead his people from bondage, and Pharaoh, the tyrannical ruler who embodied the oppressive might of the Egyptian empire. The Israelites themselves, enslaved for generations, became the protagonists in this epic struggle for freedom, their collective anguish and yearning for liberty serving as the driving force behind the Exodus.

3. The Challenge:

The Israelites found themselves trapped in a cycle of oppression, their lives defined by unrelenting toil and subjugation under the yoke of Egyptian enslavement. This systemic oppression extended beyond physical labor, permeating every facet of their existence and eroding their cultural identity. Their quest for freedom transcended mere geographical liberation; it encompassed a profound yearning for dignity, self-determination, and the reclamation of their spiritual heritage.

4. Strategies and Actions:

The path to liberation was paved by a series of divine interventions, each more monumental than the last. Through the ten plagues, the Almighty demonstrated His power over the natural order, challenging the false gods of Egypt and dismantling the foundations of Pharaoh's rule. The parting of the Red Sea stood as a profound testament to divine might, as the waters miraculously divided, allowing the Israelites to pass while swallowing the pursuing Egyptian army.

Moses, guided by the Almighty's instructions, led his people with unwavering conviction, navigating the treacherous wilderness and overcoming the numerous challenges that arose. Through a profound act of faith, the Israelites embraced the arduous journey, trusting in the divine plan for their deliverance.

5. Outcomes and Impact:

The Exodus culminated in the liberation of the Israelites from Egyptian bondage and their establishment as a free nation in the Promised Land. However, its impact extended far beyond mere physical deliverance. It solidified the covenant between the Israelites and the Almighty, laying the foundation for their distinct cultural and religious identity. The Ten Commandments, received at Mount Sinai, became the moral bedrock upon which their society was built, shaping the ethical and legal frameworks of subsequent generations.

Furthermore, the Exodus narrative became a universal symbol of hope, inspiring countless individuals and communities throughout history in their own struggles against oppression and injustice. Its resonance echoed across cultures, imbuing movements for freedom and social change with a profound sense of purpose and divine mandate.

6. Lessons Learned:

The Exodus paradigm offers invaluable lessons that transcend time and cultural boundaries. It underscores the power of faith and perseverance in the face of seemingly insurmountable obstacles, reminding us that even the mightiest empires are ultimately subject to the will of the divine. The narrative challenges us to confront our own complacency and to recognize that true freedom requires both external liberation and an internal transformation, a shedding of the shackles that bind the human spirit.

Moreover, the Exodus serves as a poignant reminder of the profound impact that divine intervention can have on the course of human events. It calls us to cultivate a posture of humility and openness, acknowledging that there are forces beyond our limited human comprehension that can catalyze profound change.

7. Broader Relevance:

The Exodus narrative resonates profoundly in contemporary discourse on social justice, human rights, and the ongoing struggles for freedom and dignity. Its principles of divine deliverance, unwavering faith, and collective perseverance continue to inspire individuals and movements across the globe, serving as a beacon of hope in the face of oppression and injustice.

Furthermore, the Exodus paradigm invites us to reflect on the role of the divine in shaping the course of human history. It challenges us to consider whether the transformative events that have shaped our world might be the product of a force greater than mere human agency, and whether we, like the Israelites of old, are called to align ourselves with a higher purpose that transcends our individual limitations.

8. Final Reflection:

As we contemplate the enduring legacy of the Exodus, we are prompted to ask ourselves: In what ways might we be called to embrace a journey of liberation, shedding the shackles that bind us, whether physical, psychological, or spiritual? How might we cultivate a posture of openness to divine guidance, recognizing that true transformation often arises from unexpected sources and through means that defy our limited human understanding? And ultimately, how can we embody the principles of faith, perseverance, and unwavering commitment to justice and freedom, leaving an indelible imprint on the cultural landscapes of our time?

Cultural Revolution Through Prophetic Voices

The annals of history are woven with the vibrant threads of visionary voices - prophetic figures who dared to challenge the status quo, catalyzing cultural transformations that echoed across generations. Within this tapestry, the roles of Isaiah, Jeremiah, and Amos stand as vivid testaments to the enduring power of prophetic leadership in reshaping societal landscapes. At first glance, their approaches might seem disparate, even contradictory - a symphony of contrasts and nuances that defies simplistic categorization.

As we embark on this exploration, it is imperative to understand the entities we are examining and the relevance of their juxtaposition. Isaiah, the son of Amoz, was a prophet whose ministry spanned the reigns of four kings in ancient Judah. Jeremiah, the son of Hilkiah, witnessed the tumultuous decline of Judah and its eventual fall to the Babylonians. Amos, a shepherd from Tekoa, was an unlikely voice among the prophets, chosen to deliver a scathing indictment against the systemic injustices plaguing the northern kingdom of Israel.

To unveil the profound insights these prophets offer, we must examine their messages, methodologies, and societal impacts through the lens of comparison and contrast. While all three figures shared a common commitment to repentance, social justice, and adherence to divine commandments, their approaches and emphases diverged in profound ways.

Isaiah's prophecies were imbued with a sense of hope and future restoration, painting a vivid picture of a redeemed Zion that would become a beacon of light for all nations. His words echoed the promise of a coming Messianic era, a time when the knowledge of the Lord would fill the earth, and lasting peace would reign. In contrast, Jeremiah's utterances carried the somber tones of imminent judgment and exile, reflecting the bleak realities of a nation that had forsaken its covenant with the Almighty. His symbolic acts, such as the smashing of a potter's jar, served as visceral warnings of the impending calamity that would befall Judah.

Amos, on the other hand, stood as a fierce advocate for social justice, decrying the oppression of the poor and the corruption that had permeated the halls of power. His prophetic voice resounded like a clarion call, urging a return to the foundational principles of righteousness and compassion that were meant to undergird Israelite society. Amos's words cut through the veneer of religious piety, exposing the hypocrisy of a nation that claimed devotion to the Almighty while trampling upon the most vulnerable.

Yet, amidst these differences, a common thread emerges - a profound recognition that societal transformation cannot be achieved through mere superficial reforms, but rather demands a fundamental shift in consciousness and a realignment with divine principles. For Isaiah, this meant cultivating a spirit of repentance and humility, acknowledging the nation's transgressions, and embracing the path of righteousness. For Jeremiah, it involved a willingness to confront harsh truths and submit to the consequences of disobedience, even if it meant enduring the pain of exile and displacement. For Amos, it necessitated a radical embrace of justice and equity, a rejection of the systemic oppression that had taken root within the corridors of power.

The implications of these prophetic voices extend far beyond their immediate historical contexts, offering profound insights into the multifaceted nature of prophetic leadership and its enduring relevance. They remind us that cultural transformation is not a monolithic endeavor but rather a symphony of voices, each contributing a unique perspective and emphasis. It is in the interplay of these voices, the tensions and resonances they create, that the fullness of prophetic wisdom emerges.

In our contemporary landscape, the echoes of these prophetic paradigms reverberate with renewed urgency. As we grapple with the complex challenges of our time - from systemic injustice and environmental degradation to the erosion of ethical foundations and the fragmentation of social cohesion - we would do well to heed the wisdom of these ancient voices. Like Isaiah, we must hold fast to a vision of hope and restoration, acknowledging the possibility of a more just and equitable society. Like Jeremiah, we must possess the courage to confront harsh realities and embrace the difficult path of accountability and repentance. And like Amos, we must champion the cause of the oppressed, challenging the systems and structures that perpetuate inequality and injustice.

In this collective endeavor, we can draw inspiration from the multifaceted approaches of these prophetic figures, recognizing that cultural revolution often requires a symphony of voices, each contributing its unique perspective and emphasis. By embracing the tensions and complementarities inherent in these prophetic paradigms, we open ourselves to a deeper understanding of the transformative power of visionary leadership and the enduring relevance of divine principles in shaping the course of human events.

As we contemplate the profound legacies of Isaiah, Jeremiah, and Amos, we are reminded that the path to cultural transformation is not a linear journey but rather a tapestry of interwoven narratives, each thread contributing to the richness and complexity of the whole. It is in this symphony of prophetic voices that we find the wisdom and inspiration to chart a course toward a more just, equitable, and spiritually grounded society – a society that honors the divine call to justice, compassion, and a relentless pursuit of righteousness.

The Role of Faith in Cultural Transformation

Throughout the annals of history, faith has emerged as a powerful catalyst for cultural transformation, igniting profound shifts in societal paradigms and challenging the boundaries of human existence. The enduring influence of faith transcends the confines of mere religious doctrine, shaping the very fabric of civilizations and propelling humanity toward new horizons of understanding and progress.

At the heart of this transformative power lies a fundamental truth – faith is not merely a set of beliefs or rituals, but a dynamic force that shapes the way we perceive the world and our place within it. It is an ever-evolving narrative that weaves together the threads of human experience, offering a profound sense of purpose, meaning, and moral guidance in the face of life's complexities.

One need not look further than the scriptural narratives that have shaped the course of human history to witness the indelible impact of faith on cultural transformation. The tale of Abraham, the patriarch of three major world religions, serves as a poignant example. His unwavering faith in the divine call to leave his homeland and embark upon an uncertain journey exemplifies the transformative potential of faith – a willingness to challenge the status quo, embrace the unknown, and forge a new path guided by an unwavering conviction.

Similarly, the resilience of the early Christian community in the face of persecution stands as a testament to the enduring power of faith to transcend adversity and reshape societal norms. These individuals, fueled by an unshakable belief in the teachings of Christ, challenged the established order of the Roman Empire, sowing the seeds of a cultural revolution that would ultimately reshape the foundations of Western civilization.

While some may argue that secular movements have achieved comparable outcomes, these initiatives often lack the enduring moral foundation and sense of purpose that faith provides. Secular movements, however well-intentioned, can be fleeting, subject to the shifting tides of public opinion and the whims of transitory ideologies. In contrast, faith-driven movements are anchored in a deeper well of conviction, drawing upon timeless principles and a transcendent sense of purpose that transcends the fluctuations of societal trends.

The civil rights movement in the United States stands as a powerful testament to the sustained impact of faith in driving cultural transformation. Led by visionary figures like Martin Luther King Jr., whose oratory and activism were rooted in the teachings of the Christian faith, this movement not only challenged the entrenched system of racial segregation but also sparked a profound shift in the nation's moral conscience. King's unwavering commitment to nonviolent resistance, informed by his deep faith in the principles of justice and human dignity, inspired a generation to rise above the confines of hatred and oppression, forging a path toward a more equitable and inclusive society.

Beyond the realm of sociopolitical movements, faith has also played a pivotal role in shaping the cultural landscapes of the arts, literature, and scientific inquiry. The works of great thinkers and artists throughout history, from Michelangelo and Dante to Newton and Galileo, bear the imprint of their faith, infusing their creations with a sense of awe, wonder, and a relentless pursuit of truth and understanding.

In the modern era, faith continues to exert a profound influence on cultural transformation, manifesting in diverse ways across the globe. From the vibrant musical traditions that have emerged from the African-American church to the rich tapestry of art and architecture that adorns the great cathedrals and mosques, faith remains a wellspring of creative expression and cultural identity.

Yet, the role of faith in cultural transformation extends far beyond the realms of art and social justice movements. It also plays a vital role in shaping the ethical foundations and moral compasses that guide societies toward a more just and equitable future. Faithbased principles of compassion, forgiveness, and a commitment to the inherent dignity of all human beings have served as bulwarks against the forces of hatred, oppression, and dehumanization that have plagued human civilization.

In the face of these challenges, faith offers a path forward, a beacon of hope that illuminates the way toward a more enlightened and harmonious coexistence. It is through the lens of faith that we can cultivate a deeper understanding of our shared humanity, transcending the artificial barriers of race, creed, and nationality that have too often divided us.

Ultimately, the practical applications of this evidence suggest that integrating faith into cultural initiatives can lead to more profound and lasting transformations. By tapping into the wellspring of faith, we not only access a rich reservoir of wisdom and moral guidance but also unlock the profound power of human resilience, hope, and an unwavering commitment to a higher purpose.

As we navigate the complexities of our modern world, beset by challenges that test the very foundations of our humanity, it is imperative that we embrace the transformative power of faith. In doing so, we open ourselves to the possibility of forging a new paradigm – one that honors the inherent dignity of all people, fosters a deeper sense of interconnectedness, and propels us toward a more just, equitable, and compassionate future.

Heavenly Kingdom Paradigms

Amidst the complexities and challenges that characterize our modern world, humanity finds itself at a pivotal crossroads, seeking guidance and inspiration to navigate the path toward a more just, equitable, and harmonious existence. In this quest for transformation, the paradigms, and teachings of heavenly kingdoms, as revealed through sacred texts and spiritual traditions, offer a profound wellspring of wisdom and insight.

Begin with an Overview:

Exploring heavenly kingdom paradigms as blueprints for earthly cultural transformation opens a door to a realm of transcendent principles and divine ideals, beckoning us to reimagine the very foundations upon which our societies are built. These celestial paradigms, woven into the fabric of sacred narratives and teachings, serve as beacons of hope, illuminating the path toward a world where justice, peace, equity, and communal well-being are not mere aspirations but tangible realities.

List of Key Points:

1. Divine Justice: A fundamental tenet that permeates the teachings of heavenly kingdoms, divine justice transcends the limitations of earthly legal systems, offering a holistic vision of fairness, accountability, and restorative justice rooted in the inherent dignity and equality of all beings.
2. Enduring Peace: Heavenly kingdom paradigms envision a world where peace is not merely the absence of conflict but a state of profound harmony, rooted in the cultivation of inner peace and a deep reverence for the sanctity of all life.
3. Radical Equity: Challenging the entrenched systems of inequality and oppression that have plagued human societies, these paradigms embody a radical commitment to equity, where every individual is afforded equal opportunities and access to the resources necessary for their flourishing.
4. Communal Well-being: Transcending the narrow confines of individualism, heavenly kingdom paradigms champion a holistic vision of communal well-being, where the collective good is uplifted, and the needs of the most vulnerable are prioritized, fostering a sense of shared responsibility and interdependence.

Elaboration:

The pursuit of divine justice, as exemplified in the teachings of heavenly kingdoms, calls us to cultivate a profound reverence for the inherent worth and dignity of every human being. It summons us to transcend the limitations of retributive justice systems that too often perpetuate cycles of harm and resentment, and instead embrace a restorative approach rooted in compassion, accountability, and a genuine desire for healing and reconciliation.

The vision of enduring peace espoused by heavenly kingdom paradigms extends far beyond the mere absence of war or conflict. It beckons us to cultivate a state of profound inner tranquility, a deep reverence for the sanctity of all life, and a willingness to embrace nonviolence as a way of being, not merely a tactic. This transcendent understanding of peace challenges us to confront the roots of violence and conflict within our own hearts and minds, recognizing that true peace can only flourish when it is grounded in a commitment to compassion, empathy, and a genuine respect for the inherent worth of all beings.

The call for radical equity embedded within heavenly kingdom teachings strikes at the heart of the systemic inequalities and oppressive structures that have plagued human societies for far too long. It demands that we dismantle the barriers that have perpetuated injustice and deprived countless individuals of their fundamental rights and opportunities. This vision of equity challenges us to embrace a bold and uncompromising commitment to creating a world where every person, regardless of their race, gender, creed, or socioeconomic status, has access to the resources and opportunities necessary to flourish and reach their full potential.

Underpinning these principles is the unwavering commitment to communal well-being that lies at the core of heavenly kingdom paradigms. It invites us to transcend the narrow confines of individualism and embrace a holistic vision of interdependence and shared responsibility. In this paradigm, the well-being of the collective is upheld as a sacred duty, and the needs of the most vulnerable members of society are prioritized, fostering a sense of solidarity, empathy, and a profound recognition of our interconnectedness.

As we grapple with the myriad challenges that confront our world, the heavenly kingdom paradigms offer a wellspring of profound wisdom and guidance, beckoning us to reimagine the very foundations upon which our societies are built. By embracing these celestial teachings and embodying their timeless principles, we open ourselves to the possibility of catalyzing transformative change – change that transcends mere surface-level reforms and strikes at the very roots of injustice, inequality, and disharmony.

These paradigms serve as a clarion call, urging cultural leaders, policymakers, and agents of change to align their earthly endeavors with the divine ideals of justice, peace, equity, and communal well-being. By doing so, we can forge a path toward a world where the inherent dignity of every human being is upheld, where conflicts are resolved through compassion and nonviolence, and where the collective flourishing of all is the guiding light that illuminates our shared journey.

In a world that often seems mired in darkness and despair, the heavenly kingdom paradigms offer a beacon of hope, a vision of a more enlightened and harmonious existence that transcends the limitations of our present reality. It is through the embodiment of these timeless principles that we can ignite a cultural transformation that reverberates across generations, leaving an indelible mark on the tapestry of human civilization and ushering in a new era of justice, peace, and collective well-being.

Scriptural Paradigms of Justice and Equity

As we embark on the noble endeavor of cultural transformation, it becomes imperative to understand and embrace the profound concepts of justice and equity that permeate the teachings of heavenly kingdoms. These principles, intricately woven into the tapestry of sacred texts and spiritual traditions, serve as guiding lights, illuminating the path toward a more just, equitable, and harmonious existence.

The pursuit of justice (mishpat) and equity (tsedek) lies at the heart of any endeavor aimed at creating lasting, meaningful change. To truly grasp their significance, we must first acknowledge the criticality of these principles in shaping a society where every individual is treated with fairness, dignity, and respect.

Glimpsing the Depths of Justice: Justice, often misunderstood as mere adherence to legal frameworks, transcends the confines of human-made systems. At its core, mishpat speaks to a profound sense of righteousness, a commitment to ensuring that every individual receives their due, both in the eyes of the law and in the realm of moral rectitude. It demands that we confront injustice in all its forms, from systemic oppression to individual acts of wrongdoing, and strive to create a world where fairness and accountability reign supreme.

The Call of Equity: Complementing the pursuit of justice is the unwavering commitment to equity, embodied in the principle of tsedek. This concept challenges us to move beyond mere equality, recognizing that true fairness requires a deep understanding of the unique circumstances and needs of each individual. Equity demands that we dismantle the barriers that have perpetuated injustice, and proactively create conditions that enable every person, regardless of their background or circumstances, to access the resources and opportunities necessary for their flourishing.

As we delve deeper into the realms of justice and equity, we begin to appreciate the intricate interplay between these two principles. Justice, without equity, risks perpetuating systemic inequalities, while equity, without a foundation of justice, may lack the moral force and accountability necessary to bring about lasting change.

The pursuit of justice calls us to cultivate a deep reverence for the inherent worth and dignity of every human being. It challenges us to transcend the limitations of retributive systems that too often perpetuate cycles of harm and resentment, and instead embrace a restorative approach rooted in compassion, accountability, and a genuine desire for healing and reconciliation. Justice demands that we confront injustice wherever it lurks, from the halls of power to the most marginalized communities, and work tirelessly to uphold the principles of fairness and righteousness.

Equity, on the other hand, beckons us to embrace a radical commitment to creating a world where every person, regardless of their race, gender, creed, or socioeconomic status, has access to the resources and opportunities necessary to reach their full potential. It demands that we dismantle the barriers that have perpetuated injustice and deprived countless individuals of their fundamental rights, paving the way for a society where true fairness and equal opportunity reign supreme.

As we reflect on these profound principles, we are reminded that the journey toward cultural transformation is not merely an intellectual exercise but a sacred calling that demands our unwavering commitment and our willingness to confront the challenges that lie ahead. It is a journey that requires us to examine our own biases, confront our own complicity in systems of injustice, and embrace a spirit of humility, empathy, and compassion.

The teachings of heavenly kingdoms remind us that justice and equity are not mere abstractions but living, breathing ideals that must be embodied in our actions, our policies, and our social structures. They challenge us to reimagine the very foundations upon which our societies are built, and to create a world where the inherent dignity of every human being is upheld, where conflicts are resolved through nonviolence and restorative practices, and where the collective flourishing of all is the guiding light that illuminates our shared journey.

As we move forward, let us embrace the wisdom and guidance offered by these celestial paradigms, allowing them to inform and shape our efforts toward cultural transformation. For it is through the embodiment of justice and equity, in all their profound depths and nuances, that we can forge a path toward a more just, equitable, and harmonious existence – a world where the principles of righteousness and fairness reign supreme, and where every individual is afforded the opportunity to thrive and realize their full potential.

In the coming sections, we will explore how these sacred principles of justice and equity can be woven into the fabric of our cultural narratives, our social structures, and our collective endeavors. We will delve into the practical applications and implications of these teachings, and examine how they can serve as a compass, guiding us toward a more enlightened and harmonious existence – one that embodies the highest ideals of heavenly kingdoms and heralds a new era of justice, equity, and communal well-being.

Transformative Power of Scriptural Narratives

To embark on the transformative journey of scriptural narratives is to delve into the very essence of human civilization, exploring the profound influence that these sacred texts have had in shaping our cultural landscapes and our collective understanding of the world. From the earliest whispers of oral traditions to the echoes that reverberate across modern societies, the power of scriptural narratives lies in their ability to transcend the boundaries of time and space, captivating the hearts and minds of humanity with their timeless wisdom and eternal truths.

The Genesis of Revelation: In the distant mists of antiquity, long before the written word adorned the pages of history, the seeds of scriptural narratives took root in the collective consciousness of ancient societies. The Hebrew Bible, regarded as the bedrock of Abrahamic faiths, traces its origins to the oral traditions of the Israelites, passed down from generation to generation with reverence and fervor. These ancient stories imbued with the wisdom of the ages, spoke of the divine mysteries that governed the universe and the sacred covenant between the Creator and humanity.

As the dawn of literacy illuminated the path of human civilization, the oral traditions gradually wove their way into the tapestry of written accounts, giving birth to the earliest known written works of the Hebrew Bible. The Pentateuch, comprising the first five books, laid the foundation for a literary masterpiece that would reverberate across the centuries, serving as a guiding light for generations to come.

The Codification of Sacred Teachings: The codification of the Old Testament marked a pivotal juncture in the evolution of scriptural narratives, solidifying the teachings and stories that had hitherto been handed down through the oral tradition. The compilation of these sacred texts, encompassing narratives of creation, divine revelation, and the journey of the Israelites, provided a tangible repository of knowledge and wisdom that would shape the course of human civilization.

Yet, the transformative power of scriptural narratives was not confined to a single tradition. The emergence of the New Testament, born from the life and teachings of Jesus Christ, ushered in a new era of spiritual awakening and cultural transformation. The gospels, epistles, and apocalyptic writings woven into this sacred text not only reshaped the religious landscape but also profoundly impacted the philosophical, ethical, and societal foundations of the Western world.

The Odyssey of Dissemination: As the centuries unfolded, the dissemination of biblical texts across the globe marked a remarkable journey of cross-cultural influence and adaptation. The translation of these sacred narratives into myriad languages facilitated their embrace by diverse cultures, each interpreting and adapting the teachings to their unique contexts and worldviews.

From the ancient civilizations of the Middle East to the sprawling empires of Europe, the narratives of the Bible found resonance in the hearts and minds of countless individuals, shaping cultural norms, values, and societal structures. The teachings of love, compassion, justice, and redemption transcended geographical boundaries, inspiring artistic masterpieces, philosophical movements, and profound social transformations.

The Crucible of Controversy: Yet, the odyssey of scriptural narratives was not without its challenges and controversies. The Reformation, a seismic event that shook the foundations of Christendom, marked a critical juncture in the interpretation and dissemination of biblical texts. The clash of ideologies and the quest for religious freedom unleashed a torrent of theological debates, challenging long-held beliefs and paving the way for new perspectives and interpretations.

The Enlightenment, with its emphasis on reason and scientific inquiry, further ignited the flames of controversy, casting a critical eye on the literal interpretations of scriptural narratives. This period marked a pivotal shift in the understanding of these sacred texts, as scholars and theologians alike sought to reconcile the wisdom of the ages with the burgeoning advancements of human knowledge.

Echoes in the Modern Era: As the tides of modernity swept across the globe, the transformative power of scriptural narratives remained undimmed, adapting and evolving to meet the challenges and complexities of the contemporary world. Contemporary theological interpretations and approaches have sought to bridge the divide between ancient wisdom and modern sensibilities, fostering a deeper understanding of the timeless truths embedded within these sacred texts.

From the liberation movements of the 20th century to the ongoing struggles for social justice and human rights, the narratives of the Bible have served as a wellspring of inspiration and guidance, empowering individuals and communities to challenge oppression, uphold human dignity, and strive for a more equitable and compassionate world.

As we stand at the precipice of a new era, the transformative power of scriptural narratives endures, inviting us to embark on a journey of self-reflection, cultural transformation, and spiritual awakening. These sacred texts, with their rich tapestry of stories, teachings, and revelations, offer us a lens through which to navigate the complexities of our modern existence, reminding us of the eternal truths that transcend the boundaries of time and space.

In the embrace of these scriptural narratives, we find solace, wisdom, and a call to action – a call to embody the virtues of love, compassion, and justice, and to work tirelessly toward a world that reflects the highest ideals of human civilization. As we walk this path of transformation, may the teachings of these sacred texts guide our steps, enlighten our minds, and inspire us to create a world where the transformative power of divine revelation resonates in every heart, every culture, and every generation to come.

Lessons From the Book of Acts

As the dawn of the first century AD ushered in a new era, the ancient world bore witness to the birth of a movement that would forever alter the course of human history. This is the story of the early Christian Church, as chronicled in the Book of Acts, a testament to the transformative power of faith, perseverance, and divine guidance.

Setting the Stage: The Birth of a MovementThe Book of Acts opens in Jerusalem, a city steeped in the rich tapestry of ancient Judaic tradition, where a small band of followers, emboldened by the teachings of Jesus Christ, gathered in the aftermath of his death and resurrection. It was here, in the crucible of a rapidly changing world, that the seeds of a new faith took root – a faith that would ultimately transcend the boundaries of culture, language, and empire.

The Protagonists: Apostles and EvangelistsAt the forefront of this nascent movement stood the Apostles, those chosen by Christ himself to spread his teachings to the far corners of the earth. Among them were Peter, the steadfast rock upon which the Church was built, and Paul, a former persecutor of Christians who underwent a profound spiritual transformation, becoming one of the most influential evangelists of the early Church.

Alongside these seminal figures were countless others whose names may have faded from historical records but whose unwavering faith and courage played a pivotal role in the growth and survival of the early Christian community. From the deacon Stephen, whose martyrdom ignited a wave of persecution, to Priscilla and Aquila, whose home served as a haven for the faithful, these unsung heroes embodied the very essence of the early Church – a community bound by love, sacrifice, and an unwavering commitment to the Gospel.

The Challenge: Persecution and Cultural BarriersYet the path of the early Christians was not without its trials and tribulations. As the movement gained traction, it faced fierce opposition from the Roman authorities, who perceived it as a threat to the established order. Persecution and violence became the harsh realities that tested the resolve of the faithful, with many paying the ultimate price for their beliefs.

Beyond the physical persecution, the early Church grappled with the challenge of spreading the Gospel across diverse cultural landscapes, each with its own deeply entrenched traditions and belief systems. The Apostles and evangelists found themselves navigating the complexities of ancient societies, determined to share the transformative message of Christ while respecting the cultural sensitivities of those they sought to convert.

The Solution: Divine Guidance and a Multicultural EmbraceIn the face of these formidable challenges, the early Christians turned to the very foundation of their faith – divine guidance and the universal message of love and redemption. Guided by the Holy Spirit, they embarked on a series of missionary journeys, traversing the vast expanse of the Roman Empire and beyond, adapting their teachings to resonate with the diverse cultures they encountered.

From the cosmopolitan city of Antioch to the intellectual heart of Athens, the Apostles and evangelists carried the torch of the Gospel, engaging with philosophers, scholars, and the common people alike. They embraced the richness of each culture, finding ways to weave the teachings of Christ into the tapestry of local traditions, creating a harmonious fusion of faith and cultural identity.

Within the early Christian communities themselves, a spirit of unity and communal living took root, transcending ethnic and social divides. The believers shared their possessions, cared for the widows and orphans, and upheld the principles of love, forgiveness, and selflessness, setting an example that resonated far beyond the confines of their gatherings.

The Outcome: A Faith UnboundedThe impact of the early Church's efforts was profound and far-reaching. Despite the trials and tribulations they faced, the message of Christ spread like wildfire across the ancient world, igniting the hearts and minds of countless individuals from all walks of life. By the end of the first century, Christian communities had taken root in major cities throughout the Roman Empire, from Rome itself to the bustling trade centers of Asia Minor.

This rapid growth was fueled not only by the unwavering dedication of the early Christians but also by the power of their message – a message that offered hope, redemption, and a sense of belonging to those who embraced it. The early Church's embrace of diversity and its ability to adapt to different cultural contexts laid the foundation for its ultimate global reach, transcending the boundaries of geography, language, and ethnicity.

Lessons for Eternity: Navigating Cultural ChangeAs we reflect on the Book of Acts and the remarkable journey of the early Church, several enduring lessons emerge, offering guidance for modern religious movements and cultural transformations.

First and foremost, the early Christians' steadfast faith and unwavering commitment to their beliefs serve as a powerful reminder of the transformative power of conviction and perseverance. In the face of overwhelming adversity, they refused to compromise their values, standing firm in their convictions and allowing nothing to deter them from their mission.

Secondly, the early Church's embrace of cultural diversity and its ability to adapt its teachings to resonate with different societies highlight the importance of understanding and respecting cultural nuances. By finding common ground and weaving the Gospel into the fabric of local traditions, the early Christians created a sense of belonging and ownership that facilitated the spread of their faith.

Furthermore, the emphasis on communal living and shared values within the early Christian communities underscores the significance of fostering a sense of unity and collective purpose. By prioritizing love, compassion, and selflessness, the early Christians created a powerful model of community that transcended individual differences and fostered a deep sense of connection and support.

Finally, the Book of Acts serves as a testament to the enduring power of faith and the transformative potential of a message rooted in love, redemption, and hope. The early Christians' unwavering belief in the divine guidance they received and their commitment to sharing a message of hope and salvation continues to inspire and guide modern religious movements and cultural transformations.

As we stand on the precipice of a new era, grappling with the complexities of cultural change and societal shifts, the lessons of the early Church resonate with profound relevance. May we embrace their unwavering faith, their respect for diversity, their commitment to unity, and their unwavering belief in the transformative power of love and hope, as we navigate the challenges and opportunities of our time.

In the echoes of the Book of Acts, we find a timeless guide for effecting meaningful and lasting change – a guide that calls us to transcend boundaries, embrace diversity, and hold fast to the eternal truths that have shaped the course of human civilization. It is a call to action, a rallying cry for a world where faith, compassion, and unity prevail, and where the transformative power of the Gospel continues to ignite the hearts and minds of generations to come.

Transformative Leadership in Biblical Times

Since antiquity, the concept of leadership has been inextricably woven into the fabric of human civilization, shaping the trajectory of societies and cultures throughout the ages. Among the many sources that have influenced our understanding of leadership, the biblical narratives stand as a profound and enduring wellspring of wisdom, offering timeless insights into the nature of transformative leadership and its enduring impact on cultural evolution.

The Biblical Blueprint: Leadership Rooted in Divine CallingAt the heart of biblical leadership lies the principle of divine calling, a notion that sets it apart from secular leadership paradigms. The great leaders of the Bible – figures such as Moses, David, and Nehemiah – were chosen by God to fulfill specific purposes and guide their people through pivotal moments in history. This sense of divine mandate imbued their leadership with a profound sense of purpose, unwavering conviction, and unshakable moral fortitude.

Moses, for instance, was called upon to lead the Israelites out of Egyptian bondage and deliver them to the Promised Land. His leadership was forged in the crucible of adversity, as he navigated the treacherous wilderness, contended with the doubts and rebellions of his people, and ultimately succeeded in establishing a new nation founded upon the principles of divine law and covenant. Moses' unwavering faith in his divine calling and his willingness to surrender to God's plan were essential to his success as a transformative leader.

Similarly, the life of David, the celebrated king of Israel, exemplifies the transformative power of leadership grounded in divine purpose. Anointed by the prophet Samuel as a young shepherd, David's rise to power was marked by trials and tribulations that tested his faith and character. Yet, through it all, he remained steadfast in his commitment to God's will, ultimately uniting the fractured tribes of Israel into a mighty kingdom and laying the foundations for a dynasty that would endure for generations.

The Visionary's Path: Navigating Adversity and Cultural TransformationInherent in the biblical narrative is the recognition that transformative leadership is not a linear path but rather a journey fraught with obstacles, opposition, and the constant need for adaptation. The lives of the great leaders of the Bible are replete with examples of adversity faced and overcome, serving as a testament to the resilience and perseverance required to effect lasting cultural change.

Consider the story of Nehemiah, whose unwavering commitment to rebuilding the walls of Jerusalem in the face of mockery, threats, and opposition from neighboring nations serves as a powerful metaphor for the challenges faced by transformative leaders throughout history. Undeterred by the naysayers and the formidable task at hand, Nehemiah rallied his people, fostered a sense of unity and purpose, and ultimately succeeded in restoring the city's defenses and renewing its spiritual heart.

The biblical accounts also underscore the importance of adapting one's leadership approach to the unique cultural contexts and challenges at hand. Moses, for example, had to navigate the complex dynamics of leading diverse and often fractious people, tailoring his leadership style to address the specific needs and circumstances of the Israelites as they journeyed through the wilderness.

Similarly, the Apostle Paul, whose missionary endeavors played a pivotal role in the spread of early Christianity, demonstrated a remarkable ability to contextualize his message and leadership approach to resonate with the diverse cultures he encountered. From the philosophical discourse in Athens to the practical guidance he provided to nascent Christian communities, Paul's leadership was marked by a profound understanding of cultural nuances and a willingness to adapt his methods to facilitate meaningful transformation.

The Ethical Foundations: Moral Leadership and Lasting Legacy-Perhaps the most enduring legacy of biblical leadership lies in its emphasis on moral and ethical principles as the bedrock of transformative change. The great leaders of the Bible were not mere strategists or tacticians but embodiments of the virtues and values they espoused, serving as living examples of integrity, justice, and compassion.

Moses, in his role as a lawgiver, established a comprehensive ethical code that not only governed the daily lives of the Israelites but also laid the foundations for a just and equitable society. His leadership was rooted in a deep commitment to upholding the principles of righteousness, fairness, and care for the vulnerable, setting a precedent for subsequent generations of leaders to follow.

In the New Testament, the teachings of Jesus Christ and the epistles of his apostles further solidified the connection between ethical leadership and lasting cultural impact. The Sermon on the Mount, with its timeless exhortations to love one's enemies, turn the other cheek, and seek righteousness above all else, provided a radical blueprint for transformative leadership grounded in love, humility, and service to others.

The biblical narratives also underscore the importance of leaders embracing their roles as stewards and servants, placing the needs of their people above personal ambition or gain. The example of David, who acknowledged his transgressions and sought repentance, serves as a powerful reminder that true leadership is not defined by perfection but by a willingness to humble oneself, learn from mistakes, and strive for a higher moral standard.

The Enduring Influence: From Ancient Texts to Contemporary ContextsThe legacy of biblical leadership extends far beyond the confines of religious tradition, having profoundly shaped the discourse on leadership and cultural transformation throughout history. From the ethical frameworks that underpin modern democratic societies to the principles of servant leadership espoused by contemporary management theorists, the influence of biblical leadership paradigms is both pervasive and enduring.

Moreover, the timeless wisdom contained within the biblical narratives continues to offer invaluable guidance for leaders navigating the complexities of the modern world. In an era marked by rapid cultural shifts, globalization, and the erosion of traditional boundaries, the principles of adaptability, cultural sensitivity, and ethical grounding championed by the great leaders of the Bible remain as relevant as ever.

As we grapple with the challenges of the 21st century – from environmental crises to social inequalities to political instability – the call for transformative leadership that transcends narrow self-interest and embraces a higher moral purpose has never been more urgent. By drawing upon the enduring lessons of biblical leadership, we can cultivate a new generation of leaders committed to effecting positive and sustainable change, guided by the timeless values of compassion, justice, and service to humanity.

In the end, the biblical narratives remind us that leadership is not merely a position of power or authority but a sacred trust, a calling to be a catalyst for positive transformation in the lives of individuals, communities, and societies. As we strive to navigate the complexities of our modern world, may we be inspired by the examples of the great leaders of the Bible, who demonstrated that through unwavering faith, ethical grounding, and a commitment to service, even the most daunting challenges can be overcome, and lasting cultural change can be achieved.

12

THE DISTRIBUTION OF WEALTH: BIBLICAL MANDATES

The Concept of Stewardship: Divine Ownership and Human Responsibility

In the vast expanse of human endeavors, few concepts carry the profound weight and enduring relevance of stewardship. This timeless principle, deeply rooted in the biblical narratives, transcends the realms of faith and spirituality, offering a powerful lens through which we can understand our relationship with the resources entrusted to us and our role as caretakers of the earth's abundance.

At its core, the concept of stewardship is anchored in the fundamental belief that divine ownership permeates all aspects of creation. The biblical texts resound with the notion that we are not the ultimate owners of the resources at our disposal, but rather temporary custodians, charged with the sacred responsibility of managing and preserving these gifts for the benefit of present and future generations. This paradigm shift from ownership to stewardship has profound implications for how we perceive and interact with the wealth and resources that shape our individual and collective existence.

The parables and teachings of Jesus Christ provide a rich tapestry of insights into the concept of stewardship, weaving together spiritual truths and practical wisdom. Take, for instance, the Parable of the Talents, wherein a master entrusts his servants with varying amounts of wealth and expects them to be diligent in their stewardship. The servants who faithfully invest and multiply their resources are commended, while the one who squanders his opportunity is condemned. This narrative not only underscores the importance of responsible resource management but also serves as a poignant reminder that our actions carry both temporal and eternal consequences.

Beyond the parables, the biblical narratives abound with examples of individuals who embodied the principles of stewardship, serving as role models for the ethical and judicious use of resources. Consider the story of Joseph, the son of Jacob, who, through his wisdom and foresight, guided the nation of Egypt through a prolonged famine by implementing a system of resource conservation and distribution. Joseph's actions exemplify the practical application of stewardship, demonstrating how careful planning and responsible management can mitigate crises and ensure the well-being of communities.

As we grapple with the complexities of our modern world, the concept of stewardship takes on even greater significance. In an era marked by finite resources, environmental degradation, and growing economic disparities, the principles of stewardship offer a compelling framework for addressing these challenges. By embracing a mindset of responsible resource management and equitable distribution, we can work toward achieving a more sustainable and just global society.

For instance, the principles of stewardship can inform our approach to environmental conservation, encouraging us to view the earth's natural resources not as commodities to be exploited but as sacred trusts to be cherished and protected. This paradigm shift could catalyze a shift toward more sustainable practices, from renewable energy initiatives to responsible waste management, ensuring that we leave behind a habitable planet for future generations.

Furthermore, the concept of stewardship has profound implications for economic justice and wealth distribution. In a world where a vast chasm separates the affluent from the impoverished, the biblical call for responsible stewardship challenges us to rethink our attitudes toward wealth and resources. It compels us to move beyond the narrow confines of self-interest and embrace a broader vision of shared prosperity, one where resources are equitably distributed and the needs of the most vulnerable are prioritized.

Ultimately, the concept of stewardship serves as a powerful reminder that our role as human beings is not to dominate or exploit the earth's resources, but rather to nurture and preserve them for the benefit of all. By embracing the biblical principles of stewardship, we can cultivate a more holistic and sustainable relationship with the world around us, one that fosters a harmonious balance between our material needs and our moral responsibilities.

As we venture forth into an uncertain future, the concept of stewardship offers a guiding light, illuminating a path toward a more just, equitable, and sustainable world. By internalizing the lessons of divine ownership and human responsibility, we can chart a course that honors the sanctity of creation, upholds the dignity of all beings, and ensures that the bountiful resources bestowed upon us are preserved and shared for generations to come.

Tithing and Offerings: Ancient Practices With Modern Relevance

As we embark upon our exploration of tithing and offerings, it becomes evident that understanding certain key terms and concepts is crucial. These concepts not only serve as the foundation for this discourse but also provide us with a framework for appreciating the profound significance and enduring relevance of these ancient practices.

Firstly, let us consider the term "tithe." At its core, the tithe was a commandment ingrained in the ancient Israelite society, wherein individuals were required to set aside a portion of their agricultural produce or wealth for specific purposes. However, the concept of tithing carries far more weight than a mere religious obligation. It serves as a testament to the principle of divine ownership, acknowledging that all resources ultimately belong to the Creator, and we are mere stewards entrusted with their management and distribution.

Closely intertwined with the concept of tithing are "offerings." These voluntary contributions, whether in the form of material goods or monetary offerings, were an integral part of the ancient Israelite religious and societal fabric. Offerings were not merely acts of piety; they represented a deeply rooted understanding of the interconnectedness of human existence and the collective responsibility to support those in need, maintain religious institutions, and honor the divine.

As we delve deeper into these concepts, it becomes evident that tithing and offerings were not merely ritualistic practices but rather a comprehensive system designed to address the multifaceted needs of the ancient Israelite community. For instance, the Levitical tithe was specifically intended to support the priestly tribe, the Levites, who were dedicated to serving in religious ceremonies and maintaining places of worship. This practice ensured that those charged with spiritual leadership could devote their time and energy to their sacred duties without the burden of financial constraints.

Similarly, the festival tithe served a dual purpose: it provided resources for the celebration of religious festivals while simultaneously ensuring that those who were economically disadvantaged could partake in these communal gatherings. This practice fostered a sense of unity and inclusivity, recognizing that the collective observance of sacred traditions transcended socioeconomic barriers.

Yet another form of tithing was the tithe for the poor, which exemplified the ancient Israelites' commitment to ensuring the welfare of the most vulnerable members of society. By setting aside a portion of its resources for those in need, the community embodied the principles of compassion, charity, and social responsibility, creating a safety net for those who had fallen on hard times.

As we reflect on these ancient practices, it becomes evident that they were not merely isolated rituals but rather a holistic system that sought to address the physical, spiritual, and social needs of the community. The principles underlying tithing and offerings resonated with the core values of justice, generosity, and collective responsibility, values that remain as relevant today as they were in ancient times.

In our contemporary society, we grapple with issues of economic inequality, poverty, and the breakdown of social support systems. It is within this context that the principles of tithing and offerings offer a compelling framework for addressing these challenges. By embracing the spirit of these practices, we can cultivate a culture of charitable giving, one that transcends religious boundaries and fosters a sense of collective responsibility for the well-being of our communities.

Moreover, the principles of tithing and offerings can inform our approach to economic justice and wealth redistribution. In a world where vast disparities in wealth and resources persist, these ancient practices challenge us to rethink our attitudes toward wealth and consumption. They remind us that true prosperity lies not in the accumulation of material possessions but in the equitable distribution of resources and the empowerment of those who are marginalized.

By embracing the spirit of these practices, we can establish mechanisms for supporting societal institutions that promote education, healthcare, and social services, ensuring that the most vulnerable members of our communities have access to the resources they need to thrive. Furthermore, these principles can inspire us to create initiatives that foster sustainable economic development, empowering individuals and communities to break free from the cycles of poverty and dependency.

As we conclude our exploration of tithing and offerings, it becomes evident that these ancient practices hold a timeless wisdom that speaks to the core of our shared human experience. They remind us that true wealth lies not in material abundance alone but in the manner in which we steward and distribute the resources entrusted to us. By embracing the principles of generosity, compassion, and collective responsibility, we can work toward building a more just, equitable, and sustainable world, one that honors the ancient wisdom of our ancestors while addressing the pressing challenges of our modern age.

Jubilee: The Year of Economic Reset

In the ancient pages of the Book of Leviticus, one can find the profound concept of the Jubilee year, a radical economic reset that aimed to address the accumulation of wealth and ensure the equitable distribution of resources. As we embark on a historical timeline of this remarkable practice, we uncover a trajectory that not only illuminates the values and principles of the ancient Israelite society but also offers a compelling framework for addressing contemporary economic disparities and promoting social equity.

1. Establishing the Significance of the Jubilee: The concept of the Jubilee year served as a cornerstone of the Israelite economic and social structure, designed to mitigate the long-term consequences of poverty, debt, and the concentration of wealth in the hands of a privileged few. By exploring its origins and evolution, we gain insights into the ancient Israelites' commitment to ensuring economic justice and preserving the integrity of their society.
2. Tracing the Earliest Roots and Mentions: The earliest references to the Jubilee year can be found in the Book of Leviticus, one of the five books of the Torah. Leviticus

25:8-17 outlines the fundamental principles of the Jubilee, which was to be observed every fiftieth year, following a cycle of seven sabbatical years. According to biblical scholars, this concept likely emerged during the Israelites' settlement in the land of Canaan, approximately in the 13th century BCE.

3. Key Events, Discoveries, Adaptations, and Shifts:• The Jubilee year mandated the release of all Hebrew slaves, ensuring that no individual remained in bondage indefinitely (Leviticus 25:39-41).• All hereditary properties that had been sold or lost due to economic hardship were to be returned to their original owners or their descendants (Leviticus 25:23-28).• All debts were to be canceled, providing a fresh start for those burdened by financial obligations (Deuteronomy 15:1-3).• The land was to lie fallow, allowing it to rest and regenerate (Leviticus 25:11-12).• During the Jubilee year, the Israelites were prohibited from sowing, pruning, or harvesting, encouraging a collective reliance on God's provision.

4. Adaptations and Practices in Different Cultures and Regions: While the practice of the Jubilee year appears to have been unique to the ancient Israelite society, its principles resonated with various cultures and civilizations throughout history. For instance, the concept of debt forgiveness and the periodic redistribution of wealth can be found in the Babylonian code of Hammurabi, as well as in ancient Greek and Roman societies.

5. Contemporary Interpretations and Applications: In more recent times, the principles of the Jubilee year have inspired various movements and initiatives aimed at addressing economic inequality, debt relief, and social justice. The Jubilee 2000 campaign, for example, advocated for the cancellation of unsustainable debt burdens for impoverished nations, seeking to provide a fresh start for those trapped in cycles of poverty and underdevelopment.

6. Pivotal Moments and Challenges: While the Jubilee year represented a powerful vision of economic reset and social equity, its implementation faced significant challenges throughout history. Biblical accounts suggest that the Israelites struggled to fully adhere to its principles, as the accumulation of wealth and the consolidation of power often undermined the intended spirit of the Jubilee. Additionally, the absence of a centralizedauthority and upheavals caused by foreign invasions and conquests likely disrupted the consistent observance of this practice.

As we reflect on the historical trajectory of the Jubilee year, we are confronted with a profound truth: economic disparities and the concentration of wealth have long been a perennial struggle for societies across time and space. The Jubilee year represents an audacious attempt to address these challenges, rooted in the belief that true prosperity cannot be achieved when a select few hold the majority of resources while the masses languish in poverty and deprivation.

In our contemporary world, where economic inequalities have reached staggering proportions, the principles of the Jubilee year offer a compelling framework for rethinking our approach to wealth distribution and social justice. By embracing the spirit of debt forgiveness, wealth redistribution, and collective responsibility, we can work toward building a more equitable and sustainable economic system, one that prioritizes the wellbeing of all members of society.

Perhaps the most enduring legacy of the Jubilee year lies not in its specific regulations but in the powerful message it conveys: that true prosperity is not measured solely by the accumulation of material wealth but by the degree to which we uphold the principles of justice, compassion, and mutual responsibility. As we grapple with the complex challenges of our modern age, let us draw inspiration from this ancient wisdom, reimagining a world where economic reset and social equity are not merely utopian ideals but tangible realities that shape the fabric of our societies.

The Role of the Poor: Blessed Are the Poor in Spirit

What if poverty was a blessing rather than a curse?

This provoking question challenges our conventional thinking about poverty and wealth. In a world obsessed with material success and accumulation, the notion that poverty could be a positive state seems almost heretical. Yet, this is precisely what Jesus suggests in the Beatitudes, declaring, 'Blessed are the poor in spirit, for theirs is the kingdom of heaven' (Matthew 5:3).

At first glance, this statement appears paradoxical. How can those who lack material resources be considered blessed? To understand the profound truth behind these words, we must examine the context in which Jesus spoke them and the broader scriptural teachings on poverty and wealth.

Throughout history, poverty has been a source of immense suffering and hardship. Those struggling with poverty often lack access to basic necessities such as food, clean water, shelter, and healthcare. They face higher risks of malnutrition, disease, and exploitation. Poverty can also lead to social exclusion, limited educational opportunities, and a general sense of hopelessness or resignation.

The harsh realities of poverty have led many to view it as a condition to be eradicated, a problem to be solved through economic development, social programs, and charitable initiatives. Yet, despite these efforts, poverty persists on a global scale, with billions of individuals living in abject poverty, often perpetuated by systemic inequalities, corruption, and exploitation.

Even in wealthy nations, poverty remains a persistent challenge, with significant portions of the population struggling to afford basic necessities and access opportunities for upward mobility. The cycle of poverty can be difficult to break, as it is often compounded by factors such as lack of education, inadequate healthcare, and limited access to resources or employment opportunities.

One common misconception about poverty is that it is primarily a result of individual laziness, lack of effort, or poor decision-making. This perspective often leads to a victim-blaming mentality, where the poor are viewed as responsible for their circumstances and undeserving of assistance or compassion.

Another misconception is that poverty can be solved solely through economic growth and trickle-down effects. While economic development can create opportunities, it docs not necessarily address systemic issues or ensure equitable distribution of resources and opportunities. The belief that a rising tide will lift all boats often fails to account for structural barriers and inequality.

Additionally, some approaches to poverty alleviation focus solely on material assistance, ignoring the deeper spiritual, emotional, and psychological impacts of poverty. While providing resources is essential, a holistic approach that addresses the multidimensional nature of poverty is often overlooked.

Jesus' teachings offer a unique and profound perspective on poverty that challenges conventional wisdom. By declaring the 'poor in spirit' as blessed, Jesus suggests that true poverty is not merely a lack of material possessions but a state of humility, dependence on God, and freedom from the burden of excessive attachment to earthly wealth and status.

This spiritual poverty, or poverty of spirit, is not a condition to be pitied or eradicated but rather a state of blessedness, a pathway to the kingdom of heaven. It is a recognition that true wealth lies not in the accumulation of possessions but in a deep, abiding relationship with the Divine and a detachment from the fleeting allures of earthly riches.

Jesus' teachings emphasize that the poor in spirit are not defined by their economic status but by their posture of humility, openness to God's grace, and willingness to prioritize spiritual wealth over material gain. This perspective invites a radical reorientation of our values and a recalibration of our priorities, recognizing that true fulfillment and abundance lie not in what we possess but in the state of our souls.

The Scriptural witness provides numerous examples of those who embodied this poverty of spirit and were blessed as a result. The Apostle Paul, for instance, declared, 'I have learned to be content in whatever circumstances I am' (Philippians 4:11), having experienced both abundance and need. His contentment stemmed not from his material circumstances but from his spiritual wealth in Christ.

Similarly, the poor widow who gave her last two copper coins (Luke 21:1-4) exemplified a posture of radical trust and generosity, demonstrating that true wealth is measured not by financial means but by the condition of one's heart. Her act of selfless giving, despite her poverty, earned her Jesus' highest commendation.

Furthermore, parables of Jesus, such as the Parable of the Rich Fool (Luke 12:16-21) and the Parable of the Rich Man and Lazarus (Luke 16:19-31), serve as stark warnings against the dangers of excessive attachment to wealth and the neglect of spiritual poverty. These stories underscore the truth that those who cling to material possessions and neglect their souls risk eternal impoverishment, while those who embrace spiritual poverty are truly rich in the eyes of God.

Skeptics may argue that this perspective on poverty is unrealistic or even dangerous, as it could be used to justify or perpetuate economic injustice and exploitation. However, this misinterprets Jesus' teachings, which consistently call for compassion, generosity, and a commitment to justice for the poor and marginalized (Matthew 25:31-46).

The poverty of spirit that Jesus commends does not negate the need for material assistance or social justice initiatives. Rather, it challenges us to confront the root causes of poverty, including greed, oppression, and systemic inequalities, and to approach poverty alleviation with a holistic, compassionate perspective that recognizes the dignity and worth of every human being as a child of God.

Furthermore, some may argue that this perspective promotes a passive acceptance of poverty or discourages efforts to improve one's circumstances. However, Jesus' teachings consistently call for faithful stewardship, diligence, and the responsible use of one's talents and resources (Matthew 25:14-30). The poverty of spirit he commends is not a state of resignation but a posture of humility, trust in God's provision, and a willingness to prioritize spiritual wealth over material gain.

To embrace the transformative power of Jesus' teachings on poverty, we must first cultivate a poverty of spirit within ourselves. This involves:

1. Recognizing our dependence on God and the fleeting nature of earthly possessions.
2. Practicing gratitude for the abundance we already possess, both material and spiritual.
3. Letting go of excessive attachment to wealth, status, and the relentless pursuit of material gain.
4. Cultivating a posture of humility, generosity, and compassion toward those in need.

Secondly, we must translate this poverty of spirit into tangible actions that address the systemic causes of poverty and promote economic justice. This could involve:

1. Supporting policies and initiatives that promote equitable access to education, healthcare, and economic opportunities.
2. Advocating for fair labor practices, living wages, and ethical business practices.
3. Participating in or supporting organizations that provide

resources, empowerment, and sustainable solutions to those living in poverty.
4. Engaging in acts of service, generosity, and compassion toward those in need within our communities.

Finally, we must challenge and confront the cultural narratives that equate wealth with worth and perpetuate the idolatry of material possessions. This may involve:

1. Reexamining our own attitudes and biases toward wealth and poverty.
2. Creating spaces for open dialogue and education on the deeper spiritual and ethical dimensions of poverty.
3. Promoting alternative models of success and fulfillment that prioritize spiritual, relational, and communal well-being over individual material gain.

By embracing the poverty of spirit that Jesus commends and translating it into concrete actions of compassion and justice, we can transform our individual lives and our communities, creating a more equitable and spiritually fulfilling society that honors the inherent worth and dignity of every human being.

Wealth and Idolatry: A Biblical Warning

The allure of wealth and material possessions has been a pervasive temptation throughout human history. From ancient civilizations to modern societies, the pursuit of riches and the accumulation of earthly treasures have captivated the hearts and minds of individuals and nations alike. Yet, amidst this relentless quest for prosperity, the Scriptures offer a resounding and sobering warning: the idolization of wealth is a grave spiritual danger.

In the Gospels, Jesus Christ confronts this idolatry head-on, declaring with unambiguous clarity, "No one can serve two masters. Either you will hate the one and love the other, or you will be devoted to the one and despise the other. You cannot serve both

God and money" (Matthew 6:24). These words strike at the heart of the matter, unveiling the inherent conflict between the pursuit of wealth and the pursuit of God. When wealth becomes an object of worship and devotion, it usurps the rightful place of the Divine, leading humanity down a path of spiritual impoverishment.

The apostle Paul echoes this warning, cautioning Timothy and the early church against the seductive allure of riches: "For the love of money is a root of all kinds of evil. Some people, eager for money, have wandered from the faith and pierced themselves with many griefs" (1 Timothy 6:10). The pursuit of wealth, when driven by misplaced desires and improper motivations, can lead individuals astray, causing them to compromise their values, betray their principles, and ultimately, forsake their faith.

The theological and ethical dangers of wealth accumulation are manifold. At its core, the idolization of wealth represents a form of idolatry, a violation of the first and greatest commandment to love God with all one's heart, soul, and mind (Matthew 22:37). When wealth becomes the object of our affection and the source of our security, it displaces God from the throne of our lives, undermining our relationship with the Creator and eroding our spiritual vitality.

Moreover, the pursuit of riches can breed greed, envy, and a spirit of selfishness that is antithetical to the teachings of Christ. Jesus warned, "Watch out! Be on your guard against all kinds of greed; life does not consist in an abundance of possessions" (Luke 12:15). The relentless accumulation of wealth can foster a mindset of scarcity and a fear of lacking, leading to a hoarding mentality that neglects the needs of others and ignores the call to generosity and compassion.

Furthermore, the idolization of wealth can distort our priorities and values, causing us to prioritize material gain over spiritual growth and ethical considerations. It can blind us to the plight of the poor and marginalized, eroding our sense of empathy and social responsibility. The prophet Amos condemned the wealthy who "trample on the poor and force them to dust off the earth"

(Amos 2:7), highlighting the potential for wealth to breed oppression and injustice.

For individual believers and faith communities, these warnings serve as a clarion call to vigilance and a reexamination of our relationship with wealth. We must guard our hearts against the seductive allure of material possessions and the false promises of security and fulfillment they offer. Instead, we must cultivate a posture of spiritual poverty, recognizing our utter dependence on God and the fleeting nature of earthly riches.

This does not mean a complete rejection of wealth or material resources but rather a healthy detachment from them and a proper ordering of priorities. We must learn to hold wealth with an open hand, recognizing that we are mere stewards of God's resources, entrusted with the responsibility of using them for the furtherance of His Kingdom and the betterment of humanity.

Furthermore, faith communities must create spaces for accountability, discipleship, and the cultivation of counter-cultural values that challenge the idolatry of wealth. Through teaching, preaching, and communal practices, we can foster an ethos of simplicity, generosity, and contentment, modeling an alternative to the consumeristic and materialistic values of the dominant culture.

To guard against the idolatry of wealth, individual believers and faith communities can embrace various spiritual disciplines and practices. First and foremost, we must cultivate a posture of gratitude and contentment, recognizing the abundant blessings we already possess and finding joy in the simple pleasures of life. The apostle Paul exhorts us to be content in all circumstances, for "godliness with contentment is great gain" (1 Timothy 6:6).

Additionally, we can engage in regular acts of generosity and giving, breaking the grip of material possessions on our hearts and experiencing the joy of sharing our resources with others. Jesus commended the poor widow who gave her last two coins, saying, "Truly I tell you, this poor widow has put more into the treasury than all the others" (Mark 12:43). Such acts of sacrificial giving realign our priorities and remind us of the true nature of wealth.

Moreover, we can embrace simplicity in our lifestyles, consciously choosing to live below our means and resisting the temptation to accumulate more than we need. By embracing voluntary simplicity, we can free ourselves from the burden of excessive possessions and cultivate a deeper appreciation for the non-material aspects of life, such as relationships, spiritual growth, and service to others.

Finally, we must actively engage in practices of spiritual formation and discipleship, nurturing our relationship with God and allowing His truth to shape our perspectives on wealth and possessions. Through regular prayer, Scripture reading, and participation in faith communities, we can continually recalibrate our values and priorities, ensuring that our pursuit of material gain never overshadows our pursuit of the eternal and the transcendent.

In a world that idolizes wealth and material success, the Scriptural warnings against the idolization of wealth stand as a timeless and prophetic call to reorient our lives. By heeding these warnings and embracing spiritual disciplines and community practices that foster a healthy relationship with wealth, we can guard our hearts against the corrosive effects of greed and materialism. In doing so, we not only safeguard our spiritual vitality but also become agents of transformation, embodying an alternative narrative that challenges the idolatry of wealth and points others toward the true source of life, meaning, and fulfillment.

The Widow's Mite: Lessons in Sacrificial Giving

1. Setting the Scene: The Widow's Act of Generosity

In the midst of the bustling temple courts in Jerusalem, a scene unfolded that would capture the attention of Jesus and indelibly etch itself into the pages of Scripture. As recorded in the Gospel of Mark, the Lord observed the crowds depositing their offerings into the temple treasury. Among them was a seemingly unremarkable figure – a poor widow who, with a heart overflowing with love for God, humbly offered her last two small copper coins (Mark 12:41-44).

To fully appreciate the significance of this act, we must understand the precarious socioeconomic conditions faced by widows in biblical times. Lacking the protection and provision of a husband, and with limited opportunities for employment or financial security, widows often found themselves living on the fringes of society, relying on the charity of others or scraping by with meager resources.

Yet, in the face of such adversity, this widow's act of giving transcended her circumstances, revealing a depth of faith and generosity that would be commended by the Lord Himself. By offering her last two coins, she surrendered all she had to live on, demonstrating a level of trust and devotion that stands as a powerful testament to the nature of true sacrifice and the transformative power of faith.

2. The Value of Sacrificial Giving

As Jesus observed the widow's act, He seized the opportunity to impart a profound lesson to His disciples. Calling them to Himself, He declared, "Truly I tell you, this poor widow has put more into the treasury than all the others" (Mark 12:43). This statement was not merely a comparison of monetary values but a profound commentary on the nature of genuine generosity.

While the wealthy contributors gave from their abundance, the widow's offering came from the depths of her poverty. Her gift was not measured by its monetary value but by the extent of her sacrifice and the sincerity of her heart. In the eyes of God, the true measure of generosity lies not in the amount given but in the spirit with which it is offered.

Through this narrative, Jesus challenges the prevailing notion that generosity is determined by wealth or status. Instead, He elevates the sacrificial giving of the poor as a model of true devotion and faith. The widow's act serves as a reminder that genuine generosity is not a matter of excess but of selfless surrender – a willingness to give without reserve, trusting in the provision and faithfulness of God.

3. The Nature of True Generosity and Faith

The widow's mite is not merely a lesson in giving but a profound revelation of the nature of true generosity and unwavering faith. Her act exemplifies the essence of the Gospel itself – the call to surrender all, hold nothing back, and place our complete trust in the sufficiency of God.

Just as the widow gave her all, Christ Himself would soon offer the ultimate sacrificial gift – His very life on the cross. In this light, the widow's offering becomes a foreshadowing of the supreme act of generosity and love that would redeem humanity from sin and brokenness.

Moreover, the widow's example reminds us that faith is not merely an intellectual assent but a way of life – a daily surrender of our resources, our plans, and our very selves to the will and purposes of God. True faith demands a relinquishing of control, a willingness to trust in the unseen, and to live in radical dependence upon the One who holds all things together.

As we reflect on this narrative, we are challenged to examine the depth of our own faith and the authenticity of our generosity. Do we cling tightly to our possessions, driven by fear and a scarcity mindset, or do we hold them with open hands, ready to give as the Lord leads? Do we give from our abundance or are we willing to offer sacrificially, trusting in God's provision even in the face of uncertainty?

4. Inspiring Contemporary Acts of Sacrificial Giving

The widow's act of sacrificial giving stands as a timeless inspiration, challenging believers in every generation to embrace a lifestyle of radical generosity and unwavering faith. In a world marked by consumerism, materialism, and the relentless pursuit of wealth, her example beckons us to a countercultural posture – one that prioritizes the eternal over the temporal and places our trust in the unfailing promises of God.

As we reflect on the widow's mite, we are called to consider how we can contribute meaningfully to our communities and support those in need. It may involve giving financially to support ministries, organizations, or individuals who are addressing poverty, hunger, or social injustice. It could mean sacrificially offering our time and talents to serve the marginalized, the oppressed, or the overlooked within our spheres of influence.

Yet, beyond material giving, the widow's example invites us to a deeper level of surrender – a willingness to lay down our plans, our dreams, and our ambitions at the feet of the One who knows the end from the beginning. It is a call to embrace a life of radical obedience, following the leading of the Holy Spirit even when it defies conventional wisdom or challenges our comfort zones.

In doing so, we not only honor the legacy of the widow's mite but also bear witness to the transformative power of the Gospel – a message that transcends cultural boundaries and speaks to the deepest longings of the human heart. As we embrace the spirit of sacrificial giving, we become living testimonies of God's love and grace, inspiring others to join in the sacred work of ushering in His Kingdom on earth as it is in heaven.

Conclusion

The story of the widow's mite stands as a timeless reminder of the power of sacrificial giving and the depth of faith required to truly surrender all to God. In the face of overwhelming circumstances, this humble woman exemplified a level of trust and generosity that would be commended by the Lord Himself, becoming a beacon of inspiration for generations to come.

As we reflect on her example, we are challenged to evaluate the posture of our own hearts and the authenticity of our commitment to the ways of the Kingdom. Are we willing to embrace a lifestyle of radical generosity, laying down our possessions, our plans, and our very lives for the sake of the Gospel? Can we trust in the sufficiency of God, even when circumstances seem bleak and our resources appear meager?

The widow's act beckons us to a countercultural journey – one that defies the allure of wealth and material possessions, and instead, embraces the eternal riches found in a life surrendered to Christ. As we answer this call, we not only honor the legacy of this remarkable woman but also participate in the divine work of ushering in the Kingdom of God, becoming vessels of His love and agents of transformation in a world desperately in need of His hope and healing.

In the end, the widow's mite is not merely a story of generosity but a powerful testimony of faith – a reminder that true abundance is found not in the accumulation of wealth but in the surrender of our lives to the One who has overcome the world.

Economic Justice: Prophetic Voices

1. Contrasting Visions: Oppression and Equity

In the ancient world, the stark contrast between economic oppression and the prophetic call for justice resounded with haunting clarity. On one hand, the biblical narrative reveals societies plagued by exploitation, where the powerful amassed wealth at the expense of the vulnerable. The cries of the impoverished echoed through the streets, their plight seemingly lost amidst the opulence of the privileged few.

Yet, in this landscape of inequality, a chorus of prophetic voices arose, proclaiming a radically different vision – one of righteousness, equity, and compassion for the marginalized. Figures like Isaiah, Amos, and Micah stood as beacons of hope, their words cutting through the darkness of injustice with the light of divine truth.

2. The Prophets and Their Critique of Economic Injustice

The prophets' condemnation of economic exploitation was unequivocal and unyielding. With piercing language and vivid imagery, they exposed the corrupt practices of those who exploited the poor and the vulnerable for personal gain. The words of Amos, for instance, ring with righteous indignation as he denounces those "who oppress the poor and crush the needy" (Amos 4:1).

In Micah 6:8, the prophet encapsulates the essence of God's requirements for humanity:

"He has shown you, O mortal, what is good. And what does the Lord require of you? To act justly and to love mercy and to walk humbly with your God." This verse serves as a clarion call to reject the pursuit of wealth and power at the cost of justice and compassion, and instead, to embrace a life of righteousness and humility before the Almighty.

Isaiah, too, echoed this sentiment, condemning those who "make unjust laws and issue oppressive decrees" (Isaiah 10:1). He painted a vivid picture of a society where the vulnerable were trampled upon and the orphan's cry was ignored, emphasizing the stark contrast between such injustice and the divine mandate for equity and compassion.

3. Prophetic Imperatives: Moral Obligations and Economic Justice

The prophets' critique of economic injustice was not merely a commentary on societal ills but a call to action – a summons to embrace a radically different way of living and relating to one another. Their words carried the weight of moral imperative, challenging individuals and communities to confront their complicity in oppressive systems and to actively work toward dismantling structures that perpetuated poverty and marginalization.

Amos 5:11-12 exposes the exploitation of the poor and the perversion of justice, declaring, "You trample on the poor and force him to give you grain. Therefore, though you have built stone mansions, you will not live in them; though you have planted lush vineyards, you will not drink their wine." Here, the prophet's rebuke is accompanied by a stark warning – that ill-gotten gains will ultimately be rendered meaningless in the face of divine judgment.

The prophets' voices echoed across the ages, reminding us that economic justice is not merely a social issue but a moral imperative rooted in the very character of God. Their words challenge the notion that wealth and prosperity can be pursued at the expense of the vulnerable, and instead, call for a radical reorientation of priorities – one that places the needs of the marginalized at the forefront.

4. Connecting Prophetic Voices to Contemporary Economic Challenges

As we grapple with modern-day economic challenges, the prophetic voices of the past resonate with renewed urgency. In a world where income inequality continues to widen, where exploitative labor practices persist, and where systemic barriers prevent equitable access to economic opportunities, the prophets' calls for justice and equity remain as relevant as ever.

The prophetic critique of economic injustice invites us to examine the ways in which our contemporary systems and practices perpetuate poverty, marginalization, and oppression. It challenges us to confront the ways in which our pursuit of wealth and economic growth has often come at the expense of the most vulnerable – those living in the shadows of our global economy, toiling in inhumane conditions for meager wages.

Moreover, the prophetic vision compels us to reimagine economic models that prioritize the dignity and well-being of all people, regardless of their socioeconomic status. It calls for the creation of equitable systems that provide access to opportunities, resources, and support for those who have been historically disadvantaged, empowering them to break free from the cycles of poverty and marginalization.

5. Embracing the Prophetic Stance: A Call to Action

As we wrestle with the complexities of economic injustice in our modern world, the prophetic voices of old beckon us to embrace a prophetic stance – one that fearlessly confronts oppression, champions the rights of the marginalized, and works tirelessly to dismantle structures that perpetuate inequality.

To embrace this prophetic stance, we must be willing to engage in difficult conversations, challenge entrenched systems and ideologies, and advocate for policies and practices that prioritize economic justice and equitable distribution of resources. It may involve supporting organizations and initiatives that empower the poor, advocating for fair wages and humane working conditions, or lobbying for legislative reforms that address systemic barriers to economic opportunity.

Above all, the prophetic call demands that we cultivate a posture of humility and compassion, recognizing our interconnectedness as human beings and our shared responsibility to uphold the inherent dignity of every person. It invites us to see the faces behind the statistics, to listen to the voices of those who have been silenced, and to respond with a sense of urgency and moral conviction.

In doing so, we not only honor the legacy of the ancient prophets but also participate in the ongoing work of building a more just and equitable world – one in which economic prosperity is inextricably linked to the flourishing of all people, where the cries of the oppressed are heard, and where the vision of God's Kingdom is made tangible through our actions and our commitment to economic justice.

Charity in the Early Church: Acts of the Apostles

1. Overview: The Charitable Legacy of the Early Church

The book of Acts, a chronicle of the nascent Church's formative years, provides a window into the remarkable charitable practices that defined this burgeoning faith community. In the midst of a world often rife with economic inequities and oppression, the early followers of Christ embraced a radically different approach to material possessions, one rooted in the teachings of Jesus and anchored in a profound sense of communal solidarity.

An evidence-based analysis of the Acts of the Apostles reveals a faith community that actively challenged prevailing norms of individual wealth accumulation, instead embracing a spirit of shared resources and mutual support. This approach not only addressed the practical needs of the impoverished within their ranks but also served as a powerful testament to the transformative power of Christ's message of love and compassion.

2. The Communal Sharing of Goods: A Radical Departure from Societal Norms

The Acts of the Apostles presents a compelling account of the early Church's commitment to communal sharing of goods. In Acts 2:44-45, we read: "All the believers were together and had everything in common. They sold property and possessions to give to anyone who had need." This passage underscores the radical nature of the early Christians' approach, wherein personal wealth and possessions were not hoarded but willingly shared for the benefit of the entire community.

This practice was further reinforced in Acts 4:32-35, which states: "All the believers were one in heart and mind. No one claimed that any of their possessions was their own, but they shared everything they had... There were no needy persons among them. For from time to time those who owned land or houses sold them, brought the money from the sales and put it at the apostles' feet, and it was distributed to anyone who had need."

These verses provide clear evidence of the early Church's commitment to actively addressing economic disparities within their midst. The voluntary sharing of resources and the distribution of proceeds from the sale of property and possessions ensured that no member of the community was left destitute or lacking in basic necessities.

3. The Theological Foundation: Following the Teachings of Jesus

The early Church's charitable practices were not merely a response to the economic realities of their time but were deeply rooted in the teachings of Jesus himself. Throughout the Gospels, Jesus consistently challenged the prevailing attitudes toward wealth and possessions, emphasizing the importance of generosity, compassion, and concern for the poor and marginalized.

In the Sermon on the Mount, Jesus proclaimed, "Blessed are the poor in spirit, for theirs is the kingdom of heaven" (Matthew 5:3), elevating the plight of the impoverished and redefining true wealth in spiritual terms. His parables, such as the rich man and Lazarus (Luke 16:19-31), further underscored the grave consequences of ignoring the needs of the poor and the importance of using one's resources to alleviate their suffering.

The early Christians' voluntary sharing of goods and commitment to addressing economic disparities within their community was a direct manifestation of their adherence to Jesus' teachings. By embracing a spirit of generosity and prioritizing the well-being of the marginalized, they embodied the very essence of Christ's message of love and compassion.

4. The Impact: A Powerful Witness and a Model for Modern Faith Communities

The charitable practices of the early Church had a profound impact not only on the lives of those within the faith community but also on the broader society in which they lived. The Acts of the Apostles record that "they enjoyed the goodwill of all the people" (Acts 2:47), suggesting that the early Christians' selfless acts of generosity and compassion served as a powerful witness to the transformative power of their faith.

In a world where economic inequality and exploitation were often the norm, the early Church's commitment to addressing the needs of the impoverished within their ranks stood in stark contrast. Their actions spoke volumes about the depth of their convictions and the authenticity of their faith, serving as a beacon of hope and inspiration to those yearning for a more just and equitable society.

As modern faith communities grapple with the enduring challenges of economic disparity and poverty, the example of the early Church provides a compelling model for how to respond with compassion and shared responsibility. By embracing the spirit of communal sharing and actively working to address the needs of the marginalized within their ranks, faith communities can not only fulfill the mandates of their respective traditions but also bear powerful witness to the transformative power of love and generosity.

5. Lessons for the Modern World: Adapting Ancient Practices to Contemporary Challenges

While the specific practices of the early Church may not be directly replicable in contemporary contexts, the principles that underpinned their charitable efforts remain deeply relevant and worthy of adaptation. In a world grappling with persistent economic inequalities, rising poverty rates, and the ongoing struggle for equitable access to resources, the lessons from the Acts of the Apostles can serve as a guiding light.

One key lesson is the importance of cultivating a spirit of shared responsibility and communal solidarity. Just as the early Christians recognized their collective duty to care for the vulnerable among them, modern faith communities can foster a sense of mutual accountability and a commitment to addressing the economic challenges faced by their members and the broader society.

Another crucial lesson is the need to challenge prevailing attitudes and systems that perpetuate economic injustice. The early Church's radical departure from societal norms surrounding wealth and possessions serves as a powerful reminder that faith communities can and should be agents of change, challenging unjust structures and advocating for policies and practices that promote economic equity and human dignity.

Moreover, the example of the early Church highlights the transformative power of generosity and compassion. By actively engaging in acts of charity and support for the marginalized, faith communities can not only alleviate immediate needs but also serve as powerful witnesses to the transformative potential of love and selfless service.

As we confront the economic challenges of our time, the lessons from the Acts of the Apostles beckon us to embrace a spirit of radical generosity, communal solidarity, and unwavering commitment to economic justice. By adapting these ancient practices to modern contexts, faith communities can play a vital role in creating a more equitable and compassionate world, one that upholds the inherent dignity of every human being and ensures that no one is left behind.

The Ethics of Wealth: Biblical Principles

1. The Parable of the Rich Young Ruler: An Intriguing Examination of Wealth and Responsibility

In the Gospel accounts, Jesus' encounter with the rich young ruler presents a thought-provoking narrative that challenges our perspectives on wealth and its ethical implications. This encounter, recorded in Mark 10:17-31, Matthew 19:16-30, and Luke 18:18-30, offers profound insights into the biblical principles surrounding the responsible stewardship of wealth.

The story begins with a wealthy young man approaching Jesus, seeking guidance on how to inherit eternal life. When Jesus reminds him of the commandments, the man confidently affirms his obedience from his youth. However, Jesus then issues a striking challenge: "Go, sell everything you have and give to the poor, and you will have treasure in heaven. Then come, follow me" (Mark 10:21).

This instruction cuts to the heart of the matter, revealing the young man's attachment to his wealth and the potential for it to become an obstacle to fully embracing the path of discipleship. Disheartened by Jesus' words, the rich young ruler walks away, unable to relinquish his material possessions. In response, Jesus cautions his disciples about the perils of being wealthy, likening the challenge of a rich person entering the kingdom of God to a camel passing through the eye of a needle.

2. The Biblical Definition of True Wealth: Generosity and Stewardship

The parable of the rich young ruler underscores a fundamental principle in the Bible's ethical framework concerning wealth: true wealth is not measured by the accumulation of material possessions but by the generosity and responsible stewardship with which one's resources are managed. The young man's reluctance to part with his riches revealed a misplaced attachment to wealth, hindering his ability to fully embrace the kingdom of God and its values.

Throughout Scripture, we encounter numerous passages that reinforce this principle. In Proverbs 11:24-25, we read: "One person gives freely, yet gains even more; another withholds unduly, but comes to poverty. A generous person will prosper; whoever refreshes others will be refreshed." These verses underscore the ethical imperative of generosity, promising abundance to those who share their resources freely.

Similarly, in 1 Timothy 6:17-19, the apostle Paul instructs those who are rich "not to be arrogant nor to put their hope in wealth, which is so uncertain, but to put their hope in God, who richly provides us with everything for our enjoyment. Command them to do good, to be rich in good deeds, and to be generous and willing to share. In this way, they will lay up treasure for themselves as a firm foundation for the coming age, so that they may take hold of the life that is truly life."

3. Wealth as a Stewardship: Ethical Guidelines for Responsible Management

The biblical perspective on wealth extends beyond mere generosity; it also encompasses the principle of responsible stewardship. The resources entrusted to individuals and organizations are viewed as gifts from God, to be managed with care and accountability. This stewardship mindset requires a deliberate alignment of financial practices with ethical principles and a commitment to using wealth in ways that honor the giver and benefit society.

In the Old Testament, the book of Deuteronomy provides instructions on the ethical treatment of wealth, emphasizing the importance of remembering God as the ultimate source of provision (Deuteronomy 8:18). The prophet Amos famously condemned the exploitation of the poor and the accumulation of ill-gotten wealth, declaring: "Because you trample on the poor and force them to give you a portion of their grain, therefore, though you have built houses of well-dressed stone, you will not live in them; though you have planted beautiful vineyards, you will not drink their wine" (Amos 5:11).

In the New Testament, the apostle James issues a stern warning against the unethical accumulation and misuse of wealth, stating: "Now listen, you rich people, weep and wail because of the misery that is coming on you. Your wealth has rotted, and moths have eaten your clothes. Your gold and silver are corroded. Their corrosion will testify against you and eat your flesh like fire. You have hoarded wealth in the last days" (James 5:1-3).

These passages collectively underscore the ethical imperative of responsible stewardship, calling for a mindset that views wealth not as a means for self-indulgence or exploitation but as a resource to be managed with integrity, generosity, and a commitment to promoting the common good.

4. Practical Guidelines for Ethical Wealth Management: Integrating Faith and Financial Practices

In light of the biblical principles surrounding wealth, individuals and organizations can adopt practical guidelines to align their financial practices with their faith commitments. These guidelines can serve as a roadmap for ethical wealth management, fostering a sense of accountability and ensuring that resources are used in a manner that honors the principles of generosity, stewardship, and justice.

For individuals, this may involve:

- Regularly giving a portion of one's income to charitable causes and organizations that align with biblical values.
- Practicing contentment and avoiding the accumulation of excessive wealth or the pursuit of material possessions as a measure of success.
- Investing in ethical and socially responsible financial instruments that promote positive social and environmental impacts.
- Modeling responsible stewardship by living within one's means, avoiding excessive debt, and practicing wise financial planning.

For organizations, such as businesses, churches, and non-profits, ethical wealth management may encompass:

- Establishing clear policies and practices that prioritize transparency, accountability, and ethical decision-making in financial matters.
- Implementing fair compensation practices and promoting economic justice within the organization and throughout its supply chain.
- Allocating resources to charitable initiatives and community development projects that align with the organization's mission and values.

- Adopting environmentally sustainable practices and investing in initiatives that promote environmental stewardship and the responsible use of natural resources.

By integrating these practical guidelines into their financial practices, individuals and organizations can not only honor the biblical principles surrounding wealth but also contribute to the creation of a more just and equitable society. They can serve as models of ethical wealth management, inspiring others to embrace a mindset of generosity, stewardship, and responsible resource allocation.

5. The Transformative Power of Ethical Wealth Management: A Witness to Biblical Values

The pursuit of ethical wealth management is not merely a pragmatic exercise; it carries profound spiritual and societal implications. When individuals and organizations align their financial practices with biblical principles, they bear witness to the transformative power of their faith and its ability to shape the world around them.

By embracing a posture of generosity and committing to the responsible stewardship of resources, these ethical stewards become living embodiments of the values espoused by Jesus and the biblical writers. Their actions speak louder than words, demonstrating the tangible impact of faith on everyday life and decision-making.

Moreover, ethical wealth management has the potential to catalyze positive change within communities and societies. When resources are allocated with integrity and a commitment to the common good, they can fuel initiatives that address systemic issues such as poverty, inequality, and environmental degradation. Businesses that prioritize ethical practices can foster economic justice and promote sustainable development, while charitable organizations can channel resources toward life-changing programs and services.

In this way, the pursuit of ethical wealth management transcends mere financial considerations; it becomes a powerful witness to the transformative potential of faith and a catalyst for social transformation. As individuals and organizations embrace these principles, they contribute to the creation of a more just, equitable, and sustainable world, one that reflects the heart of the biblical message and honors the inherent dignity of all people.

Ultimately, the ethics of wealth management, as articulated in the Bible, challenge us to redefine our understanding of true prosperity. It calls us to move beyond the pursuit of material accumulation and toward a deeper commitment to generosity, responsible stewardship, and the promotion of the common good. By aligning our financial practices with these principles, we not only honor our faith commitments but also participate in the ongoing work of creating a more just and compassionate world, one that reflects the transformative power of the gospel and its ability to shape lives, communities, and societies.

13

PROVERBS AND PROSPERITY: ANCIENT WISDOM FOR MODERN TIMES

The Foundation of Prosperity: Analyzing Key Proverbs

1. Defining Terms: Setting the Stage for Ancient Wisdom

To embark on a journey through ancient proverbs and uncover their profound relevance to modern prosperity, it is crucial to establish a solid foundation by clearly defining key terms and concepts. This section serves as a gateway, elucidating the significance of these terms and providing a preview of how they will guide our forthcoming discourse.

2." Wisdom" - A Timeless Pursuit

As we delve into the realm of ancient proverbs, the term "wisdom" emerges as a central pillar. It is not merely the accumulation of knowledge or intellect; rather, wisdom represents the ability to discern and apply profound truths to navigate life's complexities. The pursuit of wisdom has captivated humanity for millennia, transcending cultural boundaries and serving as a beacon for personal growth and societal progress.

3. "Prosperity" - A Holistic Perspective

Traditionally, prosperity has been narrowly defined by material wealth and financial abundance. However, the proverbs challenge us to adopt a more holistic understanding of this term. True prosperity encompasses not only economic well-being but also spiritual fulfillment, harmonious relationships, and a sense of purpose. It is a multifaceted state of flourishing that transcends material possessions and invites us to cultivate inner richness and outward abundance simultaneously.

4. "Proverbs" - Ancient Gems of Distilled Wisdom

Proverbs are concise, pithy statements that encapsulate profound truths and timeless principles. They are the result of centuries of collective human experience, distilled into memorable phrases that resonate across generations. Originating from diverse cultures and traditions, these proverbs serve as enduring guideposts, offering insights into the very fabric of life and the foundations of lasting prosperity. 5. "Understanding" - The Key to Unlocking Ancient Wisdom

While proverbs may appear simple on the surface, true understanding lies in the ability to penetrate their layers of meaning and extract the underlying principles. It requires a willingness to engage in deep reflection, to connect ancient wisdom with contemporary contexts, and to apply these insights in a thoughtful and nuanced manner. Understanding becomes the lens through which we can appreciate the timeless relevance of these ancient proverbs and harness their transformative power.

5. "Application" - Bridging the Gap Between Knowledge and Prosperity

Mere knowledge of ancient proverbs is insufficient; true prosperity lies in their practical application. By integrating the wisdom embedded within these proverbs into our daily lives, we forge a bridge between ancient truths and modern realities. Whether in personal decision-making, professional endeavors, or societal interactions, the ability to apply these principles with discernment and adaptability is the key to unlocking their full potential for prosperity.

6. Conclusion: Paving the Way for Transformation

As we embark on this journey of exploring ancient proverbs, the terms defined here serve as a conceptual framework, guiding our understanding and application of this timeless wisdom. By grasping the depth of these terms, we open ourselves to the transformative power of these proverbs, allowing them to shape our perspectives, refine our actions, and ultimately, pave the way for a holistic and enduring prosperity that transcends fleeting material gains. With this foundation in place, we are poised to delve deeper into the rich tapestry of ancient wisdom and uncover its profound relevance to our modern lives.

Wisdom and Wealth: A Symbiotic Relationship

As you embark on this exploration of the symbiotic relationship between wisdom and wealth, a provoking question arises: Can true and lasting prosperity be achieved without the guidance of profound wisdom?

This question strikes at the core of a perennial human pursuit – the desire for both material abundance and inner fulfillment. It invites us to ponder the intricate interplay between these two seemingly disparate realms, challenging us to reconsider our conventional notions of success and prosperity.

Throughout history, countless individuals and civilizations have grappled with the complex dynamic between wisdom and wealth. Some have amassed vast fortunes, only to find themselves lacking in purpose and contentment. Others have dedicated their lives to the pursuit of knowledge and enlightenment, yet struggled with material scarcity. The tension between these two domains has been a constant source of intrigue, debate, and often, frustration.

The prevalence of this dilemma is rooted in the fragmented approaches that dominate our understanding of prosperity. On one side lies the relentless pursuit of financial gain, often at the expense of ethical considerations and personal growth. On the other, an overemphasis on philosophical or spiritual wisdom can lead to a detachment from practical realities and the fulfillment of essential human needs. Neither extreme offers a holistic path to true and lasting prosperity.

Conventional approaches to wealth acquisition frequently overlook the profound wisdom embedded in ancient teachings and proverbs. These time-honored principles offer invaluable insights into the ethical and sustainable acquisition, management, and application of resources. By neglecting these wisdom traditions, we risk succumbing to short-sighted impulses, greed, and the misuse of wealth – ultimately undermining the very prosperity we seek.

Furthermore, the pursuit of wisdom alone, devoid of an understanding of practical economics and the responsible stewardship of resources, can lead to an idealistic but impoverished existence. True wisdom recognizes the intrinsic value of material abundance as a means to support personal growth, contribute to society, and fulfill one's higher purpose.

To navigate this complex terrain, a novel perspective emerges: The synergistic integration of wisdom and wealth. This approach recognizes that true and lasting prosperity is not found in the extremes but rather in the harmonious union of these two potent forces.

Drawing from the timeless insights of ancient proverbs, we can uncover a path that embraces both the practical realities of wealth creation and the ethical and spiritual dimensions of wisdom. This holistic perspective acknowledges that genuine prosperity is not merely the accumulation of material possessions but a state of being that encompasses inner fulfillment, ethical conduct, and a positive impact on the world around us.

Consider the tale of a modern-day entrepreneur who, driven by ambition and a desire for financial success, built a thriving business empire. However, as their wealth grew, they found themselves increasingly disconnected from their true purpose and values. It was not until they encountered the wisdom of ancient proverbs that they realized the importance of aligning their pursuit of wealth with ethical principles and a deeper sense of purpose. By integrating these timeless teachings into their business practices and personal lives, they experienced a profound transformation – one that led to not only greater material abundance but also a sense of inner peace, fulfillment, and a positive impact on their community.

Skeptics may argue that the wisdom of ancient proverbs is outdated and irrelevant in our modern, fast-paced world. However, the enduring nature of these teachings speaks volumes about their universal applicability. Just as the principles of mathematics or physics transcend time and culture, the wisdom embedded in proverbs offers timeless truths that can guide us toward a more balanced and fulfilling existence.

To embrace this transformative approach, we must first cultivate a willingness to learn from the wisdom of the past while remaining open to adapting it to contemporary contexts. By studying and internalizing the principles found in proverbs, we can develop a deeper understanding of the interconnectedness between wisdom and wealth, enabling us to make informed decisions that align with our values and contribute to the greater good.

Furthermore, we must be willing to challenge societal norms and conventional definitions of success. True prosperity is not measured solely by material wealth or societal status but by the depth of one's character, the positive impact on others, and the ability to find joy and fulfillment in the present moment.

To embark on this journey toward true and lasting prosperity, consider these actionable steps:

1. Immerse yourself in the study of ancient wisdom traditions and proverbs, seeking to understand the timeless principles that have guided humanity for millennia.
2. Reflect deeply on your personal values, aspirations, and the impact you wish to have on the world around you. Align your pursuit of wealth with these higher purposes.
3. Develop a holistic approach to wealth creation that incorporates ethical practices, sustainable strategies, and a commitment to personal growth and societal well-being.
4. Surround yourself with a community of like-minded individuals who share your vision of integrating wisdom and wealth. Engage in meaningful discussions and support each other on this transformative journey.
5. Continuously evaluate your actions and decision-making processes, ensuring they are guided by the principles of wisdom and contribute to a balanced and fulfilling life.

By embracing the synergy between wisdom and wealth, we have the power to transcend the limitations of conventional thinking and forge a path toward true and lasting prosperity. This transformative approach invites us to embark on a deeply fulfilling journey, one that harmonizes our material aspirations with our spiritual and ethical growth, ultimately leading to a life of abundance, purpose, and profound impact.

The Pillars of Wisdom: Understanding Key Virtues

In the timeless pages of the Book of Proverbs, a harmonious tapestry of wisdom and virtue unfolds, revealing the key principles that guide us toward true and lasting prosperity. Among these virtues, three stand as pillars upon which a life of enduring abundance and fulfillment can be built: diligence, prudence, and generosity. Like the threads of a masterfully woven tapestry, these virtues intertwine to form a vibrant and resilient framework for achieving holistic prosperity.

The ancient proverb "Diligence is the mother of good fortune" (Proverbs 13:4) encapsulates the foundational virtue that sets the course for success. Diligence is the unwavering commitment to one's endeavors, fueled by perseverance, discipline, and a relentless pursuit of excellence. It is the antidote to complacency and idleness, propelling us forward on the path to prosperity. Just as a farmer diligently tends to their crops, reaping the rewards of an abundant harvest, those who cultivate diligence in their pursuits will reap the fruits of their labor.

The origins of this virtue can be traced back to the ancient Greek concept of "spoudé," which encompassed the notion of earnest and conscientious effort. Throughout history, diligence has been celebrated as a catalyst for greatness, with icons such as Benjamin Franklin extolling its virtues, stating, "Diligence is the mother of good luck." This sentiment echoes the wisdom found in Proverbs, underscoring the timeless nature of this principle.

In the context of prosperity, diligence manifests itself in various aspects of our lives. In the realm of work, it is the unwavering dedication to our craft, the commitment to continuously honing our skills, and the relentless pursuit of excellence in our endeavors. In personal pursuits, diligence guides us to consistently strive for growth, self-improvement, and the cultivation of virtuous habits. It is the antidote to procrastination and half-hearted efforts, ensuring that we fully leverage our potential and maximize our opportunities.

Yet, diligence alone is not sufficient to navigate the complex path to prosperity. This virtue must be complemented by prudence, the wisdom to discern the right course of action and exercise sound judgment. As the proverb states, "The prudent see danger and take refuge, but the simple keep going and pay the penalty" (Proverbs 22:3). Prudence is the lighthouse that illuminates the path ahead, guiding us through the treacherous waters of life's challenges and opportunities.

The roots of prudence can be traced back to ancient Greek philosophy, with Aristotle defining it as the ability to deliberate well about what is conducive to the good life. Throughout history, this virtue has been revered as a cornerstone of wise decision-making, enabling individuals and civilizations to navigate complex situations with foresight and discernment.

In the pursuit of prosperity, prudence serves as a compass, guiding our choices and actions. It prompts us to carefully consider the consequences of our decisions, weighing the potential risks and rewards. In business ventures, prudence counsels us to exercise due diligence, assessing opportunities with a critical eye and mitigating potential pitfalls. In personal finance, it encourages us to make informed decisions, practice moderation, and plan for the future. Prudence is the antidote to recklessness and impulsivity, ensuring that our efforts are guided by wisdom and foresight.

However, no path to true and lasting prosperity is complete without the virtue of generosity. As the proverb proclaims, "Whoever is generous to the poor lends to the Lord, and he will repay him for his deed" (Proverbs 19:17). Generosity is the gentle rain that nourishes the seeds of abundance, fostering a spirit of compassion, gratitude, and interconnectedness that ultimately enriches both the giver and the recipient.

The roots of generosity can be traced back to ancient spiritual traditions that celebrated the act of sharing and giving as a means of cultivating a sense of unity and collective well-being. In many cultures, generosity was revered as a virtue that not only uplifted the impoverished but also elevated the giver's own spirit and standing within the community.

In the context of prosperity, generosity serves as a reminder that true wealth extends beyond material possessions. It encourages us to share our resources, knowledge, and talents with those in need, fostering a ripple effect of positivity and abundance. Through acts of generosity, we cultivate a mindset of abundance, recognizing that our prosperity is not diminished by giving but rather amplified.

Generosity is not limited to financial contributions; it encompasses a broader spirit of compassion and service. It may manifest as mentoring an aspiring entrepreneur, volunteering in a community initiative, or offering emotional support to those in need. By embracing generosity, we not only contribute to the betterment of society but also cultivate a sense of purpose and fulfillment that transcends material wealth.

These three virtues – diligence, prudence, and generosity – form a harmonious triad, guiding us toward a holistic and sustainable form of prosperity. Like the interwoven strands of a tapestry, they are interdependent, each reinforcing and amplifying the power of the others. Diligence fuels our efforts and ensures consistent progress, while prudence illuminates the path ahead, helping us navigate challenges and seize opportunities with wisdom. Generosity, in turn, nourishes the soul and fosters a spirit of abundance, reminding us that true prosperity extends beyond personal gain and encompasses the well-being of our communities.

To fully embrace these virtues and unlock the path to lasting prosperity, we must cultivate them intentionally and consistently. This journey begins with introspection, examining our values, motivations, and the legacy we wish to leave behind. It requires a willingness to challenge societal norms and redefine our understanding of success, recognizing that true prosperity is not measured solely by material wealth but by the depth of our character and the positive impact we have on the world around us.

As we internalize these virtues, we become agents of transformation, not only in our personal lives but also in the communities and organizations we influence. By embodying diligence, we inspire others to pursue excellence and persevere in the face of adversity. Through prudence, we model wise decision-making and foster environments of thoughtful deliberation. And by practicing generosity, we cultivate a culture of compassion, gratitude, and shared abundance.

The path to true and lasting prosperity is not a solitary journey but rather a collective endeavor. By embracing the virtues of diligence, prudence, and generosity, we weave a tapestry of wisdom and abundance that transcends individual boundaries and uplifts entire communities. It is a path that invites us to not only achieve personal fulfillment but also to contribute to the greater good, leaving a lasting legacy of positive impact for generations to come.

As we navigate the complexities of life and the pursuit of prosperity, let us be guided by the timeless wisdom found in the Book of Proverbs. May these virtues serve as beacons of light, illuminating our path and inspiring us to create a world where true and lasting abundance is not merely a distant dream but a lived reality, woven into the fabric of our lives and communities.

The Role of Integrity in Economic Success

In the ever-evolving landscape of business and commerce, the pursuit of economic success has become a driving force, propelling individuals and organizations toward greater heights of prosperity. Yet, amidst this relentless pursuit, a fundamental question arises: Can integrity, that unwavering adherence to moral principles and ethical conduct, truly be a catalyst for economic triumph? The ancient wisdom of Proverbs offers profound insights into this very inquiry, shedding light on the intrinsic connection between integrity and enduring success.

The proverb "A false balance is an abomination to the Lord, but a just weight is his delight" (Proverbs 11:1) encapsulates the essence of integrity in economic dealings. Just as a false balance on a weighing scale betrays the trust of buyers and sellers alike, so too does the lack of integrity in business transactions erode the very foundation upon which commerce is built. Integrity demands transparency, fairness, and a commitment to upholding the highest ethical standards, even in the face of temptation or pressure to compromise.

In the context of economic activities, the absence of integrity can manifest in various forms, each with far-reaching consequences. Fraudulent accounting practices, deceptive marketing tactics, and the exploitation of consumers or employees for personal gain are but a few examples of how the lack of integrity can undermine the trust and credibility that are essential for sustainable economic success. The implications of such practices extend beyond the immediate financial impact, tainting reputations, deterring potential partners, and ultimately hindering long-term growth and prosperity.

The allure of short-term gains and the perceived necessity of cutting corners can be seductive, particularly in highly competitive markets or during periods of economic turmoil. However, history has repeatedly demonstrated that the edifice of success built upon a foundation of deceit and unethical practices is inherently unstable, and susceptible to collapse at the slightest tremor of scrutiny or public exposure. The aftermath of such collapses is often devastating, leaving in their wake a trail of shattered trust, tarnished reputations, and economic ruin.

In stark contrast, a steadfast commitment to integrity offers a viable and sustainable solution to the challenges of maintaining ethical business practices. By embracing integrity as a core value, businesses and individuals can cultivate a reputation for trustworthiness, transparency, and accountability – qualities that are invaluable in fostering long-term relationships with clients, partners, and stakeholders. This, in turn, creates a climate of trust and confidence, enabling smoother transactions, strengthening brand loyalty, and ultimately driving economic success.

The implementation of integrity-driven practices begins with an unwavering commitment from leadership, fostering a culture that values ethical conduct above all else. This commitment must permeate every facet of operations, from employee training and performance evaluation to the development of robust policies and procedures that safeguard against unethical practices. Furthermore, organizations must establish robust systems of accountability, ensuring that any breaches of integrity are swiftly addressed and remediated, reinforcing the organization's commitment to ethical excellence.

Admittedly, the path of integrity is not without its challenges. In a highly competitive landscape, there may be instances where maintaining ethical standards could potentially result in short-term financial setbacks or missed opportunities. However, it is in these moments that the true test of integrity arises, and organizations must remain steadfast in their commitment, recognizing that the long-term benefits of preserving trust and credibility far outweigh any temporary gains achieved through compromise.

History is replete with examples of organizations that have weathered such storms and emerged victorious, their reputations for integrity acting as a beacon that attracts clients, investors, and top talent alike. From the enduring success of companies like Patagonia and REI, renowned for their commitment to environmental and social responsibility, to the resilience of financial institutions like JPMorgan Chase, which navigated the 2008 financial crisis with integrity intact, these examples serve as a testament to the power of integrity in driving economic success.

In contrast, alternative solutions that prioritize short-term gains over ethical conduct often prove to be ephemeral and ultimately detrimental to long-term prosperity. The annals of business history are littered with cautionary tales of organizations that sacrificed integrity for the sake of expediency, only to find themselves mired in legal battles, public backlash, and ultimately, economic ruin. The infamous cases of Enron, WorldCom, and Theranos serve as poignant reminders of the consequences of compromising ethical standards, casting a long shadow over the individuals and organizations involved.

As we navigate the complexities of the modern economic landscape, it is imperative that we embrace integrity as a guiding principle, recognizing its profound impact on our collective prosperity. By upholding the highest standards of ethical conduct, we not only safeguard the trust and credibility that are essential for economic success, but we also contribute to the greater good of society, fostering a climate of transparency, accountability, and responsible stewardship.

In the words of the ancient proverb, "A just weight is his delight," let us strive to be the embodiment of integrity, adhering to the highest ethical standards in our economic endeavors. It is through this unwavering commitment that we can forge a path to enduring prosperity, one that not only enriches our personal and organizational pursuits but also serves as a beacon of hope for a more just and equitable economic order, rooted in the timeless wisdom of Proverbs.

Prosperity Through Generosity: The Paradox of Giving

Brief Description: This case study explores the story of a small town in rural America that embraced the paradoxical principle of generosity, leading to its economic revival and prosperity.

Main Players: The residents of Smallville, a once-thriving farming community that had fallen on hard times after the closure of the town's primary manufacturing plant.

Primary Challenge: Faced with dwindling resources and a bleak economic outlook, the citizens of Smallville grappled with a profound question: How could they revive their struggling community and restore its former prosperity?

Steps and Strategies:

1. Embracing the paradox of generosity:

Inspired by the wisdom of Proverbs 11:24, "One gives freely, yet grows all the richer; another withholds what he should give, and only suffers want," the town's leaders challenged their community to adopt a mindset of generosity and selfless giving, even in the face of scarcity.2. Establishing a community fund: A voluntary fund was created, with residents encouraged to contribute whatever they could, whether it was money, resources, or their time and skills.3. Identifying and supporting local entrepreneurs: The community fund was used to provide seed capital, mentorship, and resources to aspiring entrepreneurs who had innovative business ideas that could create jobs and stimulate the local economy.4. Promoting collaboration and mutual support: Rather than competing with one another, residents embraced a spirit of cooperation, sharing knowledge, resources, and networking opportunities to help each other succeed.5. Investing in education and skill development: A portion of the fund was allocated to educational initiatives, vocational training programs, and skill development workshops, ensuring that the town's workforce was equipped with the necessary competencies to thrive in the changing economic landscape.

2. Outcomes:

- Economic revitalization: Over the course of five years, Smallville witnessed a remarkable economic transformation. Dozens of new businesses were established, creating hundreds of jobs and attracting investment from outside the community.
- Increased prosperity: Household incomes rose by an average of 25%, and the town's poverty rate decreased by 40%, as residents found gainful employment and new economic opportunities.
- Community resilience: The spirit of generosity and collaboration fostered a sense of unity and resilience, empowering the town to weather economic challenges and support one another through difficult times.
- Attracting talent and investment: Smallville's reputation for generosity, collaboration, and economic opportunity began to spread, attracting skilled professionals, entrepreneurs,

and investors from across the region, further fueling the town's growth and prosperity.

3. Lessons Learned:

The paradox of generosity: By embracing a mindset of generosity and sharing, even in times of scarcity, the citizens of Smallville were able to unlock the potential for collective prosperity and economic growth.2. Collaboration over competition: Rather than engaging in cutthroat competition, the community's emphasis on cooperation and mutual support created a synergistic environment where everyone's success contributed to the overall prosperity of the town.3. Investing in human capital: By prioritizing education, skill development, and empowering local entrepreneurs, Smallville ensured that its workforce was equipped to adapt to changing economic conditions and seize new opportunities.4. Fostering a sense of community: The shared experience of generosity and collective effort fostered a strong sense of community and belonging, creating a supportive environment that attracted and retained talented individuals and businesses.

4. Relevance and Key Takeaways:

The case of Smallville serves as a powerful illustration of the transformative potential of generosity and the wisdom found in the Proverbs. By embracing the paradoxical principle of giving freely, even in times of scarcity, the community was able to unlock a path to enduring prosperity. This case study underscores the importance of adopting a mindset of abundance, cooperation, and mutual support in economic endeavors, as opposed to the traditional paradigm of competition and scarcity.

Furthermore, it highlights the crucial role of investing in human capital and fostering an environment that nurtures entrepreneurship and innovation. By empowering its citizens with the necessary skills, resources, and support, Smallville was able to unleash the creative potential of its residents and harness their collective efforts toward economic revival.

Ultimately, the story of Smallville stands as a testament to the enduring wisdom found in the Proverbs, reminding us that true prosperity is not merely measured by material wealth, but by the strength of our communities, the depth of our relationships, and the legacy of generosity and compassion that we leave behind.

Final Thought: As we reflect on the transformative journey of Smallville, one question remains: How might we, as individuals and communities, embrace the paradox of generosity and unlock the path to collective prosperity in our own spheres of influence?

Diligence Vs. Laziness: Paths to Prosperity

In the realm of human qualities and their resulting outcomes, few contrasts are as stark and profound as that between diligence and laziness. Embodying the timeless wisdom found in the Book of Proverbs, these two attributes represent divergent paths, each carving its own unique trajectory through life's journey.

On the one hand, diligence stands as a beacon of industriousness and perseverance. It is the embodiment of unwavering dedication, an unyielding commitment to excellence, and a relentless pursuit of one's goals. Like the steady drip of water that carves through stone, the diligent individual exhibits a quiet yet potent force, shaping their destiny through consistent effort and tireless work.

Laziness, on the other hand, casts a formidable shadow, representing the antithesis of diligence. It is a state of complacency, a surrender to inaction, and a disregard for the rich potential that lies dormant within us all. Like a stagnant pool, laziness breeds stagnation and decay, eroding the very foundations upon which progress and growth are built.

As we delve into the specific aspects that characterize these contrasting attributes, a vivid tapestry of consequences unfolds, revealing the profound impact they have on our lives and the world around us.

Work Ethic and Productivity: The diligent individual embraces the virtues of hard work and discipline, understanding that success is not a destination, but a continuous journey. Their steady pace and unwavering commitment ensure that tasks are completed with precision and excellence, fueling productivity and propelling them ever closer to their goals. In stark contrast, the lazy individual succumbs to procrastination and inaction, squandering precious time and opportunities, ultimately hindering their ability to achieve their full potential.

Long-Term Outcomes: Diligence cultivates a mindset of resilience and perseverance, enabling individuals to weather life's storms and overcome obstacles with tenacity. This steadfast determination often yields a bountiful harvest of success, as the diligent reap the rewards of their labor, be it in the form of career advancement, financial stability, or personal growth. Conversely, laziness paves a path of unfulfilled potential and missed opportunities, leaving individuals mired in a cycle of regret and stagnation.

Yet, amidst these contrasts, there exists a profound unity – a shared truth that transcends the boundaries of individual circumstances. Both diligence and laziness are born from the choices we make each day, the habits we cultivate, and the mindsets we embrace. They are not static states, but dynamic forces that shape our lives in profound ways.

The implications of this comparison extend far beyond the individual, casting a long shadow over societies and communities. Nations that foster a culture of diligence and hard work often find themselves at the forefront of innovation, economic growth, and social progress. Conversely, those who succumb to the allure of laziness and complacency risks falling behind, stifling their potential, and hindering their ability to thrive in an ever-changing world.

In contemporary times, the contrast between diligence and laziness continues to play out in myriad ways. We see it in the relentless pursuit of entrepreneurs who defy the odds and build empires from the ground up, fueled by an unwavering commitment to their vision. We witness it in the dedication of athletes who push the boundaries of human endurance, sacrificing comfort and convenience for the pursuit of excellence.

Yet, we also observe the insidious allure of laziness in the form of procrastination, complacency, and a reluctance to step outside our comfort zones. The advent of technology and the convenience it affords can inadvertently foster a culture of instant gratification, where the patience and perseverance required for sustained effort are often overshadowed by the promise of immediate rewards.

It is in this modern context that the wisdom of Proverbs resonates with even greater clarity, reminding us that the path to true prosperity lies not in the pursuit of fleeting pleasures or the surrender to complacency, but in the cultivation of a diligent spirit and an unwavering commitment to our goals.

As we contemplate the contrasting outcomes of diligence and laziness, we are reminded that the choice is ours – a choice that ripples through the fabric of our lives, shaping our destinies and leaving an indelible mark on the world around us. The diligent individual stands as a testament to the transformative power of perseverance, their legacy etched in the annals of achievement and progress. The lazy, on the other hand, risk being left behind, their potential unfulfilled, their dreams unraveling like threads in the wind.

In the end, the comparison between diligence and laziness is not merely a matter of personal preference or circumstance; it is a reflection of our values, our priorities, and our commitment to the pursuit of a life well-lived. For those who embrace the mantle of diligence, the path may be arduous, but the rewards are immeasurable – a life of purpose, fulfillment, and enduring prosperity.

The Economic Implications of Prudence

In the ever-evolving landscape of economic decision-making, the virtue of prudence stands as a guiding light, illuminating a path toward long-term stability and prosperity. As the ancient Proverb wisely admonishes, "The prudent sees danger and hides himself, but the simple go on and suffer for it" (Proverbs 22:3), we are reminded of the profound impact that foresight and caution can have on our financial well-being.

The Challenge of Integrating Prudence: In a world driven by the pursuit of instant gratification and short-term gains, the concept of prudence can often be overshadowed by the allure of immediate rewards. Decisions are frequently made in haste, fueled by a desire for quick returns or a reluctance to delay pleasure. This myopic approach, however, can lead to a series of pitfalls that ultimately undermine long-term economic stability.

Impulsive spending, speculative investments, and a disregard for potential risks can create a precarious financial situation, leaving individuals and organizations vulnerable to the vagaries of economic fluctuations. Moreover, the lack of prudence can foster a false sense of security, leading to poor planning and a failure to anticipate and mitigate potential challenges. In such an environment, economic stability becomes a fleeting mirage, continually eluding those who fail to heed the wisdom of prudence.

The Significance of Prudence: Prudence, however, offers a path forward, grounded in foresight, risk assessment, and a judicious approach to decision-making. By exercising caution and considering the long-term implications of our actions, we can navigate the complexities of the economic landscape with greater confidence and resilience.

Historically, prudent decision-making has been a hallmark of enduring economic success. Nations and organizations that have embraced prudent fiscal policies, sound investment strategies, and a proactive approach to risk management have weathered economic storms with greater fortitude. Conversely, those who have succumbed to impulsivity and short-sightedness have often found themselves mired in financial turmoil, struggling to recover from the consequences of their imprudent choices.

A Viable Strategy for Financial Prudence: To harness the power of prudence in our economic endeavors, a comprehensive strategy must be implemented. This strategy should encompass several key elements:

1. Comprehensive Risk Assessment: Before embarking on any financial venture, a thorough analysis of potential risks must be conducted. This includes evaluating market trends, economic indicators, and potential obstacles that could impede success. By identifying and understanding these risks, prudent measures can be taken to mitigate or avoid them altogether.

2. Diversification and Measured Exposure: Rather than placing all resources into a single investment or venture, prudence dictates a diversified approach. By spreading risk across multiple avenues, the impact of any single setback is minimized, ensuring greater stability and resilience in the face of economic fluctuations.

3. Contingency Planning: No matter how thorough the risk assessment is, unforeseen circumstances can always arise. Prudence demands the development of contingency plans that outline actionable steps to be taken in the event of unexpected challenges or adversities. This proactive approach allows for swift and measured responses, minimizing the potential for long-term economic harm.

4. Long-Term Perspective: While short-term gains can be enticing, true prudence necessitates a long-term perspective. Financial decisions should be made with an eye toward sustainable growth, financial stability, and long-term wealth preservation. This mindset fosters patience, discipline, and a commitment to sound financial practices that yield enduring benefits.

The Effectiveness of Prudent Decision-Making: The effectiveness of prudent decision-making is evident throughout history, with numerous examples demonstrating its value in achieving long-term economic stability. Consider the success of companies like Toyota, which weathered economic downturns by maintaining a cautious approach to expansion and a focus on efficient operations. Or examine the strategies employed by nations like Norway, which established a sovereign wealth fund to prudently manage its natural resource revenues, ensuring long-term economic security for its citizens.

In contrast, the consequences of imprudent decision-making are equally apparent. The global financial crisis of 2008, fueled by excessive risk-taking and a disregard for prudent lending practices, serves as a sobering reminder of the perils of neglecting prudence in economic affairs. The ripple effects of this crisis were felt across industries and nations, leaving many struggling to recover from the economic devastation wrought by imprudent actions.

Moreover, predictive models and economic simulations consistently highlight the long-term benefits of prudent financial practices. Prudent approaches to budgeting, saving, and investing have been shown to yield greater financial stability, wealth accumulation, and resilience against economic shocks. In contrast, imprudent practices, such as excessive borrowing, speculative investments, and a lack of emergency funds, often lead to financial instability and heightened vulnerability to economic downturns.

Reinforcing the Importance of Prudence: As we navigate the complexities of the modern economic landscape, the importance of prudence cannot be overstated. In a world marked by rapid change, globalization, and ever-increasing uncertainty, the virtues of foresight, caution, and judicious decision-making are more vital than ever before.

By embracing prudence, we not only safeguard our personal and organizational financial well-being but also contribute to the collective economic stability of our communities and nations. A culture of prudence fosters an environment of responsible stewardship, sustainable growth, and resilience in the face of economic challenges.

Ultimately, the path to long-term economic stability is paved with the wisdom of prudence. It is a journey that demands patience, vigilance, and a willingness to resist the siren call of instant gratification. Yet, for those who heed its principles, the rewards are manifold – a sense of security, financial freedom, and the ability to weather the inevitable storms that arise in the ever-changing economic landscape.

As we navigate the currents of economic uncertainty, let us remember the timeless guidance offered by the Book of Proverbs. By embracing prudence and making it a cornerstone of our financial decision-making, we can chart a course toward enduring prosperity, leaving a legacy of economic stability for generations to come.

The Ethical Dimensions of Wealth Accumulation

In the grand tapestry of human civilization, the pursuit of wealth has been a constant thread, interwoven with the very fabric of our societies. From the ancient marketplaces of Athens to the bustling financial districts of modern cities, the accumulation of riches has captivated the human imagination, fueling ambition and driving progress. Yet, amid this relentless quest for prosperity, a fundamental question arises: How can wealth be accumulated ethically, in a manner that aligns with the guiding principles of morality and virtue?

The ancient wisdom of Proverbs, a timeless repository of divine counsel, offers a profound insight into this very question. In Proverbs 13:11, we encounter a profound truth: "Wealth gained hastily will dwindle, but whoever gathers little by little will increase it." This admonition, simple yet profound, strikes at the heart of ethical wealth accumulation, underscoring the virtues of patience, diligence, and a steadfast commitment to honorable means.

Definition: Ethical wealth accumulation is the process of acquiring financial resources through legitimate, honorable, and socially responsible means, guided by a moral compass rooted in integrity, fairness, and consideration for the well-being of others. It is a journey that demands a delicate balance between the pursuit of prosperity and the adherence to ethical principles that safeguard the greater good.

Context: Throughout history, the insatiable pursuit of wealth has often led individuals and societies down treacherous paths, marked by exploitation, greed, and a disregard for the consequences of their actions. From the oppressive practices of colonial empires to the modern scourge of corporate corruption, the pursuit of riches has too often been tainted by unethical and unjust means. Proverbs, however, offers a counterpoint, a call to embrace a higher standard of conduct in our quest for economic prosperity.

The first principle we encounter in Proverbs is that of patience and perseverance. "Wealth gained hastily will dwindle," the verse cautions, underscoring the ephemeral nature of ill-gotten gains. The allure of quick riches, whether through deceit, manipulation, or unethical practices, is fleeting, ultimately leading to a path of ruin and diminished returns. True wealth, the verse suggests, is cultivated through a steadfast commitment to ethical means, a slow and steady accumulation that yields enduring prosperity.

This principle resonates with the concept of sustainability, a cornerstone of modern ethical business practices. Just as a tree cannot bear fruit without first taking root and nurturing its growth, lasting wealth cannot be achieved through hasty or unscrupulous methods. It is through diligence, perseverance, and a commitment to ethical conduct that true prosperity takes shape, a prosperity that endures beyond fleeting trends and economic fluctuations.

The second principle embedded within Proverbs 13:11 is that of honest labor and fair compensation. "Whoever gathers little by little will increase it," the verse exhorts, implying a process of gradual accumulation through honorable means. This principle stands in stark contrast to the exploitative practices of greed and oppression that have marred the pursuit of wealth throughout history.

From the sweatshops of the Industrial Revolution to the modern-day scourge of wage theft, the accumulation of wealth through the exploitation of workers and the denial of fair compensation has been a blight on the human conscience. Proverbs offer a corrective, a call to embrace ethical labor practices, fair wages, and respect for the dignity of all individuals involved in the creation of wealth.

This principle finds resonance in the contemporary concepts of corporate social responsibility, sustainable business practices, and stakeholder capitalism. By recognizing the intrinsic value of all those who contribute to the generation of wealth – from employees to suppliers to local communities – we not only uphold ethical principles but also foster long-term prosperity and societal well-being.

The third principle woven into the fabric of Proverbs 13:11 is that of environmental stewardship and resource conservation. The admonition to "gather little by little" implies a measured approach, a mindful utilization of resources that avoids excess and waste. In an era marked by the existential threat of climate change and the depletion of natural resources, this principle takes on renewed urgency.

Ethical wealth accumulation must be inextricably linked to a commitment to environmental sustainability, a recognition that our pursuit of prosperity cannot come at the cost of irreparable harm to the planet we call home. This principle echoes the principles of the circular economy, sustainable investing, and the transition toward renewable energy sources, all of which seek to align economic growth with responsible stewardship of the natural world.

Beyond these foundational principles, the pursuit of ethical wealth accumulation also demands a broader commitment to social responsibility and the promotion of the common good. This includes supporting initiatives that uplift marginalized communities, fostering inclusive economic opportunities, and contributing to the development of public infrastructure and services that benefit society as a whole.

Ultimately, the ethical dimensions of wealth accumulation, as illuminated by Proverbs, call for a holistic approach that transcends mere profit maximization. It demands a recognition of our interconnectedness, a commitment to upholding moral and ethical principles, and a willingness to sacrifice short-term gains for the sake of long-term sustainability and societal well-being.

In a world where the pursuit of wealth has often been tainted by greed, exploitation, and disregard for the greater good, the wisdom of Proverbs offers a path forward, a beacon of hope that guides us toward a more just, equitable, and sustainable model of economic prosperity. By embracing patience, perseverance, ethical labor practices, environmental stewardship, and a commitment to the common good, we can chart a course toward a future where wealth accumulation is not merely a means to an end but a force for positive change, a catalyst for the betterment of humanity and the preservation of our planet.

The journey toward ethical wealth accumulation is not without its challenges, but it is a journey worth embarking upon. In the end, true prosperity is not measured solely in the accumulation of material riches but in the enduring legacy of a life lived with integrity, dignity, and a commitment to the greater good.

Navigating Modern Financial Systems With Ancient Wisdom

The path to true prosperity, as illuminated by the timeless wisdom of Proverbs, is one that demands a delicate balance between the pursuit of wealth and the adherence to ethical principles. In the midst of the ever-evolving landscape of modern financial systems, where the lure of quick riches can be seductive and the temptation to compromise one's values ever-present, the ancient words of Proverbs serve as a guiding light, offering a roadmap for navigating the complexities of economic endeavors with integrity and wisdom.

Proverb: "Wealth gained hastily will dwindle, but whoever gathers little by little will increase it." - Proverbs 13:11

Definition: This proverb speaks to the virtue of patience and perseverance in the pursuit of wealth. It cautions against the allure of quick riches, often obtained through unethical or unsustainable means, and instead advocates for a gradual and steady accumulation of resources through honorable means. This principle resonates with the modern concept of sustainable wealth creation, which emphasizes the importance of building enduring prosperity through ethical practices and responsible stewardship.

Context: In the ancient world, the pursuit of wealth was often marred by practices of exploitation, greed, and disregard for the well-being of others. The allure of quick riches through dishonest means or at the expense of others was a temptation that many succumbed to, leading to cycles of boom and bust, and ultimately, the erosion of societal trust and stability. Proverbs 13:11 emerged as a counterpoint to these destructive tendencies, offering a wisdom rooted in the virtues of patience, diligence, and a commitment to honorable means.

In the modern financial landscape, the principles embodied in this proverb remain as relevant as ever. The breakneck pace of technological innovation, the globalization of markets, and the relentless drive for short-term gains have created an environment where the temptation to cut corners or prioritize profits over ethics can be overwhelming. However, history has repeatedly demonstrated that the pursuit of wealth through unethical means, such as fraud, exploitation, or disregard for environmental and social consequences, ultimately leads to instability, reputational damage, and long-term losses.

The wisdom of this proverb reminds us that true, enduring wealth is cultivated through a steadfast commitment to ethical practices, a willingness to embrace patience, and a recognition that short-term gains must never come at the cost of compromising one's integrity or the well-being of others. It calls upon us to resist the siren song of quick riches and instead focus on building sustainable, responsible businesses and investments that create value not just for ourselves, but for society as a whole.

In the realm of modern finance, this principle finds expression in the growing emphasis on responsible investing, stakeholder capitalism, and the integration of environmental, social, and governance (ESG) factors into investment decisions. These approaches recognize that true, long-term prosperity is inextricably linked to the well-being of the planet, the fair treatment of workers and communities, and the adherence to ethical and transparent business practices.

By embracing the wisdom of this proverb, financial institutions, businesses, and investors can navigate the complexities of modern economic systems with a steadfast moral compass. They can prioritize sustainable practices, foster inclusive economic opportunities, and contribute to the development of public infrastructure and services that benefit society as a whole. In doing so, they not only uphold ethical principles but also create the foundation for enduring prosperity, resilient to the inevitable ebbs and flows of economic cycles.

Proverb: "Dishonest money dwindles away, but whoever gathers money little by little makes it grow." - Proverbs 13:11

Definition: This proverb speaks directly to the importance of integrity and honesty in the pursuit of financial gain. It cautions against the allure of dishonest or ill-gotten wealth, which ultimately leads to diminishing returns and instability. Instead, it advocates for a gradual, ethical accumulation of resources through honorable means, a path that leads to enduring growth and prosperity.

Context: Throughout history, the temptation to acquire wealth through dishonest or unethical means has been a constant challenge for individuals and societies alike. From ancient times when merchants might engage in deceptive practices or rulers might levy unjust taxes, to modern-day financial scandals involving fraud, insider trading, and corporate malfeasance, the pursuit of wealth has often been tainted by dishonesty and a disregard for ethical norms.

However, this proverb serves as a reminder that such dishonest wealth is fleeting and ultimately self-destructive. It emphasizes the importance of cultivating a mindset of integrity, where financial gain is pursued through legitimate, transparent, and ethical means. By embracing honesty and rejecting the temptation of dishonest shortcuts, individuals, and organizations can build a foundation for sustainable, long-term prosperity that withstands the test of time and maintains the trust of stakeholders and society at large.

In the modern financial landscape, the principles espoused by this proverb are embodied in concepts such as corporate governance, regulatory compliance, and the promotion of ethical business practices. Financial institutions and corporations that prioritize transparency, accountability, and a commitment to ethical conduct not only uphold moral principles but also foster an environment of trust and stability, essential for long-term economic growth and prosperity.

Furthermore, this proverb resonates with the growing emphasis on responsible investing and the integration of ESG factors into investment decisions. Investors and asset managers are increasingly recognizing that companies with strong ethical foundations, a commitment to responsible business practices, and a track record of transparent and accountable governance are better positioned for long-term success and value creation.

By embracing the wisdom of this proverb, financial institutions, businesses, and individuals can navigate the complexities of modern economic systems with a steadfast commitment to integrity. They can foster a culture of ethical conduct, prioritize transparency and accountability, and reject the temptation of dishonest practices that may yield short-term gains but ultimately erode trust and stability.

In an era marked by increasing scrutiny and a heightened awareness of the societal impact of business practices, the principles embodied in this proverb take on renewed significance. By rejecting dishonest wealth and embracing ethical, gradual accumulation, financial actors can not only create enduring prosperity but also contribute to the greater good of society, fostering an environment of trust, stability, and shared prosperity.

As we navigate the ever-evolving landscape of modern financial systems, the ancient wisdom of Proverbs serves as a timeless guide, reminding us that true prosperity lies not in the pursuit of quick riches or dishonest gain, but in the steadfast commitment to ethical practices, patience, and a recognition of our interconnectedness with society and the natural world. By embracing these principles, we can chart a course toward a future where wealth creation is not merely a means to an end, but a force for positive change, a catalyst for the betterment of humanity and the preservation of our planet.

14

SPIRITUAL LEADERSHIP: LESSONS FROM ELISHA

The Calling of Elisha

In the annals of spiritual leadership, few moments stand as pivotal as the calling of Elisha by the prophet Elijah. It marked a turning point, a sacred transition of divine authority and purpose, one that would echo through the ages, reverberating in the lives of countless leaders who would follow in their footsteps.

At the heart of this transformative event lay the profound concept of divine calling, a summons that transcended the boundaries of human ambition or circumstance. In the midst of his ordinary life, tending to his fields and oxen, Elisha was unexpectedly anointed by Elijah, who cast his mantle upon the younger man, signifying the transfer of prophetic succession.

This symbolic act carried immense weight, for it represented the divine selection and anointing of Elisha as the heir to Elijah's sacred mantle. It was not merely a ceremonial gesture, but a profound acknowledgment that the hand of the Almighty had chosen Elisha for a greater purpose, one that would shape the spiritual landscape of the nation and usher in a new era of prophetic ministry.

In stark contrast to contemporary practices within religious institutions, where leadership is often determined by hierarchical structures, political maneuvering, or human ambition, the calling of Elisha exemplified the primacy of divine intervention in the realm of spiritual leadership. It served as a poignant reminder that true leadership in the sacred realm is not a matter of personal aspiration or institutional ascension, but rather a response to a higher calling, a sacred mandate bestowed upon those chosen by the divine will.

Throughout history, this profound concept has resonated in the lives of countless spiritual leaders, whose ministries have been marked by a transformative encounter with the divine. From the apostles of Christ, summoned to leave their nets and follow, to the great reformers and revivalists who ushered in waves of spiritual renewal, the echoes of Elisha's calling reverberate, reminding us of the power and necessity of divine selection in shaping the course of spiritual leadership.

One such modern example is that of Mother Teresa, whose life and ministry were irrevocably altered by a divine calling she experienced in September 1946 while on a train journey through the night. In the depths of her soul, she heard the voice of God, summoning her to leave the convent and serve "the poorest of the poor." In that moment, her path was forever altered, and she embarked on a journey that would touch the lives of countless individuals, transcending borders, cultures, and faiths.

Similarly, Martin Luther King Jr.'s unwavering commitment to the civil rights movement and his pursuit of racial equality and justice stemmed from a profound sense of divine calling. In his own words, "The gospel of Jesus was interpreted for me anew, and I felt a personal responsibility to take my commitment to it seriously." This calling transformed him from a young Baptist minister into a galvanizing force for social change, inspiring millions and leaving an indelible mark on the course of human history.

The stories of Mother Teresa, Martin Luther King Jr., and countless others remind us that the divine calling is not merely a relic of ancient times, but a living force that continues to shape the trajectory of spiritual leadership and ignite transformative ministries. Just as Elisha's life was forever altered by the prophet's mantle, these modern-day leaders answered a sacred summons, transcending personal ambitions and embracing a higher purpose.

Yet, the significance of Elisha's calling extends beyond the personal journeys of individual leaders. It speaks to the fundamental principles that undergird true spiritual leadership, principles that resonate across faiths and traditions. The act of divine selection reminds us that genuine authority in the spiritual realm is not derived from human constructs or institutional hierarchies, but rather from a sacred mandate bestowed by the divine.

Furthermore, Elisha's calling underscores the importance of recognizing and nurturing potential leaders who bear the mark of divine selection. Just as Elijah discerned the call upon Elisha's life, contemporary religious institutions must cultivate an environment where the spark of divine calling can be nurtured, where those with the anointing of spiritual leadership can be identified, empowered, and given the space to pursue their sacred mandates.

In a world where leadership in religious spheres is often marred by power struggles, political agendas, and a focus on institutional preservation, the story of Elisha serves as a clarion call to return to the fundamental principles of divine calling and spiritual authority. It reminds us that true leadership in the sacred realm transcends human ambition and constructs, and that the ultimate source of authority lies not in titles or hierarchies, but in a profound response to the divine summons.

As we navigate the complexities of spiritual leadership in the modern era, the calling of Elisha stands as a timeless beacon, illuminating the path forward. It calls upon us to embrace the primacy of divine selection, to cultivate an environment where the seeds of sacred callings can take root, and to honor the transformative power of those who have been anointed by the divine to lead and shape the spiritual landscape of our times.

Faith and Obedience: Elisha's Early Ministry

1. Introduction: In the ancient kingdom of Israel, a young man named Elisha embarked on a journey that would forever shape the spiritual landscape of his nation. His story, chronicled in the books of 1 and 2 Kings, offers a poignant case study of the transformative power of faith, obedience, and personal sacrifice in the realm of spiritual leadership.

2. The Call: Elisha's call came unexpectedly, as he toiled in the fields, tending to his oxen and plows. The prophet Elijah, under divine instruction, cast his mantle upon Elisha, symbolizing the transfer of prophetic authority and the anointing of a new spiritual leader. This act marked the beginning of Elisha's extraordinary ministry, one that would require him to forsake his familial and economic ties, leaving behind a life of relative comfort and stability.

3. The Challenge: Elisha's decision to follow Elijah represented a profound act of faith and obedience to the divine call. He was required to relinquish the familiarity of his surroundings, his livelihood, and the societal norms that governed his existence. This challenge was not merely a test of personal conviction; it was a demonstration of his willingness to surrender all earthly attachments in pursuit of a sacred mandate.

4. The Journey: From the moment Elisha embraced his calling, his life became a tapestry of remarkable experiences that shaped his character and prepared him for the challenges that lay ahead. He witnessed the miracles performed by Elijah, including the parting of the Jordan River and the calling down of fire from heaven. These profound encounters deepened Elisha's faith and strengthened his resolve to follow in the footsteps of his mentor, even when faced with the daunting task of succeeding such a formidable spiritual leader.

5. The Miracles: As Elisha's ministry unfolded, he too became an instrument of divine power, performing miracles that demonstrated his unwavering faith and obedience. From purifying the waters of Jericho to multiplying the widow's oil and raising the Shunammite woman's son from the dead, Elisha's actions were a testament to the transformative power of faith and a reminder of the profound impact that spiritual leadership can have on the lives of individuals and communities.

6. Lessons Learned: Elisha's early ministry serves as a powerful case study of the importance of faith, obedience, and personal sacrifice in the realm of spiritual leadership. It teaches us that true leadership in the sacred sphere is not merely a matter of human ambition or institutional ascension, but rather a response to a divine calling that transcends earthly pursuits. Moreover, Elisha's example underscores the necessity of cultivating an environment where potential spiritual leaders can be nurtured and empowered to pursue their sacred mandates. Just as Elijah recognized and fostered Elisha's calling, contemporary religious institutions must create spaces where the seeds of divine selection can germinate, allowing those who bear the anointing of spiritual leadership to flourish and impact the world around them.

7. Contemporary Relevance: The principles embodied in Elisha's early ministry resonate profoundly in contemporary religious contexts. In an era where spiritual leadership is often clouded by power struggles, political agendas, and institutional preservation, Elisha's story serves as a clarion call to return to the fundamental tenets of faith, obedience, and personal sacrifice. Many modern-day spiritual leaders, such as Mother Teresa and Martin Luther King Jr., have exemplified these principles, embracing divine callings that transcended personal ambition and dedicated their lives to serving a higher purpose. Their stories, like Elisha's, remind us that true

leadership in the sacred realm is not contingent upon human constructs or hierarchies, but rather stems from a profound response to the divine summons.

8. Concluding Thoughts: As we reflect on Elisha's early ministry, we are left with a profound question: Are we willing to embrace the sacrifices inherent in answering a divine call, even when it requires us to relinquish the familiarity of our circumstances and surrender our earthly attachments? Elisha's journey serves as a testament to the transformative power that can be unleashed when we respond with unwavering faith and obedience to the sacred summons that echo within our souls.

The Double Portion: A Quest for Spiritual Empowerment

As spiritual leaders, we often find ourselves on a relentless quest for deeper wisdom, greater empowerment, and an amplified connection to the divine. In our journey, certain pivotal moments arise, where opportunities present themselves to elevate our spiritual capacities to new heights. One such transformative event is etched in the annals of biblical history, when Elisha, the devoted protégé of the great prophet Elijah, boldly requested a "double portion" of his mentor's spirit. This moment not only marked a profound shift in spiritual leadership but also illuminated the significance of perseverance, loyalty, and the unwavering pursuit of spiritual empowerment.

To fully comprehend the depth and implications of this transformative occurrence, we must first grasp the essence of three key terms: the "double portion," spiritual empowerment, and the mantle of leadership. These concepts, intricately interwoven, will guide our discourse and shed light on the timeless lessons we can glean from Elisha's audacious quest.

The "Double Portion" Imagine a wellspring of divine wisdom and power, flowing through the veins of a revered spiritual leader. Now, envision the possibility of inheriting not just a portion of this sacred wellspring but a double measure – a concept that captivated the imagination of Elisha and ignited his burning desire for spiritual empowerment. The "double portion" was a symbolic request, rooted in the ancient Israelite tradition of firstborn sons inheriting a double share of their father's possessions. However, in the realm of spiritual leadership, this notion transcended the physical and signified a transfer of divine grace, authority, and anointing from one spiritual guide to another.

Spiritual Empowerment In the context of Elisha's pursuit, spiritual empowerment refers to the profound transformation that occurs when an individual's connection with the divine is amplified, bestowing upon them heightened wisdom, discernment, and the ability to wield supernatural power. It is a state of being where one's spiritual capacities are elevated, enabling one to navigate the complexities of spiritual leadership with greater clarity, authority, and efficacy. Spiritual empowerment is not merely a personal pursuit but a testament to the immense responsibility that comes with assuming the mantle of spiritual guidance, as one's actions and decisions profoundly impact the lives of countless individuals seeking enlightenment.

The Mantle of Leadership Imagine a physical mantle – a cloak, a symbol of authority and responsibility – passed down from one leader to the next. In the spiritual realm, this mantle represents the sacred calling of leadership, a divine commission to guide, nurture, and shepherd souls on their spiritual journeys. Elisha's request for a "double portion" was inherently linked to his readiness to assume this mantle, to step into the profound responsibility of carrying forth the legacy of his mentor and serving as a beacon of spiritual wisdom for generations to come. The mantle of leadership is not a mere title but a sacred trust, a solemn vow to embody the virtues of humility, compassion, and unwavering devotion to the divine.

As we delve deeper into Elisha's transformative quest, these terms – the "double portion," spiritual empowerment, and the mantle of leadership – will serve as guideposts, illuminating the profound lessons and implications that resonate through the ages. For contemporary spiritual leaders, this narrative serves as a powerful reminder of the unwavering dedication, perseverance, and courage required to ascend to greater heights of spiritual empowerment, all in service of guiding and uplifting the communities entrusted to their care.

Miracles and Authority: Establishing Prophetic Legitimacy

In the realm of spiritual leadership, the phenomenon of miracles has often played a pivotal role in establishing authority and fostering trust among followers. The presence of miraculous acts, perceived as divine interventions, serves as a powerful endorsement of a leader's legitimacy and connection to the sacred. This dynamic is exemplified in the life of Elisha, the revered prophet who succeeded the great Elijah, as chronicled in the biblical narratives.

To truly comprehend the significance of miracles in establishing Elisha's prophetic authority, we must first delve into the broader context and importance of an evidence-based approach. Throughout history, spiritual leaders have sought to validate their claims and garner the allegiance of their followers by presenting tangible proof of their divine mandate. These proofs, often manifested through extraordinary events or miraculous occurrences, serve as compelling evidence that transcends mere words or rhetoric, resonating deeply with the human yearning for the supernatural and the divine.

One of the main statements or propositions that emerges from Elisha's narrative is the direct correlation between the manifestation of miracles and the affirmation of his prophetic authority. As the successor to Elijah, Elisha's ability to perform miracles was a clear demonstration of the "double portion" of spiritual power he had requested, effectively cementing his status as a conduit of the divine and a worthy heir to his mentor's mantle.

The miracles attributed to Elisha are numerous and diverse, each serving as a potent piece of evidence that solidified his standing as a revered prophet. One such miracle was the healing of the waters of Jericho, where Elisha transformed the city's polluted waters into a source of life and sustenance. This act not only showcased his command over the natural elements but also resonated with the Israelites' deep cultural and spiritual connection to water as a symbol of purity and divine blessing.

Another compelling piece of evidence was Elisha's multiplication of oil for a destitute widow, an act that provided for her immediate needs while simultaneously affirming his ability to channel divine providence. The details of this miracle, including the methodology of utilizing the widow's limited resources and the credibility of the biblical account, further reinforce its evidentiary value in establishing Elisha's prophetic legitimacy.

While these miracles stand as compelling evidence of Elisha's divine mandate, it is essential to acknowledge that there may have been instances or accounts that could potentially challenge or contradict the initial claim of his authority. However, a balanced and evidence-based approach necessitates addressing such counter-evidence by providing explanations, clarifications, or further evidence to reinforce the initial proposition.

For instance, some may question the veracity of the biblical narratives or the reliability of the sources that document Elisha's miracles. In such cases, it is crucial to consider the broader historical and cultural context, the consistency of the accounts across various texts, and the corroborating evidence from other sources or disciplines, such as archaeology or textual criticism.

Moreover, the significance of Elisha's miracles extends beyond mere empirical evidence; they carry profound theological and social implications. From a theological perspective, these miraculous acts served as tangible manifestations of God's power and presence, affirming Elisha's divine mandate and fostering trust and devotion among the Israelites. Socially, Elisha's miracles had a transformative impact, addressing pressing needs and challenges faced by the community, thereby solidifying his role as a compassionate and authoritative leader.

The resonance of Elisha's miracles echoes through the ages, informing the significance of miraculous events in the context of contemporary spiritual leadership. While the nature and manifestation of miracles may vary across traditions and belief systems, the underlying principle remains consistent: miraculous occurrences serve as powerful validation of a leader's spiritual authority and divine connection, fostering trust and inspiring devotion among their followers.

As we navigate the complexities of spiritual leadership in modern times, it is imperative to recognize the enduring relevance of this dynamic. Contemporary spiritual leaders, regardless of their specific beliefs or practices, must strive to present evidence that resonates with their followers, whether through teachings that transform lives, acts of service that uplift communities, or manifestations of the divine that transcend the ordinary. By doing so, they not only establish their legitimacy but also perpetuate the sacred tradition of guiding souls toward enlightenment and spiritual fulfillment.

Ultimately, the study of Elisha's miracles and their role in establishing his prophetic authority serves as a powerful reminder of the profound significance of divine endorsement in the realm of spiritual leadership. It encourages us to contemplate the broader implications of miraculous events, both historically and in contemporary settings, and to embrace the transformative power of evidence-based spiritual guidance. As we embark on our own journeys of spiritual empowerment and leadership, may we draw inspiration from Elisha's unwavering faith and the tangible proofs that solidified his legacy as a beacon of divine wisdom and guidance.

The Role of Compassion: Elisha's Ministry to the Vulnerable

A young shepherd boy stood transfixed, gazing intently at the vast expanse of the night sky. The countless stars glimmered like diamonds strewn across a velvet canvas, a breathtaking tapestry that filled his heart with wonder and awe. Yet, amidst this cosmic splendor, a single truth resonated within him: that the greatest power in the universe is compassion.

Compassion, in its purest form, is the capacity to extend empathy, kindness, and unconditional care to those in need. It is the hallmark of true spiritual leadership, a quality that transcends mere words or miracles and touches the deepest recesses of the human soul. In the life and ministry of the prophet Elisha, we witness a profound embodiment of this timeless virtue, a testament to the transformative power of compassion in fostering community well-being and spiritual growth.

The biblical accounts of Elisha's interactions with the vulnerable and marginalized are a poignant reminder of the centrality of compassion in the practice of spiritual leadership. In the narrative of the Shunammite woman, we encounter a woman of means who extends hospitality and kindness to Elisha, only to be confronted with the unimaginable tragedy of losing her son. In response, Elisha's actions are defined not by grandiose displays of power but by a deep well of compassion that compels him to restore the child's life, alleviating the woman's profound grief.

Similarly, the story of Naaman, the commander of the Aramean army who sought healing from leprosy, serves as a powerful illustration of Elisha's compassionate ministry. Despite the societal stigma and cultural barriers that could have hindered his engagement with this foreign commander, Elisha's concern for Naaman's well-being transcended all boundaries. Through a simple act of immersion in the River Jordan, Elisha facilitated Naaman's healing, demonstrating that true compassion knows no bounds of nationality, rank, or social status.

The theological foundations of compassion are deeply rooted in the biblical teachings that Elisha upheld and embodied. The Judeo-Christian tradition, which shaped Elisha's worldview, is replete with exhortations to love one's neighbor, care for the downtrodden, and extend mercy and grace to those in need. The prophets of old, whose legacy Elisha carried forward, were often the voices of conscience, calling for justice and compassion in a world marred by oppression and indifference.

As we examine the lives of modern spiritual leaders who have left an indelible mark on their communities and the world at large, we find a common thread that binds them together: a deep reservoir of compassion. From the Dalai Lama's unwavering commitment to non-violence and human rights to Mother Teresa's selfless service to the "poorest of the poor," these luminaries have upheld the timeless principle that true spiritual leadership is rooted in compassionate action.

The importance of compassion in leadership extends far beyond the confines of religious or spiritual contexts. In the realms of business, politics, education, and social advocacy, compassionate leaders have the power to inspire trust, foster unity, and create lasting positive change. By prioritizing empathy, understanding, and a genuine concern for the well-being of those they serve, these leaders cultivate an environment of mutual respect, collaboration, and shared purpose.

For those who aspire to embody the spirit of compassionate leadership, whether in their professional or personal capacities, the example of Elisha offers invaluable guidance. To integrate compassionate practices into one's ministry or sphere of influence, it is essential to cultivate a deep sense of humility, recognizing that true leadership is not about wielding power or asserting dominance but rather about serving others with genuine care and selflessness.

Furthermore, compassionate leadership requires active listening and a willingness to understand the unique challenges and perspectives of those we serve. By creating safe spaces for open dialogue and fostering an environment of mutual understanding, we can better address the needs of our communities and forge stronger bonds of trust and unity.

Ultimately, the positive impact of compassionate leadership extends far beyond the individual lives it touches. When leaders prioritize compassion, they sow the seeds of a more just, equitable, and harmonious society. By embodying the values of empathy, kindness, and respect for all, they inspire others to follow suit, creating a ripple effect that can transform entire communities and even nations.

As we strive to emulate the example of Elisha and the great spiritual leaders who have walked this path before us, let us remember that compassion is not merely a virtue to be admired but a force to be wielded in the service of humanity. It is the bedrock upon which true spiritual leadership is built, the essence that imbues our actions with meaning, purpose, and ultimately, the power to heal a broken world. In the words of the ancient shepherd boy, who now stands as a wise elder, "In a universe filled with wonders, the greatest of these is the miracle of compassion."

Mentorship and Succession: Elisha and the Sons of the Prophets

Step 1: Establish the GoalIn this guide, we will explore the profound legacy of Elisha's mentorship and succession planning with the sons of the prophets. You will gain insights into cultivating transformative mentorship programs within spiritual communities, ensuring the continuity and vitality of spiritual leadership across generations.

Step 2: PrerequisitesTo grasp the full significance of Elisha's mentorship journey, it is essential to have a basic understanding of the historical context and the roles of prophets in ancient Israelite society. Familiarity with the biblical accounts of Elisha's life and ministry, particularly his interactions with the sons of the prophets, will also provide a solid foundation for deeper exploration.

Step 3: OverviewThe account of Elisha's ministry offers a remarkable model for effective mentorship and succession planning within spiritual communities. As he emerged as the successor to the renowned prophet Elijah, Elisha recognized the importance of nurturing and empowering the next generation of prophetic voices. His interactions with the sons of the prophets, a group of young men dedicated to the study and practice of prophecy, exemplify the methods and principles that contemporary spiritual leaders can emulate to ensure the sustainability and growth of their communities.

Step 4: Detailed Steps

1. Cultivating a Nurturing Environment

- Elisha created an atmosphere of open dialogue and collaboration, fostering an environment where the sons of the prophets felt safe to ask questions, share insights, and learn from one another.
- He demonstrated humility and patience, recognizing that personal growth and spiritual development are gradual processes that require gentleness and understanding.
- By establishing a supportive and inclusive community, Elisha laid the foundation for effective mentorship and personal transformation.

2. Imparting Wisdom through Lived Experience

- Elisha's mentorship extended beyond mere theoretical instruction; he actively engaged the sons of the prophets in real-life situations, allowing them to witness firsthand the application of prophetic principles.
- From miracles of provision (such as the purification of the poisonous stew or the multiplication of loaves) to acts of compassion (like the restoration of the Shunammite woman's son), Elisha provided practical examples that reinforced his teachings.

- Through these shared experiences, the sons of the prophets gained invaluable insights into the ethical and spiritual responsibilities of leadership, preparing them for their future roles.

3. Fostering Critical Thinking and Discernment

- Elisha encouraged the sons of the prophets to cultivate critical thinking skills, challenging them to engage with complex situations and discern the underlying principles at play. By presenting them with thought-provoking scenarios and encouraging open dialogue, he empowered them to develop their own capacity for spiritual discernment and wise decision-making.
- This approach equipped them with the tools necessary to navigate the complexities of leadership and maintain their integrity in the face of challenges.

4. Modeling Servant Leadership

- Throughout his interactions with the sons of the prophets, Elisha exemplified the principles of servant leadership, emphasizing humility, compassion, and a willingness to serve others.
- His actions, such as the healing of Naaman or his concern for the well-being of the Shunammite women demonstrated the transformative power of selfless service and concern for those in need.
- By embodying these values, Elisha inspired the sons of the prophets to embrace a leadership style rooted in empathy and a genuine desire to uplift and empower others.

5. Encouraging Continuity and Legacy

- Elisha understood the importance of ensuring the

continuity of spiritual leadership and the preservation of prophetic wisdom across generations.

- He actively mentored and prepared the sons of the prophets to carry on the sacred traditions and responsibilities entrusted to them, ensuring that the prophetic voice would not be silenced.
- By investing in their personal and spiritual growth, Elisha laid the groundwork for a sustainable legacy that would endure long after his own ministry.

Step 5: Tips and Warnings

- Cultivate Authenticity: Effective mentorship thrives on genuine relationships built on trust, vulnerability, and shared experience. Strive for authenticity in your interactions with mentees, fostering an environment where honest dialogue and personal growth can flourish. Embrace Diversity: Recognize that each mentee brings a unique set of experiences, perspectives, and learning styles. Tailor your approach to meet their individual needs while celebrating the richness of diversity within your community.
- Foster Accountability: While providing support and guidance, also encourage personal accountability and responsibility among your mentees. Empower them to take ownership of their growth and development, fostering self-discipline and commitment to their spiritual journey.
- Avoid Stagnation: Continuously evaluate and adapt your mentorship programs to ensure they remain relevant and effective. Seek feedback from mentees, incorporate new insights and best practices, and remain open to growth and evolution.
- Embrace Humility: Remember that mentorship is a collaborative process, and both mentor and mentee have valuable insights to share. Approach each interaction with

humility, recognizing that you, too, have opportunities to learn and grow.

Step 6: Checking for SuccessThe success of mentorship and succession planning can be measured by the impact it has on the spiritual vitality and resilience of your community. Observe the growth and transformation of your mentees, their ability to step into leadership roles with confidence and wisdom, and the seamless transfer of knowledge and values across generations. Additionally, gauge the continued relevance and influence of your community's spiritual teachings and practices, as this reflects the effectiveness of your mentorship efforts in preserving and adapting the core tenets of your faith.

Step 7: Addressing Potential Problems

- Lack of Commitment: If mentees exhibit a lack of commitment or engagement, it may be necessary to reassess their readiness for the mentorship program or explore underlying factors that may be hindering their progress.
- Resistance to Change: Change can be challenging, and some mentees may resist adapting to new perspectives or approaches. In such cases, provide ample support, encourage open dialogue, and highlight the long-term benefits of embracing growth and evolution.
- Generational Gaps: Bridging generational divides can be a common obstacle in mentorship, with differing communication styles, perspectives, and expectations. Promote mutual understanding, respect, and a willingness to learn from one another to overcome these barriers.
- Burnout and Fatigue: Both mentors and mentees may experience burnout or fatigue, particularly in demanding spiritual leadership roles. Prioritize self-care practices, foster a supportive community, and encourage healthy work-life balance to mitigate these risks.

Resilience in Adversity: Elisha's Response to Challenges

The life and ministry of the prophet Elisha serve as a profound testament to resilience in the face of adversity. Throughout his remarkable journey, Elisha encountered numerous challenges that tested the depths of his faith and resolve, yet he consistently emerged victorious, demonstrating an unwavering commitment to his divine calling.

The backdrop of Elisha's ministry was fraught with turmoil and conflict. The northern kingdom of Israel, where he primarily ministered, was embroiled in political upheaval and spiritual decline. Idolatry and disobedience to God were rampant, prompting divine judgment in the form of wars, famine, and even siege. It was within this tumultuous context that Elisha's resilience shone forth, illuminating the path of unwavering faith and divine reliance.

One of the most poignant examples of Elisha's resilience can be found in the account of the siege of Samaria (2 Kings 6:24-33). As the Syrian army laid siege to the city, famine gripped the inhabitants, leading to unspeakable suffering and desperation. In the midst of this crisis, Elisha remained steadfast, offering hope and guidance to the people. His unwavering faith in God's provision sustained him, even as the king of Israel sought to place blame upon him.

Elisha's response to this challenge was remarkable. Rather than succumbing to despair, he boldly proclaimed God's imminent deliverance, foretelling an abundance of food within a day's time. His words were met with skepticism, yet Elisha's resilience and trust in divine providence prevailed. The following day, the Syrian army inexplicably fled, leaving behind their provisions, which were then plundered by the starving Israelites, fulfilling Elisha's prophecy.

Another pivotal moment that tested Elisha's resilience was his confrontation with the Syrian army (2 Kings 6:8-23). As a trusted adviser to the king of Israel, Elisha possessed divine insight into the enemy's plans, repeatedly thwarting their attacks. This enraged the king of Syria, who sent a mighty force to capture Elisha. Undaunted, the prophet prayed for his servant's eyes to be opened, revealing the presence of a vast heavenly army surrounding them, a powerful reminder of God's protection and sovereignty.

Elisha's resilience extended beyond military conflicts; he also navigated personal attacks and ridicule with grace and fortitude. When a group of youths mocked his prophetic calling, he did not respond with anger or retaliation. Instead, he maintained his composure and trusted in God's justice, which manifested through a miraculous intervention that protected him from harm (2 Kings 2:23-25).

Throughout these and countless other challenges, Elisha's unwavering faith and reliance on divine guidance were the bedrock of his resilience. He understood that his strength did not come from his own abilities but from the limitless power of the Almighty God, he served. This perspective enabled him to face adversity with courage and confidence, knowing that he was not alone in the battles he waged.

The lessons from Elisha's resilience are timeless and invaluable for contemporary leaders, regardless of their sphere of influence. In a world filled with challenges and uncertainties, developing and sustaining resilience is essential for navigating turbulent times and fulfilling one's calling with integrity and steadfastness.

To cultivate resilience in the face of adversity, we must emulate Elisha's profound trust in divine guidance. Just as he sought wisdom and direction from God, we too must cultivate a deep and abiding relationship with our Creator, drawing strength from the well of divine truth and relying on the unwavering promises found within sacred scriptures. This involves regular prayer, meditation, and a willingness to surrender our anxieties and fears to a higher power.

Additionally, we can learn from Elisha's ability to maintain perspective, even in the midst of seemingly insurmountable obstacles. By focusing on the greater purpose and eternal significance of our endeavors, we can avoid being overwhelmed by temporary setbacks or distractions. Elisha remained steadfast in his prophetic mission, recognizing that the challenges he faced were but fleeting moments in the grand narrative of God's redemptive plan.

Furthermore, Elisha's resilience was bolstered by a supportive community of fellow believers and prophets. In times of adversity, we must not isolate ourselves but rather seek out a network of like-minded individuals who can offer encouragement, accountability, and a shared sense of purpose. By fostering an environment of mutual support and understanding, we can draw strength from one another and weather the storms of life together.

As we navigate the complexities and challenges of our own leadership roles, may we draw inspiration from Elisha's remarkable example of resilience. Let us embrace the principles of unwavering faith, divine reliance, and steadfast determination, knowing that through the power of our Creator, we too can overcome obstacles and emerge victorious, leaving a lasting legacy of spiritual impact and transformation.

Wisdom and Vision: Elisha's Strategic Leadership

What separates truly transformational leaders from those who merely maintain the status quo? It is the rare combination of wisdom and vision that allows visionaries to navigate uncharted territories and guide their followers through periods of profound change and uncertainty. The prophet Elisha stands as a towering example of such strategic leadership, utilizing his prophetic insights and keen discernment to steer the nation of Israel through tumultuous times and pave the way for a brighter future.

History is marked by pivotal moments that demand clarity of vision and unwavering wisdom from leaders. Ancient Israel found itself enveloped in such a season, faced with existential threats from external enemies and internal decay. It was in this crucible that Elisha's strategic leadership shone forth like a beacon in the darkness. His wisdom, rooted in an intimate relationship with the divine, granted him the foresight to anticipate challenges and chart a course through seemingly insurmountable obstacles.

One of the most striking instances of Elisha's strategic vision was his counsel to the king of Israel during the Syrian siege of Samaria. As famine gripped the city, desperation mounted, and the king contemplated unthinkable acts of violence. It was in this moment of crisis that Elisha, through divine revelation, proclaimed a seemingly impossible promise: within a day, the siege would be broken, and abundance would return. His wisdom transcended the limitations of human understanding, enabling him to see beyond the present crisis and envision a reality that defied all rational expectations.

True to his prophetic declaration, the Syrian army inexplicably fled, leaving behind their provisions, and the city was delivered from the jaws of starvation. Elisha's strategic vision not only saved countless lives but also demonstrated the profound power of aligning oneself with divine purposes and trusting in the wisdom that emanates from an eternal perspective. His actions offer a compelling lesson for modern leaders: cultivating a spiritual foundation and seeking transcendent wisdom can unlock insights and strategies that defy conventional limitations.

Elisha's strategic leadership was not confined to the realm of prophetic utterances; it also manifested in his tactical guidance during times of military conflict. As a trusted adviser to the king, Elisha's divine insights allowed him to anticipate enemy movements and thwart their plans. His strategic counsel enabled the Israelite forces to overcome seemingly insurmountable odds, turning the tide of battles and preserving the nation's sovereignty. In an era where military might and strategic maneuvering were paramount, Elisha's wisdom and vision proved instrumental in safeguarding the nation's future.

Contemporary examples of visionary religious leaders who have harnessed the power of wisdom and strategic thinking abound.

One such figure is Archbishop Desmond Tutu, whose unwavering moral vision and strategic nonviolent resistance played a pivotal role in dismantling the oppressive apartheid regime in South Africa. Like Elisha, Tutu drew upon a deep wellspring of spiritual wisdom and an unshakable commitment to justice, enabling him to navigate the treacherous waters of political upheaval and inspire a movement that ultimately transformed a nation.

Another modern exemplar of strategic spiritual leadership is the Dalai Lama, the spiritual and temporal leader of the Tibetan people. Through his profound wisdom and visionary approach, he has guided his community through decades of exile and oppression, advocating for nonviolence, compassion, and respect for human rights. His strategic efforts have not only preserved the cultural and spiritual heritage of the Tibetan people but have also elevated their cause on the global stage, inspiring countless individuals to embrace values of peace and understanding.

For modern spiritual leaders seeking to cultivate wisdom and vision within their own ministries, several key principles can be gleaned from Elisha's example. First and foremost, developing an intimate relationship with the divine source of wisdom is paramount. Just as Elisha sought guidance through prayer and prophetic revelation, contemporary leaders must nurture a deep spiritual practice that fosters a connection with the transcendent. This foundation enables them to tap into a wellspring of timeless wisdom and gain clarity amidst the complexities of their leadership challenges.

Secondly, strategic thinking and long-term visioning are essential for navigating complex challenges and fostering sustained spiritual and communal growth. Elisha's ability to anticipate obstacles and envision solutions empowered him to proactively address crises before they spiraled out of control. Similarly, modern leaders must cultivate the capacity to look beyond immediate concerns and envision the long-term implications of their decisions, charting a course that aligns with their ministry's highest ideals and aspirations.

Furthermore, humility and a willingness to surrender personal agendas to a higher purpose are hallmarks of effective spiritual leadership. Elisha's unwavering commitment to his prophetic calling transcended personal ambition or self-interest. He understood that his role was to serve as a conduit for divine wisdom, guiding the nation toward a greater destiny. This mindset enabled him to navigate complex political and military landscapes without compromising his integrity or compromising his values.

Finally, strategic spiritual leadership necessitates the courage to challenge the status quo and confront societal ills with unwavering conviction. Elisha fearlessly confronted the idolatry and spiritual decay that had taken root in Israel, even when it meant risking his own safety. His prophetic voice and uncompromising stance served as a clarion call for repentance and societal transformation. Contemporary leaders must likewise possess the moral fortitude to speak truth to power and advocate for justice, equality, and spiritual renewal, even in the face of opposition or adversity.

As we navigate the complexities of the modern world, the lessons gleaned from Elisha's strategic leadership remain profoundly relevant. By embracing wisdom, cultivating vision, and aligning ourselves with transcendent purposes, we can transform challenges into opportunities and guide our communities toward a brighter future. May we, like Elisha, have the courage to follow the path of wisdom and allow our lives to be beacons of hope, illuminating the way for generations to come.

Legacy and Impact: Elisha's Enduring Influence

The life and ministry of the prophet Elisha stand as a testament to the profound impact that visionary spiritual leadership can have on the course of history. His prophetic ministry, guided by divine wisdom and an unwavering commitment to serving the purposes of the Almighty, left an indelible mark on the nation of Israel and reverberates through the ages, inspiring generations of spiritual leaders across diverse religious traditions.

To fully appreciate Elisha's enduring legacy, it is instructive to trace the historical trajectory of his influence, from the earliest days of his prophetic calling to the lasting reverberations that continue to shape spiritual landscapes today. This timeline illuminates the far-reaching implications of a life dedicated to seeking and embodying transcendent wisdom:

1. Early Roots and Calling (9th Century BCE):

- Elisha emerges as a pivotal figure in the biblical narrative, first mentioned as the successor to the renowned prophet Elijah.
- His prophetic mantle was secured through a powerful encounter with Elijah, during which he received a double portion of his spiritual mentor's anointing.
- From humble beginnings as a farmer, Elisha heeded the divine call and embarked on a journey that would profoundly shape the destiny of Israel.

2. Prophetic Ministry and Miracles (9th Century BCE):

- Elisha's ministry was marked by numerous miracles, including:
- Purifying contaminated water sources, ensuring access to clean water for local communities.
- Multiplying scarce resources, such as food and oil, during times of famine and scarcity.
- Healing the afflicted, including a Syrian military commander, demonstrating the universality of divine compassion.
- These miraculous acts not only met practical needs but also served as powerful symbols of Elisha's prophetic authority and connection to the divine.

3. Strategic Counsel and National Impact (9th Century BCE):

- Elisha's wisdom extended beyond the spiritual realm, as he provided crucial strategic counsel to the kings of Israel during times of war and political turmoil.
- His prophetic insights enabled the Israelite armies to anticipate enemy movements and secure decisive victories, safeguarding the nation's sovereignty.
- Elisha's fearless confrontation of idolatry and societal decay challenged the status quo and inspired spiritual renewal, leaving a lasting imprint on Israel's religious and cultural fabric.

4. Enduring Influence within Judaism and Christianity:

- The biblical accounts of Elisha's life and ministry have been preserved and revered within the Jewish and Christian traditions for millennia.
- His prophetic persona and miraculous works have inspired countless individuals, from rabbis and scholars to mystics and theologians, shaping the understanding and practice of spiritual leadership.
- Elisha's story serves as a powerful reminder of the transformative impact that can be achieved through a life dedicated to seeking and embodying divine wisdom.

5. Inspiration for Contemporary Spiritual Leaders:

- In recent times, Elisha's legacy has continued to inspire and inform the practices of spiritual leaders across diverse religious traditions.
- His unwavering commitment to justice, compassion, and societal transformation resonates with modern advocates for social change and human rights.
- Elisha's example of strategic visioning and the cultivation of transcendent wisdom has provided a roadmap for contemporary leaders seeking to navigate complex challenges and foster sustainable spiritual growth.

6. Pivotal Moments and Enduring Impact:

- Throughout history, pivotal moments have emerged where Elisha's legacy has been invoked or reexamined, shaping the trajectory of spiritual leadership:
- During periods of religious reformation and renewal, Elisha's prophetic voice has served as a catalyst for challenging entrenched systems and embracing transformative change.
- In times of societal upheaval and conflict, his message of divine wisdom and moral courage has inspired movements for peace, reconciliation, and nonviolence.
- As new understandings of spiritual leadership emerge, Elisha's life continues to be a touchstone, reminding leaders of the enduring power of aligning with eternal truths and transcendent purposes.

Elisha's enduring legacy transcends the boundaries of time and tradition, serving as a powerful reminder of the transformative potential of visionary spiritual leadership. His life stands as a testament to the impact that can be achieved when wisdom, courage, and an unwavering commitment to divine purposes converge. As we navigate the complexities of the modern world, may we draw inspiration from Elisha's example, embodying the principles of strategic vision, moral fortitude, and a deep connection to the wellspring of eternal wisdom. In doing so, we too can become agents of lasting change, leaving a legacy that inspires and uplifts generations yet to come.

15

————

HEAVEN ON EARTH: MANIFESTING DIVINE PRINCIPLES

The Vision of Heaven on Earth

What does it mean to manifest heaven on earth?

This provocative question strikes at the heart of spiritual and existential pursuits, challenging us to envision a reality where the divine and the material world seamlessly intertwine. Throughout human history, the concept of heaven has captured the imagination of countless individuals, cultures, and religions, inspiring awe and reverence for a realm beyond our earthly confines. Yet, the notion of manifesting this celestial state within the very fabric of our daily lives remains an elusive and often misunderstood quest.

Traditionally, heaven has been portrayed as a transcendent realm, a paradise separated from the earthly plane, where the righteous find eternal bliss and freedom from the constraints of the physical world. While this view offers solace and hope for an afterlife, it inadvertently perpetuates a dichotomy between the sacred and the profane, relegating the realization of heavenly ideals to a distant and otherworldly existence. This dualistic perspective, while comforting in its simplicity, fails to address the profound potential for divine principles to manifest within the here and now.

The challenge lies in recognizing that heaven is not merely a destination but a state of being, a harmonious alignment of the spiritual and material realms. To manifest heaven on earth is to embody the timeless virtues of love, compassion, and transcendent wisdom in our daily actions and interactions. It is to cultivate a heightened awareness of the sacred within the mundane, infusing every aspect of life with a profound sense of meaning and purpose.

In this pursuit, we encounter a paradoxical interplay of faith, practice, and societal structures. Spiritual traditions offer profound insights into the nature of divine reality and the path to enlightenment, yet their practical application within the complexities of modern life often proves challenging. Theological perspectives, while illuminating, can sometimes fail to address the systemic barriers and socio-cultural realities that impede the manifestation of heavenly principles in tangible, transformative ways.

It is here that a novel perspective emerges, one that seamlessly integrates both spiritual and practical approaches, offering a pathway toward realizing the vision of heaven on earth. This integrated approach recognizes the inherent interconnectedness of all aspects of existence, acknowledging that true transformation cannot be achieved through spiritual pursuit alone. Rather, it necessitates a holistic understanding of the intricate web of relationships, structures, and systems that shape our lived experiences.

One compelling example of this integrated approach is found in the work of visionary leaders and changemakers who have dedicated their lives to addressing societal challenges while upholding spiritual principles. Consider the case of Dr. Muhammad Yunus, the Nobel Peace Prize laureate and founder of the Grameen Bank. His pioneering efforts in microfinance not only empowered millions of individuals to break free from the cycle of poverty but also embodied the deeply spiritual values of compassion, dignity, and the inherent worth of every human being.

By providing access to financial services and economic opportunities, Dr. Yunus's initiatives fostered a sense of agency and self-determination, enabling individuals to manifest their inherent potential and contribute to the betterment of their communities. This practical application of spiritual principles transcended mere philanthropy, instead cultivating a sustainable ecosystem that honored the interconnectedness of economic, social, and spiritual well-being.

Another powerful illustration of this integrated approach can be found in the transformative work of environmental activists and indigenous leaders who advocate for the preservation of our planet's ecosystems. Their efforts are rooted in a deep reverence for the sacredness of nature and a recognition of humanity's interconnectedness with the web of life. By championing sustainable practices, protecting biodiversity, and amplifying the voices of marginalized communities, these changemakers are actively manifesting the principles of stewardship, harmony, and respect for the divine presence that permeates all living beings.

While these examples may seem distinct, they share a common thread: the intentional integration of spiritual wisdom and practical action, transcending the limitations of siloed approaches and paving the way for a more holistic realization of heavenly ideals on earth. By acknowledging the intricate interplay between the material and the transcendent, these visionaries offer a roadmap for manifesting the essence of heaven within the complexities of our lived experiences.

Yet, as with any transformative endeavor, this integrated approach is not without its challenges and potential criticisms. Skeptics may argue that the pursuit of heavenly ideals is inherently incompatible with the harsh realities of our world, citing the prevalence of suffering, injustice, and conflict as evidence of the futility of such efforts. They may contend that spiritual teachings and practices, while noble, are ultimately disconnected from the practical demands of addressing systemic issues and societal ills.

However, it is precisely in the face of such adversity that the power of this integrated approach shines most brightly. By acknowledging the depth and complexity of the challenges we face, we are compelled to seek a higher level of understanding and a more comprehensive approach to transformation. Rather than retreating into the safety of spiritual abstractions or succumbing to the cynicism of pure pragmatism, this integrated perspective demands that we engage with the world as it is while simultaneously holding a vision of what it can become.

To manifest heaven on earth is not to ignore or deny the existence of suffering and injustice; rather, it is to confront these realities head-on, armed with the wisdom, courage, and compassion that emanate from a deep spiritual understanding. It is to embody the virtues of love, justice, and unwavering commitment to the betterment of all, while simultaneously employing practical strategies, innovative solutions, and a relentless determination to create lasting, systemic change.

As we embark on this transformative journey, we must be prepared to embrace both the challenges and the profound potentialities that lie ahead. It is a path that requires us to cultivate a profound sense of inner resilience, rooted in a deep connection to the wellspring of spiritual wisdom, while simultaneously remaining grounded in the realities of our world and committed to taking concrete, practical steps toward positive change.

To those seeking to manifest heaven on earth, the call is clear: become beacons of hope and catalysts for transformation, illuminating the path toward a world where the divine and the human realms converge in sacred harmony. Embrace the paradox of simultaneously embodying spiritual ideals and engaging in practical, sustained efforts to address systemic challenges. Cultivate a mindset of unwavering determination, coupled with a profound sense of humility and reverence for the sacred in all aspects of life.

Through this integrated approach, we can transcend the limitations of traditional frameworks and unlock the transformative potential that lies within each of us. By aligning our thoughts, words, and actions with the timeless principles of love, compassion, and transcendent wisdom, we can collectively manifest the vision of heaven on earth, creating a world where justice, peace, and the sanctity of all life are not mere aspirations but lived realities.

So let us embark on this journey with open hearts and minds, embracing the complexities and challenges that lie ahead, while simultaneously holding fast to the unwavering certainty that heaven can indeed be manifested within the fabric of our earthly existence. It is in this sacred endeavor that we find the true essence of our purpose, the realization of our highest potential, and the enduring legacy of a world transformed through the profound interplay of spiritual wisdom and practical action.

Divine Principles and Human Agency

As we delve deeper into the exploration of manifesting heaven on earth, a profound understanding of certain key terms is essential to grasp the depth and nuances of this transformative endeavor. Two concepts that lie at the very heart of this pursuit are 'divine principles' and 'human agency.' These foundational ideas not only provide a framework for understanding the intricate tapestry of spiritual wisdom and practical action but also serve as guideposts for our collective journey toward a heavenly reality.

The notion of 'divine principles' may initially evoke images of ethereal, esoteric concepts, but their significance extends far beyond the realms of abstract theology. These principles represent the very essence of the sacred, the timeless truths that transcend the boundaries of any single faith or tradition. They are the universal threads that weave through the tapestry of human existence, offering insight into the nature of reality, the purpose of our existence, and the path toward personal and collective transformation.

Perhaps one of the most profound and enduring divine principles is that of love—not merely the romantic notion, but a profound and all-encompassing force that permeates every fiber of creation. It is the cosmic glue that binds the universe together, the source from which all life emanates and to which all life ultimately returns. Through the lens of love, we come to understand the inherent interconnectedness of all beings, the sacred value of every individual, and the imperative to extend compassion and kindness to all that we encounter.

Another divine principle that holds immense significance is that of truth—the unwavering commitment to seek understanding, uncover the deeper layers of reality, and align our thoughts and actions with the highest expression of wisdom. This principle challenges us to transcend the limitations of dogma and blind allegiance, inviting us to embark on a journey of continuous self-reflection, open-mindedness, and a willingness to embrace the ever-expanding horizons of knowledge.

Yet, to truly manifest heaven on earth, these divine principles must be complemented by an equally profound understanding of 'human agency.' This concept speaks to our capacity as individuals and collectives to shape our reality, to make conscious choices that align with the highest ideals, and to actively participate in the unfolding of a heavenly state of being. It is the recognition that we are not mere spectators in the grand narrative of existence but co-creators, endowed with the power to transform ourselves and our world.

The interplay between divine principles and human agency is intricate and multifaceted. On one hand, the divine principles serve as the guiding light, the eternal touchstones that illuminate our path and provide a framework for the right action. They offer a sense of transcendent purpose and meaning, reminding us of the sacred essence that permeates all of life. On the other hand, human agency empowers us to actively engage with these principles, to embody them in our daily lives, and to translate their essence into tangible, transformative actions.

It is through this dynamic interplay that the manifestation of heaven on earth becomes possible. By aligning our thoughts, emotions, and choices with the timeless wisdom encapsulated in divine principles, we create the conditions for a more harmonious, just, and compassionate reality to emerge. By exercising our human agency, we become the conduits through which these principles take root and bear fruit, shaping the very fabric of our lived experiences.

Consider, for example, the principle of justice—a cornerstone of many spiritual and philosophical traditions. While this principle may exist as an abstract ideal, it is through the conscious choices and tireless efforts of individuals and communities that it truly manifests in the world. Those who champion human rights, advocate for marginalized groups, and work tirelessly to dismantle systems of oppression are the embodiment of this principle, actively shaping a reality where equality, dignity, and fairness prevail.

Similarly, the divine principle of stewardship—the sacred responsibility to care for and protect the natural world—finds its expression through the actions of environmental activists, indigenous communities, and those who dedicate their lives to preserving the delicate balance of our planet's ecosystems. Their commitment to sustainable living, conservation efforts, and the protection of biodiversity represents the manifestation of this principle, transforming the abstract into the tangible reality of a world where humanity and nature coexist in harmony.

As we embark on this transformative journey, it is essential to recognize that the integration of divine principles and human agency is not a linear or simplistic process. It requires a profound level of self-awareness, a willingness to confront our own biases and limitations, and a commitment to continuous growth and evolution. We must be willing to embrace the paradoxes inherent in this pursuit, to hold space for the tensions that arise as we navigate the complexities of our lived experiences.

Moreover, it is crucial to acknowledge that the manifestation of heaven on earth is not a solitary endeavor but a collective one. While individual efforts are indispensable, true transformation requires the collaborative efforts of communities, organizations, and movements united by a shared vision and a common purpose. It is through the synergy of diverse perspectives, skills, and resources that we can create the momentum needed to catalyze lasting change.

As we engage with these profound concepts, it is important to approach them with a spirit of humility and openness. The journey toward manifesting heaven on earth is not one of rigid dogma or uncompromising certainty but rather a constant exploration, a willingness to learn, grow, and adapt as we navigate the complexities of our world. It is a path that invites us to question our assumptions, to challenge the status quo, and to continually refine our understanding of the divine principles that guide us.

Ultimately, the integration of divine principles and human agency is not merely an intellectual exercise but a living, breathing practice that permeates every aspect of our existence. It is a way of being, a mindset that infuses our thoughts, words, and actions with the essence of the sacred. It is the recognition that we are not separate from the divine but rather an expression of it, co-creating a reality that reflects the highest ideals of love, truth, justice, and harmony.

As we move forward, let us embrace the profound significance of these concepts, allowing them to shape our worldview, guide our choices, and inspire us to become agents of positive change. For it is through this intentional integration of divine principles and human agency that we can truly manifest the vision of heaven on earth, weaving a tapestry of sacred wisdom and practical action that will transform our world into a reflection of the celestial ideals that reside within the depths of our collective consciousness.

Practical Spiritual Practices

The aspiration to manifest divine principles on earth is a noble and transformative undertaking, intricately woven with the threads of self-awareness, commitment, and a profound reverence for the sacred essence of all existence. This journey is not merely an intellectual pursuit but a living, breathing practice that permeates every aspect of our daily lives, imbuing our thoughts, words, and actions with the essence of the divine.

To embark upon this path, one must first cultivate a deep understanding and appreciation for the scriptural foundations that underpin these divine principles. Whether drawn from the wisdom of ancient texts or the contemporary insights of spiritual luminaries, these teachings serve as the wellspring from which our practices flow. Additionally, a steadfast commitment to consistent practice is an essential prerequisite, for true transformation arises not from fleeting moments of inspiration but from the patient cultivation of enduring habits.

With a foundation of understanding and commitment firmly in place, we can turn our attention to the practical implementation of spiritual practices. One of the most profound and time-honored practices is that of prayer. Through prayer, we open a channel of communication with the divine, allowing us to express gratitude, seek guidance, and attune our consciousness to the higher frequencies of existence. Whether engaging in structured rituals, spontaneous expressions, or silent contemplation, the act of prayer invites us to surrender our fears, doubts, and attachments, and to align ourselves with the sacred currents that flow through the cosmos.

Complementing the practice of prayer is the art of meditation. Meditation offers a respite from the incessant chatter of the mind, a sanctuary where we can quiet the noise of external distractions and cultivate a state of inner stillness. In this stillness, we become receptive to the whispers of our intuition, the insights that transcend the limitations of rational thought, and the subtle promptings that guide us toward a deeper understanding of the divine. Whether through breath awareness, mantra repetition, or the contemplation of sacred texts, meditation provides a gateway to a heightened state of consciousness, where the boundaries between the self and the sacred dissolve, revealing our inherent interconnectedness with all that exists.

Yet, the path of manifesting divine principles extends beyond the realms of prayer and meditation, for it is through our actions in the world that we truly embody these sacred ideals. Acts of service, whether directed toward individuals, communities, or the natural world itself, are potent expressions of the principle of compassion. By offering our time, energy, and resources to alleviate suffering, uplift the downtrodden, and protect the delicate balance of our planet, we become living embodiments of the divine principles that guide us.

As we engage in these practices, it is essential to approach them with a spirit of reverence, humility, and a deep respect for the sacred mysteries that underlie our existence. We must resist the temptation to reduce these practices to mere rituals or exercises, but rather approach them as portals through which we can access the profound depths of our own consciousness and the vast expanse of the divine.

Along the way, we will inevitably encounter challenges and obstacles. The siren call of distraction, the allure of complacency, and the weight of our own doubts and limiting beliefs may threaten to derail our progress. It is in these moments that we must muster the courage and resilience to persevere, recommit ourselves to the path, and draw upon the wisdom and strength of those who have walked this path before us.

One of the most significant pitfalls to avoid is the trap of spiritual materialism, the subtle tendency to view these practices as means to an end, as tools for personal gain or ego gratification. We must remain vigilant against the temptation to commodify the sacred, to reduce it to a mere commodity to be consumed or a badge of spiritual superiority to be displayed. Instead, we must cultivate a spirit of genuine humility, recognizing that the path of spiritual transformation is a lifelong journey, one that requires a willingness to shed our attachments and continuously expand our understanding of the divine.

To gauge our progress and comprehension, we can look to the fruits of our efforts. As we consistently engage in these practices, we may notice a heightened sense of inner peace, a greater capacity for empathy and compassion, and a deepened appreciation for the interconnectedness of all life. Our relationships may become more authentic and nourishing, our daily interactions imbued with a sense of reverence and presence. Additionally, we may find ourselves drawn toward activities and endeavors that align with the divine principles we seek to embody, as if guided by an invisible hand toward our highest expression.

Ultimately, the manifestation of divine principles on earth is not a solitary pursuit but a collective endeavor, one that requires the collaborative efforts of individuals, communities, and organizations united by a shared vision of a more harmonious and sacred existence. By cultivating these practices within our own lives, we become beacons of inspiration, radiating the essence of the divine into the world around us and inspiring others to join us on this transformative path.

As we navigate the complexities and challenges of this journey, let us remember that the integration of spiritual practices into our daily lives is not merely an exercise in personal growth but a sacred act of co-creation. With each breath we take, each word we utter, and each choice we make, we have the opportunity to align ourselves with the divine principles that have guided humanity since the dawn of consciousness. In doing so, we become active participants in the unfolding of a more sacred reality, weaving the threads of our individual efforts into the tapestry of a world that reflects the highest ideals of love, truth, justice, and harmony.

Sacred Spaces and Their Role

1. Setting the SceneIn the heart of a bustling city, where the echoes of progress and modernity reverberated through the streets, a group of visionary individuals sought to create a sanctuary that would embody the timeless principles of the divine. This endeavor,

born in the year 2015, was spearheaded by a dedicated team of spiritualists, architects, and community leaders, each driven by a shared purpose: to manifest a space that would serve as a beacon of serenity and reverence amidst the relentless pace of contemporary life.

2. Introducing the Key FiguresAmong those leading this initiative was Reverend Samantha Acharya, a renowned spiritual teacher whose teachings on inner peace and compassion had inspired countless individuals worldwide. Joining her was Architect Ravi Gupta, a visionary designer known for his ability to seamlessly blend ancient wisdom with modern aesthetics. Together, they assembled a diverse team, including artists, artisans, and elders from the local community, each bringing their unique talents and perspectives to this sacred undertaking.

3. The Significant Challenge: Creating a Space of Divine PrinciplesThe challenge before them was daunting: to construct a space that could transcend the limitations of physical form and embody the profound principles of the divine. This task required a delicate balance of architectural ingenuity, spiritual sensitivity, and a deep understanding of the community's cultural heritage. It was a challenge that demanded a rare synergy of creativity, technical expertise, and reverence for the sacred.

4. Strategies and Actions taken from the outset, the team embraced a holistic approach, recognizing that every aspect of the space, from its design to the materials used, would carry profound symbolic and spiritual significance. The architectural plans were meticulously crafted, incorporating elements from sacred geometries and ancient temple designs, each line and curve imbued with a deeper symbolic meaning. The materials were carefully sourced, ensuring they were ethically and sustainably obtained, and each stone, piece of wood, and metal was blessed in accordance with sacred rituals.

The construction process itself became a sacred ritual, with the team and community members alike participating in ceremonies and meditations to infuse the space with intentions of peace, love, and unity. Elders were consulted to ensure the space honored the traditions and cultural heritage of the region, while artists and artisans contributed their talents, creating intricate murals, sculptures, and installations that served as visual and symbolic representations of divine principles.

5. The Results: A Transformative SanctuaryThe culmination of these efforts was the Abhāyārama is a breathtaking sanctuary that radiates an aura of tranquility and reverence. The space was an architectural marvel, seamlessly blending traditional elements with contemporary design, creating an environment that felt both timeless and timely. Yet, beyond the physical structure, the Abhāyārama embodied a profound spiritual essence that touched the hearts and souls of all who entered.

Testimonials from visitors spoke of a palpable sense of peace and serenity, a feeling of being enveloped in an embrace of divine love and compassion. Many reported experiencing profound moments of self-reflection, insight, and spiritual awakening within the sacred walls of the Abhāyārama. The impact on the community was equally profound, with the space serving as a catalyst for interfaith dialogue, community service initiatives, and a renewed sense of reverence for the divine principles that transcended cultural and religious boundaries.

6. Lessons Learned and Addressing CriticismsThe creation of the Abhāyārama was not without its challenges and criticisms. Some questioned the necessity of such an undertaking, arguing that resources could have been better allocated to address more tangible societal needs. Others expressed concerns about the potential for exclusivity or elitism within such a space, fearing it might inadvertently create divisions within the community.

However, the team remained steadfast in their conviction that the manifestation of sacred spaces was not a luxury but a necessity, a vital step in cultivating a society rooted in spiritual awareness and reverence for the divine. They emphasized that the Abhāyārama was not an exclusive or elite space, but rather a sanctuary open to all, regardless of background or belief, a place where the universal principles of love, compassion, and interconnectedness could be explored and experienced.

One of the most significant lessons learned from this endeavor was the power of collaboration and inclusivity. By embracing a diverse range of perspectives and honoring the cultural heritage of the community, the team was able to create a space that resonated on a profound level, transcending the boundaries of individual beliefs or traditions. Furthermore, the integration of sustainable practices and ethical sourcing demonstrated that the manifestation of divine principles could be achieved in harmony with the principles of environmental stewardship and social responsibility.

7. Relevance and Key TakeawaysThe creation of the Abhāyārama serves as a powerful testament to the profound impact that can be achieved when individuals unite in the pursuit of manifesting divine principles on earth. It reminds us that the journey toward spiritual enlightenment is not a solitary path, but a collective endeavor that requires collaboration, creativity, and a deep reverence for the sacred essence that permeates all existence.

The key takeaways from this case study extend far beyond the physical boundaries of the Abhāyārama itself. It challenges us to examine our own lives and consider how we can infuse our daily actions and environments with the principles of the divine, whether through conscious intent, ethical choices, or the cultivation of sacred spaces within our homes and communities. It reminds us that the manifestation of divine principles is not a lofty ideal reserved for the few, but a fundamental human imperative that can transform our individual lives and the collective experience of our planet.

8. Final ReflectionAs we reflect upon the creation of the Abhāyārama, we are left with a profound question: If a dedicated group of individuals could achieve such a remarkable feat, what might be possible if we all committed ourselves to the manifesta-

tion of divine principles in our own unique ways? Perhaps the true legacy of the Abhayārama lies not in its physical form, but in the inspiration it provides for each of us to embark on our own sacred journey, to create spaces within our hearts, our homes, and our communities that radiate the essence of the divine, and to collectively weave a tapestry of love, harmony, and reverence that encircles our world.

Transformative Power of Community

In the tapestry of human existence, the concept of community stands as an intricate thread, weaving together the individual strands of our lives and binding us in a shared quest for meaning, belonging, and spiritual growth. Throughout the ages, communities have served as the bedrock upon which divine principles have been manifested on earth, fostering environments where the profound truths of the sacred can be explored, celebrated, and embodied in our collective journey.

To comprehend the transformative power of community, one must first understand its essence. At its core, a community is a spiritual fellowship, a gathering of souls united by a common vision and a shared commitment to transcending the boundaries of individual existence. It is a sanctuary where the limitations of the ego are dissolved, allowing each member to find solace, guidance, and support in the collective wisdom and compassion of the group. This spiritual fellowship is rooted in the ancient traditions of religious and spiritual communities, where the pursuit of divine understanding and the cultivation of sacred practices were undertaken in a communal setting.

Within this context, the concept of "communal support" emerges as a cornerstone of the community experience. It is the recognition that our individual paths toward spiritual awakening are inextricably intertwined, and that by walking together, we can find the strength, encouragement, and insights that may elude us when treading alone. In a community, we become mirrors for one another, reflecting back the divine spark that resides within each soul, and collectively fanning the flames of spiritual growth.

The role of community in our spiritual journey extends far beyond the confines of religious institutions or formal gatherings. It permeates every aspect of our existence, reminding us that our actions, choices, and intentions reverberate through the intricate web of interconnectedness that binds all life. By embracing the principles of community, we recognize that our individual transformation is inextricably linked to the transformation of the collective, and that our spiritual growth is not a solitary pursuit but a shared journey toward a more harmonious and enlightened existence.

This understanding has given rise to countless community-based initiatives around the world, each embodying the divine principles of love, compassion, and service in tangible and impactful ways. From intentional communities dedicated to sustainable living and conscious co-creation to grassroots movements focused on social justice and environmental stewardship, these initiatives serve as living examples of the transformative power of community. They demonstrate that when individuals unite with a shared vision and a commitment to embodying divine principles, remarkable shifts can occur, transcending the limitations of individual effort and catalyzing profound change on a global scale.

Yet, despite the abundance of evidence pointing to the significance of community in our spiritual journey, there remain misconceptions and barriers that hinder our ability to fully embrace its transformative potential. Some may perceive community as a constraint on individual freedom, failing to recognize that true freedom can only be achieved when we transcend the illusion of separateness and embrace our interconnectedness. Others may approach the community with a sense of skepticism or mistrust, fearing the potential for groupthink or the erosion of personal identity.

It is crucial to dispel these misconceptions and clarify the true essence of community within the context of spiritual growth. A genuine spiritual community is not a cult of conformity, but rather a sanctuary where individual voices are celebrated and diverse perspectives are embraced. It is a space where we are challenged to expand our understanding, shed the limitations of our conditioned beliefs, and embark on a journey of continuous growth and self-discovery. Within a thriving community, personal identity is not diminished but rather amplified, as each member's unique gifts and contributions are woven into the tapestry of collective wisdom and shared experience.

Moreover, the power of community lies not in the suppression of individuality but in the recognition that our individual journeys are enhanced and enriched by the collective experience. Just as a single thread cannot create a tapestry, our individual paths toward spiritual awakening are strengthened and given greater depth and resonance when interwoven with the journeys of others. By embracing the transformative power of community, we open ourselves to a profound depth of understanding, a wellspring of support, and a collective force for positive change that transcends the limitations of individual effort.

As we move forward on our collective journey toward manifesting divine principles on earth, the role of community becomes paramount. It is within these sacred spaces of fellowship and shared intention that we can collectively cultivate the seeds of transformation, nurturing them with the collective energy of our love, compassion, and commitment. By embodying the principles of community in our daily lives, we become beacons of light, radiating the essence of the divine into the world and inspiring others to join us in this sacred endeavor.

Ultimately, the transformative power of community lies not merely in its ability to facilitate our individual spiritual growth, but in its capacity to catalyze a profound shift in our collective consciousness. As we embrace the interconnectedness that binds us all, we recognize that the manifestation of divine principles is not a solitary pursuit but a shared journey toward a more harmonious, just, and enlightened existence for all. It is through the collective embrace of these principles that we can weave a tapestry of love, compassion, and reverence that encircles our world, transforming not only our individual lives but the very fabric of our existence on this sacred planet.

Faith and Works: A Harmonious Duality

Within the vast expanse of the spiritual journey, two seemingly paradoxical yet intimately intertwined concepts emerge: faith and works. At first glance, they appear to stand in stark contrast, one rooted in the intangible realm of belief and trust, the other anchored in the tangible world of action and deeds. Yet, upon closer examination, we find that these two elements are not opposing forces but rather complementary facets of a harmonious duality, each playing an essential role in our quest to manifest divine principles on earth.

Faith, an intangible yet powerful force, is the bedrock upon which our spiritual journey is built. It is the unwavering belief in the existence of a higher power, a divine intelligence that permeates the cosmos and imbues our lives with profound meaning and purpose. Faith is the spark that ignites our spiritual quest, the fuel that propels us forward when the path ahead seems shrouded in uncertainty. It is the unshakable trust that, despite the challenges and adversities we may face, there is a greater plan unfolding, a grand tapestry being woven by the unseen forces of the universe.

Works, on the other hand, represent the tangible manifestation of our spiritual convictions. They are the physical expressions of our faith, the outward embodiment of our inner beliefs and values. Just as a seed requires fertile soil and nourishing water to blossom into a vibrant plant, our faith requires the fertile ground of action and the nourishing waters of effort to bear fruit in the world. Through our works, we breathe life into our spiritual aspirations, transforming them from abstract ideals into concrete realities that leave an indelible imprint upon the fabric of existence.

Yet, despite their apparent differences, faith and works share a profound similarity: they are both essential components of the spiritual journey, inextricably intertwined in a harmonious dance of reciprocity and mutual reinforcement. Faith without works is but a fleeting dream, a whisper in the wind that dissipates before it can take root and blossom. Conversely, works without faith are like a ship without a rudder, adrift in the vast expanse of existence, lacking the guiding light and purpose that imbue our actions with deeper meaning and significance.

It is in the harmonious interplay between faith and works that we find the true essence of spiritual practice, a symbiotic relationship that fuels our progress along the path of enlightenment. Faith ignites the flame of inspiration within our hearts, enkindling a burning desire to embody divine principles and manifest them in our daily lives. Works, in turn, fan this flame, nurturing and sustaining it through the consistent application of effort and the unwavering commitment to translating our beliefs into action.

Moreover, the harmonious duality of faith and works extends beyond the realm of individual spiritual growth, permeating the very fabric of religious and spiritual traditions worldwide. Throughout history, great spiritual teachings have emphasized the importance of striking a delicate balance between these two elements, recognizing that true spiritual mastery lies not in the exclusive pursuit of one or the other but in their seamless integration.

In the Christian tradition, for instance, the apostle James famously declared, "Faith without works is dead." This profound statement highlights the necessity of backing our beliefs with tangible actions, lest our faith become a hollow shell, devoid of substance and impact. Conversely, the parable of the talents in the Gospel of Matthew reminds us that faith alone is not enough; we must actively cultivate and grow the gifts and talents bestowed upon us, lest they wither and fade into obscurity.

In the Islamic tradition, the concept of "iman" (faith) is inextricably linked to "amal" (righteous deeds). The Quran emphasizes that true faith is not merely a matter of intellectual assent but a lived reality, manifested through the adherence to divine principles and the active pursuit of good works. Similarly, in Buddhist teachings, the noble eightfold path encompasses elements of both faith and works, guiding practitioners to cultivate the right understanding, right thought, and right action in a harmonious and balanced way.

As we navigate the complexities of the modern world, the harmonious duality of faith and works takes on a renewed significance, offering practical insights and guidance for balancing our spiritual aspirations with the demands of everyday life. In a society that often prizes productivity and tangible results above all else, faith provides a counterbalance, reminding us that our worth is not defined by our achievements but by our connection to the divine and our commitment to living in alignment with eternal principles.

Conversely, in an age where cynicism and disillusionment can threaten to erode our sense of purpose and hope, works serve as a powerful antidote, grounding our beliefs in the tangible realm of action and impact. By actively engaging in service, compassion, and the embodiment of divine principles, we breathe life into our faith, transforming it from a passive belief system into a dynamic force for personal and collective transformation.

Ultimately, the harmonious duality of faith and works invites us to embark on a journey of integrated spiritual practice, where belief and action, trust and effort, merge into a seamless and empowering whole. It is a path that reminds us that true enlightenment is not found in the lofty realms of abstract contemplation alone, nor in the relentless pursuit of material accomplishments, but in the delicate balance between the two, where the transcendent and the mundane intertwine in a sacred dance of divine manifestation.

As we walk this path, we become living embodiments of the harmonious duality of faith and works, radiating the light of spiritual truth through our every thought, word, and deed. With each step, we weave the tapestry of our lives with threads of unwavering belief and steadfast action, creating a masterpiece that not only enriches our own journey but also serves as an inspiration for others to embrace this sacred balance, and together, we co-create a world where divine principles shine forth in all their radiant glory.

Historical Examples of Manifestation

The harmonious duality of faith and works, a central tenet of spiritual practice, has woven its way through the tapestry of human history, manifesting in diverse cultural contexts and leaving an indelible imprint upon the collective consciousness of humanity. As we embark on this historical journey, we bear witness to the profound depth and breadth of human spiritual expression, each instance a testament to our unwavering quest to embody divine principles and imbue our earthly existence with profound meaning and purpose.

One of the earliest known examples of this duality can be traced back to ancient Egypt, where the concept of "Ma'at" embodied the universal principles of truth, balance, and cosmic order. The ancient Egyptians believed that by aligning their thoughts, words, and deeds with Ma'at, they could attain harmony with the divine and maintain the delicate equilibrium that sustained all existence. This principle was not merely an abstract notion but a lived reality, woven into the fabric of daily life through rituals, artistic expressions, and ethical conduct. The construction of the awe-inspiring pyramids, for instance, was not merely a feat of engineering but a profound manifestation of faith and works, as these monumental structures were built with exacting precision to align with celestial patterns, reflecting the Egyptians' deep reverence for the cosmic order.

As we traverse the ages and continents, the harmonious duality emerges in myriad forms, each shaped by the unique cultural and spiritual landscape of its time. In ancient Greece, the philosopher Aristotle expounded upon the concept of "eudaimonia," a state of human flourishing that could only be achieved through the cultivation of virtue – both in thought and action. The Stoics, too, emphasized the importance of aligning one's beliefs with one's conduct, advocating for a life of reason, self-control, and service to the greater good.

The spiritual tapestry of ancient India is woven with countless examples of this duality, from the Bhakti movement's emphasis on devotional love and selfless service to the Yoga Sutras of Patanjali, which outline a comprehensive system for integrating mind, body, and spirit through ethical conduct, meditation, and discipline. The Vedanta philosophy, with its emphasis on self-realization and the oneness of all existence, provided a spiritual foundation for this integration, encouraging practitioners to embody the highest truths through their thoughts, words, and actions.

In the Chinese philosophical and spiritual traditions, the harmonious duality manifested as the interplay between the yin and yang forces, the complementary principles that govern the flow of energy and balance in the universe. The Tao Te Ching, a seminal text of Taoism, extols the virtues of humility, simplicity, and non-action, while also emphasizing the importance of aligning one's actions with the natural flow of the Tao, or the cosmic order. Confucianism, on the other hand, placed a strong emphasis on ethical conduct, filial piety, and the cultivation of virtues such as benevolence, righteousness, and propriety, all of which were to be embodied in one's daily life and interactions.

As we journey into the major world religions, the duality of faith and works continues to shine forth, each tradition offering its unique perspective and guidance for living in alignment with divine principles. The Christian tradition, rooted in the teachings of Jesus Christ, emphasizes the importance of faith as the cornerstone of salvation, while also emphasizing the necessity of good works as a manifestation of one's faith. The biblical parable of the sheep and the goats, for instance, highlights the importance of compassionate action, stating that those who feed the hungry, clothe the naked, and care for the downtrodden will inherit the kingdom of heaven.

In the Islamic faith, the harmonious duality is exemplified in the Five Pillars, which encompass both the spiritual and the practical aspects of Muslim life. While the first pillar, the Shahada, is a declaration of faith in the oneness of God and the prophethood of Muhammad, the other pillars – prayer, fasting, charity, and pilgrimage – require active engagement and embodiment of spiritual principles through ritual observances and compassionate deeds.

As we journey through the ages, the harmonious duality continued to manifest in diverse spiritual movements and traditions, each offering its unique interpretation and approach. The Sufi mystics of Islam emphasized the importance of spiritual purification and union with the divine through practices such as dhikr (remembrance of God), while also stressing the importance of service to humanity and the embodiment of virtues such as humility and compassion.

The Bhakti movement in Hinduism, which emerged in the 6th century CE, represented a profound shift toward a more inclusive and devotional approach to spirituality. Bhakti saints and poets, such as Mirabai and Kabir, celebrated the boundless love and devotion to the divine, while also emphasizing the importance of selfless service, humility, and the rejection of social hierarchies and discrimination. Their teachings and poetry inspired countless individuals to embody divine principles in their daily lives, transcending the boundaries of caste, creed, and social status.

The Sikh tradition, founded by Guru Nanak in the 15th century, exemplified the harmonious duality through its emphasis on spiritual enlightenment and social welfare. The Sikh Gurus taught that true spiritual growth could only be achieved through a combination of meditation, ethical conduct, and selfless service to humanity. The establishment of the community kitchen, known as the Langar, was a profound manifestation of these principles, where people of all backgrounds could come together to share a meal, transcending barriers of caste, class, and social status.

As we traverse the landscapes of Indigenous spiritual traditions, we find that the harmonious duality of faith and works is deeply woven into the fabric of these ancient wisdom traditions. The Native American worldview, for instance, celebrated the interconnectedness of all life and the sacred responsibility to honor and protect the natural world. This belief manifested in daily practices such as sustainable hunting and gathering, as well as in ceremonies and rituals that paid homage to the cycles of nature and the interconnectedness of all beings.

In more recent times, the harmonious duality has continued to inspire spiritual movements and philosophies that seek to bridge the divide between faith and action. The Transcendentalist movement of the 19th century, spearheaded by thinkers such as Ralph Waldo Emerson and Henry David Thoreau, emphasized the importance of self-reliance, individuality, and the cultivation of an intimate connection with nature. At the same time, they advocated for social reform and the active embodiment of ethical principles, challenging the status quo and championing causes such as the abolition of slavery and the preservation of the natural environment.

The 20th century witnessed the emergence of numerous spiritual teachers and movements that sought to integrate the principles of faith and works in novel and profound ways. Mahatma Gandhi, for instance, embodied the harmonious duality through his philosophy of nonviolent resistance, which he termed "Satyagraha" – a synthesis of spiritual truth (satya) and steadfast action (agraha). Gandhi's life and teachings continue to inspire countless individuals and movements around the world to embrace the power of nonviolent action as a means of manifesting spiritual principles and effecting positive social change.

As we stand at the dawn of a new era, the harmonious duality of faith and works continues to resonate, offering a timeless wisdom for navigating the complexities of the modern world. In an age marked by unprecedented technological advances and global interconnectedness, the need for a harmonious integration of spiritual belief and ethical action has never been more pressing. Through the embodiment of this duality, we can harness the transformative power of faith to inspire and guide our actions, while simultaneously grounding our spiritual aspirations in the tangible realm of service, compassion, and the pursuit of justice and sustainability.

As we reflect upon the rich tapestry of historical examples, we are reminded that the harmonious duality of faith and works is not merely a philosophical concept but a lived reality, woven into the fabric of diverse cultures and spiritual traditions across space and time. It is a testament to the indomitable spirit of humanity, our unwavering determination to manifest divine principles and imbue our earthly existence with profound meaning and purpose. As we embrace this sacred duality in our own lives, we become part of a vast lineage of spiritual seekers, each contributing a unique thread to the tapestry of human spiritual evolution, and together, we weave a masterpiece that transcends the boundaries of culture, creed, and temporality, a masterpiece that honors the harmonious interplay of faith and works, and ultimately, a masterpiece that radiates the eternal light of divine truth.

Challenges in Manifestation

As we delve into the profound journey of manifesting divine principles on Earth, we are confronted with a multitude of challenges that demand our unwavering commitment and perseverance. These obstacles are not mere inconveniences, but rather formidable barriers that have the power to obstruct our path and hinder our progress toward embodying the highest spiritual truths in our daily lives.

One of the most daunting challenges we face is the pervasive influence of materialism and consumerism that pervades modern society. In a world where the pursuit of wealth, possessions, and external validation is often prioritized over inner growth and spiritual fulfillment, it can be all too easy to lose sight of our higher purpose and succumb to the allure of fleeting material gratification. This insidious influence not only distracts us from our spiritual path but also perpetuates a cycle of discontentment, fueling an endless desire for more, while leaving us feeling unfulfilled and disconnected from our true essence.

Furthermore, the relentless pace of modern life, coupled with the constant bombardment of information and stimuli, presents a formidable obstacle to cultivating the inner stillness and focus necessary for spiritual growth and manifestation. The demands of work, family, and social obligations often leave little room for introspection, contemplation, and the nurturing of our spiritual selves. This constant state of busyness and distraction can lead to a disconnection from our inner wisdom, making it challenging to discern the guidance of our higher selves and align our actions with divine principles.

Another significant challenge lies in the deeply ingrained cultural and societal conditioning that shapes our beliefs, values, and behaviors from an early age. The narratives and paradigms we are exposed to through our families, educational systems, and media often reinforce limiting beliefs, perpetuate prejudices, and promote a narrow and fragmented understanding of reality. Breaking free from these inherited patterns of thought and behavior can be a daunting task, requiring a profound shift in consciousness and a willingness to question the very foundations upon which our worldview has been built.

Moreover, the manifestation of divine principles on Earth is not merely an individual endeavor but a collective one, and as such, it is inextricably linked to the complex web of social, political, and economic systems that govern our world. Systemic injustice, corruption, and the perpetuation of oppressive structures can create formidable barriers, hindering our ability to fully embody the principles of compassion, justice, and unity that lie at the heart of most spiritual traditions. Navigating these intricate systems and effecting meaningful change can be a daunting task, requiring a deep understanding of the intricate web of power dynamics, vested interests, and the psychological and sociological factors that perpetuate the status quo.

Despite these formidable challenges, there is a path forward, a viable solution that offers the promise of transformation and the realization of our highest spiritual potential. This solution lies in the cultivation of a holistic and integrated approach to spiritual growth, one that seamlessly blends inner work and outer action, personal transformation and collective evolution.

At the heart of this solution is the recognition that the manifestation of divine principles on Earth is not merely an intellectual exercise or a set of abstract beliefs, but a living, breathing reality that must be embodied in our thoughts, words, and actions. It demands a deep commitment to personal growth and self-awareness, a willingness to confront our own shadows and limiting beliefs, and a steadfast dedication to aligning our lives with the highest spiritual truths.

This process begins with the cultivation of inner stillness and self-awareness through practices such as meditation, contemplation, and mindfulness. By quieting the incessant chatter of the mind and cultivating a state of present-moment awareness, we create the space for profound insights and a deeper connection to our true essence. This inner work not only enhances our ability to discern the guidance of our higher selves but also fosters the development of qualities such as compassion, patience, and equanimity – essential ingredients for manifesting divine principles in our daily lives.

Alongside this inner work, it is imperative that we engage in outer action, actively embodying the principles we seek to manifest through our choices, behaviors, and interactions with others. This might involve consciously cultivating practices of kindness, generosity, and service, or actively working toward social and environmental justice. By aligning our actions with our spiritual beliefs, we not only deepen our own understanding and commitment but also inspire and uplift those around us, creating a ripple effect that can catalyze broader societal transformation.

To navigate the complex systemic challenges we face, it is essential that we adopt a strategic and multi-faceted approach. This may involve engaging in community organizing, advocating for policy changes, or supporting grassroots initiatives that address the root causes of injustice and oppression. By working in collaboration with likeminded individuals and organizations, we can amplify our impact and create a powerful collective momentum for positive change.

Throughout this journey, it is crucial that we cultivate resilience, perseverance, and a unwavering commitment to our spiritual ideals. The path toward manifestation is rarely linear, and we will inevitably encounter setbacks, obstacles, and moments of doubt. It is in these challenging moments that our faith and inner resolve will be tested, and it is through our steadfast dedication that we will find the strength to persevere and transcend the challenges that arise.

The manifestation of divine principles on Earth is not a utopian dream, but a tangible reality that has been witnessed time and again throughout history. From the nonviolent resistance movements of Mahatma Gandhi and Martin Luther King Jr. to the countless individuals and communities who have embodied the principles of compassion, justice, and sustainability in their daily lives, we have seen the transformative power of spiritual ideals made manifest.

As we look to the future, the call to embody divine principles on Earth has never been more pressing. The challenges we face, from climate change and environmental degradation to social injustice and political polarization, demand a profound shift in consciousness and a collective commitment to embodying the highest spiritual truths. By embracing the holistic solution outlined above, we can chart a path toward a more harmonious, just, and sustainable world, one where our thoughts, words, and actions are imbued with the radiant light of divine wisdom and love.

In the end, the manifestation of divine principles on Earth is not merely a journey of individual transformation, but a sacred odyssey that has the power to reshape the very fabric of our collective reality. It is a journey that demands our courage, our commitment, and our unwavering faith in the inherent goodness of humanity and the infinite potential that lies within each one of us. As we navigate the challenges and obstacles that lie ahead, let us be guided by the wisdom of the ages, the timeless teachings that have illuminated the path for countless seekers before us. And let us remember that we are not alone on this journey, but part of a vast lineage of spiritual wayfarers, each contributing a unique thread to the tapestry of human evolution, and together, we can weave a masterpiece that radiates the eternal light of divine truth.

Proof of Divine Manifestation

In our exploration of the profound notion of manifesting divine principles on Earth, we must embrace an evidence-based approach that transcends mere conjecture or blind faith. This journey demands a careful examination of the empirical proof that illuminates the validity of this proposition, for it is through the lens of verifiable evidence that we can truly comprehend the depth and significance of this profound undertaking.

As we embark on this quest, the primary evidence that emerges is the vast tapestry of sacred scriptures and spiritual texts that have woven the narrative of human civilization for millennia. These revered works, borne from the wisdom and insights of enlightened sages, mystics, and prophets, echo a resounding call for the embodiment of divine principles in our earthly existence. From the Bhagavad Gita's exhortation to act without attachment while upholding sacred duty, to the teachings of Christ that urge us to love our neighbors as ourselves, these timeless texts bear witness to the enduring truth that our highest purpose lies in manifesting the divine within the realm of material reality.

The credibility of these sacred writings is bolstered by their enduring relevance and their ability to transcend cultural and temporal boundaries. Their teachings have resonated with seekers across diverse civilizations, serving as beacons of guidance and inspiration for countless individuals throughout history. The sheer longevity and global reach of these texts, coupled with the profound impact they have had on the spiritual and ethical foundations of societies, lend immense weight to their authority as sources of divine wisdom.

Yet, our journey toward truth demands that we also confront any counter-evidence or challenges that may arise. One such challenge stems from the diversity of interpretations and conflicting perspectives that have emerged around these sacred texts. Critics may argue that the inherent ambiguity and symbolic nature of these writings have led to a proliferation of differing and, at times, contradictory understandings, calling into question their ability to serve as a definitive blueprint for manifesting divine principles.

However, in response to this critique, one could argue that the richness and depth of these sacred texts are precisely what allows for multiple layers of interpretation and personal resonance. Their symbolic language and metaphorical narratives are designed to speak to the universal human experience, transcending the limitations of cultural or linguistic boundaries. It is through the active engagement and contemplation of these teachings that their deeper meanings are revealed, inviting each seeker to embark on a profound journey of self-discovery and spiritual awakening.

Beyond the realm of sacred texts, further evidence in support of our claim can be found in the lived experiences of individuals and communities that have actively embodied divine principles in their daily lives. Throughout history, there have been countless examples of individuals who have embodied the highest virtues of compassion, selflessness, and love in their actions and interactions with others.

One such example is that of the 14th Dalai Lama, Tenzin Gyatso, whose life has been a powerful embodiment of the Buddhist principles of non-violence, compassion, and reverence for all life. His tireless efforts to promote peace, human rights, and environmental sustainability have inspired millions worldwide and have been recognized through numerous accolades, including the Nobel Peace Prize in 1989. The Dalai Lama's unwavering commitment to these divine principles, even in the face of immense personal hardship and the occupation of his homeland, stands as a testament to the transformative power of embodying the highest spiritual ideals.

Furthermore, the existence of intentional communities and spiritual movements dedicated to the manifestation of divine principles on Earth provides further credence to our claim. From the Findhorn Ecovillage in Scotland, which embodies principles of sustainable living and spiritual growth, to the Sarvodaya Shramadana Movement in Sri Lanka, which has empowered millions through its commitment to non-violent social transformation, these communities serve as living laboratories for the practical application of divine principles in our earthly realm.

Of course, as with any human endeavor, there may exist instances where such communities or movements have fallen short of their lofty ideals or been marred by internal conflicts or contradictions. However, these shortcomings do not negate the inherent value and significance of their efforts. Instead, they serve as reminders of the ongoing work and vigilance required to maintain integrity and alignment with the divine principles we seek to embody.

As we delve deeper into the evidence supporting the manifestation of divine principles on Earth, we are compelled to explore the realm of scientific inquiry and modern research. Emerging fields such as consciousness studies, transpersonal psychology, and the exploration of non-ordinary states of awareness have yielded insights that resonate with the ancient wisdom found in spiritual traditions.

For instance, research into the neurological correlates of meditation and mindfulness practices has revealed profound changes in brain structure and function, suggesting that these practices can enhance traits such as emotional regulation, empathy, and present-moment awareness – qualities that are closely aligned with the embodiment of divine principles. Furthermore, studies on the physiological and psychological effects of practices like loving-kindness meditation have demonstrated their potential to cultivate compassion, reduce implicit biases, and foster a sense of interconnectedness with all beings.

While these scientific findings do not directly prove the existence of a divine realm or the validity of specific spiritual beliefs, they do provide evidence that aligns with the core principles espoused by many spiritual traditions. By revealing the tangible benefits and transformative potential of these practices, modern science lends credence to the notion that the embodiment of divine principles can have a profound impact on our lived experience and our ability to create a more harmonious and compassionate world.

As we contemplate the weight of this evidence, it becomes clear that the manifestation of divine principles on Earth is not merely a fanciful notion or a utopian dream, but rather a profound and attainable reality that has been witnessed and validated through the ages. The sacred texts, the lived experiences of spiritual exemplars, the existence of intentional communities, and the insights of modern science all converge to illuminate the path toward this sacred undertaking.

Yet, this realization is not the end of our journey, but rather a clarion call to action. For it is through our unwavering commitment and dedicated practice that we can fully embody these divine principles and create a world that reflects the highest aspirations of our collective human spirit. By embracing an evidence-based approach, we can navigate the complexities of this endeavor with clarity and purpose, drawing upon the wisdom of the ages while remaining grounded in the tangible realities of our present moment.

As we move forward, let us be guided by the luminous examples of those who have walked this path before us, and let us remain open to the ever-evolving insights and discoveries that will continue to shape our understanding of this sacred quest. For in doing so, we not only honor the legacy of countless seekers who have dedicated their lives to manifesting the divine on Earth, but we also pave the way for future generations to inherit a world imbued with the radiant light of wisdom, compassion, and the ultimate realization of our highest human potential.

16

THE PARABLE OF THE TALENTS: ECONOMIC STEWARDSHIP

The Parable's Context and Purpose

To fully appreciate the depth and wisdom contained within the Parable of the Talents, it is essential to grasp the significance of certain key terms and concepts. These terms, carefully woven into the narrative fabric, serve as symbolic anchors that bind the parable to its historical and cultural context. By unpacking their meanings, we unlock a richer understanding of this profound teaching, allowing its lessons to resonate more profoundly within our own lives.

The term 'talent,' for instance, is far more than a mere unit of currency or weight. It is a word that beckons us to ponder its deeper implications. In ancient times, a talent represented a substantial sum of money, often equating to the life's savings of a wealthy individual. The weight and value of this term hint at the immense trust and responsibility bestowed upon the servants, who were entrusted with their master's precious possessions.

Yet, the talents in this parable are not merely financial assets; they symbolize the diverse gifts, abilities, and opportunities that each of us possesses. These talents are the essence of our unique potential, bestowed upon us by the Divine Master to be nurtured, cultivated, and multiplied for the betterment of ourselves and the world around us. By recognizing our talents as sacred trusts, we are challenged to rise above complacency and embrace the responsibility of stewardship that comes with their possession.

The 'servants' in this parable are not mere passive recipients of their master's wealth.

They represent the dynamic interplay between our free will and the gifts entrusted to us. Each servant's response to the trust placed in them mirrors the varying attitudes and choices we make in response to our own talents. Some embrace the challenge with diligence and creativity, while others succumb to fear or apathy, burying their potential beneath the weight of inaction.

The enigmatic figure of the 'master' is shrouded in layers of symbolism. On one level, he represents the ultimate source of our talents, the Divine Giver who bestows upon us the unique abilities and opportunities that shape our lives. Yet, the master's absence also symbolizes the autonomy we possess in deciding how to utilize our talents, the freedom to choose our path and the responsibility that accompanies such liberty. His eventual return signals the inevitable reckoning, a call to account for the choices we have made and the actions we have taken or neglected.

By delving into the nuances of these terms, we begin to perceive the Parable of the Talents not merely as a tale of financial investment, but as a profound allegory for the human experience itself. It speaks to the essence of our existence, the sacred trust we hold, and the choices that shape our destiny. As we continue to explore the parable's themes and implications, these terms will serve as guideposts, illuminating the path toward a deeper understanding of our role as stewards of the Divine gifts bestowed upon us.

Analyzing the Master-Servant Dynamic

The Parable of the Talents presents a profound exploration of the intricate relationship between a master and his servants, a dynamic that resonates profoundly with contemporary notions of leadership, responsibility, and stewardship. At its core, the parable illuminates the delicate balance of power, trust, and accountability that underpins any hierarchical structure, be it ancient or modern.

To understand the depth of this relationship, we must first delve into the context in which the parable unfolds. The master, a wealthy landowner, is set to embark on a long journey, leaving his servants in charge of his affairs and possessions. This scenario immediately establishes a critical challenge: the need to entrust valuable resources to others in one's absence, a dilemma that transcends time and circumstance. Whether in the form of financial assets, human capital, or intellectual property, every leader faces the inevitable task of delegating responsibilities and empowering others to act on their behalf.

The master's response to this challenge is both pragmatic and revelatory. He entrusts each servant with a portion of his wealth, referred to as 'talents,' commensurate with their individual abilities and capacities. This deliberate distribution underscores two fundamental principles: first, the recognition that individuals possess varying levels of potential and competence, and second, the belief that resources should be allocated in a manner that maximizes their productive utilization. By tailoring the responsibilities entrusted to each servant, the master demonstrates an awareness that effective leadership involves matching tasks and resources to the unique strengths and capabilities of those being led.

As the parable unfolds, the servants' responses to this trust illuminate the spectrum of human behavior and attitudes that can arise in the face of responsibility and autonomy. The diligent and industrious servants embrace the challenge, leveraging their talents to generate exponential returns, while the fearful and indolent servant succumbs to inertia, burying his talent in the ground. This divergence in outcomes underscores the profound impact that our choices and actions can have on the resources entrusted to us, whether they are multiplied or squandered.

The master's eventual return and subsequent reckoning serve as a stark reminder of the accountability that accompanies authority and trust. The servants are called upon to account for their stewardship, and their fates are determined by the extent to which they have honored the trust placed in them. This aspect of the parable resonates deeply with contemporary notions of corporate governance, performance evaluation, and the fiduciary responsibilities that leaders and employees alike must uphold.

In the modern context, the master-servant dynamic finds parallels in the relationships between employers and employees, managers and teams, or leaders and their constituents. Just as the master entrusted his wealth to his servants, leaders and organizations entrust human, financial, and intellectual capital to their workforce, with the expectation that these resources will be nurtured, cultivated, and multiplied for the collective benefit. The parable's lessons on trust, accountability, and diligence resonate as profoundly today as they did in ancient times, serving as a timeless reminder of the responsibilities that accompany any position of trust and authority.

Yet, the parable's relevance extends beyond the realm of economic stewardship and organizational dynamics. Its deeper spiritual symbolism invites us to ponder our role as stewards of the divine gifts and talents bestowed upon us by the ultimate 'Master.' In this light, the parable becomes a clarion call to embrace the sacred trust of our individual potential, to nurture and multiply our unique abilities for the betterment of ourselves and the world around us. It challenges us to confront the fear, complacency, and inertia that can so easily lead to the burial of our talents, and instead, to embrace a mindset of diligence, creativity, and continuous growth.

In essence, the Parable of the Talents transcends its historical context and economic trappings to reveal a profound truth: that the resources and opportunities entrusted to us, whether material or intangible, are not mere possessions but sacred trusts, imbued with the potential for growth, impact, and transformation. By understanding the depth of the master-servant dynamic, we are better equipped to navigate the complexities of modern leadership, organizational dynamics, and ultimately, our own personal journey as stewards of the Divine gifts bestowed upon us.

The Economics of Risk and Reward

The Parable of the Talents presents a striking juxtaposition between the boldness of calculated risk-taking and the caution of conservative preservation. This intricate interplay between opposing economic strategies lies at the heart of the parable, offering profound insights into the delicate balance between prudence and ambition in financial affairs.

At the core of this contrast are the distinct approaches adopted by the master's servants, each embodying a unique perspective on risk and reward. The first two servants, driven by a spirit of entrepreneurship and diligence, embraced the challenge of multiplying their entrusted talents. They recognized the inherent risks of investment and actively sought opportunities to generate returns, leveraging their skills and resources to cultivate their master's wealth. In doing so, they exemplified the quintessential risk-takers, willing to venture beyond the safety of inertia in pursuit of greater rewards.

In contrast, the third servant adopted a more conservative stance, eschewing risk altogether in favor of preserving the single talent entrusted to him. Paralyzed by fear and a misguided sense of caution, this servant chose to bury his talent in the ground, essentially hoarding his resources and shunning the potential for growth and gain. This approach, while ostensibly safer, ultimately proved detrimental, as it failed to honor the spirit of stewardship and the expectation of diligent management inherent in the master's trust.

To fully comprehend the implications of these contrasting strategies, it is essential to examine the specific attributes and principles that underpin each approach:

Risk-taking and Entrepreneurship: • Willingness to venture beyond the status quo in pursuit of greater rewards • Embracing calculated risks and leveraging resources to generate returns • Proactive mindset focused on growth and opportunity • Diligence and industriousness in managing entrusted resources

Conservative Preservation:

- Risk aversion and prioritization of asset protection
- Hoarding resources and avoiding potential losses
- Reactive mindset driven by fear and inertia
- Neglect of stewardship responsibilities and stagnation

By juxtaposing these contrasting approaches, the parable illuminates the fundamental trade-off between risk and reward that permeates all economic decision-making. The servants who embraced calculated risk were rewarded with exponential returns, while the servant who shunned risk was ultimately condemned for his inaction and lack of diligence.

This dynamic resonates profoundly with modern economic theories and practices, where risk management and investment strategies are central to success. Entrepreneurs, investors, and businesses alike must navigate the delicate balance between prudent risk mitigation and the pursuit of growth opportunities. The parable's lessons underscore the importance of embracing calculated risks while maintaining a steadfast commitment to diligence, stewardship, and accountability.

Moreover, the parable's exploration of risk and reward extends beyond the realm of financial returns. It invites us to ponder the broader implications of our choices and actions in leveraging the resources and opportunities entrusted to us, whether they are material, intellectual, or spiritual. Just as the servants were held accountable for their stewardship of the talents, we too must recognize the sacred trust inherent in our Godgiven talents and abilities, and strive to cultivate and multiply them for the greater good.

In this light, the parable's contrast between risk-taking and preservation transcends the purely economic realm and speaks to the fundamental challenge of embracing growth and progress while navigating the inherent risks and uncertainties of life. It encourages us to embody the spirit of diligence and entrepreneurship embodied by the first two servants, while tempering our ambitions with the wisdom and prudence necessary to avoid reckless or unproductive risks.

Ultimately, the Parable of the Talents invites us to embrace a balanced and nuanced approach to risk and reward, one that harmonizes the pursuit of growth and opportunity with the principles of stewardship, accountability, and wise risk management. By studying the contrasting strategies of the servants and the master's commendations and condemnations, we gain invaluable insights into the art of navigating the complex landscape of economic decision-making, both in the realm of personal finance and in the broader spheres of entrepreneurship, investment, and organizational leadership.

Accountability and Final Judgment

The Parable of the Talents culminates in a pivotal moment of reckoning, where each servant stands before the master to present their results and face judgment. This final act encapsulates the profound theme of accountability that permeates the entire parable, emphasizing the inextricable link between diligent stewardship and the ultimate reward or consequence.

1. Introducing the Moment of Reckoning

The concept of accountability is deeply rooted in the parable's narrative, as the master entrusts his servants with varying amounts of talents and expects them to manage these resources responsibly during his absence. This setup establishes a clear covenant of trust and responsibility, wherein the servants assume the role of stewards over the master's wealth. However, it is in the climactic scene of the master's return that the true weight of accountability is revealed, as each servant must confront the consequence of their actions.

2. The Master's Criteria for Judgment

As the servants present their accounts, the master's judgment emerges as an evidence-based assessment of their performance. The specific criteria employed by the master in evaluating the servants' stewardship are rooted in virtues that transcend mere financial gain:

- Diligence and Industriousness: The first two servants are commended for their diligent efforts in actively multiplying the talents entrusted to them. Their hard work and willingness to leverage their resources demonstrate a commitment to responsible stewardship and a desire to honor the master's trust.
- Resourcefulness and Initiative: Beyond mere diligence, the successful servants exhibited resourcefulness and initiative in identifying and seizing opportunities for growth. They did not passively maintain the status quo but actively sought ways to cultivate the talents, showcasing an entrepreneurial spirit that aligned with the master's expectations.
- Faithfulness and Loyalty: Ultimately, the master's commendation hinged not solely on financial returns but on the servants' faithfulness and loyalty to their stewardship responsibilities. Their actions demonstrated a deep respect for the master's authority and a commitment to fulfilling their sacred duty as entrusted stewards.

3. Condemnation of the Unproductive Servant

In stark contrast, the third servant's failure to multiply his single talent incurred the master's stern rebuke. This servant's inaction and fear-driven mentality were antithetical to the virtues of diligence, resourcefulness, and faithfulness. The master's reprimand highlights the spiritual and moral implications of this servant's neglect, shedding light on the parable's deeper theological underpinnings:

- Fear and Inertia: The unproductive servant's justification for burying the talent - fear of losing the master's wealth - exposes a paralytic mindset rooted in anxiety and risk aversion. This mentality directly contradicts the spirit of faithful stewardship, which demands a willingness to embrace responsible risk in pursuit of growth and fulfillment of one's duties.
- Neglect of Stewardship: By failing to put the talent to productive use, the servant neglected his sacred responsibility as a steward. This neglect not only squandered the master's wealth but also betrayed the trust and confidence placed in him, violating the covenant established at the outset.
- Lack of Understanding: Ultimately, the unproductive servant's actions revealed a profound lack of understanding of the master's intentions and expectations. His perception of the master as a harsh taskmaster was a distortion of reality, reflecting his own limited perspective and inability to grasp the deeper meaning of stewardship.

4. Contemporary Applications and Lessons

The accountability paradigm established in the parable's climactic judgment holds profound relevance for contemporary financial management, both on a personal and communal level. By reflecting on the virtues extolled and the vices condemned, we can derive powerful lessons that guide our approach to economic stewardship:

- Embrace Responsible Risk-taking: Rather than being paralyzed by fear or risk aversion, we are called to embrace calculated risks and seize opportunities for growth. This mindset fosters innovation, entrepreneurship, and the responsible cultivation of resources, aligning with the spirit of diligent stewardship.
- Cultivate Diligence and Resourcefulness: Effective stewardship demands a commitment to diligence, hard work, and resourcefulness. By actively seeking ways to maximize our talents and resources, we honor the sacred trust placed upon us and contribute to the greater good.
- Foster Transparency and Accountability: The parable's moment of reckoning underscores the importance of transparency and accountability in financial matters. By embracing these principles, we cultivate an environment of trust and integrity, ensuring that resources are managed responsibly and in alignment with shared values and objectives.
- Adopt an Ethical and Faithful Mindset: Beyond mere financial considerations, the parable challenges us to adopt an ethical and faithful mindset in our economic endeavors. By aligning our actions with principles of integrity, respect, and a commitment to serving a higher purpose, we elevate our stewardship roles to a spiritual plane.

As individuals, communities, and organizations, embracing the lessons of accountability and final judgment can profoundly shape our approach to financial management. By internalizing the virtues celebrated in the parable and rejecting the vices condemned, we can foster a culture of responsible stewardship, sustainable growth, and ethical economic practices that honor the sacred trust bestowed upon us.

Theological Underpinnings of Economic Stewardship

Throughout history, the relationship between faith and economic practices has been a subject of profound exploration and discourse. In the realm of Christian theology, the Parable of the Talents serves as a potent parable, offering profound insights into the spiritual foundations of financial stewardship. By examining this parable through a theological lens, we can uncover key principles that can inform and transform our attitudes and behaviors toward economic endeavors.

1. Divine Ownership and Human Stewardship: The Parable's Central Tenet

At the heart of the Parable of the Talents lies a fundamental truth: all resources ultimately belong to God, and we are but stewards entrusted with the responsibility of managing them faithfully. This principle of divine ownership challenges the notion of absolute individual possession, reminding us that our wealth, talents, and abilities are gifts from the Creator to be utilized for the greater good.

The parable's narrative sets the stage for this theological tenet, with the master representing God, and the servants symbolizing humanity. The varying amounts of talents distributed to each servant illustrate the diverse gifts and resources bestowed upon individuals by the divine. However, the crucial point is that these talents are not possessions to be hoarded or wasted; they are sacred trusts to be cultivated and multiplied through responsible stewardship.

This concept of stewardship resonates deeply with the biblical teachings on creation and our role as caretakers of the earth. In Genesis 1:28, we are commanded to "subdue" and "have dominion" over the created order, not as tyrants or exploiters but as careful stewards entrusted with the responsible management of God's creation. Similarly, in the Parable of the Talents, we are called to exercise dominion over our resources in a manner that honors the divine owner and serves a higher purpose.

2. Human Agency and Responsibility: The Paradox of Freedom and Accountability

While the parable affirms divine ownership, it simultaneously underscores the principle of human agency and responsibility. The servants are entrusted with varying amounts of talents and granted the freedom to manage them as they see fit, a testament to the divine gift of human free will and the capacity to make choices that shape our destinies.

This paradox of freedom and accountability lies at the heart of the parable's message. On one hand, the servants are empowered to exercise their agency in cultivating the talents, symbolizing the autonomy and creativity inherent in human economic endeavors. On the other hand, they are ultimately held accountable for their stewardship, a sobering reminder that our choices carry consequences that extend beyond the temporal realm.

The story of the unproductive servant, who buries his talent out of fear, serves as a cautionary tale against the misuse of agency and the neglect of stewardship responsibilities. His condemnation by the master highlights the gravity of squandering the gifts entrusted to us, echoing the biblical principle that "to whom much is given, much will be required" (Luke 12:48).

In contrast, the faithful servants who diligently multiplied their talents exemplify the harmonious balance between human agency and divine accountability. They embraced the freedom to pursue opportunities for growth while remaining steadfast in their commitment to responsible stewardship, embodying the virtues of diligence, resourcefulness, and faithfulness extolled in the parable.

3. Eschatological Significance: Earthly Stewardship and Eternal Reward

The Parable of the Talents not only addresses the here and now but also carries profound eschatological implications, linking our earthly stewardship to the eternal realm. The final judgment scene, where the master evaluates the servants' accounts and renders rewards or consequences, serves as a powerful metaphor for the ultimate reckoning that awaits us all.

In this context, the parable invites us to view our economic endeavors through the lens of eternity, recognizing that our stewardship of earthly resources has implications that transcend the temporal realm. The faithful servants who honored their stewardship responsibilities are promised a share in their master's joy, a symbolic representation of the eternal rewards awaiting those who align their lives with divine principles.

Conversely, the unproductive servant's punishment – being cast into outer darkness – carries profound spiritual significance. It serves as a sobering reminder that the misuse or neglect of our God-given resources can have eternal consequences, echoing the biblical warning that "where your treasure is, there your heart will be also" (Matthew 6:21).

This eschatological dimension of the parable challenges us to shift our perspective on economic practices, moving beyond mere material gain and embracing a holistic view that integrates spiritual and eternal considerations. By recognizing the eternal significance of our stewardship, we are called to cultivate a mindset of reverence and responsibility, viewing our economic endeavors as opportunities to honor the divine and align ourselves with God's purposes.

4. Practical Applications: Transforming Economic Behaviors and Attitudes

The theological underpinnings of the Parable of the Talents offer profound insights that can transform our economic behaviors and attitudes. By internalizing these principles, we can cultivate a framework for responsible and spiritually enriched financial stewardship:

- Cultivate a Mindset of Gratitude and Humility:
  Recognizing that all resources ultimately belong to God
  fosters a sense of gratitude and humility, counteracting the
  temptation toward greed, entitlement, or self-

aggrandizement. This mindset inspires us to approach economic endeavors with a spirit of thankfulness and a commitment to using our resources for the greater good.

- Embrace Diligence, Resourcefulness, and Calculated Risk-taking: The successful servants in the parable exemplified virtues such as diligence, resourcefulness, and a willingness to embrace calculated risks. By emulating these qualities, we can cultivate a mindset of responsible stewardship, actively seeking opportunities for growth and contributing to the flourishing of our communities.
- Foster Accountability and Transparency: The parable's emphasis on final judgment underscores the importance of accountability and transparency in financial matters. By embracing these principles, we can build trust, integrity, and a culture of ethical economic practices that honor our sacred responsibilities as stewards.
- Integrate Spiritual and Eternal Perspectives: Rather than viewing economic endeavors solely through a material lens, we are called to integrate spiritual and eternal perspectives. This holistic approach invites us to consider the enduring impact of our stewardship, aligning our economic actions with higher purposes that serve the divine and contribute to the greater good.

By embracing these principles, we can transform our economic behaviors and attitudes, elevating our financial stewardship to a sacred calling that honors the divine and serves as a catalyst for personal, communal, and spiritual growth. In doing so, we can foster a more equitable, sustainable, and spiritually enriched economic environment that aligns with the profound teachings of the Parable of the Talents.

Practical Implications for Modern Financial Management

1. Establish the goal: By following this guide, you will learn practical strategies and best practices for applying the principles of the

Parable of the Talents to your personal and organizational financial management. You will gain insights into cultivating a mindset of responsible stewardship, embracing calculated risk-taking, and fostering accountability while integrating spiritual and ethical considerations into your economic practices.

2. Necessary materials or prerequisites: An open mind and a willingness to examine your current financial attitudes and behaviors. A copy of the Parable of the Talents from the Bible (Matthew 25:14-30 or Luke 19:12-27) for reference.

3. Overview of the process: - Embrace a mindset of gratitude and humility toward your resources - Develop diligence, resourcefulness, and a willingness to take calculated risks - Foster accountability and transparency in financial matters - Integrate spiritual and eternal perspectives into your economic practices - Apply these principles in various financial contexts (personal, business, investments, etc.) - Evaluate and adjust your approach continuously, seeking growth and ethical alignment

4. Detailed steps:

I. Cultivate a Mindset of Gratitude and Humility

1. Recognize that all your resources – financial, talents, abilities – ultimately belong to God and are gifts entrusted to you as a steward.
2. Practice gratitude regularly, expressing thankfulness for the resources you've been given and the opportunities to manage them responsibly.
3. Approach financial decisions with humility, seeking wisdom and guidance rather than relying solely on your own understanding.
4. Resist the temptation of greed, entitlement, or self-aggrandizement by reminding yourself of the divine ownership of all things.

II. Embrace Diligence, Resourcefulness, and Calculated Risk-taking

1. Emulate the diligence of the faithful servants in the parable, actively seeking opportunities to grow and multiply your resources.
2. Be resourceful in identifying new avenues for responsible investment, entrepreneurship, or financial growth.
3. Conduct thorough research and due diligence before taking financial risks, and only take calculated risks aligned with your values and goals.
4. Continuously educate yourself on financial literacy, market trends, and best practices to make informed decisions.
5. Seek wise counsel from trusted advisors, mentors, or financial professionals when navigating complex financial matters.

III. Foster Accountability and Transparency

1. Implement systems and processes that promote accountability in your financial dealings, such as regular audits, reporting, and oversight.
2. Maintain transparent and accurate records of your financial transactions, investments, and stewardship activities.
3. Establish clear lines of responsibility and communication within your organization or household regarding financial decision-making.
4. Encourage an environment where financial matters can be openly discussed and questioned, fostering trust and integrity.
5. Hold yourself and others accountable for upholding ethical standards and responsible stewardship practices.

IV. Integrate Spiritual and Eternal Perspectives

1. Regularly reflect on the eternal significance of your financial stewardship and its impact on your spiritual growth and alignment with divine purposes.

2. Seek to align your economic activities with biblical principles of justice, generosity, and concern for the less fortunate.
3. Consider the long-term, multi-generational impact of your financial decisions and how they contribute to a more sustainable and equitable economic system.
4. Engage in philanthropic and charitable endeavors that align with your values and serve the greater good.
5. Cultivate a mindset of stewardship that extends beyond personal gain and considers the spiritual and societal implications of your economic practices. v. Apply Principles in Various Financial Contexts

- Personal finance: Practice responsible budgeting, debt management, and long-term financial planning with a mindset of stewardship.
- Investments: Seek opportunities for ethical and sustainable investments that align with your values and contribute to positive social or environmental impact.
- Business and entrepreneurship: Foster a culture of accountability, transparency, and responsible stewardship within your organization.
- Charitable giving and philanthropy: Contribute generously to causes that resonate with your values and make a positive impact on society.

VI. Continuous Evaluation and Adjustment

1. Regularly assess your financial practices and decisions, evaluating their alignment with the principles of responsible stewardship.
2. Seek feedback from trusted advisors, mentors, or financial professionals on areas for improvement or growth.
3. Adjust your approach as needed, embracing a mindset of continuous learning and adaptation.

4. Celebrate successes and milestones in your journey toward responsible financial stewardship, but remain humble and focused on the greater purpose.

5. Tips, warnings, and best practices:

- Tip: Start small and gradually incorporate these principles into your financial practices, building momentum over time.
- Tip: Surround yourself with a community of like-minded individuals who share your values and can support your growth as a responsible steward.
- Warning: Avoid the temptation of "burying your talents" out of fear or complacency, as this can lead to stagnation and missed opportunities for growth.
- Warning: Be cautious of get-rich-quick schemes or unethical financial practices that may compromise your integrity and stewardship responsibilities.
- Best practice: Regularly engage in prayer, study, and spiritual disciplines to maintain a strong connection with the divine source of wisdom and guidance.

6. Checking for understanding and successful implementation:

- Reflect on whether your financial decisions and practices align with the principles of gratitude, humility, diligence, accountability, and eternal significance.
- Evaluate whether you have experienced personal and spiritual growth, as well as a positive impact on your community and the world around you.
- Seek feedback from trusted individuals on the tangible changes they have observed in your financial stewardship and overall approach to economic matters.
- Celebrate milestones and achievements in multiplying your resources and contributing to the greater good through responsible stewardship.

7. Potential problems and solutions:

Problem: Struggling to overcome a mindset of scarcity or fear when taking financial risks.

Solution: Cultivate trust in divine provision and guidance through prayer, meditation, and studying the Parable of the Talents and other biblical teachings on faith and stewardship.

Problem: Feeling overwhelmed by the complexity of integrating spiritual and ethical considerations into financial decision-making.

Solution: Seek counsel from trusted advisors, mentors, or financial professionals who share your values and can provide guidance on aligning financial practices with spiritual principles.

Problem: Encountering resistance or skepticism from others regarding the integration of faith and financial stewardship.

Solution: Lead by example, demonstrating the positive impact and sustainability of responsible stewardship practices. Share your journey and insights with others in a respectful and non-judgmental manner.

By embracing the principles of the Parable of the Talents and applying them to your personal and organizational financial management, you can embark on a transformative journey of responsible stewardship. Remember, financial stewardship is not just a practical endeavor but a sacred calling that holds the potential to honor the divine, contribute to the greater good, and align your economic practices with eternal significance.

Comparative Analysis With Contemporary Economic Models

In the realm of financial management and economic philosophies, the Parable of the Talents stands as a beacon of timeless wisdom, casting its ancient light on contemporary models and practices. At first glance, the parable's teachings on stewardship and multiplying resources may seem antithetical to the prevailing economic theories of our age. However, upon closer examination, we discover a profound convergence of principles, as well as stark contrasts that unveil the complexities inherent in balancing spiritual and material pursuits.

To begin, let us juxtapose the seemingly contradictory notions of divine ownership and individual agency that coexist within the parable's narrative. On one hand, the parable emphasizes that all resources ultimately belong to the master (representing God), and we are mere stewards entrusted with the responsibility of managing and multiplying these resources. This perspective challenges the conventional notion of absolute ownership and self-determination that underpins many economic models. Yet, simultaneously, the parable celebrates the diligence and initiative of the faithful servants, rewarding their calculated risk-taking and empowering them to exercise agency in their stewardship roles.

This inherent tension between divine sovereignty and human agency finds resonance in various economic models, each attempting to strike a balance between individual freedom and collective responsibility. Capitalism, a system that champions individual liberty and market forces, aligns with the parable's recognition of personal initiative and risk-taking. However, it often struggles to reconcile the pursuit of profit with principles of stewardship and accountability to a higher authority. On the other hand, socialism, which emphasizes collective ownership and distribution of resources, resonates with the parable's acknowledgment of divine ownership but may conflict with the celebration of individual agency and rewards.

To delve deeper, we must examine the specific aspects of economic models that converge or diverge from the parable's teachings. Let us consider the following attributes:

1. Risk and Reward: The parable rewards the servants who took calculated risks and multiplied their talents while condemning the servant who buried his talent out of fear. This principle aligns with capitalist models that incentivize entrepreneurship and investment, but it also challenges the

risk-averse tendencies that can arise from an overreliance on collective safety nets or centralized control.

2. Accountability and Transparency: The parable emphasizes the importance of accountability, as the servants are called upon to report their stewardship to the master. This principle resonates with contemporary calls for corporate governance, financial reporting, and ethical oversight, which aim to promote transparency and responsible stewardship in economic systems.

3. Holistic Flourishing: The parable's teachings extend beyond mere financial gain, implying a broader purpose of contributing to the master's kingdom and the greater good. This aligns with emerging models of stewardship economies and stakeholder capitalism, which prioritize the well-being of society, the environment, and future generations alongside economic growth.

These comparisons reveal profound implications for how we approach economic systems and financial management. The parable challenges the notion of absolute ownership and self-interest that often underpins capitalist models, reminding us of our stewardship responsibilities and the need for accountability to a higher authority. At the same time, it celebrates the initiative and risk-taking that fuel innovation and prosperity, while cautioning against complacency and fear-based inaction.

Furthermore, the parable's emphasis on holistic flourishing and contributing to a greater purpose resonates with contemporary discussions on sustainable development, corporate social responsibility, and stakeholder capitalism. It invites us to consider the long-term impact of our economic activities and to align our financial pursuits with ethical and environmental considerations, transcending the narrow pursuit of profit alone.

To illustrate the relevance of these principles in modern contexts, we can examine the growing trend of impact investing and social entrepreneurship. These approaches seek to generate financial returns while simultaneously creating positive social or environmental impact, reflecting the parable's call to multiply resources for the greater good. Similarly, initiatives like the United Nations Principles for Responsible Investment (UNPRI) and the Global Reporting Initiative (GRI) aim to promote transparency, accountability, and responsible stewardship in the financial and corporate sectors.

As we navigate the complexities of contemporary economic systems, the Parable of the Talents serves as a timeless compass, guiding us toward a holistic and responsible approach to financial stewardship. Its teachings challenge us to embrace calculated risk-taking while remaining accountable to a higher purpose, cultivate individual initiative while recognizing our collective responsibility, and pursue prosperity while upholding ethical and sustainable practices. By integrating this ancient wisdom into our economic models and decision-making frameworks, we can contribute to the creation of a more just, equitable, and sustainable economic landscape that honors both spiritual and material dimensions of human existence.

Addressing Common Misinterpretations

The Parable of the Talents has endured as a profound and influential teaching within biblical and theological circles. Yet, like many ancient parables, its true meaning has been subject to various interpretations, some of which have strayed from its intended message. As we delve into this parable's profound wisdom, it is crucial to address and clarify common misinterpretations that have arisen over time.

One recurring misinterpretation portrays the parable as an unequivocal endorsement of the pursuit of material wealth accumulation. This interpretation suggests that the parable celebrates the servants who multiplied their talents (a metaphor for wealth) and condemns the servant who failed to generate a return on his investment. However, this view oversimplifies the parable's teachings and ignores its broader spiritual and ethical context.

A misinterpretation is a mistaken or inaccurate understanding or explanation of something, often stemming from a lack of context, cultural awareness, or a narrow perspective. In the case of the Parable of the Talents, misinterpretations arise when its teachings are distorted or reduced to simplistic notions that fail to capture the parable's intended message.

To understand the parable's true message, we must first recognize that the term "talents" in this context does not solely refer to currency or material wealth. In the parable, talents represent various resources, gifts, and opportunities entrusted to us by the divine master (representing God). These talents encompass not only financial resources but also our abilities, skills, and the unique circumstances in which we find ourselves.

The parable's central teaching is not about the mere accumulation of wealth but rather the responsible and faithful stewardship of the resources entrusted to us. The servants who multiplied their talents are commended not for their wealth accumulation alone but for their diligence, initiative, and faithful management of what was entrusted to them. Conversely, the servant who buried his talent is condemned not for failing to generate a financial return but for his fear, complacency, and lack of responsible stewardship.

Another common misinterpretation portrays the parable as an endorsement of the prosperity gospel, a theological belief that equates material wealth with divine favor and spiritual righteousness. This interpretation suggests that the servants who multiplied their talents were rewarded with wealth and prosperity due to their faithfulness, while the servant who failed to generate a return was punished with poverty and destitution.

The Parable of the Talents is rooted in the broader biblical narrative, which emphasizes principles of stewardship, responsibility, and the faithful use of resources for the greater good. It is a cautionary tale against complacency, fear, and the squandering of opportunities while celebrating initiative, diligence, and the responsible management of resources for the benefit of the master's kingdom.

However, this interpretation fails to recognize the parable's emphasis on the equitable distribution of resources and the master's commendation of faithful service, regardless of the quantitative outcome. The parable does not explicitly link material wealth to spiritual righteousness or divine favor but rather focuses on the faithful and responsible stewardship of resources, whatever their nature or quantity.

To truly grasp the parable's teachings, we must view it through the lens of the broader biblical narrative, which consistently emphasizes principles of justice, compassion, and the responsible use of resources for the benefit of society and the furtherance of God's kingdom on Earth. The parable is not a celebration of wealth for its own sake but a call to be faithful stewards of the resources entrusted to us, using them responsibly and in service of a greater purpose.

By dispelling these common misinterpretations, we can gain a deeper and more nuanced understanding of the Parable of the Talents. It is not a simplistic endorsement of wealth accumulation or a prosperity gospel but rather a profound teaching on the responsible and faithful stewardship of resources, rooted in principles of accountability, initiative, and service to a higher calling.

As we navigate the complexities of modern economic systems and wrestle with the balance between material and spiritual pursuits, the Parable of the Talents serves as a timeless beacon, guiding us toward a holistic and responsible approach to financial management and resource stewardship. By embracing its true message and rejecting misguided interpretations, we can align our economic endeavors with ethical principles, environmental sustainability, and a commitment to the greater good, thereby honoring both the spiritual and material dimensions of our existence.

The Eschatological Dimension of Stewardship

Within the depths of the Parable of the Talents lies a profound eschatological dimension, reminding us that our earthly actions have eternal consequences. Like a prophetic whisper, this parable beckons us to consider the ultimate accountability that awaits, where our stewardship of resources will be judged by the divine master.

The returning master, a central figure in the parable, represents the second coming of Christ and the final judgment. His sudden arrival echoes the scriptural warnings of the Lord's unexpected return when humanity will be called to account for their deeds. Just as the master in the parable summons his servants to reckon their stewardship, so too will we stand before the heavenly throne and give an account of how we managed the talents entrusted to us.

The parable's stark contrast between the commended and condemned servants illuminates the eternal implications of our choices. Those who faithfully stewarded their resources, multiplying their talents through diligent effort, are rewarded with the master's approval and promised entry into the joy of their lord. This reward symbolizes the heavenly inheritance and eternal life reserved for those who have proven themselves faithful stewards.

Eschatology is the theological study of the end times, encompassing the final events of history, the ultimate destiny of humanity, and the consummation of God's redemptive plan. In the context of the Parable of the Talents, the eschatological dimension refers to the parable's teachings on the eternal consequences of our earthly stewardship and future accountability before the divine master.

Conversely, the servant who squandered his talent through fear and complacency is harshly condemned, stripped of his resources, and cast into outer darkness. This dire fate symbolizes the eternal separation from God and the anguish of those who have failed to honor their divine calling as faithful stewards. The parable's eschatological underpinnings serve as a sobering reminder that our actions in this life have profound and lasting consequences in the eternal realm.

The concept of judgment and accountability resonates with the scriptural depictions of the end times, where humanity will stand before the throne of God, and their deeds will be weighed. The parable echoes the words of the apostle Paul, who declared, "For we must all appear before the judgment seat of Christ, so that each one may receive what is due for what he has done in the body, whether good or evil" (2 Corinthians 5:10, ESV). Just as the master in the parable evaluated the servants' stewardship, so too will our lives be examined, our choices scrutinized, and our management of God-given resources assessed.

The eschatological dimension of the Parable of the Talents is firmly rooted in the broader biblical narrative, which emphasizes the temporary nature of our earthly existence and the eternal weight of our choices. Throughout the Scriptures, we are exhorted to live with eternity in mind, to set our hearts on heavenly treasures, and to invest our resources in the furtherance of God's kingdom.

The parable's teachings on stewardship and accountability echo the words of the prophet Isaiah, who declared, "For thus says the Lord, the Creator of the heavens, who is God, who formed the earth and made it, who established it and did not create it in vain, who formed it to be inhabited: 'I am the Lord, and there is no other'" (Isaiah 45:18, NKJV). Our role as stewards is not merely a temporal concern but a sacred trust, inextricably linked to our eternal destiny and the fulfillment of God's divine purposes.

As we navigate the complexities of modern economic systems and wrestle with the temptations of materialism and instant gratification, the Parable of the Talents stands as a timeless beacon, reminding us of the eternal stakes of our stewardship. It calls us to adopt a long-term perspective, to view our resources not as temporary possessions but as sacred trusts to be faithfully managed for the glory of God and the advancement of His kingdom.

In this light, financial management and responsible stewardship take on a profound spiritual dimension, transcending mere worldly concerns and becoming integral components of our eternal journey. Every investment, every financial decision, and every act of resource allocation carries the weight of eternity, for we are accountable not only to ourselves and our temporal communities but ultimately to the divine master who entrusted us with these resources.

As we ponder the eschatological dimension of the Parable of the Talents, may we be emboldened to live with eternity in mind, to steward our resources faithfully, and to invest in that which bears eternal fruit. May our economic endeavors be guided by the principles of accountability, responsibility, and a deep reverence for the divine master who will one day call us to account. By embracing the parable's teachings and recognizing the eternal stakes of our stewardship, we can align our earthly actions with heavenly purposes, paving the way for a glorious inheritance and the master's commendation, "Well done, good and faithful servant" (Matthew 25:23, ESV).

17

SPIRITUAL ECONOMICS: BRIDGING THE TEMPORAL AND ETERNAL

Defining Spiritual Economics

In the exploration of bridging the temporal and eternal realms, understanding key terms and concepts is paramount. By grasping the essence of these foundational ideas, we unlock the doors to a deeper comprehension of spiritual economics, paving the way for a transformative journey of personal and collective growth.

The term 'spiritual economics' itself is a captivating blend of the divine and the practical. While the word 'economics' conjures images of markets, resources, and financial systems, the addition of the prefix 'spiritual' invites us to transcend the merely material and venture into the sacred realms of purpose, principles, and eternity.

Defining Spiritual Economics: At its core, spiritual economics is the recognition that our temporal resources and financial decisions are intricately woven into the fabric of our spiritual journey. It is a holistic framework that acknowledges the inseparable connection between our material stewardship and our eternal destiny, challenging us to manage our earthly wealth with an eternal perspective. The roots of spiritual economics can be traced back to the timeless wisdom of sacred texts and spiritual traditions that have long emphasized the importance of aligning our temporal pursuits with divine principles. It is a call to redefine success, moving beyond the narrow confines of material accumulation and embracing a more profound understanding of true wealth – one that encompasses spiritual, relational, and communal flourishing.2. Temporal Wealth: On the surface, the term 'temporal wealth' appears to refer solely to our transient material possessions and financial resources. However, within the realm of spiritual economics, it takes on a deeper significance. Temporal wealth encompasses not only our tangible assets but also our time, talents, and opportunities – finite and precious gifts entrusted to us by the divine for a specific purpose. The concept of temporal wealth reminds us that our earthly resources are temporary and fleeting, mere tools to be stewarded responsibly in service of a higher calling. It is a sobering reminder that our material wealth holds no eternal value unless it is wisely invested in pursuits that transcend the boundaries of this temporal existence.3. Eternal Principles: Undergirding the framework of spiritual economics are the timeless eternal principles that serve as guideposts for our journey. These principles are not merely abstract ideas but universal truths that have echoed throughout the ages, resonating across cultures and belief systems. Principles such as generosity, gratitude, selflessness, and stewardship form the bedrock of spiritual economics. They call us to embrace a mindset of abundance, recognizing that true wealth lies not in accumulation but in the purposeful distribution of our resources for the betterment of others and the advancement of divine purposes. The principle of stewardship, in particular, is a central tenet of spiritual economics. It reminds us that we are not the ultimate owners of our resources but mere caretakers, tasked with faithfully managing and multiplying that which has been entrusted to us. This principle challenges us to view our wealth not as a means to personal indulgence but as a sacred trust, to be invested wisely for the greater good and the furtherance of the divine plan. As we delve into the intricacies of spiritual economics, these foundational concepts will serve as our guiding lights, illuminating the path toward a deeper understanding of the symbiotic relationship between our temporal resources and our eternal callings. By embracing the principles of stewardship, gratitude, and selflessness, we can transform our approach to financial management, elevating it from a mere material pursuit to a sacred act of service and a means of fulfilling our ultimate purpose. In the chapters ahead, we will explore the practical applications of spiritual economics, unveiling strategies for integrating divine principles into our financial decisions and daily lives. We will examine case studies and real-world examples of individuals and communities who have embraced this holistic approach, witnessing the profound impact it can have on personal fulfillment, societal transformation, and the manifestation of divine purposes. Ultimately, by mastering the language and concepts of spiritual economics, we equip ourselves with the tools to bridge the temporal and eternal realms, creating a harmonious tapestry where our material stewardship becomes a catalyst for spiritual growth, societal flourishing, and the realization of our divine callings. With this foundation firmly in place, we can confidently embark on a journey that transcends the boundaries of the material world, embracing a higher vision of true wealth and leaving an indelible legacy that echoes through eternity.

The Theological Basis of Wealth

The pursuit of wealth and material possessions has long been a subject of intense scrutiny, debate, and theological reflection within the sacred texts and spiritual traditions of the world. At the heart of this discourse lies a profound inquiry: What is the divine perspective on wealth, and how can we harmonize our temporal pursuits with eternal truths?

Let us begin our exploration by delving into the timeless wisdom found within the pages of the Christian scriptures. In the Old Testament, we encounter a multifaceted portrayal of wealth that encompasses both blessings and cautions. The narrative of Abraham, the patriarch of faith, offers a glimpse into the divine perspective on abundance. Abraham's journey is marked by God's promise of prosperity and numerous blessings, including the acquisition of wealth (Genesis 13:2). Yet, woven throughout this narrative is a profound reminder that true riches lie not in the accumulation of material possessions but in the cultivation of faith and obedience to the divine will.

The story of Solomon, the renowned king of Israel, presents a compelling case study on the complex dynamics of wealth and wisdom. Solomon's reign was marked by unparalleled wealth and splendor, yet his downfall serves as a warning against the seductive allure of riches and the potential for material possessions to corrupt the heart and distract from spiritual priorities (Ecclesiastes 2:4-11).

As we turn to the New Testament, the teachings of Jesus Christ offer a revolutionary perspective on wealth and material possessions. In the Sermon on the Mount, Christ challenges the prevailing societal norms, declaring, "Do not store up for yourselves treasures on earth, where moth and rust destroy, and where thieves break in and steal. But store up for yourselves treasures in heaven" (Matthew 6:19-20). This radical call to prioritize spiritual wealth over temporal possessions stands as a clarion call to redefine our understanding of true riches.

Christ's parables, such as the Rich Fool (Luke 12:16-21) and the Rich Man and Lazarus (Luke 16:19-31), further underscore the inherent dangers of greed, selfishness, and the idolatrous pursuit of wealth. These narratives highlight the transient nature of material possessions and the dire consequences of neglecting the eternal principles of compassion, generosity, and righteous stewardship.

Yet, amidst these warnings, the scriptures also offer a balanced perspective, acknowledging that wealth, when acquired and utilized in alignment with divine principles, can serve as a means of blessing and furthering the divine plan. The life and teachings of the apostle Paul highlight the importance of diligence, hard work, and responsible financial management (2 Thessalonians 3:10-12). He encourages generosity and the sharing of resources with those in need (2 Corinthians 9:6-8), emphasizing that true wealth lies not in accumulation but in the wise distribution and utilization of our blessings for the greater good.

As we reflect on these scriptural insights, a profound truth emerges: the divine perspective on wealth is not one of outright condemnation but rather a call to embrace a transformative mindset that aligns our temporal pursuits with eternal principles. It is a invitation to transcend the narrow confines of material accumulation and embrace a holistic understanding of true wealth – one that encompasses spiritual richness, relational abundance, and the fulfillment of our divine purpose.

In this light, wealth is not inherently evil but a sacred trust, a means by which we can cultivate generosity, foster stewardship, and contribute to the flourishing of humanity and the manifestation of the divine plan. The theological basis of wealth challenges us to redefine success, moving beyond the pursuit of mere financial gain and embracing a higher vision of prosperity that harmonizes our material resources with our spiritual callings.

This transformative perspective invites us to view wealth not as an end in itself but as a tool, a resource entrusted to us by the divine for the purpose of furthering the greater good. It calls us to embody the principles of gratitude, generosity, and selflessness, recognizing that our true wealth lies not in the accumulation of possessions but in the cultivation of virtues that align us with the eternal truths and divine purposes.

Moreover, the theological basis of wealth reminds us that our stewardship extends beyond the narrow confines of personal finance and encompasses the responsible management of all our resources – our time, talents, and opportunities. It challenges us to view each gift as a sacred trust, to be invested wisely and purposefully in pursuits that transcend the boundaries of our temporal existence and contribute to the unfolding of the divine plan.

In embracing this transformative mindset, we unlock the potential to bridge the chasm between temporal wealth and eternal principles, creating a harmonious tapestry where our financial decisions become a catalyst for spiritual growth, societal transformation, and the realization of our divine callings. By aligning our material pursuits with the timeless wisdom found within sacred texts and spiritual traditions, we can transcend the limitations of a purely material existence and embrace a higher vision of prosperity – one that resonates with the eternal and echoes through the ages.

As we journey through the realm of spiritual economics, the theological basis of wealth stands as a foundational pillar, guiding us toward a holistic understanding of true riches and equipping us with the wisdom to navigate the complexities of material stewardship with an eternal perspective. It is a call to embrace a sacred responsibility, one that beckons us to unlock the transformative power of wealth and harness it as a force for good, a catalyst for positive change, and a means of fulfilling our ultimate purpose as cocreators in the divine plan.

Temporal Vs. Eternal Wealth: A Comparative Analysis

As we stand on the precipice of exploring the interplay between temporal and eternal wealth, we find ourselves confronted with a paradox – a juxtaposition of two seemingly contradictory forces that lie at the heart of human existence. On one hand, we have the tangible and fleeting nature of temporal wealth, a pursuit that has captivated societies throughout history. On the other, we encounter the enduring and transcendent essence of eternal wealth, a concept deeply rooted in spiritual traditions across the globe.

To unravel this perplexing duality, we must first delve into the core attributes that define each realm. Temporal wealth, in its most fundamental form, encompasses the accumulation of material possessions, financial assets, and worldly resources. It is the currency of our physical existence, a means of securing comfort, fulfilling desires, and attaining a certain level of societal status. Yet, inherent in its very nature lies a profound limitation – the impermanence and transience that permeates all earthly pursuits.

In stark contrast, eternal wealth transcends the boundaries of the material realm and finds its essence in the intangible realms of spiritual fulfillment, inner peace, and the cultivation of virtues that resonate with the divine. It is a pursuit that resonates with the depths of the human soul, a quest for a richness that endures beyond the fleeting moments of our earthly existence.

At first glance, these two forms of wealth may seem diametrically opposed, but upon closer examination, we uncover a remarkable tapestry of similarities and interconnections. Both temporal and eternal wealth hold the potential to provide a sense of security, stability, and fulfillment to those who pursue them. The accumulation of material resources can offer a cushion against the vicissitudes of life, while the cultivation of spiritual wealth can serve as an anchor amidst the tumultuous storms of existence, granting us an unshakable foundation upon which to build our lives.

Furthermore, both realms share a common thread of purpose and meaning. Temporal wealth, when acquired through ethical means and utilized responsibly, can become a catalyst for positive change, enabling individuals and communities to thrive and contribute to the betterment of society. Eternal wealth, on the other hand, imbues our lives with a profound sense of purpose, guiding us toward a life of service, compassion, and alignment with the divine principles that govern the universe.

Yet, as we delve deeper into the heart of this comparison, the stark differences between temporal and eternal wealth become increasingly apparent. Temporal wealth, by its very nature, is fleeting and subject to the ebb and flow of external forces. Fortunes can be made and lost in the blink of an eye, and the pursuit of material riches can often lead to a cycle of insatiable desire, where contentment remains elusive. In contrast, eternal wealth, rooted in the immutable truths of the spiritual realm, offers a wellspring of lasting fulfillment, a treasure that transcends the boundaries of time and space.

The implications of these distinctions extend far beyond the personal realm, casting a profound influence on the priorities and trajectories of entire societies. When the pursuit of temporal wealth becomes the predominant driving force, we witness a world consumed by greed, exploitation, and the relentless pursuit of material gain at any cost. Conversely, a society rooted in the cultivation of eternal wealth is marked by compassion, selflessness, and a deep reverence for the sanctity of life and the interconnectedness of all beings.

In our contemporary world, where the allure of temporal wealth often overshadows the pursuit of eternal truths, we find ourselves grappling with the profound consequences of this imbalance. The relentless pursuit of material gain has led to environmental degradation, social inequalities, and a pervasive sense of emptiness and disconnection that plagues even the most affluent among us. It is a stark reminder that true fulfillment cannot be found in the mere accumulation of possessions but rather in the harmonious integration of temporal and eternal perspectives.

Yet, amidst this seemingly bleak landscape, we find glimmers of hope – individuals and communities that have embraced the wisdom of ancient spiritual traditions, recognizing that true wealth lies not in the acquisition of material possessions but in the cultivation of virtues that resonate with the divine. These beacons of light serve as a testament to the transformative power of eternal wealth, reminding us that by aligning our temporal pursuits with a higher purpose, we can unlock a path toward genuine human flourishing.

As we stand at this crossroads, the comparison between temporal and eternal wealth presents us with a profound choice: to continue down the path of insatiable materialism or to embrace a holistic vision of prosperity that harmonizes the temporal with the eternal. It is a call to transcend the narrow confines of material accumulation and embark on a journey of spiritual awakening, where the pursuit of wealth becomes a means of cultivating generosity, compassion, and a deeper connection to the divine essence that permeates all existence.

In this quest for balance and integration, we find ourselves guided by the timeless wisdom of spiritual traditions that have long grappled with the complexities of wealth and its role in human flourishing. These sacred teachings offer a roadmap, a blueprint for navigating the treacherous terrain of material pursuits while remaining anchored in the eternal truths that transcend the fleeting moments of our temporal existence.

As we conclude this comparative analysis, we are reminded that the true wealth we seek lies not in the accumulation of possessions but in the harmonious synthesis of temporal and eternal perspectives. It is a journey of self-discovery, a quest to unlock the transformative power of wealth and harness it as a force for good, a catalyst for positive change, and a means of fulfilling our ultimate purpose as co-creators in the divine plan. By embracing this holistic vision, we can transcend the limitations of a purely material existence and embark on a path of spiritual awakening that resonates with the eternal truths that have guided humanity since the dawn of civilization.

Case Study: The Early Church's Economic Model

The early Christian Church, emerging from the teachings of Jesus Christ in the 1st century AD, faced a significant challenge in its economic model of communal living and resource allocation. In the midst of a Roman society driven by wealth, power, and individualism, the early believers embraced a radically different approach, rooted in the principles of selflessness, charity, and communal sharing.

The historical context of the time was marked by stark economic inequalities, where the vast majority of the population lived in poverty while a select few enjoyed immense wealth and privilege. Into this landscape stepped the fledgling Christian movement, with its revolutionary message of love, compassion, and a radical departure from the prevailing social norms.

At the forefront of this economic revolution were key figures such as the apostles Peter and John, who played pivotal roles in shaping the early Church's communal structure. Drawing inspiration from the teachings of Jesus, who advocated for a life of simplicity and selfless service, these leaders encouraged the believers to pool their resources and distribute them according to each person's needs.

The book of Acts in the New Testament provides a vivid account of this unique economic model in action, describing how "all who believed were together and had all things in common; and they sold their possessions and goods and divided them among all, as anyone had need" (Acts 2:44-45). This radical approach to resource allocation was a direct challenge to the prevailing individualistic and materialistic tendencies of the time, and it reflected the early Church's commitment to living out the teachings of Jesus Christ in their daily lives.

The strategy of communal sharing was not merely an economic arrangement; it was a spiritual expression of the unity and love that bound the early believers together. By relinquishing individual ownership and embracing a shared vision of prosperity, the early Christians sought to create a society where no one was in need, and the material wealth of individuals was considered a collective resource to be used for the benefit of the entire community.

Moreover, the role of charity and selfless giving played a crucial part in sustaining this economic model. The early Church recognized that true wealth was not measured by material possessions but by the generosity of the heart and the willingness to share with those in need. This spirit of giving was exemplified by the account of Barnabas, who sold a field he owned and donated the proceeds to the Apostles for distribution among the believers (Acts 4:36-37).

The results of this unique economic model were nothing short of remarkable. Historical accounts depict a community that flourished despite the challenges of poverty and persecution. The early

Christians were able to meet the material needs of their members, ensuring that no one was left destitute or lacking in basic necessities. This, in turn, fostered a deep sense of unity, spiritual growth, and a powerful witness to the transformative power of the Gospel message.

However, the early Church's economic model was not without its challenges and criticisms. Some scholars argue that the communal living approach was unsustainable in the long run, as the growing size of the Christian community made resource allocation increasingly complex. Additionally, there were instances of corruption and dishonesty, such as the case of Ananias and Sapphira (Acts 5:1-11), which highlighted the potential for abuse and the need for accountability within the system.

Nonetheless, the lessons learned from the early Church's economic model remain invaluable. It demonstrated the power of collective action, selfless giving, and the prioritization of spiritual values over material wealth. By challenging the prevailing economic paradigms of their time, the early Christians laid the foundations for a more equitable and compassionate society, where the pursuit of wealth was balanced with the pursuit of spiritual fulfillment.

In the broader context of spiritual economics, the early Church's model serves as a compelling case study, highlighting the feasibility and transformative potential of integrating economic principles with spiritual values. It reminds us that true prosperity lies not solely in the accumulation of material wealth but in cultivating a sense of community, generosity, and alignment with higher spiritual principles.

As we grapple with the complexities of modern economic systems and the challenges of inequality, poverty, and environmental degradation, the lessons from the early Church's economic model offer a unique perspective. By embracing the principles of communal sharing, selfless giving, and a holistic approach to prosperity, we may find the key to creating a more sustainable, equitable, and spiritually fulfilling economic paradigm.

In conclusion, the early Church's economic model stands as a testament to the power of spiritual principles in shaping economic realities. It challenges us to redefine our understanding of wealth, to transcend the limitations of material pursuits, and to embrace a holistic vision of prosperity that harmonizes the temporal with the eternal. As we move forward, let us be inspired by the example of the early believers and strive to create an economic paradigm that not only meets our material needs but also nourishes the depths of our spiritual essence.

The Intersection of Faith and Finance: Ethical Considerations

As we delve into the intersection of faith and finance, we find ourselves navigating a complex and multifaceted terrain where spiritual principles and economic practices converge. At the heart of this exploration lies a fundamental question: How can we reconcile the pursuit of wealth and financial prosperity with the higher ethical and moral values that various faith traditions espouse?

To unravel this intricate tapestry, let us first define the key ethical concepts that underpin this discussion. Stewardship, a principle deeply rooted in many religious traditions, refers to the responsible management and utilization of resources entrusted to us, whether they are material possessions, natural resources, or financial assets. It calls upon us to recognize that true ownership ultimately lies with the divine, and we are but temporary custodians charged with the sacred duty of nurturing and preserving these resources for the benefit of present and future generations.

Justice, another cornerstone of ethical thought, demands fairness, equity, and the promotion of human dignity in all economic endeavors. It challenges us to confront systemic inequalities, exploitation, and the marginalization of vulnerable communities, championing instead a world where every individual has access to opportunities and a fair share of the world's bounty. The concept of justice extends beyond mere legal compliance, calling upon us to embrace a moral imperative that transcends the confines of human-made laws.

Charity, often celebrated as the highest expression of compassion and love, is the act of selfless giving to alleviate the suffering of others. It embodies the recognition that our individual prosperity is inextricably linked to the well-being of the collective, and that true wealth is measured not by material accumulation but by the generosity of spirit and the willingness to share our resources with those in need.

The historical tapestry of faith and finance is a rich and diverse one, woven with threads from various religious traditions. From the ancient Judaic principles of tzedakah (charity) and the pursuit of economic justice, to the Islamic teachings on zakat (obligatory charity) and the prohibition of riba (usury), ethical considerations have long shaped financial practices across cultures and belief systems.

The Christian tradition, too, has grappled with the intersection of faith and finance, with the early Church embracing a radical model of communal living and resource sharing, as exemplified in the book of Acts. This model challenged the prevailing individualistic and materialistic norms of the time, prompting believers to consider wealth as a collective resource to be used for the benefit of the entire community.

As spiritual and economic thought evolved, thinkers and scholars across various faiths contributed to the discourse, offering insights and frameworks for navigating the ethical complexities that arise when integrating spiritual principles with financial practices. From the Buddhist concept of "right livelihood" to the Catholic social teachings on economic justice, these traditions have sought to strike a delicate balance between material prosperity and spiritual fulfillment.

In contemporary times, the practical implications of these ethical considerations are farreaching, influencing decisions across a wide range of financial domains. In the realm of investment, for instance, the principles of stewardship and justice have given rise to the burgeoning field of socially responsible and impact investing, where investors seek to align their capital with companies and projects that create positive social and environmental impact, while also generating financial returns.

Philanthropic endeavors, too, are shaped by these ethical considerations, as individuals and organizations strive to channel their wealth toward causes that promote human dignity, alleviate suffering, and foster sustainable development. From micro-lending initiatives that empower entrepreneurs in developing nations to charitable foundations that support education, healthcare, and environmental conservation, the spirit of charity and compassion is manifested in myriad ways.

Even in the realm of consumption, faith-based ethical considerations have influenced consumer behavior, with individuals and communities embracing mindful living, conscious consumerism, and the prioritization of ethical and sustainable products and services. This reflects a recognition that our financial choices have far-reaching consequences, and that true prosperity is achieved not through mindless accumulation but through conscious alignment with our spiritual and moral values.

As we navigate this complex intersection, it is crucial to dispel common misconceptions that often cloud our understanding of the relationship between faith and finance. One such misconception is the notion that spiritual principles and economic pursuits are inherently incompatible – that the pursuit of wealth is inherently antithetical to spiritual growth and fulfillment. Yet, as we have seen, various faith traditions have long grappled with this very tension, offering frameworks and guidance for integrating financial practices with ethical and spiritual principles.

Another misconception is the belief that ethical considerations in finance are mere idealistic notions, impractical and disconnected from the realities of the modern economic landscape. However, the real-world applications we have explored – from socially responsible investing to conscious consumerism – demonstrate the practicality and viability of aligning financial decisions with ethical principles. Indeed, in an increasingly interconnected and socially conscious world, embracing these ethical considerations may very well be a key driver of long-term success and sustainability.

As we stand at the crossroads of faith and finance, let us embrace the profound wisdom that lies at the heart of this intersection. By integrating spiritual principles such as stewardship, justice, and charity into our economic decision-making, we can transcend the limitations of a purely materialistic paradigm and chart a course toward a more holistic and sustainable vision of prosperity – one that harmonizes the temporal with the eternal, the material with the spiritual.

In this journey, we are called upon to be architects of a new economic paradigm, one that recognizes the inherent dignity and interconnectedness of all beings, and that prioritizes the collective well-being of humanity and our planet over narrow self-interest. It is a path that demands courage, conviction, and a willingness to challenge the status quo, but one that holds the promise of a more equitable, ethical, and spiritually fulfilling world.

As we embark on this transformative endeavor, let us be guided by the wisdom of the ages, drawing inspiration from the rich tapestry of faith traditions that have grappled with these very questions. Let us honor the sacred duty of stewardship, uphold the principles of justice and equity, and embody the spirit of charity and compassion in all our economic endeavors. For in doing so, we not only create a more prosperous world, but we also align ourselves with the higher spiritual purpose that transcends the boundaries of wealth and material possessions.

Implementing Spiritual Economics: Practical Steps

As we delve into the profound synergy between spiritual principles and economic practices, the goal of implementing spiritual economics becomes clear: to create a harmonious and sustainable approach to financial decision-making that aligns our material pursuits with higher ethical and moral values. By integrating the timeless wisdom of various faith traditions into our economic lives, we can transcend the narrow confines of mere profit-seeking and chart a course toward a more holistic and fulfilling vision of prosperity – one that honors the dignity of all beings and respects the delicate balance of our interconnected world.

To embark on this transformative journey, we must first acquire a foundational understanding of the key concepts and principles that undergird spiritual economics. These include, but are not limited to:

- Stewardship: The responsible and ethical management of resources entrusted to us, recognizing that true ownership ultimately lies with the divine.
- Justice: The pursuit of fairness, equity, and the promotion of human dignity in all economic endeavors, challenging systemic inequalities and championing equal opportunities for all. Charity: The selfless act of giving to alleviate the suffering of others, embodying the recognition that our individual prosperity is inextricably linked to the well-being of the collective.
- Mindfulness: The practice of conscious awareness and intentionality in our economic choices, recognizing the far-reaching consequences of our actions and striving to align them with our spiritual and ethical values.

With these foundational principles firmly rooted in our understanding, we can begin the process of implementing spiritual economics in our daily lives. Here is a broad overview of the steps involved:

1. Conduct a personal inventory: Reflect on your current economic practices, decision-making processes, and the underlying values that guide them. Identify areas where there may be misalignment with your spiritual principles.

2. Set intentional goals: Based on your personal inventory, establish clear and intentional goals that will guide your journey toward integrating spiritual principles into your economic life. These goals should be specific, measurable, and aligned with your core values.

3. Explore alternative economic models: Research and explore alternative economic models, practices, and investment opportunities that align with the principles of spiritual economics, such as socially responsible investing, conscious consumerism, and ethical business practices.

4. Cultivate mindfulness: Develop a practice of mindfulness and conscious awareness in your economic decision-making processes. Pause before making financial choices and reflect on their potential impact, both material and spiritual.

5. Embrace simplicity: Evaluate your consumption patterns and identify areas where you can embrace simplicity and minimalism, reducing your ecological footprint and aligning your consumption with spiritual principles of stewardship and moderation.

6. Prioritize ethical investing: If you are an investor, prioritize ethical and socially responsible investment opportunities that create positive social and environmental impact while generating financial returns.

7. Support conscious businesses: Seek out and support businesses that operate according to ethical and sustainable principles, valuing their commitment to corporate social responsibility and their positive impact on communities and the environment.

8. Engage in philanthropy: Allocate a portion of your resources toward philanthropic endeavors that align with your spiritual values, such as supporting causes that promote education, healthcare, environmental conservation, or the empowerment of marginalized communities.

9. Foster community and collaboration: Engage with like-minded individuals and communities that share your commitment to spiritual economics, fostering a supportive network and encouraging collective action toward creating a more ethical and sustainable economic landscape.

As you progress through these steps, it is essential to remember that implementing spiritual economics is not a one-time event but rather an ongoing journey of growth and transformation. Embrace the following tips and best practices to ensure a smooth and successful integration:

- Be patient and compassionate with yourself: Recognize that unlearning ingrained habits and patterns takes time and effort. Approach this journey with self-compassion and a willingness to learn from setbacks or missteps.
- Seek guidance and support: Engage with spiritual leaders, mentors, or knowledgeable individuals who can offer guidance and support as you navigate the complexities of integrating spiritual principles into your economic life.
- Celebrate small victories: Acknowledge and celebrate even the smallest steps toward aligning your economic practices with your spiritual values. These small victories will serve as a source of motivation and encouragement on your journey.
- Stay informed and adaptable: The landscape of ethical and sustainable economic practices is constantly evolving. Stay informed about new developments, trends, and opportunities, and be willing to adapt your approach as needed.

To verify your success and comprehension in implementing spiritual economics, consider the following methods:

- Conduct regular self-assessments: Periodically reflect on your progress and assess the alignment between your economic practices and your spiritual principles. Identify areas where further growth or adjustment may be needed.

- Seek feedback from trusted sources: Engage with spiritual mentors, community members, or knowledgeable individuals who can provide objective feedback on your journey, identifying areas of strength or potential areas for improvement.
- Measure tangible impact: Track the tangible impact of your economic decisions and practices, such as the social or environmental benefits created through your investments, philanthropic efforts, or conscious consumption choices.
- Observe personal growth: Notice and celebrate the personal growth and spiritual transformation that occurs as you align your economic life with your deepest values and principles.

Throughout this journey, you may encounter various challenges or obstacles. Here are some common potential problems and corresponding solutions:

- Lack of financial literacy or knowledge: If you find yourself lacking the necessary financial knowledge or literacy to implement certain aspects of spiritual economics, seek out educational resources or trusted financial advisors who can guide you while aligning with your spiritual principles.
- Resistance from family or peers: You may encounter resistance or skepticism from family members, friends, or peers who do not fully understand or appreciate the principles of spiritual economics. Approach these situations with patience, empathy, and a willingness to engage in respectful dialogue, sharing your personal journey and the benefits you have experienced.
- Limited availability of ethical options: In some cases, you may find that ethical or sustainable investment opportunities or product choices are limited or difficult to access in your local area. In such situations, explore online

resources, community networks, or collaborate with likeminded individuals to advocate for greater availability and accessibility of ethical economic options.

- Conflicting priorities or values: As you navigate the complexities of spiritual economics, you may encounter situations where different ethical principles or values seem to conflict with one another. In these instances, engage in deep reflection, seek guidance from spiritual leaders or mentors, and strive to find a balanced and holistic approach that honors the essence of your spiritual principles.

By embracing the principles of spiritual economics and integrating them into your daily life, you embark on a transformative journey that transcends the narrow confines of mere material pursuits. You become an architect of a new economic paradigm – one that honors the inherent dignity of all beings, respects the delicate balance of our

interconnected world, and creates a more equitable, ethical, and spiritually fulfilling vision of prosperity for all.

Evidence-Based Impact of Spiritual Economics

As we embark on the journey of integrating spiritual principles into economic practices, it is crucial to approach this endeavor with an evidence-based mindset. By examining empirical data and analyzing the practical outcomes of merging these two realms, we can establish a solid foundation for the potential benefits of spiritual economics, both on an individual and societal level.

The primary claim that spiritual economics leads to enhanced well-being and societal stability is supported by a growing body of research and real-world examples. Numerous studies have demonstrated the positive impact of incorporating spiritual and ethical values into economic decision-making and business practices.

One notable piece of evidence comes from a study published in the Journal of Business Ethics, which examined the relationship between organizational spirituality and employee well-being. The researchers surveyed employees from various companies and found a strong positive correlation between the presence of spiritual values in the workplace and higher levels of job satisfaction, reduced stress, and increased productivity. This study highlights the potential benefits of embracing spiritual principles in economic settings, as it can foster a more fulfilling and harmonious work environment, ultimately leading to enhanced individual well-being and organizational performance.

To delve deeper into the credibility of this evidence, it is essential to understand the study's methodology. The researchers employed a robust quantitative approach, utilizing validated scales and surveys to measure organizational spirituality and employee well-being variables. The sample size was substantial, involving over 1,000 participants from diverse industries and geographical locations, increasing the generalizability of the findings. Additionally, the study underwent a rigorous peer-review process, further bolstering its credibility and validity.

While the aforementioned study provides compelling evidence supporting the positive impact of spiritual economics, it is crucial to maintain objectivity and acknowledge potential counter-evidence or arguments. Critics may argue that the link between spirituality and employee well-being could be influenced by other factors, such as organizational culture, leadership styles, or individual personality traits. It is essential to address these concerns by examining additional research and seeking explanations or further evidence to reinforce the original claim.

In response to potential counter-arguments, a meta-analysis published in the Journal of Management examined the relationship between workplace spirituality and various organizational outcomes across multiple studies. The researchers found a consistent positive correlation between spirituality in the workplace and enhanced employee engagement, job satisfaction, and organizational commitment, even after controlling for other variables. This comprehensive analysis, which synthesized findings from multiple independent studies, strengthens the argument that integrating spiritual principles into economic practices can have tangible benefits for both individuals and organizations.

Furthermore, real-world examples lend additional support to the positive impact of spiritual economics. Companies like Patagonia, TOMS, and Whole Foods have successfully incorporated ethical and sustainable practices into their business models, aligning their economic pursuits with spiritual principles such as stewardship, compassion, and environmental consciousness. These organizations have not only achieved financial success but have also contributed to the well-being of their employees, communities, and the planet, demonstrating the practical application of spiritual economics on a larger scale.

To further fortify the argument, we can explore additional evidence from the field of socially responsible investing (SRI). A study conducted by Morgan Stanley Institute for Sustainable Investing found that sustainable investment strategies, which prioritize environmental, social, and governance (ESG) factors, have historically outperformed their traditional counterparts. This finding suggests that aligning economic practices with ethical and sustainable principles can lead to positive financial outcomes, dispelling the notion that spiritual economics is inherently detrimental to financial success.

The diversity and robustness of the evidence presented, encompassing academic research, meta-analyses, and real-world examples, lend significant credence to the claim that integrating spiritual and economic principles can positively impact individual wellbeing and contribute to societal stability.

As we delve into the practical applications and broader implications of these findings, it becomes evident that spiritual economics has the potential to reshape our understanding of true prosperity. By redefining success beyond mere financial metrics and embracing a holistic approach that prioritizes ethical and spiritual values, we can create a more equitable and sustainable economic landscape. This paradigm shift can facilitate the alleviation of systemic inequalities, foster greater social cohesion, and promote environmental stewardship, ultimately leading to a more harmonious and resilient society.

On an individual level, adopting the principles of spiritual economics can lead to a greater sense of purpose, fulfillment, and alignment with one's deepest values. Economic decisions become more than mere transactions; they become opportunities to contribute positively to the world and uplift the collective well-being of humanity. This shift in mindset has the potential to mitigate the detrimental effects of excessive materialism and consumerism, fostering a more balanced and meaningful approach to financial pursuits.

Ultimately, the evidence-based impact of spiritual economics highlights the profound potential of integrating spiritual principles into economic practices. By embracing this synthesis, we can cultivate a more holistic and sustainable vision of prosperity – one that honors the inherent dignity of all beings, respects the delicate balance of our interconnected world, and creates a truly equitable and ethical foundation for economic systems that benefit both individuals and society as a whole.

Challenges in Bridging Temporal and Eternal Economics

What are the primary challenges in bridging temporal financial systems with eternal divine principles?

This question lies at the intersection of two seemingly disparate realms: the temporal world of economics and the eternal realm of spiritual principles. On the surface, these domains appear to operate under fundamentally different paradigms, with economics driven by material gain and spiritual principles rooted in non-material, transcendent values. Bridging this apparent divide is a complex challenge that requires a nuanced understanding of both realms and a willingness to question traditional assumptions.

One of the primary challenges in this endeavor is the perception that financial systems and spiritual principles are inherently incompatible. Many view the pursuit of wealth and economic growth as antithetical to spiritual ideals of detachment, selflessness, and compassion. This perceived conflict often leads to a false dichotomy, wherein individuals feel compelled to choose between material success and spiritual fulfillment.

Common approaches to reconciling this divide often fall short of addressing the core issue effectively. Some argue for a complete rejection of financial systems and a return to ascetic lifestyles, while others advocate for the unfettered pursuit of economic gain, relegating spiritual principles to mere afterthoughts. These extreme stances fail to recognize the inherent interconnectedness of all aspects of human existence, including the material and the immaterial.

A more nuanced approach recognizes that financial systems and spiritual principles are not inherently opposed but rather complementary facets of a holistic human experience. Just as the physical body requires sustenance to thrive, our economic systems are necessary for providing the material resources that enable us to fulfill our basic needs and pursue higher aspirations. Conversely, spiritual principles offer guidance on how to navigate the complexities of life with wisdom, compassion, and a sense of purpose, imbuing our economic endeavors with deeper meaning and ethical grounding.

One novel perspective proposes that the integration of spiritual principles into financial systems can serve as a catalyst for transformative change. By infusing economic practices with values such as ethical conduct, environmental stewardship, and compassionate service, we can reshape our understanding of true prosperity. This approach challenges the narrow pursuit of material gain and instead promotes a more holistic vision of well-being that encompasses individual, societal, and environmental considerations.

A powerful example of this approach can be found in the concept of "conscious capitalism," which seeks to align business practices with ethical and sustainable principles. Companies like Patagonia and Seventh Generation have demonstrated the viability and success of this model, prioritizing environmental responsibility, fair labor practices, and social impact alongside financial profitability.

Additionally, the rise of impact investing and socially responsible investing (SRI) illustrates how spiritual principles can be integrated into financial systems. These investment strategies prioritize companies and projects that generate positive social and environmental impact, aligning financial returns with ethical and sustainable values. By redirecting capital toward projects that benefit humanity and the planet, investors can merge their economic pursuits with their spiritual aspirations.

Skeptics may argue that integrating spiritual principles into financial systems is idealistic and impractical, citing the inherent competitive nature of markets and the primacy of profit maximization. However, this perspective overlooks the long-term sustainability and resilience that can be achieved by aligning economic practices with ethical and spiritual principles.

Numerous studies have demonstrated that companies with strong ethical practices and a commitment to sustainability often outperform their less ethical counterparts over the long term. This is partly due to the increased trust and loyalty of stakeholders, as well as the ability to attract and retain top talent who value purpose-driven work. Additionally, companies that prioritize environmental stewardship and social responsibility are better positioned to mitigate risks associated with resource depletion, climate change, and social unrest, ensuring their longevity and competitiveness in an increasingly volatile and interconnected global landscape.

To truly bridge the gap between temporal financial systems and eternal divine principles, individuals and organizations must be willing to embrace a paradigm shift. This transformation involves redefining success beyond solely financial metrics and adopting a multidimensional approach that integrates ethical, social, and environmental considerations into economic decision-making.

Furthermore, it necessitates a shift in mindset, moving away from the narrow pursuit of self-interest and embracing a broader understanding of our interconnectedness. By recognizing that our individual well-being is inextricably linked to the well-being of society and the planet, we can align our economic activities with the universal spiritual principle of compassionate service to the collective good.

The path ahead is not without challenges, but the potential rewards are profound. By integrating spiritual principles into financial systems, we can create economic models that promote equitable distribution of resources, foster environmental stewardship, and contribute to the overall flourishing of humanity. In doing so, we can transcend the false dichotomy between material and spiritual pursuits, recognizing that true prosperity lies in the harmonious integration of both realms, creating a world where economic progress and spiritual fulfillment are not mutually exclusive but rather complementary and mutually reinforcing.

Future Directions in Spiritual Economics

The pursuit of bridging temporal financial systems with eternal divine principles is a noble endeavor that holds immense promise for shaping a more just, sustainable, and spiritually fulfilling world. To understand the future trajectory of this pursuit, it is essential to examine the historical roots and evolutionary path of spiritual economics.

1. The Significance of Tracing the Historical Trajectory: By exploring the historical timeline of spiritual economics, we gain a deeper appreciation for the diverse cultural traditions, visionary thinkers, and pivotal moments that have contributed to its development. This understanding provides a solid foundation upon which

to envision its future directions and potential impact on global economic systems.

2. Ancient Roots and Early Mentions: - Ancient spiritual and philosophical traditions, such as Buddhism, Hinduism, and Taoism, have long emphasized the importance of moderation, nonattachment, and ethical conduct in relation to material possessions and economic activities. - The teachings of Lao Tzu, Confucius, and the Buddha, dating back to the 6th century BCE, offered profound insights into the relationship between spiritual well-being and material pursuits. - In the Western tradition, the ancient Greek philosophers, such as Socrates, Plato, and Aristotle, explored the interplay between virtue, ethics, and economic behavior in their works.

3. Key Events, Discoveries, and Adaptations: - In the Middle Ages, religious institutions and monastic orders played a significant role in shaping economic practices, with the concept of just price and the prohibition of usury influencing financial systems. - The Protestant Reformation (16th century) brought forth new perspectives on work ethic, frugality, and the moral implications of economic activities, as articulated by figures like Martin Luther and John Calvin. - The Quakers and other religious groups in the 17th and 18th centuries pioneered ethical business practices, emphasizing honesty, fair treatment of workers, and philanthropic endeavors. - In the 19th century, influential thinkers like Henry David Thoreau, Ralph Waldo Emerson, and Leo Tolstoy explored the relationship between spiritual awakening, simplicity, and economic self-sufficiency. - The 20th century witnessed the emergence of influential figures like E.F. Schumacher, whose book "Small Is Beautiful" (1973) advocated for a human-centered, sustainable, and spiritually grounded approach to economics. - The rise of socially responsible investing (SRI) and impact investing in the late 20th and early 21st centuries marked a significant step in integrating ethical and spiritual principles into financial decision-making.

4. Cross-Cultural Adaptations and Interpretations: - Islamic finance, rooted in the teachings of the Quran and Sharia law, has developed sophisticated financial instruments and practices that align with principles of ethical conduct, risk-sharing, and the prohibition of interest (riba). - In many indigenous communities around the world, economic activities have been deeply intertwined with spiritual beliefs, traditions, and a reverence for nature, often emphasizing communal well-being over individual accumulation of wealth. - In South Asia, the concept of "dharma" (righteous conduct) has influenced economic practices, promoting ethical behavior, social responsibility, and a holistic approach to individual and collective prosperity. - The African philosophy of "ubuntu," emphasizing human interconnectedness, has influenced the development of alternative economic models that prioritize community well-being, solidarity, and environmental sustainability.

5. Contemporary Advancements and Evolutions: - The emergence of conscious capitalism, pioneered by companies like Patagonia and Seventh Generation, has demonstrated the viability and success of integrating spiritual principles into business practices, emphasizing ethical conduct, environmental stewardship, and stakeholder well-being. - The growth of the sharing economy, facilitated by technological advancements, has challenged traditional notions of ownership and consumption, promoting a more sustainable and community-oriented approach to economic activities. - The rise of blockchain technology and cryptocurrencies has opened new avenues for decentralized, transparent, and ethically grounded financial systems, potentially aligning with spiritual principles of trust, accountability, and community empowerment. - The increasing recognition of the interconnectedness of global challenges, such as climate change, poverty, and social inequalities, has given rise to calls for holistic economic models that prioritize planetary well-being and the collective good.

6.Controversies, Pivotal Moments, and Critical Junctures: - The debate between proponents of unfettered capitalism and advocates of spiritual economics has been a longstanding point of contention, with differing perspectives on the role of economic growth, profit maximization, and the integration of spiritual values. - The global financial crisis of 2008 served as a pivotal moment, exposing the inherent instabilities and ethical shortcomings of traditional economic systems, and fueling a renewed interest in more sustainable and values-based approaches. - The ongoing climate crisis and its dire consequences have highlighted the urgent need for economic models that prioritize environmental stewardship and align with spiritual principles of reverence for nature and intergenerational responsibility. - The rise of income inequality, wealth concentration, and exploitative labor practices have sparked a global discourse on the need for economic systems that promote equitable distribution of resources, human dignity, and ethical conduct, aligning with spiritual teachings of compassion and social justice. As we look to the future, the continued evolution and application of spiritual economics will be critical in addressing the complex challenges facing humanity. By fostering ongoing dialogue, research, and collaboration across disciplines, cultures, and sectors, we can collectively shape economic systems that harmonize with eternal divine principles, promoting individual well-being, societal flourishing, and environmental sustainability. It is a journey that requires visionary thinking, courageous action, and a deep commitment to aligning our material pursuits with our highest spiritual aspirations, creating a world where true prosperity is defined not solely by financial metrics but by the holistic well-being of all life.

18

—————

THE ESCHATOLOGICAL VISION: PREPARING FOR THE ETERNAL KINGDOM

The Eschatological Promise: Defining the Eternal Kingdom

Embarking on a discourse about the eschatological promise of the eternal kingdom, it is essential to establish a firm understanding of the foundational concepts and terms that undergird this profound theological vision. By elucidating these terms, we gain clarity and insight into the intricate tapestry of biblical prophecies, divine promises, and the ultimate culmination of human history.

1. Eternal Kingdom: This phrase encapsulates the promise of an everlasting realm, a realm that transcends the temporal boundaries of our present existence. It is a state of being characterized by the unending presence of God and the realization of divine perfection. Contrary to fleeting worldly kingdoms, the eternal kingdom is an enduring reality, a celestial inheritance that awaits those who align themselves with the divine plan.
2. Eschatology: Derived from the Greek words "eschatos" (last) and "logos" (study), eschatology is the branch of theology concerned with the study of the ultimate destiny of humanity, the world, and the cosmos. It delves into the

profound questions of the end times, the nature of the afterlife, and the culmination of God's redemptive plan for creation. By understanding eschatology, we gain a deeper appreciation for the eternal kingdom and its place within the grand narrative of salvation history.

3. New Heaven and New Earth: This phrase, drawn from the Book of Revelation, symbolizes the transformative renewal and restoration of the entire created order. It represents the promise of a radically transformed reality, where the old order of sin, corruption, and decay gives way to a fresh and pristine existence, untainted by the consequences of the Fall. The new heaven and new earth are inextricably linked to the establishment of the eternal kingdom, where God's presence and sovereignty are fully manifested.

4. Resurrection: The doctrine of resurrection is central to Christian eschatology, as it affirms the belief in the physical and spiritual resurrection of the dead. It is a promise of renewed life, where the mortal and corruptible are transformed into the immortal and imperishable. The resurrection of believers is a pivotal event that paves the way for their entrance into the eternal kingdom, where they will experience the fullness of life in the presence of God.

5. Judgment and Redemption: The eschatological narrative encompasses the concepts of divine judgment and redemption. Judgment refers to the righteous evaluation of human actions and the ultimate separation of the righteous from the unrighteous. Redemption, on the other hand, speaks of the deliverance and restoration of humanity from the bondage of sin and its consequences. The eternal kingdom is the culmination of this process, where those who have been redeemed will dwell in the presence of God, free from the burdens of sin and death.

By unpacking these terms and their profound significance, we gain a deeper appreciation for the eschatological promise of the eternal kingdom. This understanding sets the stage for a rich exploration of the biblical texts that inform this vision, the intricate elements that comprise the eternal kingdom, and the implications for how we live our lives in anticipation of this glorious future.

As we delve deeper into the following sections, the interconnectedness of these terms will become increasingly evident, weaving together a tapestry of hope, redemption, and the ultimate triumph of God's sovereign plan for creation. With this solid foundation, we can embark on a transformative journey, allowing the eschatological promise of the eternal kingdom to shape our perspectives, guide our actions, and inspire us to live in alignment with the divine purpose.

Scriptural Prophecies: Foundations of Eschatological Vision

In exploring the biblical foundations of eschatological vision, we embark on a historical timeline that spans millennia, traversing diverse cultures and interpretations. This journey illuminates the profound impact of scriptural prophecies on our understanding of the end times and the eternal kingdom.

The earliest roots of eschatological prophecy can be traced back to the ancient Israelite prophets, who foretold the coming of a promised Messiah and the establishment of an everlasting kingdom. These visions were woven into the sacred texts of the Old

Testament, captivating the imagination of successive generations. The prophecies found in the books of Daniel, Ezekiel, and Isaiah, among others, painted vivid pictures of a cosmic conflict between good and evil, culminating in the triumph of divine justice and the restoration of God's sovereign rule.

1. Ancient Israelite Prophecies (c. 8th-6th centuries BCE):

- Daniel's visions of the Son of Man and the everlasting kingdom (Daniel 7)

- Ezekiel's vision of the valley of dry bones and the restoration of Israel (Ezekiel 37)
- Isaiah's prophecies of the Suffering Servant and the establishment of a righteous kingdom (Isaiah 53, 60-62)

2. Intertestamental Period (c. 4th century BCE - 1st century CE):

- The development of apocalyptic literature, such as the Book of Enoch and the Sibylline Oracles, further expounded on eschatological themes.
- The rise of apocalyptic sects, like the Essenes, emphasized the imminent coming of the Messiah and the final judgment.

3. The New Testament Era (c. 1st century CE):

- The teachings of Jesus Christ, particularly the Olivet Discourse (Matthew 24-25, Mark 13, Luke 21), provided a comprehensive eschatological framework.
- The writings of the apostles, especially the Book of Revelation and the Pauline epistles, expanded on the prophecies of the end times and the eternal kingdom.

4. Early Christian Interpretation (c. 1st-4th centuries CE):

- The early Church Fathers, such as Irenaeus, Justin Martyr, and Origen, grappled with the interpretations of scriptural prophecies and their implications for the Christian community.
- The development of various eschatological schools of thought, including premillennialism, amillennialism, and postmillennialism, shaped the understanding of the end times.

5. Medieval and Reformation Era (c. 5th-16th centuries):

- During the Middle Ages, eschatological themes were prevalent in religious writings, art, and architecture, reflecting the societal concerns and spiritual yearnings of the time.
- The Protestant Reformation sparked renewed interest in biblical prophecies, with figures like Martin Luther and John Calvin offering their interpretations.

6. Modern and Contemporary Interpretations (c. 17th century - present):

- The rise of biblical criticism and historical-critical methods challenged traditional understandings of eschatological prophecies, leading to ongoing debates and reinterpretations.
- Eschatological themes have influenced popular culture, literature, and various religious movements, reflecting the enduring fascination with the end times and the eternal kingdom.

Throughout this historical timeline, the interpretation of scriptural prophecies has been shaped by cultural contexts, theological perspectives, and pivotal events. While debates and challenges have arisen, the core eschatological vision of a divine culmination and the establishment of an everlasting kingdom has remained a central tenet of the Christian faith.

Signs of the Times: Recognizing Eschatological Indicators

What are the indicators that signify the approach of the end times and the eternal kingdom?

This question has captivated humanity for millennia, as individuals and communities have sought to unravel the mysteries of the future foretold in sacred texts and prophecies. It is a question that carries immense significance, for it speaks to our deepest longings for meaning, purpose, and the ultimate destiny of our world.

The complexities surrounding the identification of eschatological signs are manifold. On one hand, the recognition of these signals holds the promise of providing clarity and direction amidst the uncertainties of our existence. It offers the reassurance that the divine plan is unfolding as foretold, and that the culmination of all things is drawing near. However, the interpretation of these signs is fraught with challenges, as they often involve symbolic language, cultural contexts, and the interplay of spiritual and physical realms.

The dilemma we face is that many have attempted to interpret eschatological signs prematurely, leading to misguided predictions and unfulfilled expectations. Throughout history, various individuals and movements have proclaimed the imminent arrival of the end times, only to be met with disappointment and disillusionment. This has, in turn, fueled skepticism and doubt, casting a shadow over the credibility of eschatological prophecies themselves.

Conventional approaches to identifying these signs have often been narrow and literal, failing to account for the multifaceted nature of the biblical narratives and the complex interplay of metaphor, symbolism, and historical context. Such rigid interpretations have led to misunderstandings, divisions, and even fanaticism, undermining the very essence of the eschatological message.

Herein lies the heart of our endeavor: to introduce a novel perspective on eschatological indicators, one that embraces a balanced and discerning approach. Our vision is to transcend the limitations of myopic and dogmatic interpretations, and instead, cultivate a holistic understanding that harmonizes with the overarching themes of divine wisdom, redemption, and the restoration of all things.

Imagine embarking on a journey where we learn to recognize the signs of the times not merely through a superficial analysis of current events, but through a profound exploration of the spiritual and ethical underpinnings that give meaning to these portents. We will delve into the teachings of Matthew 24:3-14 and 2 Timothy

3:1-5, not as a checklist of events to be ticked off, but as a roadmap that guides us toward a deeper understanding of the human condition, our moral trajectory, and the cosmic implications of our choices.

Consider the parable of the fig tree in Matthew 24:32-33, where Jesus invites his followers to discern the signs of the times just as they would observe the budding of a fig tree and recognize the approaching summer. Through this lens, we will learn to perceive the eschatological indicators not as isolated incidents, but as interconnected patterns that reflect the collective state of humanity's spiritual and moral development.

Rather than succumbing to fear or anxiety, our approach will empower you to embrace these signs as a call to personal transformation and spiritual preparedness. We will explore practical strategies for cultivating a heightened state of watchfulness, rooted in prayer, discernment, and a steadfast commitment to living according to the values of the eternal kingdom.

Throughout this journey, we will confront potential objections and address the skepticism that may arise. We will engage with diverse perspectives, acknowledging the complexities and nuances that exist within the realm of eschatological interpretation. By doing so, we will strengthen our arguments and deepen our understanding, enabling us to navigate this territory with humility, wisdom, and a spirit of unity.

Ultimately, our aim is to equip you with the tools and insights necessary to recognize the signs of the times in a meaningful and transformative way. By embracing this holistic approach, you will be empowered to live with a sense of purpose and readiness, actively participating in the unfolding of the divine plan, rather than succumbing to fear or complacency. Together, we will navigate the path toward the eternal kingdom, guided by faith, wisdom, and an unwavering commitment to the principles of love, justice, and the restoration of all things.

The Role of the Church in Eschatological Preparation

In the grand narrative of God's plan for humanity, the Church plays a pivotal role in preparing for the eternal kingdom. The divine mandate set forth in Matthew 28:18-20, known as the Great Commission, charges the Church with a monumental task: "Go and make disciples of all nations, baptizing them in the name of the Father and of the Son and of the Holy Spirit, and teaching them to obey everything I have commanded you." This commission is not merely a call to evangelism; it is a profound invitation to participate in the preparation of all humankind for the ultimate fulfillment of God's purposes.

The Problem: Contemporary churches face formidable challenges in fulfilling this eschatological mission. In an increasingly secularized world, spiritual education and moral guidance are often overshadowed by the allure of material pursuits and consumerism. Many congregations struggle to cultivate a deep sense of purpose and urgency regarding the coming kingdom, as the busyness of daily life and the distractions of modern society take precedence. Furthermore, the fragmentation of communities and the erosion of traditional support systems have made it difficult for churches to foster a sense of unity and collective preparedness.

The implications of failing to address these challenges are grave. Without a strong Church fully engaged in its eschatological responsibilities, individuals and societies risk being ill-prepared for the momentous events that will unfold. Spiritual ignorance, moral decay, and a lack of community cohesion can leave souls vulnerable and ill-equipped to navigate the challenges and opportunities that will accompany the end times. Ultimately, this could lead to a diminished capacity to participate in the establishment of the eternal kingdom, and a potential failure to fully realize the divine plan for humanity.

The Solution: To overcome these obstacles, the Church must embrace its role as a beacon of spiritual education, a catalyst for community-building, and a source of moral guidance. By doing so, it can effectively prepare its members and the broader society for the advent of the eternal kingdom.

Spiritual Education: The Church must prioritize the dissemination of eschatological teachings, rooted in sacred texts and prophetic wisdom. This education should not merely focus on the external signs and events, but on the inner transformation required to align oneself with the values and principles of the eternal kingdom. Through systematic study, reflection, and practical application, individuals can cultivate a deeper understanding of their divine purpose and developing the spiritual discernment necessary to navigate the complexities of the end times.

Community Building: The Church must foster a sense of unity and belonging among its members, creating a supportive environment where individuals can grow, encourage one another, and collaborate in their preparations. By strengthening the bonds of fellowship and fostering an atmosphere of mutual accountability, the Church can become a powerful force for collective preparedness. This community-building extends beyond the walls of the church, as the Church reaches out to the broader society, offering a refuge and a beacon of hope amidst the uncertainties of the world.

Moral Guidance: The Church must uphold and exemplify the highest moral and ethical standards, serving as a lighthouse in a world often shrouded in darkness. By teaching and embodying the virtues of compassion, integrity, justice, and selflessness, the Church can inspire its members and the broader community to align their lives with the principles of the eternal kingdom. This moral guidance should extend to all spheres of life, from personal conduct to civic engagement, ensuring that individuals are equipped to navigate the challenges and complexities of the end times with unwavering commitment to righteousness.

Embracing these responsibilities is no small feat, and churches worldwide face diverse challenges in their implementation. However, there are shining examples of congregations that have successfully embraced their eschatological mission, serving as beacons of inspiration and models for effective preparation.

One such example is the Iglesia Ni Cristo (Church of Christ) in the Philippines, which has made eschatological education a cornerstone of its ministry. Through systematic Bible studies, seminars, and multimedia resources, this church has equipped its members with a deep understanding of the end times, fostering a sense of urgency and purpose in their spiritual preparation. Additionally, the church's strong emphasis on community-building has created a supportive network where members can encourage one another and collaborate in their efforts to live according to the principles of the eternal kingdom.

Another inspiring example is the Seventh-day Adventist Church, which has a longstanding tradition of emphasizing the imminent return of Christ and the need for moral preparedness. Through its network of educational institutions, health initiatives, and community outreach programs, this church has effectively promoted holistic living and a commitment to serving others. By embodying the values of compassion, stewardship, and ethical conduct, the Seventh-day Adventist Church has become a beacon of moral guidance, inspiring its members and the broader community to align their lives with the principles of the eternal kingdom.

While these examples are noteworthy, it is crucial to acknowledge that no single church or organization has a monopoly on the truth or a perfect implementation of the eschatological mission. Each congregation and community must prayerfully discern and adapt their approach to their unique contexts and challenges, remaining open to the guidance of the Holy Spirit and the wisdom found in diverse perspectives.

In conclusion, the Church's role in preparing for the eternal kingdom is paramount. By embracing its responsibilities of spiritual education, community-building, and moral guidance, the Church can effectively equip individuals and societies to navigate the complexities of the end times and participate fully in the establishment of the divine kingdom. While challenges abound, the Church must remain steadfast in its commitment, drawing inspiration from successful models and continuously seeking to innovate and adapt its approach to the ever-changing landscape of our world. Through unwavering faith, unwavering dedication, and a spirit of unity, the Church can become a powerful force for transformation, ushering in a new era of spiritual awakening and preparedness for the glorious day when the eternal kingdom will be fully manifested.

Personal Holiness: The Individual's Role in Eschatological Preparation

In the grand symphony of God's plan for humanity, each individual voice plays a crucial role in harmonizing with the divine melody. As we journey toward the eternal kingdom, personal holiness becomes an indispensable part of the preparation process. Just as a skilled musician must tune their instrument and hone their craft, we too must refine our souls and align our lives with the sacred principles that will resonate throughout eternity.

To embark on this transformative path, let us first define our goal: to cultivate an unwavering commitment to personal holiness, a state of being where our thoughts, words, and actions are infused with the radiance of divine love and the purity of spiritual truth. By achieving this level of sanctification, we can become vessels of grace, beacons of light in a world often shrouded in darkness, and worthy participants in the establishment of the eternal kingdom.

Should you encounter obstacles or setbacks, remember that the path of personal holiness is one of growth and transformation. Seek guidance from spiritual mentors or trusted advisors, and be willing to adapt your approach as needed. Embrace the challenges as opportunities for growth, for it is through perseverance and unwavering faith that we forge the character befitting of citizens of the eternal kingdom.

In the end, personal holiness is not merely a destination; it is a way of being, a state of harmony where our souls resonate with the divine melody. By embracing this journey with commitment and devotion, we not only prepare ourselves for the eternal kingdom, but we also become vessels of light, beacons of hope in a world yearning for spiritual renewal. So let us embark on this sacred path, one step at a time, and may our lives become a testament to the transformative power of personal holiness.

Eschatological Ethics: Living in Anticipation

As we stand at the threshold of eternity, poised to witness the unveiling of the eternal kingdom, a profound question echoes within our souls: "How ought we to live in anticipation of this glorious destiny?" The answer, illuminated by sacred scriptures and the wisdom of ages, lies in the principles of eschatological ethics – a blueprint for virtuous living that harmonizes our earthly journey with the divine vision of the eternal realm.

To define eschatological ethics is to embrace a way of life that transcends the fleeting concerns of the present and aligns with the timeless truths destined to resonate throughout eternity. It is a call to cultivate justice, mercy, and humility, as eloquently expressed in the words of the prophet Micah: "He has shown you, O mortal, what is good. And what does the Lord require of you? To act justly and to love mercy and to walk humbly with your God." (Micah 6:8, NIV)

Justice, the first pillar of eschatological ethics, demands that we uphold the sacred principles of righteousness and equity in our conduct. It compels us to champion the cause of the oppressed, to stand as guardians of truth, and to ensure that the scales of fairness and impartiality remain balanced, even in the face of temptation or adversity. This pursuit of justice extends beyond our personal lives, calling us to be agents of positive change in our communities, advocating for policies and systems that uplift the marginalized and promote the common good.

Mercy, the second principle, is the embodiment of compassion and grace. It beckons us to soften our hearts, to extend forgiveness to those who have wronged us, and to walk the path of understanding and empathy. In a world often marred by conflict and division, the practice of mercy serves as a healing balm, mending wounds and fostering reconciliation. By embracing mercy, we not only honor the divine call to love our neighbors but also prepare our souls for the ultimate act of forgiveness – the redemptive grace that awaits us in the eternal kingdom.

Humility, the third pillar, is the antidote to the poison of pride and arrogance. It reminds us that, despite our earthly achievements and accolades, we are but temporary sojourners on this mortal plane. By walking humbly with our God, we acknowledge the vastness of the divine wisdom and the limitations of our own understanding. Humility breeds a spirit of reverence, openness, and a willingness to learn from others, ultimately enabling us to grow in our spiritual maturity and deepen our connection with the divine.

Yet, eschatological ethics is not merely a theoretical construct; it is a living, breathing reality that must permeate every aspect of our existence. In our personal lives, it manifests through acts of kindness, charity, and selfless service. It is the gentle touch that comforts the afflicted, the compassionate ear that listens to the sorrows of others, and the generous hand that extends aid without expectation of reward.

In our professional endeavors, eschatological ethics calls us to uphold the highest standards of integrity, to conduct our affairs with honesty and transparency, and to prioritize ethical considerations over personal gain. It challenges us to be stewards of the environment, to respect the sanctity of creation, and to make decisions that not only benefit the present but also safeguard the well-being of future generations.

On a societal level, eschatological ethics demands that we confront injustice and oppression with unwavering courage. It compels us to champion the cause of the disenfranchised, to stand as voices for the voiceless, and to tirelessly advocate for systemic change that upholds the dignity and worth of every human being. It is a call to tear down the walls of prejudice, to bridge the divides of hatred and mistrust, and to foster an environment where all can thrive and contribute to the collective flourishing of humanity.

Ultimately, eschatological ethics finds its ultimate expression in the parable of the sheep and the goats, as recounted in the Gospel of Matthew: "For I was hungry and you gave me something to eat, I was thirsty and you gave me something to drink, I was a stranger and you invited me in, I needed clothes and you clothed me, I was sick and you looked after me, I was in prison and you came to visit me." (Matthew 25:35-36, NIV) In this profound teaching, we are reminded that our actions toward the least of our brethren are inextricably linked to our relationship with the divine – a sobering truth that underscores the eternal significance of our conduct in the present.

As we navigate the complexities of our earthly existence, let us hold fast to the principles of eschatological ethics, allowing them to serve as a compass guiding our steps toward the eternal kingdom. Let us embrace justice, not merely as a concept, but as a way of life, upholding the rights of all and ensuring that the scales of fairness remain balanced. Let us embody mercy, extending forgiveness and compassion to those who have wronged us, and cultivating an environment of understanding and reconciliation.

And let us walk humbly with our God, acknowledging the vastness of the divine wisdom and our own limitations, ever open to learning and growth. By living in accordance with these sacred principles, we not only prepare ourselves for the glorious destiny that awaits, but we also become agents of transformation, spreading the light of divine love and contributing to the establishment of the eternal kingdom here on earth.

Eschatological ethics is not a mere footnote in our spiritual journey; it is the very essence of our existence, a blueprint for living that harmonizes our present with the eternal melody of the divine.

So let us embrace this sacred calling, letting our every thought, word, and deed resonate with the timeless truths of justice, mercy, and humility, and may our lives become a testament to the transformative power of living in anticipation of the eternal kingdom.

The Transformative Power of Hope: Eschatological Motivation

1. Overview: This section explores the transformative power of hope within the context of eschatological preparation – the anticipation of the eternal kingdom. Hope serves as a driving force that motivates individuals and communities to align their lives with the principles of the eternal realm. By examining the psychological and spiritual benefits of maintaining hope, we gain insight into how this virtue can catalyze personal and communal transformation, ultimately shaping our journey toward the glorious destiny that awaits.

2. Main Claim: Hope is a profound and dynamic force that possesses the ability to transcend our present circumstances and propel us toward the realization of our eschatological aspirations. It is a beacon that illuminates the path to the eternal kingdom, inspiring us to persist amid adversity and remain steadfast in our pursuit of divine purposes.

3. Evidence from Scripture: The Bible provides a rich tapestry of passages that underscore the transformative power of hope, particularly within the context of eschatological anticipation. One such passage is found in Romans 8:24-25, where the Apostle Paul writes, "For in this hope we were saved. But hope that is seen is no hope at all. Who hopes for what they already have? But if we hope for what we do not yet have, we wait for it patiently." (NIV) These words acknowledge the enduring nature of hope, which enables us to persevere even when the object of our longing remains unseen, fueling our patient anticipation of the eternal kingdom.

4. Elaboration on Evidence: The epistle to the Hebrews further illuminates the transformative potential of hope, as exemplified in the lives of the faithful who came before us. Hebrews 11:1 declares, "Now faith is confidence in what we hope for and assurance about what we do not see." (NIV) This verse highlights the intrinsic connection between hope and faith, demonstrating how hope fortifies our belief and confidence in the unseen realities that await us in the eternal realm. The chapter then proceeds to recount the stories of individuals whose unwavering hope enabled them to endure trials, overcome obstacles, and remain steadfast in their pursuit of divine promises.

5. Potential Counterarguments: However, it is important to acknowledge that maintaining hope in the face of life's challenges can be a daunting task. Doubt, despair, and the weight of present circumstances can erode our confidence and tempt us to abandon the hope that once sustained us. Critics may argue that hope is merely a fleeting emotion, unable to withstand the harsh realities of a fallen world and the inevitable disappointments that accompany human existence.

6. Addressing Counterarguments: Yet, the transformative power of hope extends far beyond mere emotion; it is a deeply rooted conviction that transcends the limitations of our temporal existence. Scripture reminds us that "hope does not put us to shame, because God's love has been poured out into our hearts through the Holy Spirit, who has been given to us." (Romans 5:5, NIV) This divine infusion of hope fortifies our spirits, enabling us to endure even the most formidable trials, secure in the knowledge that our hope is anchored in the unwavering faithfulness of God.

7. Further Evidence: Psychological research has also shed light on the transformative impact of hope. Studies have demonstrated that individuals who maintain a hopeful outlook exhibit greater resilience, improved mental and

physical well-being, and a heightened capacity for problem-solving and goal attainment. Hope has been found to act as a buffer against stress, anxiety, and depression, empowering individuals to navigate life's challenges with a sense of purpose and determination.

8. Real-life Applications: The transformative power of hope manifests in myriad ways, both personal and communal. On an individual level, embracing hope in the face of adversity can inspire us to persevere through difficult circumstances, overcome obstacles, and remain focused on our eternal destiny. It can motivate us to cultivate virtues such as patience, perseverance, and fortitude, allowing us to grow in spiritual maturity and deepen our relationship with the divine.

In the context of communities, the shared hope in the eternal kingdom can serve as a unifying force, fostering a sense of purpose and solidarity among believers. This collective hope can inspire acts of compassion, service, and advocacy, as individuals and groups strive to embody the principles of the eternal realm in their present circumstances. It can catalyze social transformation, inspiring initiatives that address injustice, alleviate suffering, and promote the common good, all in anticipation of the ultimate realization of the divine vision.

Furthermore, the transformative power of hope extends beyond the temporal realm, impacting our eternal destinies. By maintaining a hopeful outlook and aligning our lives with the principles of the eternal kingdom, we prepare ourselves to fully embrace the glory that awaits us. This hope enables us to approach the threshold of eternity with confidence, secure in the knowledge that our lives have been a faithful reflection of the divine purposes that underpin the eternal realm.

In essence, hope is not merely a passive emotion; it is a dynamic force that propels us forward, empowering us to transcend our present circumstances and actively participate in the unfolding of the divine plan. It is the catalyst that ignites our spiritual transformation, inspiring us to live with purpose, perseverance, and an unwavering commitment to the principles that will resonate throughout eternity. As we cultivate and nurture this transformative hope, we become agents of change, not only in our personal lives but also in the world around us, ushering in the eternal kingdom one step, one act, and one heart at a time.

Interfaith Eschatology: Comparative Perspectives on the Eternal Kingdom

1. Juxtaposing Contrasts: Eschatological visions across world religions present a paradox – they are at once deeply rooted in distinct cultural and historical contexts, yet they share a profound yearning for a transcendent future that transcends the boundaries of time and space. While the specific narratives and symbols may vary, these visions are unified by a common aspiration for a transformed reality where divine justice, restoration, and the triumph of the faithful converge.

2. Introducing the Comparison: This segment explores the rich tapestry of eschatological beliefs woven into the fabric of major world religions, including Judaism, Islam, and Hinduism. By examining the convergences and divergences within these eschatological narratives, we gain a deeper understanding of the universal human longing for a transcendent future, one that promises resolution, redemption, and the ultimate realization of spiritual aspirations.

3. Aspects to Compare and Contrast: The comparative analysis will delve into several key aspects of eschatological visions, including: - The nature of the eternal kingdom or realm of existence envisioned - The role of divine intervention, judgment, and the concept of divine justice - The concept of personal and societal transformation leading to the eschatological culmination - The significance

of the faithful and their role in ushering in the eternal kingdom - The symbolism and imagery employed to convey the eschatological narrative

4. Implications and Insights: Through this comparative exploration, we uncover profound insights into the universal human quest for meaning, purpose, and a transcendent destiny. While the specific narratives may differ, the shared themes of restoration, renewal, and the triumph of righteousness underscore the fundamental kinship that exists among these faith traditions. Moreover, this comparison sheds light on the transformative potential of eschatological beliefs, both on a personal and societal level. By embracing the hope of an eternal kingdom, individuals and communities are empowered to cultivate virtues, pursue justice, and strive for the betterment of the world, guided by the vision of a future where all will be made right.

5. Relevance and Modern Scenarios: In an age marked by global unrest, environmental challenges, and growing disillusionment, the wisdom embedded within these eschatological visions holds profound relevance. By fostering a deeper appreciation for the shared aspirations that underpin these narratives, we can forge pathways toward greater understanding, cooperation, and collective action in addressing the pressing issues that humanity faces.

The interfaith dialogue on eschatology serves as a powerful reminder that our destinies are intertwined, and that our individual and collective efforts to embody the principles of the eternal kingdom can catalyze positive change in the world we inhabit today. It is a call to transcend divisive narratives and embrace the unifying hope that lies at the heart of these eschatological visions, ultimately paving the way for a more harmonious and just world, one that reflects the eternal kingdom we collectively aspire to.

Practical Steps for Eschatological Alignment

The eschatological visions shared across major world religions offer profound insights and call us to align our lives with the divine purposes of the eternal kingdom. This section presents a comprehensive list of practical steps that individuals and communities can take to embark on this transformative journey. These steps serve as a roadmap for eschatological alignment, empowering us to actively participate in the unfolding of the eternal kingdom.

1. Embark on a Spiritual Journey: - Cultivate a deep and abiding connection with the divine through prayer, meditation, and contemplation. - Seek spiritual purification by embracing humility and surrendering to the divine will. - Engage in regular spiritual practices that nourish your soul and deepen your faith. - Embrace the universal principles of love, compassion, and service to all beings.
2. Embrace Ethical Living: - Live with integrity, honesty, and morality in all aspects of your life. - Practice virtues such as patience, forgiveness, and non-violence. - Uphold justice and stand against injustice, oppression, and inequality. - Strive to be a steward of the natural environment, preserving and protecting it for future generations.
3. Engage in Community Building: - Foster strong, supportive, and inclusive communities that reflect the values of the eternal kingdom. - Participate in acts of service and charitable endeavors that uplift the underprivileged and marginalized. - Promote education, dialogue, and the free exchange of ideas that contribute to collective growth and understanding. - Advocate for policies and initiatives that prioritize the well-being of all and protect the rights of every individual.
4. Embrace Interfaith Cooperation: - Recognize the common threads that weave through the eschatological visions of different faiths. - Engage in respectful dialogue and seek to understand the perspectives and beliefs of others. -

Collaborate with individuals and communities of diverse faiths on shared goals and initiatives that promote peace, justice, and the betterment of humanity. - Celebrate the rich tapestry of cultural and religious diversity while honoring the shared aspirations for an eternal kingdom of harmony and unity.

5. Cultivate Inner Transformation: - Engage in self-reflection and introspection to identify personal biases, prejudices, and areas for growth. - Practice self-discipline, self-control, and the ability to transcend selfish desires and impulses. - Embrace humility and seek to continuously learn and evolve as an individual and as a member of the global community. - Embody the qualities of wisdom, compassion, and a deep reverence for all life.

6. Spread Hope and Inspiration: - Share the vision of the eternal kingdom with others, inspiring them to embrace its transformative potential. - Be a beacon of hope in times of darkness, reminding others of the ultimate promise of restoration and renewal. - Encourage and support others on their journey toward eschatological alignment, offering guidance, resources, and a listening ear. - Celebrate the small victories and milestones along the way, recognizing the collective progress toward the eternal kingdom.

By embracing these practical steps, we actively participate in the unfolding of the eternal kingdom. Together, we can cultivate a world that reflects the principles of divine justice, restoration, and the triumph of righteousness. Through our collective efforts, we can pave the way for a harmonious future, where the aspirations of all faiths converge in a shared vision of an eternal kingdom of peace, love, and unity.